Excavations at Boxfield Farm, Chells, Stevenage, Hertfordshire.

Plate 1   The Chells coin hoard (British Museum).

Excavations at Boxfield Farm, Chells, Stevenage, Hertfordshire.

by
C.J. Going & J.R. Hunn

With contributions by
Roger Bland, Mark Corney, Sally Cottam,
Brenda Dickinson, Julia Green, Steven Greep,
Jonathan Hunn, Glenys Lloyd-Morgan,
Jacqueline McKinley, Peter Murphy, Marta Moreno-Garcia,
Jennifer Price, Christopher Saunders, Angela Wardle,
Karen Waugh, David Williams, Nick Winder.

**Hertfordshire Archaeological Trust
Report No. 2
1999**

Published by: Hertfordshire Archaeological Trust
The Seed Warehouse, Maidenhead Yard, The Wash, Hertford, SG14 1PX

© 1999 Hertfordshire Archaeological Trust
All rights reserved

ISBN 09514334 1 5

Produced by: Hertfordshire Archaeological Trust
Printed by Stephen Austin & Sons Limited, Hertford

Contents

List of figures vi
List of tables vii
List of plates vii

ACKNOWLEDGEMENTS: 1

INTRODUCTION: 2

TOPOGRAPHY AND SETTING 4

THE EXCAVATIONS, *by* Chris Going
        Summary 8
        Methods and Conventions 9
        Phasing 10
        Area 1 13
        Area 2 22
        Area 3 27
        The Cemetery 29
        Discussion 35

THE FINDS:
        Coins, *by* Mark Corney 40
        Coin hoard, *by* Roger Bland 45
        Brooches, *by* Mark Corney 51
        Copper-alloy objects, *by* Angela Wardle
        (with a contribution on the mirror, *by* Glenys Lloyd Morgan) 54
        Iron objects, *by* Christopher Saunders 62
        Lead objects, *by* Julia Green 68
        Objects of bone and antler, *by* Stephen Greep 70
        Roman glass, *by* Jennifer Price *and* Sally Cottam 74
        Objects of shale, *by* Julia Green 80
        Quernstones and honestones, *by* David Williams 82
        Samian, *by* Brenda Dickinson 84
        Roman coarse pottery, *by* Karen Waugh 88
        Plant remains and macrofossils, *by* Peter Murphy ... 136
        Cremated human bone, *by* Jacqueline McKinley 144
        Animal bone, *by* Nick Winder and Marta Moreno-Garcia 146

BIBLIOGRAPHY 157

Figures

Figure 1:	Site location, site environs and extent of archaeological work	3
Figure 2:	Topography and neighbouring Roman sites	5
Figure 3:	Excavation, overall plan	8
Figure 4:	Overall plan: Periods I–IV	11
Figure 5:	Overall plan: Periods V & VI	12
Figure 6:	Area 1: Periods I & II, overall plan and principal sections	14
Figure 7:	Area 1: Period III, overall plan and principal sections	16
Figure 8:	Area 1: Well CAB, section	17
Figure 9:	Area 1: Period IV, overall plan and principal sections	18
Figure 10:	Area 1: Periods V & VI, overall plan and principal sections	22
Figure 11:	Area 2: Periods I–IV, overall plan and principal sections	24
Figure 12:	Area 2: Period V corn drier and associated features	26
Figure 13:	Area 2: Pit DBB, plan and section	27
Figure 14:	Area 3: all periods, overall plan and principal sections	28
Figure 15:	Cemetery: overall plan	30
Figure 16:	Histogram showing the pattern of coin loss from the site	40
Figure 17:	Brooches, 1–15	52
Figure 18:	Objects of copper alloy, 1–33	57
Figure 19:	Objects of copper alloy, 34–53	59
Figure 20:	Objects of copper alloy, 54–66	61
Figure 21:	Objects of iron, 1–15	63
Figure 22:	Objects of iron, 16–29	64
Figure 23:	Objects of iron, 30–43	65
Figure 24:	Objects of iron, 44–55	67
Figure 25:	Objects of lead	69
Figure 26:	Objects of bone and antler, 3–25	71
Figure 27:	Objects of bone and antler, 26–30	73
Figure 28:	Roman glass, 1–18	78
Figure 29:	Roman glass, 20–22	79
Figure 30:	Objects of shale	81
Figure 31:	Decorated samian	86
Figure 32:	Samian potters' stamps	87
Figure 33:	Fabric occurrence by weight percentage and R.EVE, Well CAB, Ceramic phase 3	99
Figure 34:	Occurrence of vessel forms, Well CAB, Ceramic phase 3	99
Figure 35:	Fabric occurrence by weight percentage and R.EVE, Well CAB, Ceramic phase 5.2	103
Figure 36:	Occurrence of vessel forms, Well CAB, Ceramic phase 5.2	103
Figure 37:	Fabric occurrence by weight percentage and R.EVE, Quarry EAA, Ceramic phase 3	103
Figure 38:	Occurrence of vessel forms, Quarry EAA, Ceramic phase 3	105
Figure 39:	Fabric occurrence by weight percentage and R.EVE, Pond GK, Ceramic phase 5.2	105
Figure 40:	Occurrence of vessel forms, Pond GK, Ceramic phase 5.2	105
Figure 41:	Fabric occurrence by weight percentage and R.EVE, Ditch ABO, Ceramic phase 5.2	106
Figure 42:	Occurrence of vessel forms, Ditch ABO, Ceramic phase 5.2	106
Figure 43:	Roman pottery; 1–24, Well CAB	112
Figure 44:	Roman pottery; 25–47, Well CAB	114
Figure 45:	Roman pottery; 48–79, Well CAB	116
Figure 46:	Roman pottery; 80–94, Well CAB: 95–108, Period III features	118
Figure 47:	Roman pottery; 109–131, ABL–ABM, VM, TF, EBB, RW, AAJ4, EAN	120
Figure 48:	Roman pottery; 132–143, EAB, ECQ, DCF, EAU, DC: 144–168, Quarry EAA	122
Figure 49:	Roman pottery; 169–199, Quarry EAA	125
Figure 50:	Roman pottery; 200–230, ABR, TB1, TQ1, EBS1, JK, ABQ, EAO, TT/YL/JE	127

Figure 51: Roman pottery; 231–268, ABO, DDX, RC, YH, DAD, GF 129
Figure 52: Roman pottery; 269–271, HB: 272–312, Pond GK 132
Figure 53: Roman pottery; 313–332, Pond GK: 333–347, other late Roman
 & unstratified pottery 134
Figure 54: Roman pottery; 348–355, Cemetery 135
Figure 55: Corn drier: location of samples from the basal flue fill 143
Figure 56: Scattergram of cattle metacarpal distal thickness against distal width 155
Figure 57: Scattergram of cattle metatarsal distal thickness against distal width 155
Figure 58: Percentage number of bone fragments for the main domesticates
 per period 156

Tables

Table 1: Catalogue of Iron Age and Roman coins 41
Table 2: Composition of the Chells hoard 49
Table 3: Comparison of the Chells hoard with other contemporary hoards 50
Table 4: Catalogue of quernstone and millstone fragments 83
Table 5: Ceramic phases and their dates 88
Table 6: Quantities of samian from the site, by origin 97
Table 7: Fabric incidence from stratified contexts 98
Table 8: Dating of features discussed in the pottery report 100
Table 9: Minimum number of vessels within Well CAB 101
Table 10: Fabric incidence from the Cemetery 107
Table 11: Totals of assemblages for each Ceramic phase 107
Table 12: Fabric incidence by Ceramic phase 108
Table 13: Plant remains and other macrofossils from corn drier Flue GF,
 Stokehole JA, and overlying Deposit JE 138
Table 14: Carbonised plant remains and other macrofossils from Well CAB 140
Table 15: Cemetery: human and other bone 145
Table 16: Fragmentation of cremated bone 145
Table 17: General description of the bone assemblage, by period 146
Table 18: Quantification of the animal bone assemblage 147
Table 19: Distribution of bone by period/context type 148
Table 20: Skeletal element per taxa in Well CAB 150
Table 21: Skeletal element per taxa in Pond GK 151
Table 22: Factors affecting bone breakage 152
Table 23: Cattle epiphyseal fusion data 153
Table 24: Cattle measurements 153

Plates

Plate 1: Chells coin hoard .... *frontispiece*
Plate 2: Ditch JJ, section, from south-east. 13
Plate 3: Well CAB, after excavation, from east 19
Plate 4: Chalk Raft ABR, from south 19
Plate 5: Circular Enclosure DAA, from east 23
Plate 6: Corn Drier GF, after excavation, from south 25
Plate 7: Quarry EAA, after sectioning, from east 29
Plate 8: Cemetery: Cremation GAM after excavation 29
Plate 9A: A selection of coins from the hoard, discussed in the report 47
Plate 9B: Contemporary forgeries of base silver radiates of Postumus (AD 260–9) 48

Acknowledgements

Hertfordshire Archaeological Trust and the directors of the fieldwork phases of this project (Stewart Bryant, Ralph Mills and Jonathan Hunn), are most grateful to English Heritage and the developers, Hubert C. Leach Ltd and Moody Homes Ltd, for funding work on the site, and the management and staff of the latter organisations for their forbearance during the works themselves. The exceptional generosity of Hubert C. Leach in donating the hoard of coins discovered during the excavations – in the first trench cut by the new Trust – to Stevenage Museum is gratefully acknowledged. Thanks are extended also to Stevenage Borough Council and to English Heritage, who between them underwrote the excavation and field costs, and to English Heritage for covering the entire cost of the project's post-excavation phase.

Jonathan Hunn thanks Stewart Bryant, Kate Flavin, Nichola Godwin, Julia Green, Ralph Mills, Mike Morris, Mike Napthan, Christine Osbourne, Jane Sandoe, John Sims, Cathy Walker, Karen Waugh, and Nick Winder for help during both fieldwork and post-excavation phases of the project. Of the specialists, Dr Glenys Lloyd-Morgan extends thanks to Dr Tim Potter and Adrian Havercroft for allowing access to unpublished material in their charge. Peter Murphy is grateful to M.van der Veen for making available the text of her paper on charred grain assemblages from Romano-British corn driers in advance of its publication. Thanks are due to the Stevenage Archaeology Group, the local metal detector users' circle, Martin Mawhinney and Stevenage Museum for their labours in connection with almost all aspects of the field work, particularly the cemetery.

The present version of this report was prepared by Chris Going from original drafts by Jonathan Hunn and the various specialist contributors, and further edited by Bob Zeepvat. Both would like to acknowledge the assistance of other Trust staff, both past and present, and of Deborah Priddy, English Heritage Inspector, and Rob Perrin, Project Monitor for English Heritage. Of the specialists, particular thanks are due to Karen Waugh, (pottery), Nick Winder, (animal bone), and to Marta Moreno-Garcia for skilfully editing the latter report.

Preparation of the published drawings was commenced by Jane Sandoe and Clare Venables, and completed by Karen Guffogg.

Introduction
Chris Going

In 1972 crop-marks were noted on a 1:2500 vertical air photograph. In consequence the site, centred on TL 266 259 (Fig. 1), was designated as an Area of Archaeological Significance in 1984 (*AAS 49*). Projected expansion of Stevenage in the later 1980s led to the granting of permission for the site to be developed for residential housing, following which the developers, Hubert C. Leach Ltd and Moody Homes Ltd, sought advice from the Archaeological Section of Hertfordshire County Council. This led to the newly-formed Hertfordshire Archaeological Trust being commissioned to undertake a site evaluation, which was duly carried out under the direction of Stewart Bryant in September/October 1986. Because the field was still under cultivation, disturbance was kept to a minimum. The three principal 1 m-wide evaluation trenches revealed a number of important features of Roman date, including Well CAB and feature EAA. A scatter of Roman coins was noted in the ploughsoil to the south of Trench 1, and a supplementary trench, sited where they seemed densest, revealed that their source was a shallow pit (EAO) containing the remains of a pot (Fig. 50.227). It contained a hoard of over 2,600 coins, principally *denarii* and *antoniniani* of the third century AD.

The results of the evaluation, and of a geophysical survey carried out the following spring by the University of Bradford (Pocock 1987), suggested that the site was a Romano-British farmstead. This was sufficiently encouraging to persuade Leach/Moody, Stevenage Borough Council, and English Heritage to allocate funds for large-scale excavation, which began eighteen months later in the early Spring of 1988. Under the direction of Ralph Mills, a series of nine parallel east-west trenches were cut, together with a 300 m-long NW–SE trench in the area to be developed by Leach/Moody, while to the south-west of this four trenches were also opened up within the area to be developed by Stevenage County Council as a public utility (Fig. 1). The latter were found to be essentially sterile, and no further work was carried out in this area. In April, Corn Drier GF was found and excavated. At the same time a *c.*60 × 50 m area to the west of the drier which had shown up in the 1986 trial-pits as a zone of comparatively high activity was machine-stripped (Area 1). Unfortunately staff were fully stretched at this time and only part of this area, some 625 sq. m, was fully excavated.

The final season began in late May 1989, under the direction of Jonathan Hunn, and lasted for fifteen weeks. At this time some 2650 sq. m was machine stripped. Two areas were examined in detail: a *c.*750 sq. m parcel in the vicinity of the corn drier (Area 2), and a *c.*1000 sq. m area to the north of the principal 1988 trench, near the location of the coin hoard (Area 3). In addition to these areas a number of dispersed trenches were sited over the cropmarks of the principal ditches in order to section them and recover good dating evidence if possible, and some other parts of the 1.6 ha cropmark complex were also sampled. In the following year (1990) the remains of a Romano-British cemetery was discovered during earth-moving operations on the line of what is now Valerian Drive (Fig. 1). The almost ploughed-out burials were excavated by members of the *Stevenage Archaeological Group*.

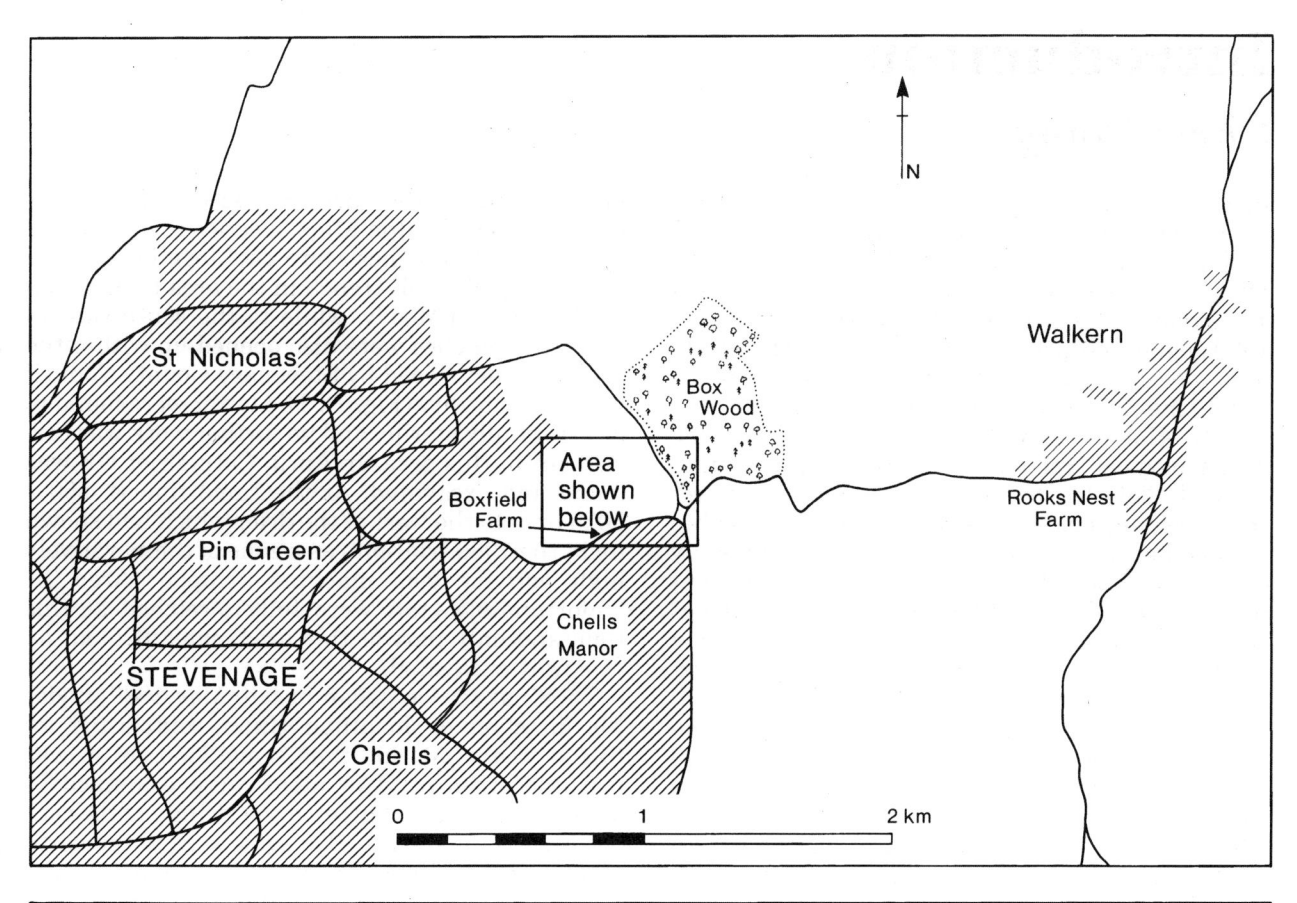

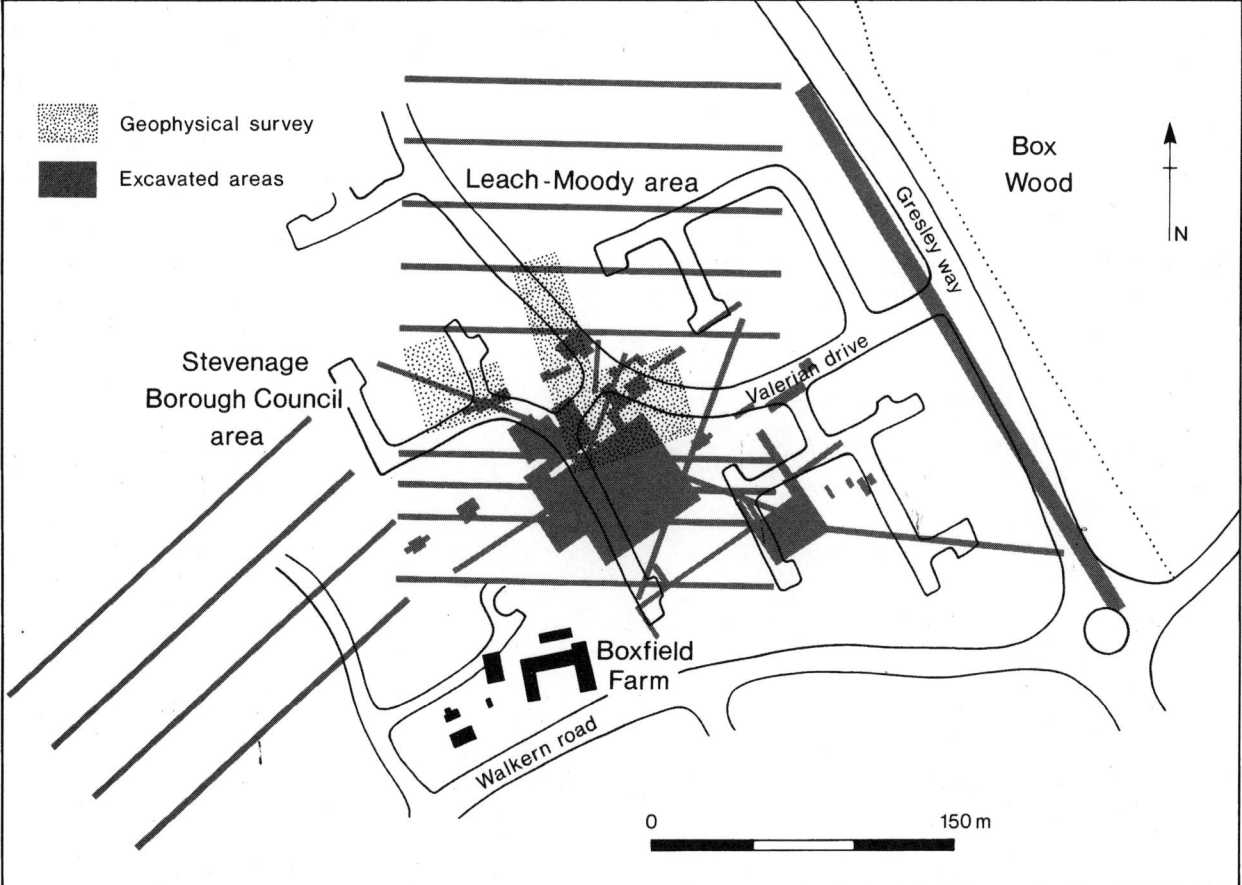

Figure 1 (above) *Site location:* (below) *Site environs and extent of archaeological work.*

Topography and Setting
Chris Going

The site lies in a terrain of gentle slopes and slight hills on the south-east side of a north–south trending spur of the dissected plateau of the East Anglian heights (Fig. 2). It overlooks the slight valley of the river Beane, which flows some 2 km to the east. Here the natural subsoil is chalk topped by boulder clay. The valley floors are covered with glacial or river-borne sands and gravels. In some parts of the valley there are chalk exposures. The water table is high and the boulder clay is effectively porous, with springs at its base.

The principal soils in the vicinity of Stevenage are therefore derived from chalk, boulder clay and gravels. The present-day pedological assessment of these soils is that they are 'moderately well-drained and imperfectly well-drained soils' (Tomason and Avery 1970, 14) and consist of a 'dominantly fine loam or silt with clay subsoils' (non calcareous). In the vicinity of Boxfield Farm the soils have a tendency to waterlogging, which is particularly noticeable in the late winter and early spring. In a wet spring, spring barley can be adversely affected, and even in a dry period cereals are only moderately affected by drought (*ibid*, 283–4). However, the rainfall, at 650 mm, is about average for the area, and summer rainfall is as high as or even higher than in winter. The temperature range permits a growing season of about 240 days (*ibid*). The combination of relief, soils and climate govern the kind of farming undertaken, and the region, with its Grade 3 land, is best suited for growing 'less demanding horticultural crops', although it is good grassland. (*ibid*, 16).

An assessment of the evidence provided by plant remains and macrofossils recovered during the excavation suggests that this picture remains more or less unchanged from the Roman period. The presence of open grassland is indicated, along with the cultivation of barley, spelt and bread-wheat, while Pit RC contained duckweed seeds, indicating waterlogging.

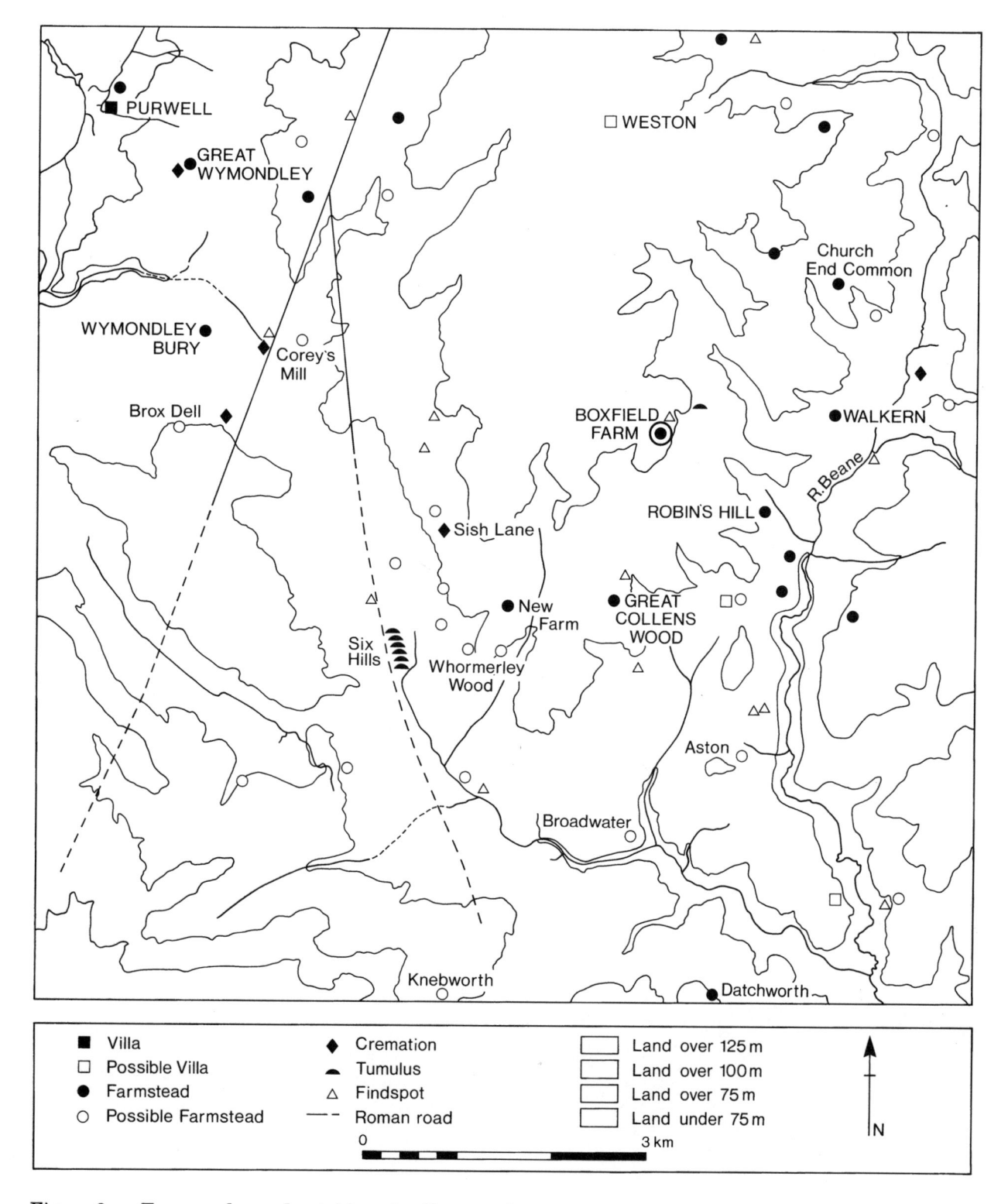

Figure 2   Topography and neighbouring Roman sites.

The Excavations

Summary

Chris Going

Excavations carried out between 1986 and 1990 by Hertfordshire Archaeological Trust in advance of housing development revealed the traces of an agricultural landscape which had been noted from the air some years previously as a cropmark complex (Fig. 3).

While time constraints precluded detailed examination of the earliest phases of the site, some evidence of prehistoric activity was recovered in the form of flint *debitage,* and enough data was obtained to suggest that the cropmark complex was primarily a palimpsest of Romano-British agricultural enclosures, elements of which may date to the end of the pre-Roman Iron Age (Fig. 4a). Two features of this date, a well and a possible trackway, were partly explored in the southern central part of the site (Area 1). The excavation dealt principally with the Romano-British landscape, which developed from a more or less irregularly-shaped ditched enclosure, datable to the later first century AD, which was extended greatly during the second century AD (Period IV: Fig. 4b). During this time, water supply to the site was changed from a well to a series of ponds.

After the middle of the second century, evidence of domestic activity on the site appears to diminish substantially. A small cremation cemetery, established on the northern part of the site during the Flavian period, appears to have gone out of use by the closing decades of the Antonine era, and for much of the ensuing century site activity appears to have been reduced to a minimum. However, during this time (probably around 261) one wholly exceptional feature was dug on the site – Pit EAO, which contained a substantial coin hoard, concealed in a pottery vessel. Apart from this remarkable find there are few indications of activity on the site, and little evidence of general maintenance at this time. It seems probable that the apparent diminution of site activity resulted from the domestic settlement being shifted further away and the site

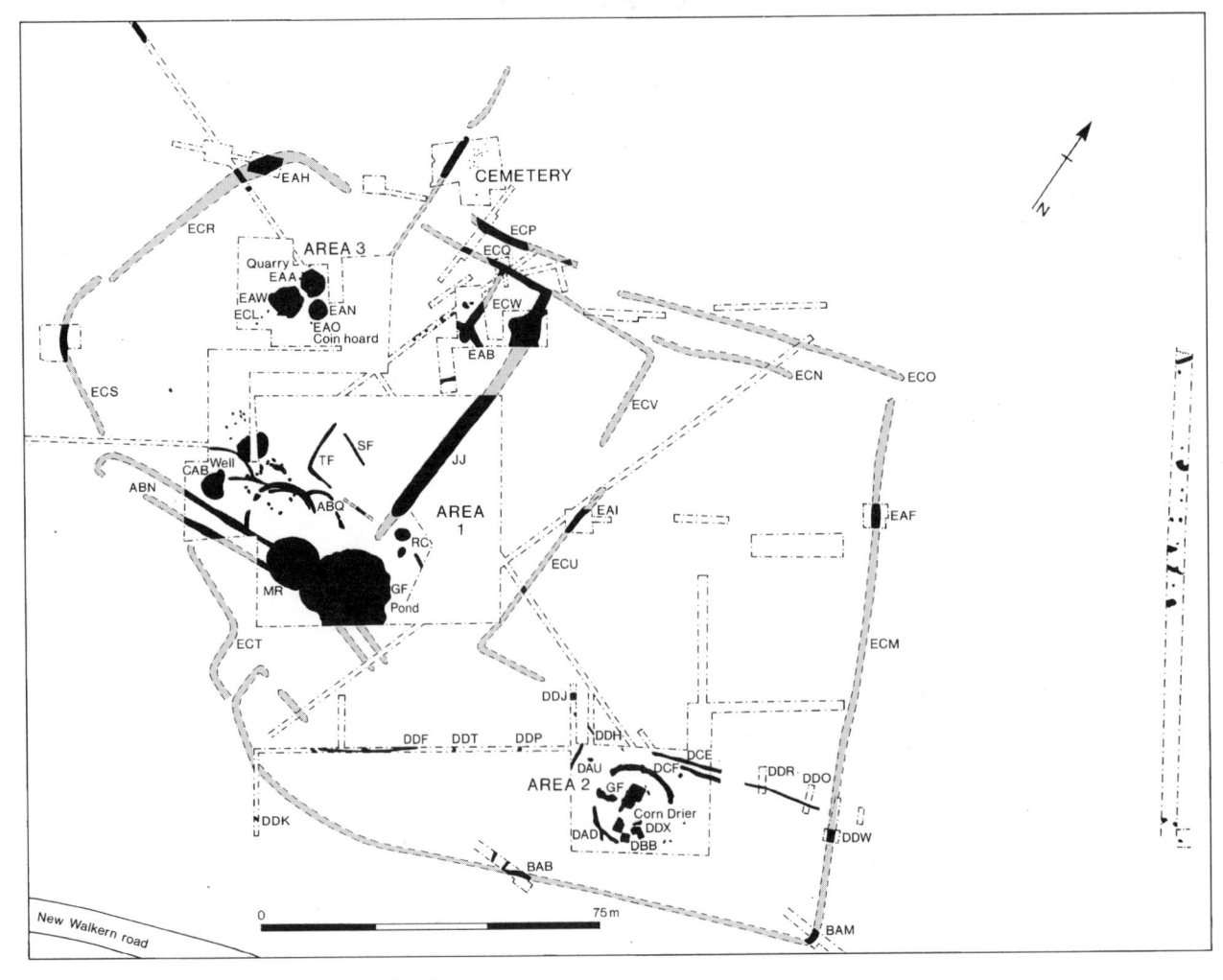

Figure 3   Excavation, overall plan.

being increasingly devoted to agriculture, at a time when the countryside in general appears to have suffered a significant and lengthy farming decline.

However, in the later Roman period (Period V: Fig. 5a), site activity appears to increase. In the southern part of the site a series of penannular gullies and other isolated features attest to renewed activity in the later third to fourth centuries, while in the south-east part of the site a corn drier was constructed to process spelt wheat. At some date probably in the middle of the fourth century the large second-century pond was extensively refurbished and lined with chalk, while the corn drier in the east part of the site was also remodelled, probably at about the same time.

This period of activity appears to have been comparatively short-lived, ending at a point in the 370s when the pond, the well weathering cone, and the last of the sequence of gullies in Area 1 appear to have been backfilled with a mixture of domestic debris and other detritus, including the remains of a substantial number of cattle, which suggests the site suffered some kind of calamity. At about the same time the corn drier in Area 2 appears to have been destroyed by fire. Activity appears to have continued on the site a little longer, but it seems to have been limited to sporadic pit cutting. No attempt seems to have been made to reclaim the pond or to reconstruct the drier, and by the end of the fourth century the Roman landscape was effectively abandoned. The next recognisable activity on the site comprises an isolated pond and a few small features of medieval date (Fig. 5b). The area remained under agricultural use until the excavations.

Methods and Conventions

Excavation methods employed at Chells were, in general terms, identical to those currently in use in British archaeology. Trial trenching and the removal of topsoil from excavation areas was carried out mechanically, followed by manual cleaning and the excavation of archaeological features. Site recording techniques were also largely conventional, although the system of context and small-finds numbering requires some explanation.

The Chells excavations were recorded using an alphanumeric context recording system. The sequence of contexts used for trial trenching begins at AA, progresses to AZ, thence to BA, and so on. A second sequence was used for the excavations, commencing at AAA. Contexts thus identified are subdivided, where necessary, by the addition of a numeric suffix, *eg* EAA 1. There is no single small-finds numbering system; small finds within each context are numbered from 1, the context number thus supplying the unique part of their identification. In the following reports, square brackets are used solely for context numbers in text; small finds numbers are attached to context numbers following an oblique stroke, hence:

ABC 1/1 = Context ABC, subdivision 1, small find 1

The publication numbers of particular finds appear in text in bold type, prefixed as necessary by their finds category, *eg* **CuAlloy 12**.

Phasing

For ease of description the site has been divided into four, Areas 1–3 and the Cemetery (Fig. 3). Each area is described by period (Table 5): Period V has additionally been subdivided into phases. It is stressed that these phases are stratigraphically derived, and are therefore not applicable across the site as a whole. Thus *Area 1, Period V, Phase 2* is not necessarily the same date as *Area 2, Period V, Phase 2*. For each period and/or phase there is a table summarising the dating evidence for the features assigned to them. This includes salient pottery and coins, and also objects of interest in other finds categories (*eg* metalwork, shale, glass, environmental, etc). These tables are followed by a brief discussion of the dating evidence for the phase, where the time-pressed reader will find a synthesis which weighs up the subtle nuances of dating not always readily presentable in tabular form. The pottery was reported on by Dr Karen Waugh, but the original spot-dating was undertaken by C. Going. In this context it is important to note that her 'ceramic phases' are wholly independent of the site periods and phases, as they do not include the earlier stratigraphic phases, which produced no diagnostic pottery. For the dates of these phases and their correlation with the structural phasing the reader is referred to Table 5, which fronts Dr Waugh's report.

Chells Chronological Phasing

Period	Date	Area 1	2	3	CMY
I	Prehistoric	–	–		–
II	Iron Age	–	–	*	–
----AD 43----					
III	Early Roman	*	*	*	*
----c.AD 125----					
IV	Roman	*	*	*	*
----c.AD 200/10----					
V	Later Roman	1 2 3	1 – 2	1	–
----c.AD 400/10----					
VI	Post-Roman	*	–	–	–

Key:
- – absence of activity
- * presence of activity
- 1–3 phase (see note in *Phasing*).

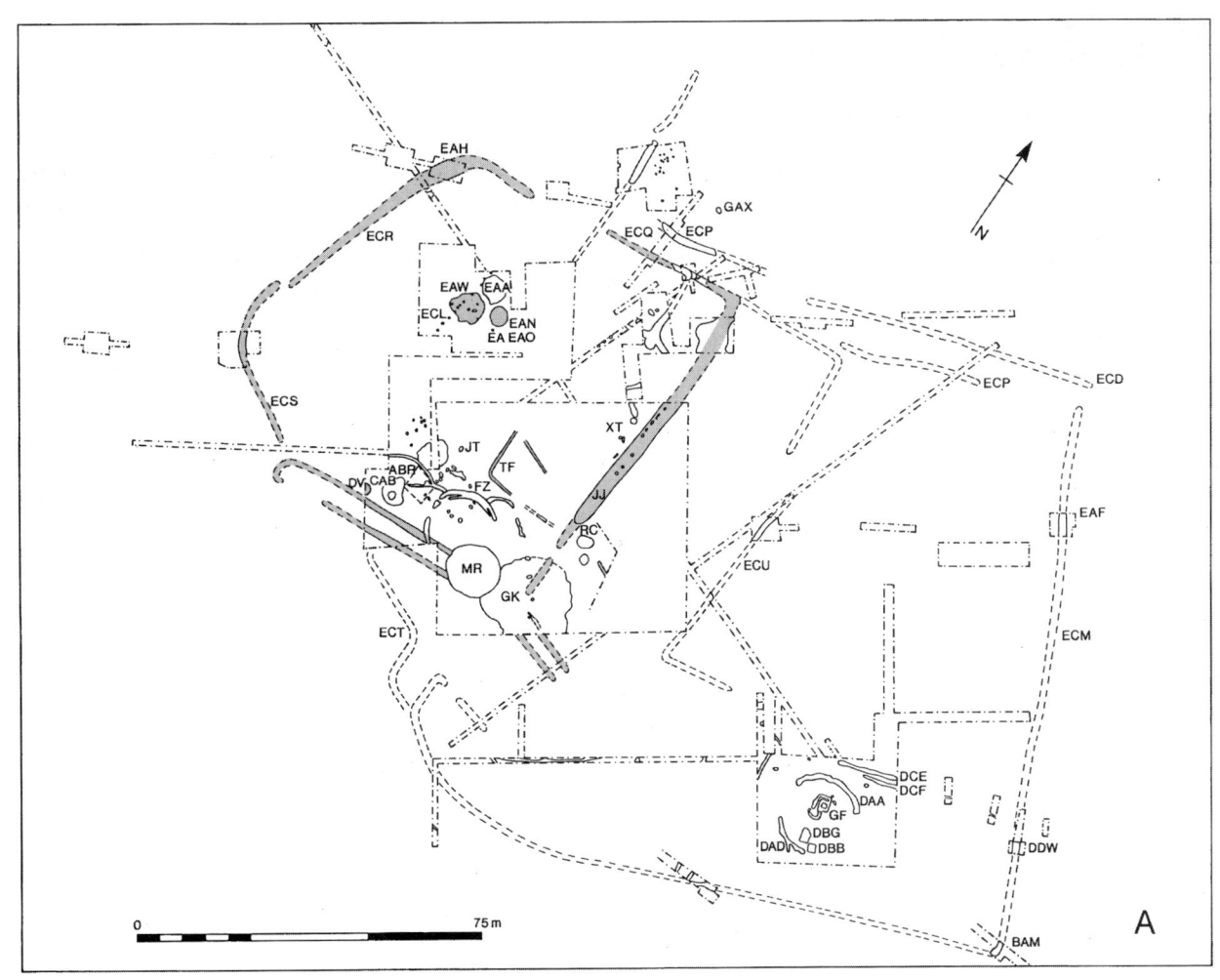

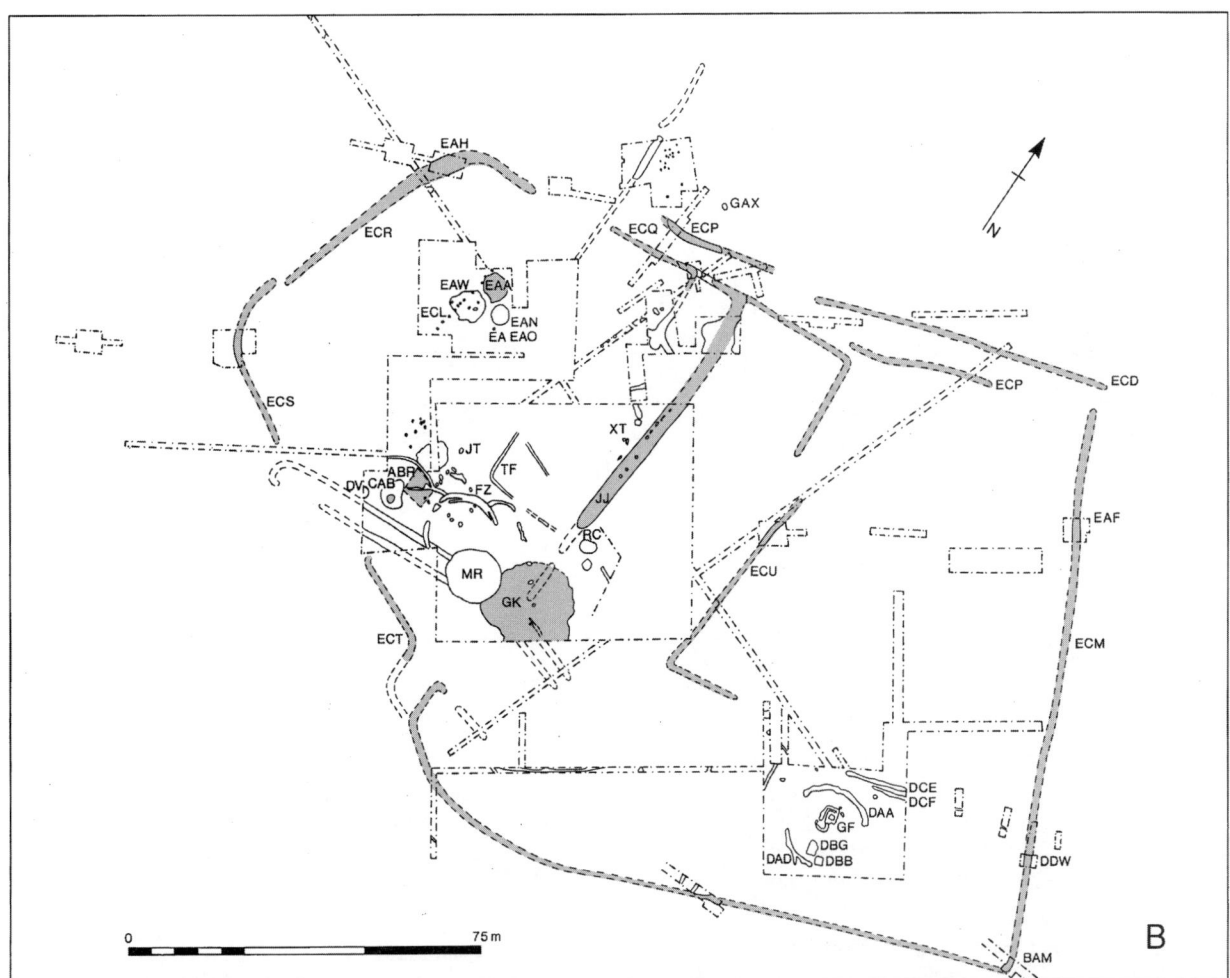

Figure 4 Overall plan: (a) Periods I & II; (b) Periods III & IV.

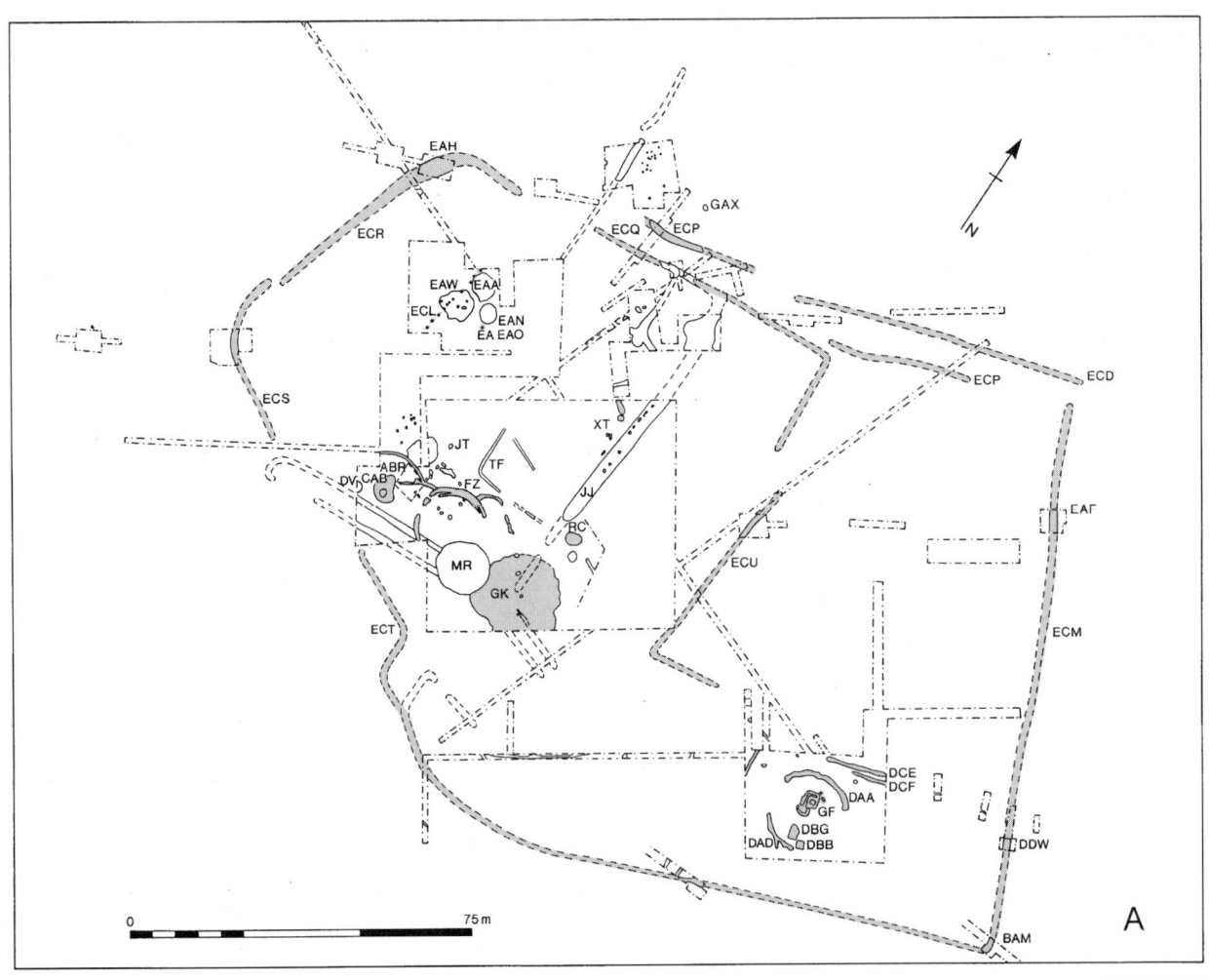

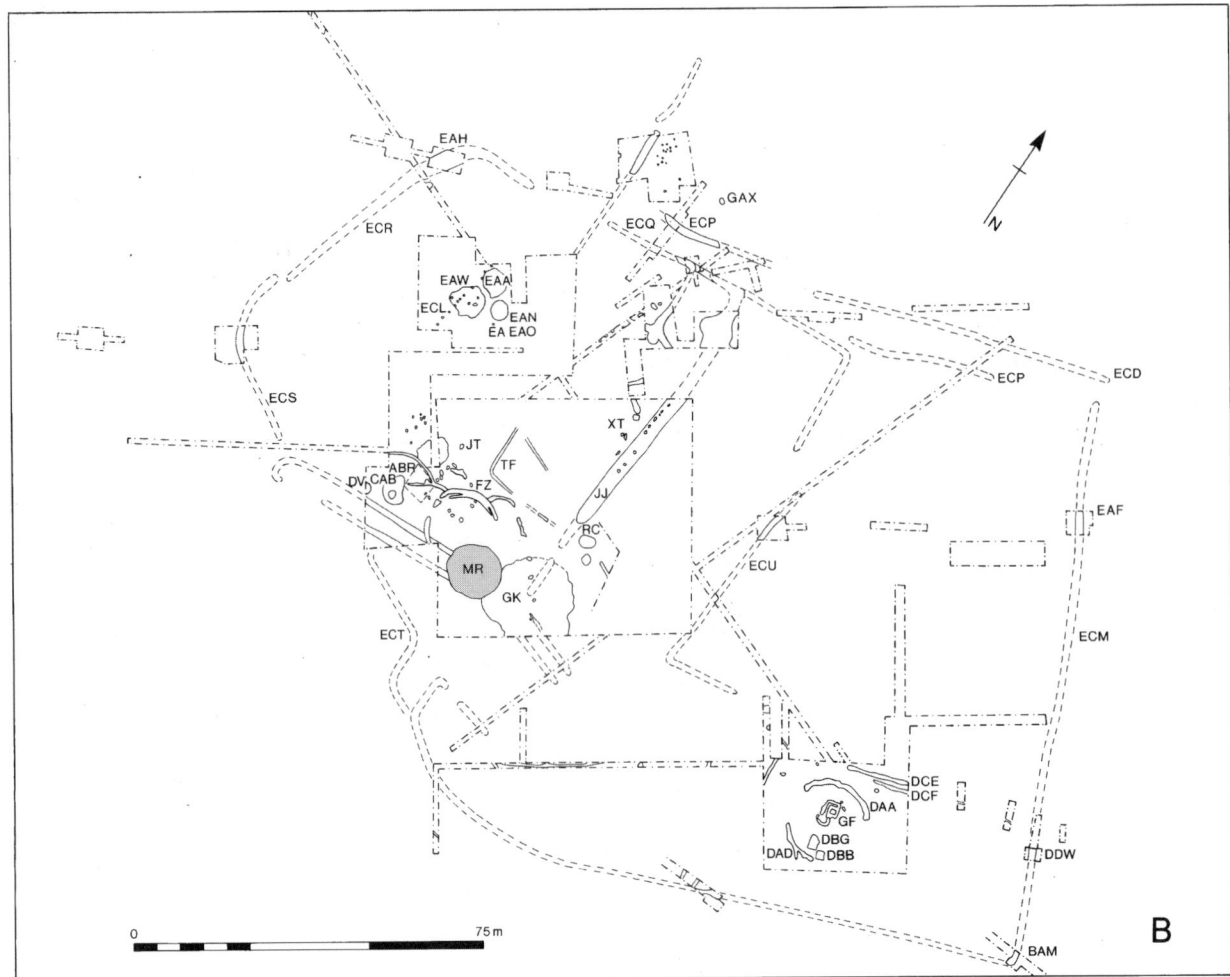

Figure 5   Overall plan: (a) Period V; (b) Period VI.

Description
Chris Going

Area 1

Period I (prehistoric)

While finds of prehistoric flint *debitage* including tools and the occasional sherd of flint-gritted pottery attest to activity on or close to the site in the prehistoric period, no definite Period I features were recognised in this area of the site. It is probable, however, that some of the small and, for the most part, stratigraphically isolated hollows [*eg* EB, JW, and TV], with their possibly leached fills are assignable to this phase (Fig. 6).

Period II (Iron Age)

In Period II, as in Period I, there was no definite evidence of site activity, save perhaps for a few discrete features. Gully DQ pre-dates trackside Ditch ABL, and thus must date to the pre-conquest period, but it contained no finds and is not closely datable. To its north, sharply curved Gully DV, which contained two sherds of pottery datable to the later Iron Age, may also pre-date the trackway, although at no point was any stratigraphic relationship between them determined. The trackway itself [ABL–ABM], which ran obliquely across Area 1, may in its inception date to this period, and although it has no definite relationship with the other enclosure ditches it appears on morphological grounds to pre-date them, and thus may provide the main excavated system with a Roman *terminus post quem* (Fig. 6).

Period III (Roman: AD 43–c.125)

In the eastern part of this area two gullies were excavated [SF and TF] (Fig. 7). It is clear from their converging alignments that they represent two episodes of activity, but in the absence of any stratigraphic relationship between them it is unclear which of the two was the earlier. Both east and west terminals of Gully SF are lost, but its alignment is adopted for a short distance by a later gully [AAJ]. Perhaps significantly, pottery from AAJ 4, the 'primary fill' of this feature, dated to *c.*AD 75–110, is described as 'fresh' (Fig. 47). The alignment is probably a continuation of SF, here at least once recut. It is possible that SF continues further to the east, and a possible length of it was noted. It is almost certainly earlier than the possible enclosure Ditch JJ, but as it cuts across the latter at the point where it is interrupted by a causeway their relationship cannot be proved.

Gully TF ran for some 10 m on a NE/SW heading before turning eastwards through roughly 90 degrees. This eastwards alignment was traced for about one metre, before it was lost in a series of later features. On morphological grounds it seems probable that TF was the later of the two gullies, and that it was linked with the earliest cut of Ditch JJ.

Ditch JJ (Plate 2), which nearly bisects Area 1, appears to be an integral component, perhaps the original east side, of Enclosure ECR (Fig. 4b). The southern side of this enclosure runs obliquely to Trackway ABL–ABM, but their stratigraphic relationship was not determined. By this period the two trackway ditches [ABL–ABM] appear to have been abandoned and allowed to silt up, a process which was apparently largely complete by the early second century (for the pottery from the ditch fills, *see* Fig. 47).

Plate 2   Ditch JJ, section, from south-east (HAT).

The primary and early fills of Ditch JJ [JJ 3–4, 6–7] contain later first to early second-century pottery. It probably formed a sub-division of Enclosure ECR together with Ditch/Gully TF, and is thus perhaps datable to the later first century AD. If so, this provides Gully SF with a date in the early post-conquest period, a date which the pottery from AAJ 4 supports. However, the interior of the enclosure appears to have been largely unexplored, and no features appear to be definitely associated with its earliest phase, although on the west side of JJ are a number of pits and hollows. Some of them may belong to this period, although their finds are undiagnostic.

OTHER FEATURES

A number of features may be dated to this period on the evidence of their fills. These discrete features include the small Pits DN and DX, and also Hollows EW, HX/CAH, and MZ. Pit JT, which was cut into the possibly natural Hollow JV, may also be assignable to this phase. To the north of this area was a complex cluster of discrete postholes and small irregularly-shaped pits. Most of these lacked finds [*eg* CAT, CBD, CBG, PG, PQ, PT, and

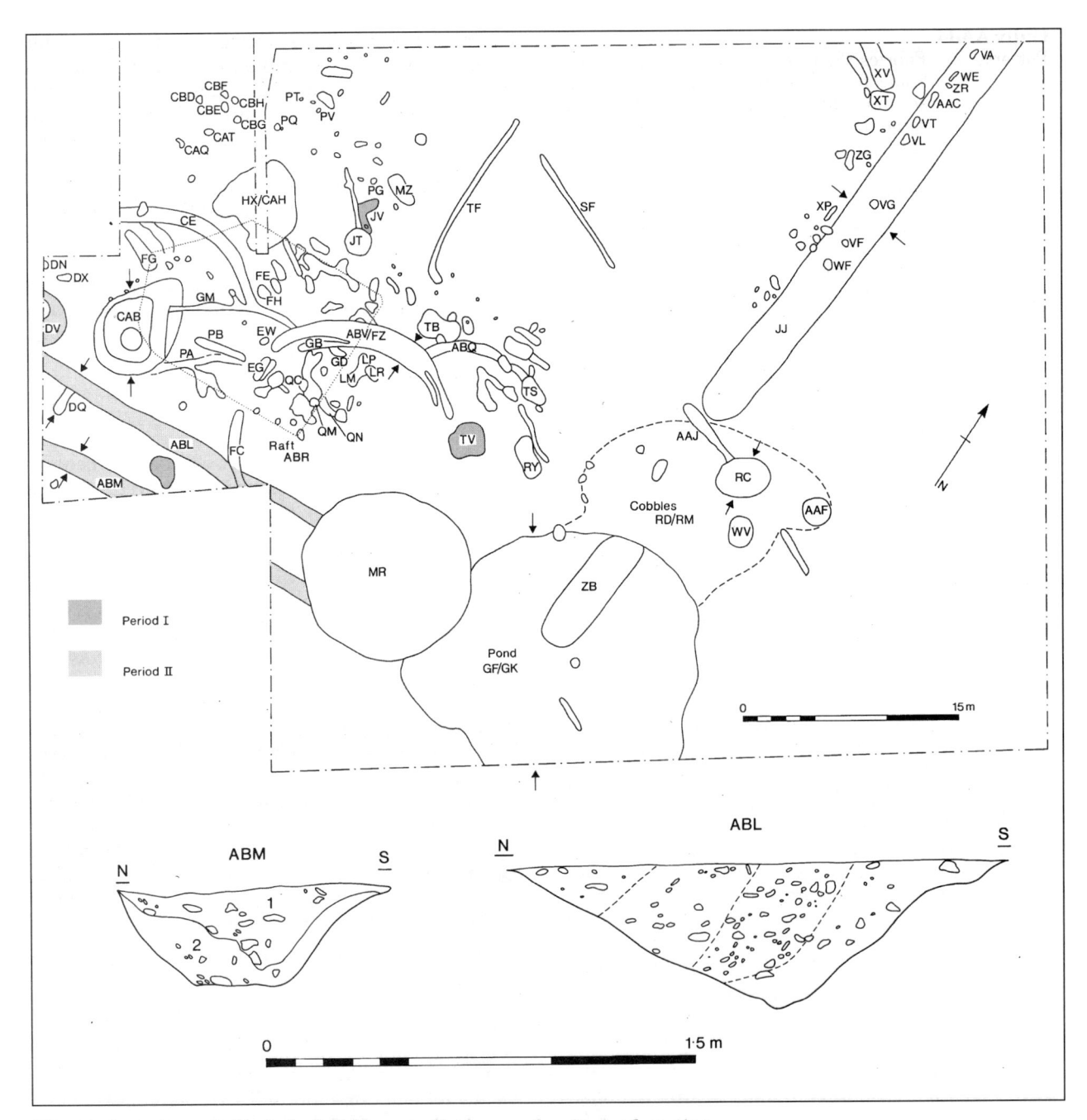

Figure 6   Area 1, Periods I & II, overall plan and principal sections.

PV], but several of the remainder [CAQ, CBE, CBF, and CBH] produced pottery of this date, admittedly in very small quantities, and may thus be assignable to Period III. While they have no discernible pattern, they may represent earthfast structures.

Perhaps also datable to the early Roman period in Area 1 is Well CAB (Fig. 8). While the well shaft was excavated to a depth of 14.5 m, it was not bottomed, so that contexts associated with its construction and the shaft lining were not reached. Material from the lowest levels reached during the excavation of the shaft, at a depth of some 13 m, are datable to the first century AD, suggesting that the shaft had begun to be filled up by the end of the first century or shortly after, possibly when Area 3 features EAW/EAN were constructed. If so, the well is datable to the first century. To the east of the well a number of features [*eg* Gully PA and Hollow PB] were cut. These contained pottery of the later first and early second centuries.

Period III Dating Evidence

Ditch JJ [primary fills JJ6, JJ7]
Pottery: Fabrics 19, 20a, 34, 37, 39, 49, 52, 53, 56, 57 *(not illustrated)*.
Samian: First century AD; Trajanic-Hadrianic.

Pit JT
Pottery: Fabric 57. Fig. 46.95.

Gully SF
Pottery: *c.*first to second centuries AD *(not illustrated)*.

Gully TF
Pottery: First century AD *(not illustrated)*.
Samian: Antonine – ?intrusive.

Gully AAJ4
Pottery: Fabrics 33, 34, 49, 53, 57. Fig. 47.121–127. Some fresh sherds of later first to early second-century shell-tempered pottery came from this feature, which may be equivalent to Gully SF.
Samian: First century; Flavian; Flavian or Flavian-Trajanic.

Pits CAQ, CBE, CBF, CBH
Pottery: Very small quantities, first to early second century *(not illustrated)*.

Ditch ABL *(trackway)*
Pottery: Fabrics 5a, 9, 34, 52, 53, 57. Fig. 47.99–108.
Samian: Claudio-Neronian.

The range of early shell-tempered, bead-rimmed jars (Fabric 57) and grog-tempered vessels (Fabric 53), together with the samian *(Samian report)*, seems to date the infill of ABL to the Neronian or the early Flavian periods (ie c.AD 50/60–75). Two worn sherds of Gallo-Belgic pottery are the only early imports to the site. However, the context also produced a few abraded sherds of Nene valley ware and oxidised Hadham ware (Fabrics 5a, 9). These are unlikely to be earlier than the third to fourth century, and are almost certainly intrusive in what was, after all, an open feature.

Ditch ABM *(trackway)*
Pottery: Fabrics 20a, 35, 56. Fig. 47.109–111.
Samian: First to second century.

The presence in ABM of Highgate Wood ware (Fabric 38) and the two-handled flagon from Brockley Hill (Fabric 20a) suggests that filling of the primary ditch did not occur much before c.AD 60–75. The Trajanic samian dish from the lowest fill [MM4] could well be derived from the rather mixed levels above. The middle layer contained a ring-necked flagon sherd (not illustrated). The samian appears to be residual. Although most material from the upper layers of the ditch is Flavian-Trajanic in date, vessels dating until at least Ceramic phase 3 (130–180/200) are present.

Well CAB [Lowest fills CAB 16–19]
Pottery: Fabric 53, first century AD. Fig. 43.1, 2.

PERIOD III DISCUSSION
The pottery from the trackway ditch fills [ABL, ABM] suggests that the feature went out of use some time in the later first century AD. Ditch SF, if it is to be identified with AAJ 4, may be dated to the later first century, while it seems probable that Ditch JJ was in existence by the early second century. The exact sequence of the well is difficult to define. Although no lining packing (and thus pre-well fills) were found, it could be deduced from the pottery recovered from the lowest excavated fills that this major construction was a comparatively early undertaking, and that its infilling and disuse also occurred at a comparatively early stage. It has been suggested that the sherd links within these fills suggest 'a single dumping episode' rather than general infilling in use Pottery from the lowest shaft fills [CAB 16–19] included two grog-tempered jars hardly likely to be current much after the Neronian period. After initial filling, the well may have been left open (but presumably top sealed; it was still some 5 m deep) and backfilled towards the end of the second century with some 10 m of spoil containing residual first-century material. In addition, however, the assemblage contained samian of Hadrianic to early Antonine date, which has been suggested as 'intrusive, probably having sunk down from deposits above' (Coarse Pottery Report, below). This is an unlikely event in a deposit of this nature, and an alternative theory is that the well did not go out of use until Period IV, when the shaft was filled during two separate dumping events [CAB 16–19: CAB 6–13], in the early and mid- to late second century respectively. The weathering cone may therefore have developed subsequently, as would be expected in such circumstances, being finally infilled in the fourth century [CAB 2–5, etc].

Period IV (c. 125–200/10)

During the second quarter of the second century the small complex of shallow features (Fig. 9) lying just to the east of the well [FH1, GD1, KL1, LK1, LM1, LP1, LR1, QC1, QM1 and QN1] was sealed with a raft of packed flints and patches of chalk [ABR], covering some 10 × 14 m. The precise function of this spread, which included Layers EV, EF and FF, and appears to have been between 200–250 mm in thickness, is not known. No foundations were discovered in connection with this feature, but a number of postholes to the north-east may, perhaps, be associated with it. It is either a simple hard-standing, perhaps partly roofed, or part of a structure.

Probably connected with this reorganisation was the rearrangement of the water supply. The shaft of Well CAB (Plate 3) was deliberately backfilled, presumably close to the original ground surface, with largely sterile spoil [CAB 6–13]. The topmost strata of this infilling [principally CAB 11], contained a substantial assemblage of coarse pottery and samian, together with a quantity of animal bones which included the remains of three dogs of domestic breeds and three horses' heads *(Bone Report)*. This deposit, which is datable to c.150–190, is unlikely to be straightforward domestic debris, and is perhaps best interpreted as a sealing or closing deposit, created when the well was replaced as a water source by Pond GF, which was cut some 40 m to the west at about this time.

POND GF
This feature, a bowl-shaped hollow measuring approximately 11.5 × 12.5 m, was excavated into the clay subsoil. A small number of features were sealed by the initial lining of the pond, but it is not clear whether they predated it, and as they lacked finds their date is not certain. The initial pond lining [TX] comprised a 100 mm-thick layer of stones, which in one area appears to have been packed into a hollow [ZB], best identified as a southern extension of Ditch JJ. This initial lining appears to have extended north and north-east of the pond as a spread of cobbles [RD, RM]. In the area of the ditch the pond appears to have been consolidated with fills [JQ, TW, KE, and KA], each shot in from the north, all sealed lastly by chalk Layer KB. The pond was cut across the southern extension of

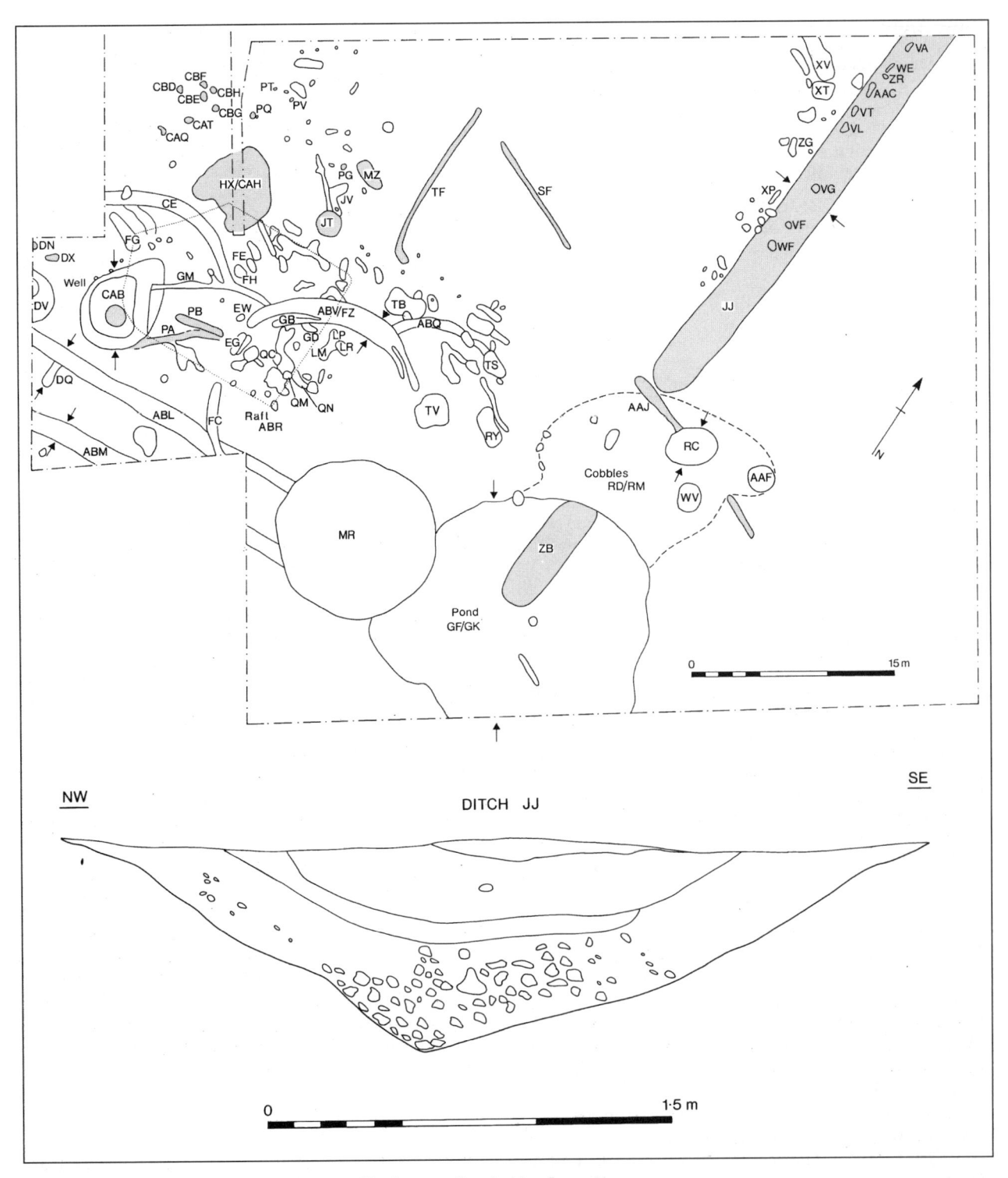

Figure 7 Area 1, Period III, overall plan and principal sections.

Ditch JJ, which seems either to have been allowed to silt up, or to have been backfilled, at about this time. The final ditch fill [JJ1] was composed of chalky rubble similar to that used to line its hollow in the pond itself.

Period IV Dating Evidence
Features FH, KL, LP, LR *[predating Raft ABR]*
Pottery: Fabrics 8, 9, 19, 20A, 33, 37–9, 46–50, 52–3, 56, 58. Later first to second century.

Well CAB *[Shaft filling: CAB 6–13]*.
Pottery: Fabrics 12, 13, 19, 25, 30, 31, 37, 38, 39, 41, 48, 52, 59. Fig. 43.3–24; Fig. 44.25, 26.
Samian: Mainly Antonine.
Iron: **Iron 16,** also some hobnails, probably from a discarded sandal or shoe.

Pond GF *[lining: TX 1–5; TA 1–4, RA1]*
Pottery: Fabrics 56–7 *(not illustrated)*.
Quern: **Querns 51.**

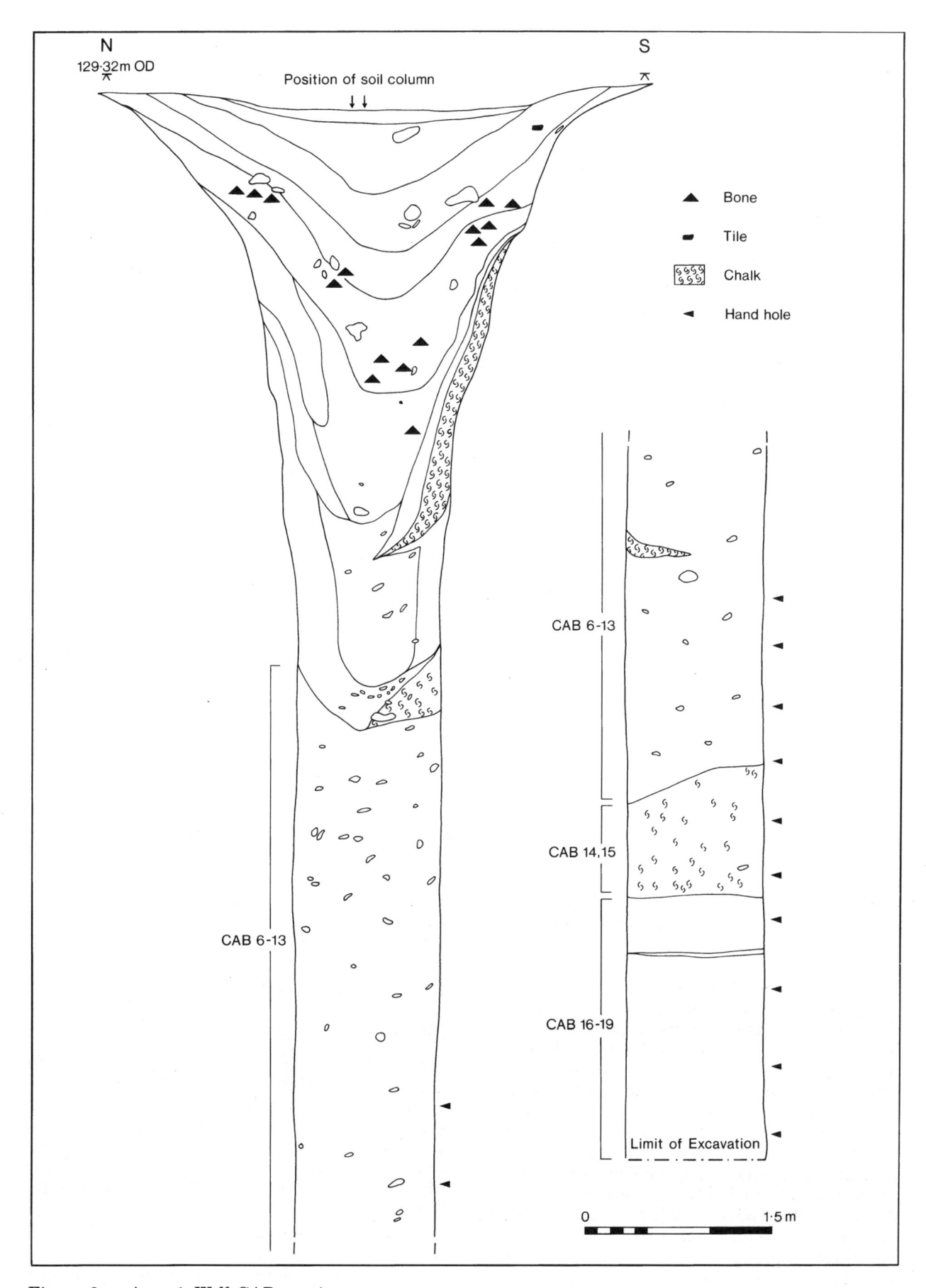

Figure 8   Area 1: Well CAB, section.

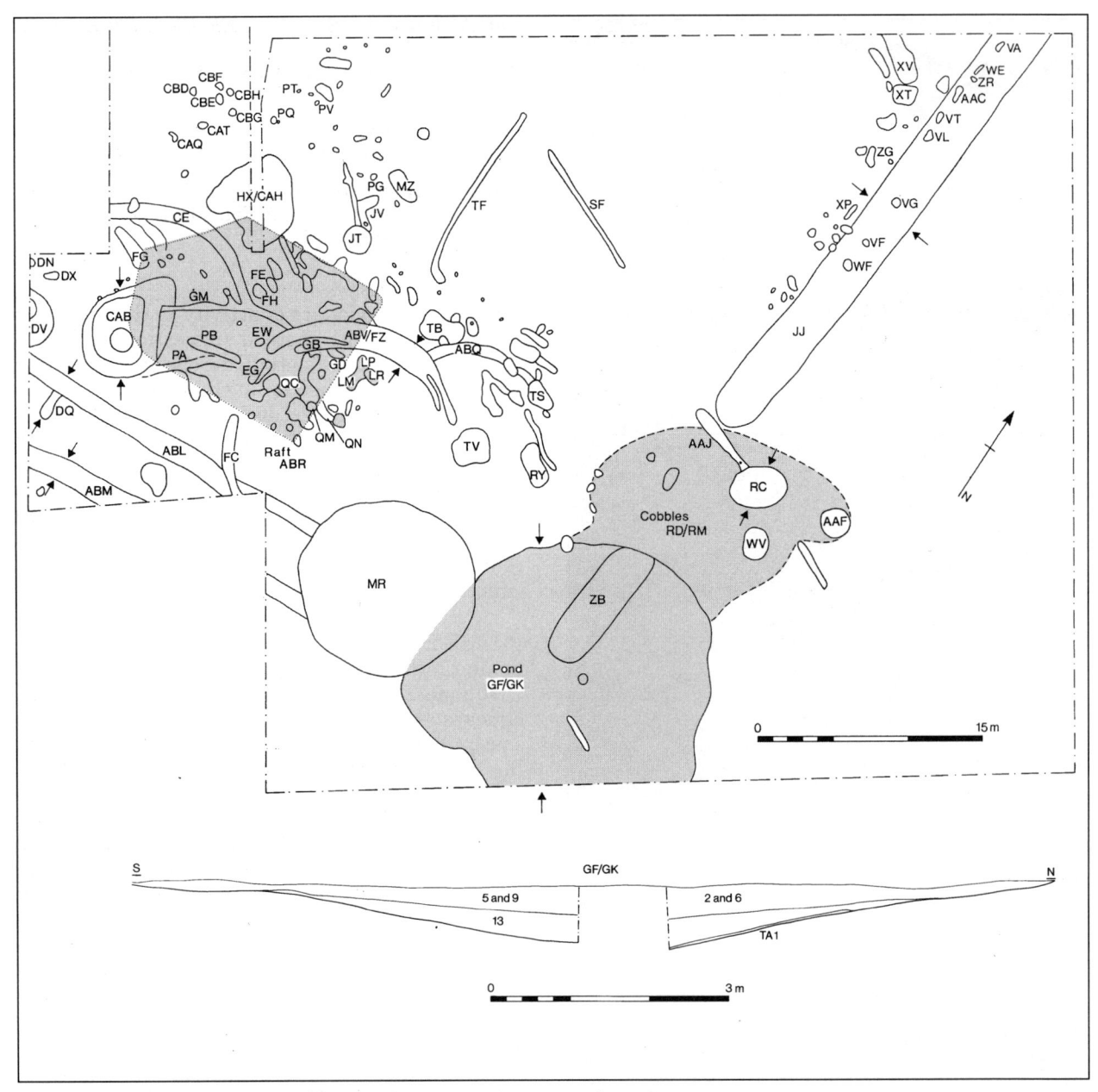

Figure 9   Area 1, Period IV, overall plan and principal sections.

PERIOD IV DISCUSSION

The pottery from the features sealed by Raft ABR (Plate 4) was restricted in the main to wares of the first–early second centuries, the latest datable to the period c.115–30. This is presumably the date for the construction of the raft. Although some later pottery was found, it was recovered from under what appears to have been later patching [*ie* FH 1] and should not be regarded as sealed beneath the primary raft. The chronological evidence, sparse though it is, suggests that Well CAB, which had been partly infilled in the late first or early second century, was finally backfilled in a single operation in the later Antonine period, at approximately the same time that feature EAA (Area 3) was abandoned and infilled, and Raft ABR was constructed over the features to its north. At this time, Pond GF was also constructed and lined. The pottery from the lining contexts is generally of a first to second-century date.

Period V (c. 200/10–400)

PHASE 1

Some time during the third century Raft ABR ceased to be patched and repaired, and over it formed a dark, organic accumulation [EK 2], on top of which in some areas stony patches appear to have been laid [*eg* FE, FH]. However, for the most part Layer EK2 remained unsealed, producing pottery datable into the fourth century (Fig. 10).

Further to the east, the line of Ditch JJ appears to have remained in use as a boundary, marked now by a ragged 12 m-long gully [JK] and, perhaps, postholes supporting a fence-line. This gully appears to have fallen out of use towards the end of the third century, producing one of the few site assemblages of pottery datable to this phase.

Plate 3   Well CAB, after excavation, from east (HAT).

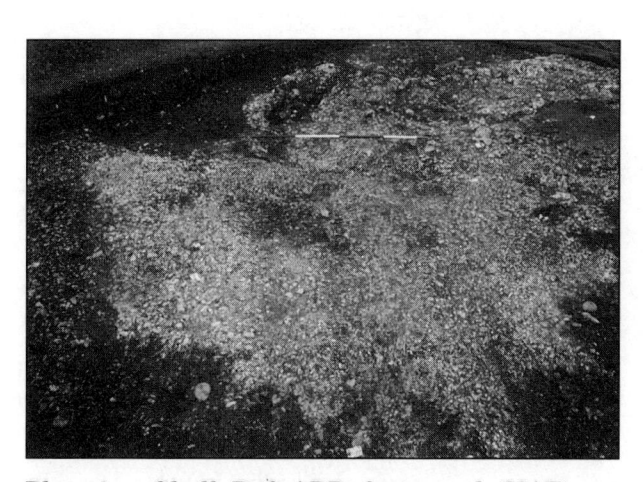

Plate 4   Chalk Raft ABR, from south (HAT).

Phase 1 Dating Evidence
Gully JK *[JK 1, VJ 1]*
Pottery: Fabrics; 20a, 37, 39, 58, 58a.
             Fig. 50.215–223.
Samian   Hadrianic–early Antonine; Antonine.
Coin: **Coin 83**, 268–70.
Iron: **Iron 5, 6, 32, 45.**

Raft ABR *[CE 2, CE 5, CE 6, EF, EF 2, ET, EV 2, FE, FF]*
Pottery: Fabrics 5B, 31, 32, 46, 53, 56, 57.
             Fig. 50.200–206.

Soil Spread EK2
Coins: **Coin 105,** 268–75: **141,** 324–330.

Gully Complex ABQ *[TJ, TL, TR, TS]*
Pottery   Fabrics 5, 8, 9. Fig. 50.224–226.
Quern: **Quern 47.**

Phase 1 Discussion
There is little evidence of activity in the early part of this period, with instead suggestions of lack of maintenance if not actual dereliction. The yard surface, while patched for a while, appears to have been allowed to go into decline at about this time. The pottery from the components of Gully Complex ABQ is of third-century or later date, with residual samian and second-century coarse wares. However, the sherds are fairly abraded and the contexts fairly mixed, suggesting secondary redeposition rather than primary dumping. There is little sign of continued site development.

PHASE 2
Some time after the raft went out of use a small, wishbone-shaped complex of gullies [CE/GM] appears to have been cut into it (Fig. 10). The southern of the two gully arms [CE] leads towards the well, but its relationship with the latter remains uncertain. By this period, settlement of the earlier infilling of the well shaft had led to the formation of a weathering cone, into which Gully CE may have drained. The northern, sharply recurved arm of the gully complex skirts the well weathering cone to the west, but its terminus is not known for it passes beyond the excavation limits. The gully complex bears off at a tangent to the later penannular gullies GB and ABV/FZ.

The penannular gullies
Some time in the later Roman period, Gully Complex ABQ [TL/TJ, and TR and TS] appears to have been superceded by a further complex of penannular gullies. Of these, the earliest is the imperfectly known ABV, which was seen in sections of the latest Gully FZ. Fills of FZ which have been identified retrospectively as components of Gully ABV are FZ 11, which consisted of an orangey clay matrix, and FZ 17, a 'grey silty loam', sealed beneath FZ 7. This gully sequence appears to clip Raft ABR, and thus to post-date it, and is probably contemporary with the drainage complex CE/GM, which cuts it. Within the gully complex a number of features were excavated including pits and postholes, but none of them formed a regular pattern suggesting any recognisable kind of structure.

After a period of use, silt build-up appears to have necessitated a relining of Pond GF. This was done in a similar manner to the first lining [TA]. After this time the pond slowly mired up in use, initially with a series of silty deposits [GK7–9, 12–15], and subsequently with darker, loamy deposits.

Phase 2 Dating Evidence
Gully CE
Coins: **Coin 12**: 161–80; **120**: 268–70; **129**: c.270+; **182, 184, 186**: 341–348; **293**: late third to late fourth.

Gully GM
Worked bone: **Bone 28** (knife handle).
Copper alloy: **CuAlloy 34** (mirror).

Pond consolidation KA
Coin: **Coin 248**: 367–78.
Querns: **Quern 52**.

Pond relining TA
Copper alloy: **CuAlloy 4**: (bracelet): **48**: (needle).
Iron: **Iron 17**: (socketed knife).

Gully TL
Coin: **Coin 302**: late third to late fourth.
Copper alloy: **CuAlloy 7**: (bracelet).

Phase 2 Discussion
Pond GF relining [TA] appears to follow a sequence of dumps in the hollow formed by the former Ditch JJ [ZB]. One of these [KA] contained a coin of Valentinian. While it is not clear whether this context was wholly sealed by the stratigraphically later relining, it strongly suggests that the pond was refurbished some time in the third quarter of the fourth century. To the west of the pond, Raft ABR was cut by gullies which drained into the sump of Well CAB. It is difficult to date these with any confidence, but it seems probable that they were cut some time in the second or third quarters of the fourth century. The pennanular gully sequence is not easy to date very closely: the earliest of them [TL] produced a coin of the later third to fourth centuries and was clearly still open at this time, which suggests that the gully complex which replaced it [GB/FZ] dates to the fourth century. The gully appears to have been recut on two occasions, but no finer chronological distinctions may be made, other than observing that each must be of fourth-century date.

PHASE 3

The latest activity on the site appears to be restricted mainly to deliberate infilling. To this phase may be dated the final infilling of Well CAB's weathering cone (Fig. 8) and the abandonment and subsequent infilling of the final pennanular Gully FZ, which also contained a substantial assemblage of material. Among the features open into the later fourth century were Pit RC, measuring 1 × 1.8 × 0.5 m, and Gully AAJ, which debouched into it, Pit AAF, 2 m in diameter and shallow, and Hollow GW. These features produced important collections of material, including substantial amounts of animal bone: approximately 85–90% of the animal bone assemblage from the site came from contexts dated to the later fourth century (*Animal Bone*). However, in terms of both volume of material involved and of finds, the most substantial deposits are those dumped onto the later fourth-century pond silts [GK 1–6, 10–11]. These dark anaerobic fills produced large collections of bone and pottery datable to the end of the Roman period, contemporary with the weathering cone of Well CAB.

Further to the east, a few late post-ditch features were noted to the west of the former Ditch JJ. These comprised four pits [XP, XV, XT and ZG], which produced later fourth-century material including, from Pit XV, a coin of Theodosius (**Coin 253**). However, none of these features formed a coherent pattern, and it is not certain that any were used for structural purposes. The old course of Ditch JJ may at this time have been marked by fence lines, including Postholes VA, WE, ZR, AAC, ?VF, VG, ?VL, VT and WF. Two within the old ditch [VA and VJ] contained fourth-century material.

Both Winder and Murphy (*Animal Bone* and *Plant Remains*) noted the lack of molluscan evidence from the site. Murphy felt that the site soil conditions might have destroyed them. Winder, however, concluded that this was unlikely on the evidence of the uneroded and comparatively fresh condition of the animal bone from features such as GF and CAB, and concluded that their lack was more probably due to the fact that the carcasses and bones of the deposits had been buried quickly, before decomposition set in. It is impossible to be certain, but the interpretation Winder puts on the bone assemblage, that it may represent the aftermath of some local disaster, fits the facts as well as any. Site activity during this final phase may well have ended in a comparatively dramatic episode.

Phase 3 Dating Evidence
GK+ (Unstratified over pond)
Pottery: Fabrics 5, 57, 58. Fig. 53.327–332.

Pond GK [fills GK 1–6, 10–11]
Coins: **Coin 213, 223, 230, 232, 234–236**: 364–78.
Pottery: Fabrics 5a, 5b, 8, 9, 10, 12, 16, 19, 21, 28, 37, 39, 48, 58. Fig. 52.272–312; Fig. 53.313–326.
Copper alloy: **CuAlloy 6, 11, 13, 14, 17**: (bracelets); **38**: (tweezers); **43**: (scoop/spatula); **47**: (miniature stand?); **53**: (chain).
Worked bone: **Bone**: (comb).
Brooches: **Brooch 15**: first century BC to third AD.
Glass: **Glass 10**: (bowl); **22**: (hairpin shaft).
Shale: **Shale 3**: (bracelet); **8**: (spindle whorl).
Lead: ?slag.
Iron: **Iron 14**: (?chisel); **18–23**: (knives).
Quern: **Quern 5–7**: (Mayen Lava); **15, 18–20, 35, 37**: (millstone grit); **64**: (Hertfordshire puddingstone).

Pit RC
Coins: **Coin 150**: 330–335; **193**: 348–354; **225**: 364–378; **244–45**: 367–78.
Pottery: Fabrics 9, 16, 39. (* 13, 16, 35, 58, 61, 231, 42). Fig. 51.252–257.
Hone: **Stone 1**.
Copper alloy: **CuAlloy 5**: (bracelet).
Iron: **Iron 15**: (tanged awl or punch).
Environmental: From RC 4 came some preserved seeds of duckweed (*Lemna* sp), suggesting that the feature was waterlogged.

Gully FZ
Coins: Coin **88, 119**: 268–70; **99**: c.268–75; **133**: 287–93; **137**: 305–6; **152**: 330–35; **188**: 341–48.
Pottery: Fabrics 5b, 9, 13, 19, 34, 37, 39, 45, 48, 49, 58, 58a. Fig. 51.231–250.
Shale: **Shale 3**: (bracelet).
Querns: **Quern 36, 60, 62**: (millstone grit).
Iron: **Iron 3**: (fragmentary socket, possibly from a reaping hook).

Gully FC
Shale: **Shale 7**: (plano-convex spacer bead).

Pit XT
Coin: **Coin 124**: 268–70.

Pit XV
Coin: **Coin 253**: 388–402.

Well CAB *[weathering cone: components EC1–2, ES1 (BX1); ES2 (ES3)]*
Coins: **Coin 27**: 253–60; **33**: 253–68; **84**: 268–70; **101, 108, 109**: c.268–75; **164**: 330–335.
Pottery: Fabrics 5a–c, 8, 9, 19, 22, 37, 39, 41, 42, 43, 46, 48, 49, 55, 58. Figs 44–46, 27–94.
Copper alloy: **CuAlloy 3**: (bracelet); **40**: (ligula); **50**: (vessel?).
Iron: **Iron 12**: (set?); **13**: (hammer); **29**: (stylus); **33**: (padlock case); **46**: (joiner's dog).
Shale: **Shale 6**: (spindle whorl, possibly post-Roman).
Quern: **Quern 40, 41**: (millstone grit).

Phase 3 Discussion
While there are a number of straightforward later fourth-century features on the site, such as pits, the latest features appear to be dumping episodes, when substantial quantities of pottery and animal bone including, perhaps, some largely complete carcasses, appear to have been deposited in the pond, the top of the well, to backfill the final curvilinear Gully FZ, and so on. Winder (*Bone report*) has noted the fact that the bone assemblage is not obviously the result of domestic activities, and suggests that it might have resulted from the processing of the carcasses of animals from more than one site, or that some small-scale disaster necessitated the disposal of the remnants of a large number of livestock. Corney (*Coin report*) has commented on the apparent frequency of coins of the period 364–88 (Coin period XIV), something the site has in common with the rural site at Cow Roast, Herts, but not with villas in the Verulamium region. Interestingly, the comparatively large coin samples from Phase 3 deposits FZ, CAB and GK do not include any of 388–402 (Coin period XV). Even if the coinage supply to the site was diminishing then, the likelihood that there should be *no* issues of this date-bracket in these deposits suggests that they were laid down early in Period XV at the latest. That some activity persisted later than this on the site is clear; Pit XV produced a coin of Theodosius, and other pits nearby are probably of a similar date.

If one had to hazard a guess as to what all this means, then it seems probable that, when quite a lot of the Period XIV coinage was circulating, an event occurred on the site which resulted in the well and other features such as the pond being backfilled with debris including the remains of numerous recently-perished animals, and that these were sealed with chalk. At about this time, too, the corn drier appears to have been destroyed by fire and not rebuilt. After this, site activity fell off almost completely, only a very few features being datable to Coin period XV or later.

Period VI (post-Roman)
Within Area 1 only a few post-Roman features were found or identified. Pit FG contained a sherd of medieval pottery which, if not intrusive, assigns the feature firmly to the medieval period. Perhaps the most important post-Roman feature on the site is Pond MR. This was c. 11 m in diameter, and contained quantities of later Roman finds in addition to medieval and post-medieval material. The feature was still evident as a shallow depression prior to the excavation, suggesting that it was not infilled until comparatively recent times. It has been identified as a medieval or post-medieval pond. The quantities of late Roman pottery from within it perhaps derive from a segment of Gully FZ, which it would certainly have cut through and destroyed.

Period VI Dating evidence
Pit FG
Pottery: Sherd of ?Saxo-Norman shell-tempered ware.

Pond MR
Pottery: Includes post-medieval white glazed wares and willow-pattern sherds.
Copper alloy: **CuAlloy 61**: (mount); **71**: (double spiked loop); **82**: (sheeting).

Period VI Discussion
There is very little indication of any activity on the site, still less of occupation, much after the end of the fourth century. By this time, Roman pottery, like coinage, was essentially a thing of the past. Hand-made wheel-thrown wares, found in some parts of the region (*eg* Foxholes, Herts), are not attested here, and while there are some possible post-Roman objects on the site (*eg* **Shale 6**), it is impossible to point to much archaeological evidence for activity on the site in the six or seven centuries following the Roman era. There is no evidence of chaff-tempered wares or later Saxon pottery. The land possibly continued to be farmed, until by the Saxo-Norman period the first features of the medieval landscape make their appearance, among them being Pond MR, dug to the west of the older Roman pond. Interestingly the latter feature, with its nutritious fills, should have survived as a crop mark; why was it not used as a pond foundation?

21

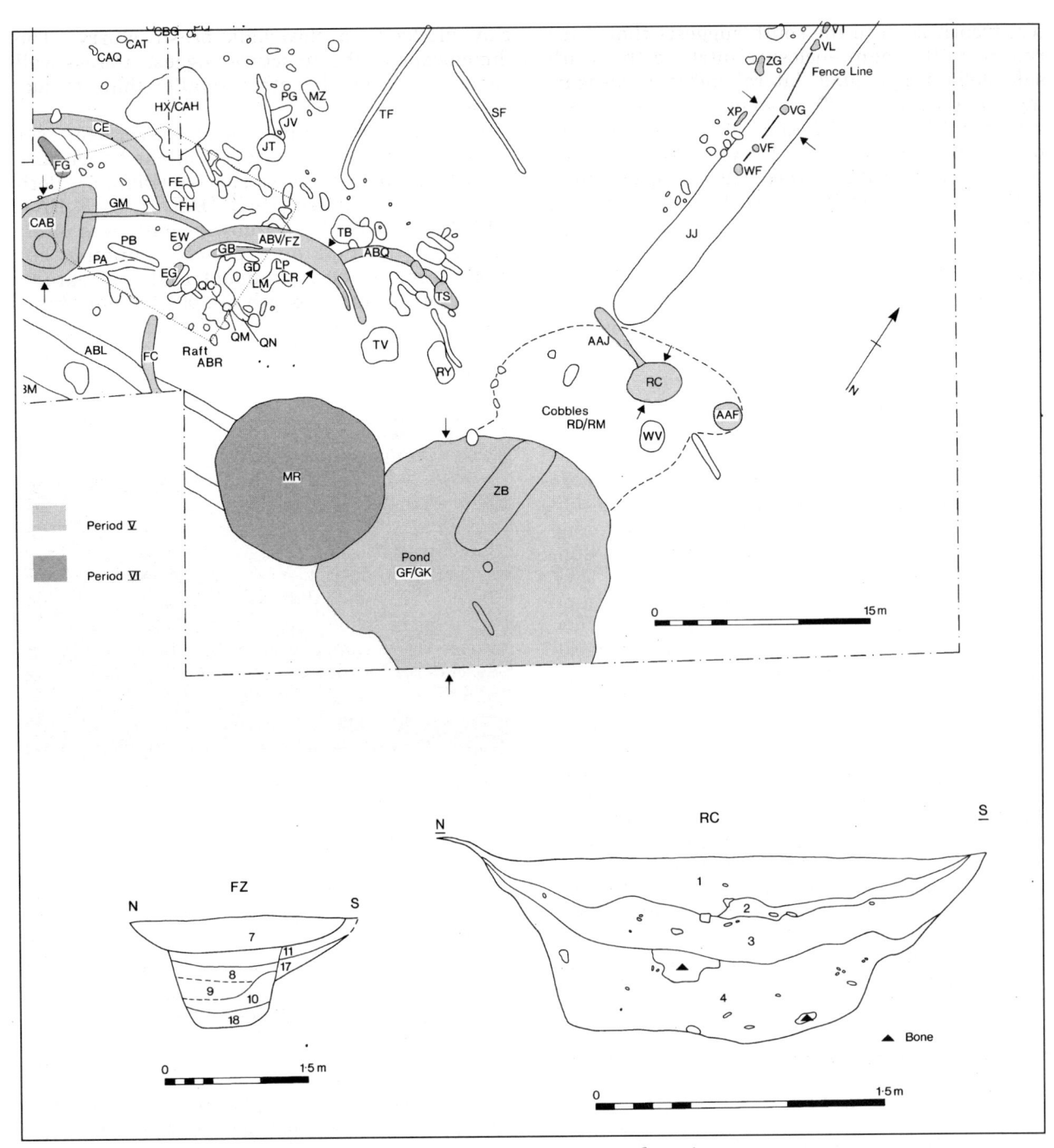

Figure 10   Area 1, Periods V & VI, overall plan and principal sections.

Area 2

Periods I–III (prehistoric to pre-AD 125)

There was virtually no datable stratified evidence of pre-Period IV activity on this part of the site. However, as in Area 1 there were a number of small isolated aceramic features, generally also devoid of other finds, which probably date to this period (Fig. 11). The only definite pre-enclosure activity on this part of the site was Posthole DBA, which was cut by the possible sub-enclosure Gully DAU.

Period IV (125–200/10)

The Sub-Enclosure

The earliest features in the south-eastern part of the site appear to be the two parallel Ditches DCE and DCF (Fig. 11). Two small trenches to the east of the open area each revealed a single linear feature on the same general alignment as DCE [DDR and DDO]. These were probably a continuation of that feature to the eastern main enclosure Ditch ECM, a distance of some 28 m. On the western side of the open area, north-south trending Gully DAU, probably forms the western side of the sub-enclosure, and a short length of similar ditch in a test trench 24 m to the south suggests that it too ran up to the main enclosure ditch on the south side, delimiting a quadrilateral enclosure measuring approximately 30 × 40 m. It is not clear whether Ditches DCE and DCF were contemporary, but the narrow gap between them suggests that one succeeded the other. The dating evidence, such as it is, suggests that DCE is the earlier of the two.

Period IV Dating evidence
Ditch DCF
Pottery: COAR, *c.*first to early/mid second century *(not illustrated).*

Gully DCE *[Components: DBH, DCC, DCD]*
Pottery: Fabric 9. Fig. 48.140.

Period IV Discussion
From the evidence that the main field system was not enlarged before the second century, these sub-divisions cannot predate the Hadrianic–Antonine period (117–161). Neither feature produced substantial amounts of datable pottery. Ditch DCF [cut DCI] produced a burnt sherd of Antonine samian, but other cuts produced only a few ceramic sherds. It is probable that the sub-enclosure was created at about the time that this part of the field system was given over to cereals processing (*Plant Remains*). While activity related to the corn drier continues into the fourth century, it is less clear how long these ditches remained open or in use. However, Ditch DCE [Section DBH] produced a crushed, but otherwise largely complete Hadham ware 'Braughing jar', probably datable to the third century, suggesting backfilling not before *c.*225/50. There is a general lack of domestic debris from this part of the site between the later second and mid fourth centuries, and the features described above could have remained open well into Period V.

Period V (c. 200/10–400/10)

PHASE 1

The first corn drier and associated features
Approximately 10 m south-west of the north *termini* of the sub-enclosure ditch were the remains of a structure identified as a corn drier. The carbonised plant remains from the later Phase 2 structure suggest it was used almost exclusively for the processing of spelt wheat, *Triticum spelta,* so the earlier drier is presumed to have had the same function. The first phase of the structure (Fig. 12), is represented by fairly fugitive evidence, as most of it had been removed during the Phase 2 remodelling. Surviving traces include part of the stokepit [GF 25] on the north side of the structure, and some parts of the flue walling which coincide with the later flue. Of the cross-wall, only the terminal survives where it projects westwards beyond the edge of the Phase 2 stokepit. Only at this point did any ashy fill survive. The structure appears to have been built of clay blocks in a clay/chalk brash 'slurry'. The dimensions of the structure suggest a cross-wall some 2 m in length, rather smaller than its successor.

The corn drier appears to have been set roughly centrally in a circular ditched enclosure [DAA], of which two arcs survive (Plate 5). Both lengths were emptied [DAB, DAE–H, DAF, DAJ, DBI, DBM–DBV]. This 1 m-wide gully was interpreted at the time as a possible building, but there seems to be little doubt that the feature, which survived to a depth of 200–300 mm, functioned as a drainage ditch. On its south-west side a 2.5 m-long subsidiary feeder gully [DAK] drains into it.

Plate 5   Circular Enclosure DAA, from east (HAT).

Phase 1 Dating Evidence
The date of the first corn drier is problematical. There is no record of pottery in the first stokepit backfill [GF 25], which would provide a firm *terminus post quem* for the construction of the Phase 2 drier. The excavator noted that the structure, by which is presumably meant the second-phase installation, was cut through a surface [LF] which contained first to second-century material. This surface may be contemporary with the earlier corn drier, but it was unsealed. The circular enclosure ditch itself contained remarkably little material in its primary or indeed in any other of its fills, but it is clearly associated with the drier and datable either to the later second or, perhaps, the third century.

PHASE 2

The second corn drier and associated features
The first corn drier was eventually demolished and replaced on the same spot by a larger structure facing in the opposite direction, with its stokepit to the south (Fig. 12: Plate 6). Morphologically it appears to have closely resembled its predecessor, having an 'L'-shaped flue with 600 mm-wide 'walls'. The flue width varied from 600 mm at the mouth to *c.*450 mm at its mid-point. The structure was built of chalk blocks of varying size up to 150 × 200 mm, set in a matrix of puddled clay and chalk fragments. Traces of rendering were noted

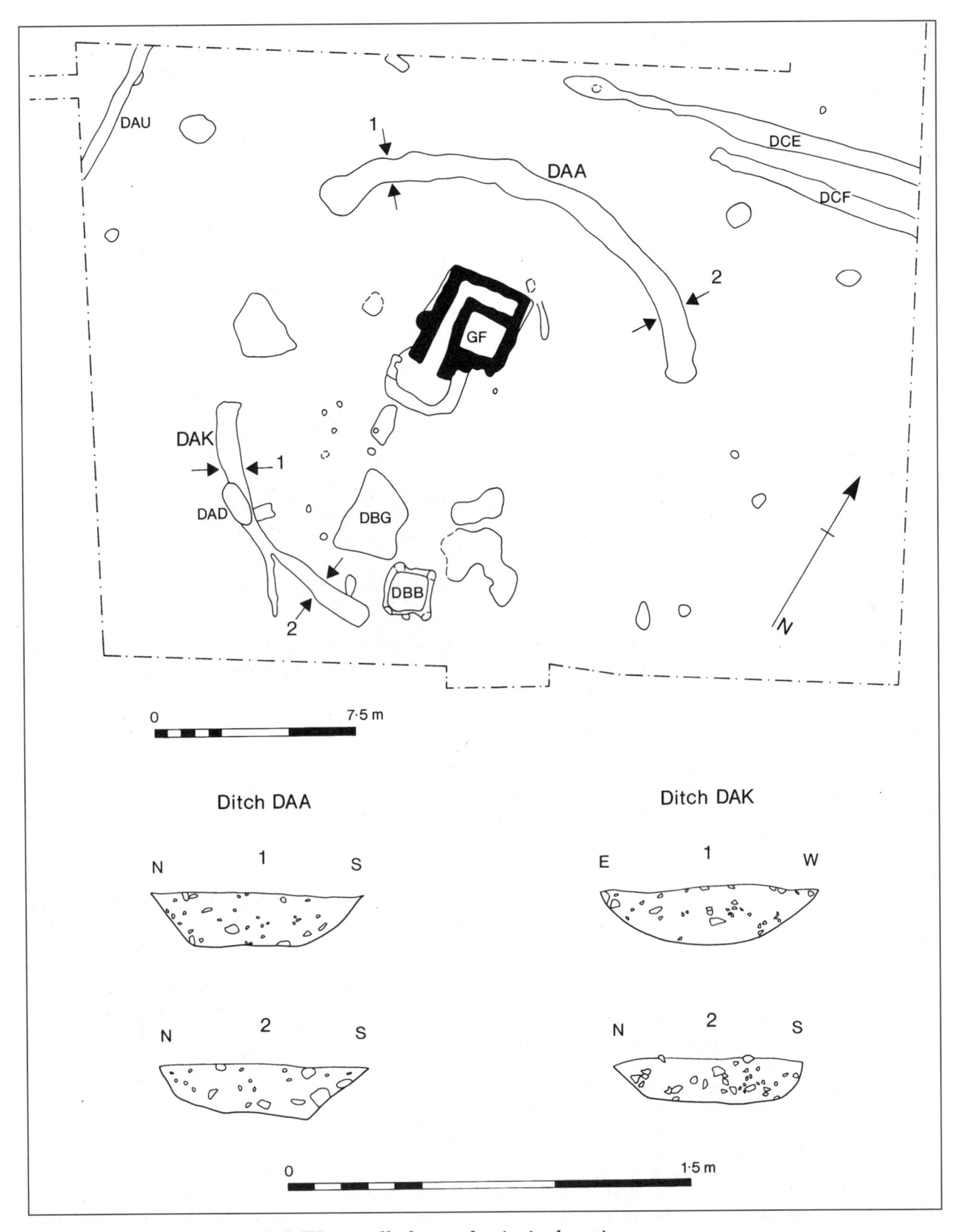

Figure 11   Area 2: Periods I–IV, overall plan and principal sections.

Plate 6   Corn Drier GF, after excavation, from south (HAT).

at the base of the flue, in the throat of which were a number of sandstone blocks. The stokehole [JA] consisted of a 'D'-shaped pit 2.3 × 1.5 × 0.6 m deep. It had steeply sloping sides and a flat base, which was lined, like the flue, with rammed chalk, on which were traces of burning. Cutting through the lowest stokepit fill and piercing its lower sides were three ragged rows of stakeholes [YF], the uprights of hurdle fencing intended as a windbreak. Plumes of fuel ash, sucked into the flue by convection, were still detectable in its basal fills [*eg.* GF 18]. Analysis of these, and of samples retrieved from the stokehole itself, indicate that the fuel comprised spelt chaff mixed with wood or charcoal (*Plant Remains*), while the remains of prime grain were found in the drier itself [*eg.* GF 16], suggesting drying prior to milling. That the latter process was carried out on this part of the site is attested by the number of quern fragments found in the area, *eg.* in GF 6, Pit RY, and in the corn drier backfill/destruction levels [*eg.* HG1–2].

A number of other features in the immediate area of the corn drier are probably assignable to this phase. Three irregular, comparatively shallow hollows [DAO, DBF and YJ] contain burnt clay fragments and charcoal, possibly fuel ash; in the case of DBF sufficient to suggest that the feature served as a hearth. The precise function of the other features is not certain. More clearly datable to this period, if more enigmatic, are Pits DBB and DBG. DBB (Figs. 12, 13) was roughly rectangular, measuring approximately 1.5 × 1.8 m, and surviving to a depth of 0.36 m below natural. At each corner were four postholes of approx 200 mm diameter [DCM, DCS, DBJ and DBK], which clearly carried some kind of superstructure. The primary pit fill [DBB 4] consisted of a black loamy clay containing a high percentage of charcoal, above which were three further dark grey and yellowish brown fills [DBB 2–4]. It may have been a latrine, but no clear cess deposits appear to have been recorded. Pit DBG lay immediately to the north-west of this structure. It measured 1.3 × 1.1 × 0.37 m in depth. Its north-east edge appears to have been revetted with chalk. The fill was a very dark, loamy clay.

Phase 2 Dating Evidence
Pit DAD
Pottery: Fabric 48. Fig. 51.264.
Coin: **Coin 44**: 253–55.

Pit DBB
Pottery: Fabrics include 8 and 59, suggesting post c.360 date *(not illustrated)*.
Coin: **Coin 168**: 337–341; **180**: 341–48.

Stakeholes YF
Querns: **Quern 33a, b**: (millstone grit)

Pit YJ
Pottery: Fabrics 5a, 37, 39. Sherds date to late third to fourth centuries *(not illustrated)*.

Corn Drier GF
[JA 1: stokehole top fill]
Pottery: Fabrics 5a, 5b. Fig. 51.260.
[HG 1–2; YH 1: spread over]
Pottery: Fabrics 8, 9, 21. Fig. 51.265–268.
Querns: **Quern 14, 28, 34**: (millstone grit).
[GF 1: debris layer over]
Pottery: Fabrics 9, 37, 58. Fig. 51.258, 259, 261.
Coin: **Coin 123**: 268–70.

Ditch DAA
Shale: **Shale 5**: (bracelet fragment).

Phase 2 Discussion
While the exact date-span of the second corn drier is not clear, it evidently cannot have been constructed much before the third century, and it is unlikely that it remained in use much beyond the later fourth century. Pottery from the stokehole fill [JA] was comparatively sparse, and what was recovered was clearly residual, being of second and third-century date. As only the topmost stokehole filling [JA 1] produced later fourth-century material, it is probable that at that time the stokehole was allowed to choke up with accumulated soot and ash from a number of firings. This may have happened fairly quickly: in the layer overlying the structure was found oak and ash charcoal was derived from mature wood, and some 20–25 mm-diameter hazel roundwood, which may have come from a superstructure (*Plant Remains*). It is possible that the structure burnt down. Whatever the exact reason for the drier falling from use, the stokehole pit was finally filled with debris-laden spoil datable to the later fourth century or after, this being the date of the pottery from the layers which sealed the structure [GF 1, HG1–2, and YH 1]. If there was a fire, it is possible that it involved more than just the corn drier: it was noted (*Quernstones*) that some of the millstone grit fragments from Gully FZ 2 [CG 1] and the pond [GF 20] were burnt, while burnt pottery of this period has also been identified (*Pottery*). This suggests that an area where corn milling was carried out may have been affected as well. An unintentional conflagration of some kind, perhaps involving more than one structure, evidently occurred on the site.

Late activity attested by other features is fairly minimal. The pottery from the nearby pits seems to be mostly residual, but that from possible Latrine DBB and Hollows YJ and DAO is clearly

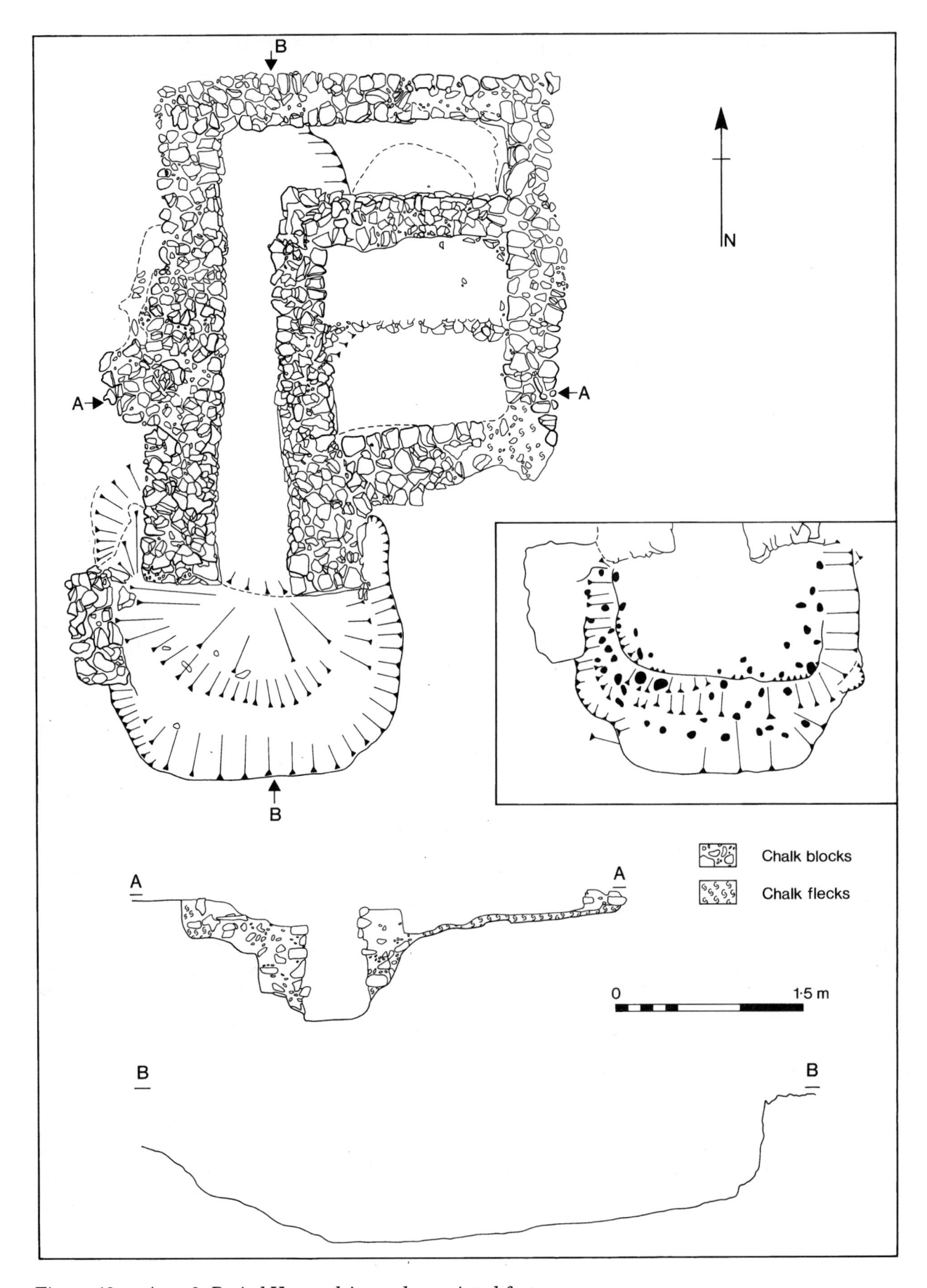

Figure 12   Area 2: Period V corn drier and associated features.

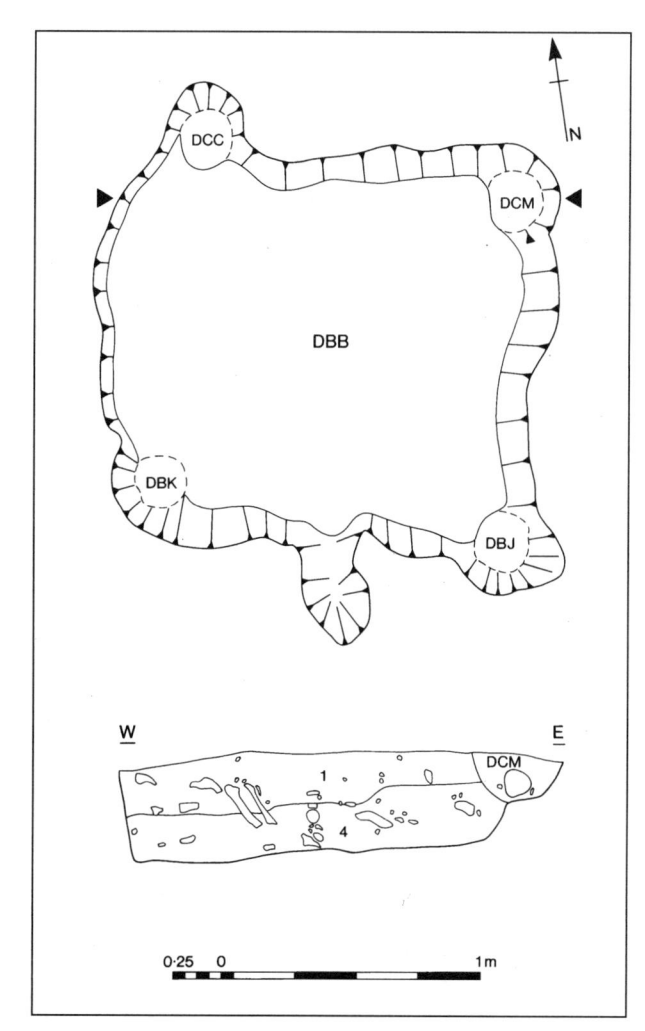

Figure 13   Area 2: Pit DBB, plan and section.

datable to the fourth century, as is perhaps the pottery from Pit DBG. Despite being very largely emptied, enclosure Ditch DAA produced very little ceramic material (0.95 kg) which, interestingly, did not include any fourth-century sherds. If the ditch had been kept open beyond the turn of the fourth century it is extremely unlikely that later Roman pottery would have failed to get into it, suggesting that the feature was probably backfilled or allowed to silt up by the end of the third century or early in the fourth century, perhaps when the later corn drier was constructed. Pit DAD, which cuts the western arc of the enclosure, had a *terminus post quem* of 253–255, but it cannot be earlier than the fourth century, and may be of a yet later date.

Area 3

Periods I–II (prehistoric to Iron Age).

The excavation appears to have produced a thin scatter of flints of prehistoric date, but in no part of the site does this material appear to have been stratified in contemporary contexts. Two of the more notable pre-conquest artefacts to come from the site were found in this area, a La Tène III brooch (**Brooch 1**) and an Iron Age coin (**Coin 1**), both from Roman Pit EAW. No contexts, however, appear to be of pre-Roman date.

Period III (AD 43 to pre-125).

Little activity was observed in the Roman period in this part of the site (Fig. 14). The natural subsoil in Area 3 appears to have been generally more sandy than elsewhere, and the three most notable features within it appear to have been sand quarrying or 'borrow' pits. Of these, the earliest was the irregularly shaped Hollow EAW, the earliest fills of which produced material dated to the later first century AD. Of slightly later date, although not linked stratigraphically, was Depression EAN, a flat-bottomed depression 4.2 m in diameter and surviving to a depth of 0.5 m. Its fill was a dark greyish-brown soil with sparse, small pebbles.

Period III Dating Evidence

Pit EAW
Pottery: Fabrics: 33, 34, 52, 56, 57. Fig. 46.105.

Only small scraps of pottery were recovered, all dating to the first century. EAW 3 contained a handmade bead-rim jar fragment (Fabric 57) of pre- or early Flavian date.

Coin: **Coin 1**: *c*.AD10–40.
Brooches: **Brooch 1**: (la Tène III fibula); **12**: (Colchester Derivative).

Pit EAN *[Components EAN 1–3, BBB]*
Pottery: Fabrics 9, 11, 17, 19, 20a, 23, 33, 34, 36, 37, 39, 42, 49, 52, 53, 56, 57, 58a.
               Fig. 47.128–131. Pottery from this feature was dated later first to early second century.
Glass: **Glass 2**: (conical bodied jug).
Brooches: **Brooch 5**: (Colchester); **10**: (Hod Hill).
Iron: **Iron 7**: (Linch pin).

Period III Discussion
Judging by the dating evidence, both features may be assigned to the later first century or slightly later, unless the chalky spoil fill of EAW is datable to later on in the second century. If so, one might have anticipated some later pottery, so on balance an earlier date is to be preferred.

Period IV (c.125–200/10).

To this phase certainly belongs the approximately circular bowl-shaped feature EAA, which measured 5.5 m in diameter (Plate 7). This lay a few metres to the north of EAW. Its initial fill appears to have been a layer of clay some 200 mm in thickness; above this were numerous fills (nine were identified), all of which appeared to have been tipped in from the south. The shape of this feature strongly suggests that it had been dug as a dew pond, and lined with clay because it was cut into sand. If so, EAA does not appear to have retained this function for very long, probably being superceded by Pond GK. The main fills of the feature contained a substantial assemblage of pottery, shell (mainly oyster), and bone, and an important group of bone pins (**Bone 3–13**). The uppermost fill [EAA 1], consisted of a starkly contrasting flint and chalk matrix, possibly a consolidation.

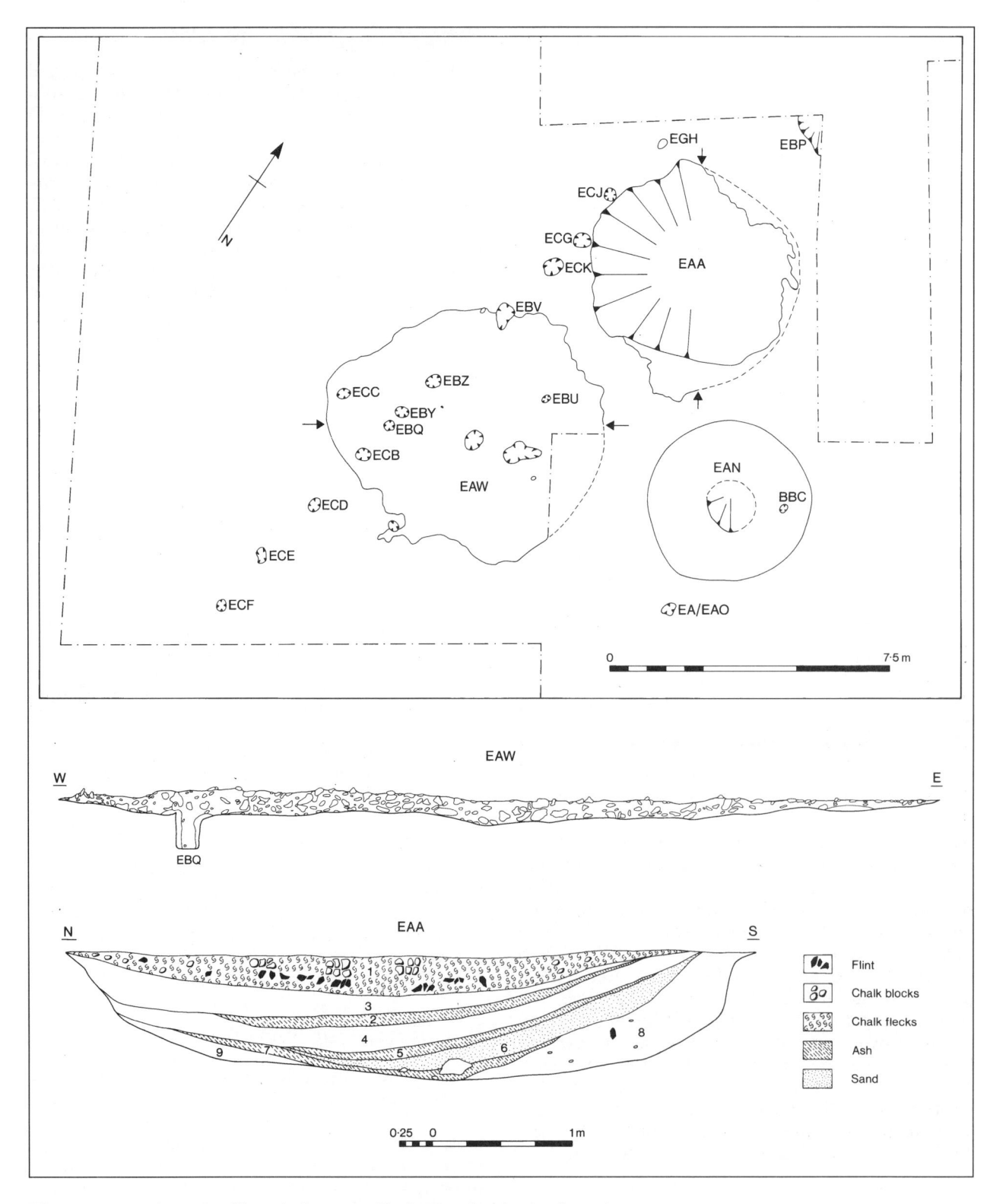

Figure 14   Area 3: all periods, overall plan and principal sections.

Period IV Dating evidence

Feature EAA *[Components: EAA, EAA1–19; 40; EAA 301–305]*

Pottery:	Fabrics: 1,4, 5a–b, 9, 12, 13, 15,16, 19, 20a, 33–41, 48–9, 51–8, 60, 61. Figs 48, 49, 144–199.
Samian:	AD 60–70; 130–160

The homogenous nature of this large (61 kg) pottery assemblage, with its many sherd links, suggests that it was a single act of dumping during the Antonine period, like that from the Well CAB upper shaft deposit (Area 1, CAB 6–13).

Brooches:	**Brooch 7**: (Thistle brooch).
Copper alloy:	**CuAlloy 21, 22**: (hairpins); **26, 35**: (nail cleaners); **37**: (tweezers).
Iron:	**Iron 10**: (hipposandal wing).
Worked bone:	**Bone 3–13**: (hair pins); **21, 22**: (needles).
Environmental:	268 of the 342 oyster shells and mussels were found in this context.

Plate 7   Dew pond/Quarry EAA, after sectioning, from east (HAT).

Period V+ (later Roman and post-Roman)

After the end of the second century, activity on this part of the site was extremely scant. Some time after the two main pits were backfilled, Fence Line ECL was constructed. Internal dating evidence for this feature was non-existent, but posts of the alignment were identified cutting the fills of Pits EAA and EAW, providing it with a *terminus post quem* of the final decades of the second century. It is possible that the fence line is contemporary with the fence which appears to replace or to continue the alignment established by Ditch JJ, but this is not certain. The only other feature in this area datable to after the second century was Pit EAQ, sited close to the earlier Pit EAN. This contained a Hadham ware jar (Fig. 50.227), in which was found a hoard of 2,579 coins sealed, and thus presumably buried, c.261 (Coin Hoard).

Period V+ Dating evidence

Pit EAQ

Pottery:	Fabric 39. Hadham ware jar. Base and lower walls only. Fig. 50.227.
Coins:	**Coin hoard**: 2579 *antoniniani* and *denarii*, up to c.AD 263.
Copper alloy:	**CuAlloy 28**: (hairpin, fragmentary).

Plate 8   The Cemetery; Cremation GAM after excavation (HAT).

The Cemetery

The cemetery (Fig. 15) was excavated in 1990 in circumstances which have been described in the *Introduction*. It lay east of Ditch GAK and north of Ditch ECP, in what was almost certainly the corner of a small field enclosure by the later second century. It comprised some twenty-five cremation burials in a compact cluster, together with two outliers [GAP and GAX]. It is likely that the cemetery was originally more extensive, but the area had been extremely badly plough-damaged. The surviving grave pits (Plate 8) were extremely shallow (it proved impossible to record sections or to plan individual cremation groups in detail) and several burials had almost certainly been completely ploughed away. Obviously these burials, and those which did not contain grave goods, will have been overlooked.

No attempt is made here to phase the burials on the evidence of their somewhat meagre grave goods: the pitfalls of such an exercise have recently been starkly published (Going 1993). Instead, a broad date range is given for each burial on the basis of the finds, with the proviso that it represents a trend only. This point will be discussed further (below).

The following summary description of the interments is rather formulaic. Reference should be made to the appropriate specialist reports for additional information on the various categories of find. For the specific meaning of the terms *adult*, *mature adult*, etc. the reader is referred to the definition given by Mackinley (*Cremated Human Bone*). Grave pit measurements are diameter × depth.

Catalogue

GAB

Grave pit:	280 × 90 mm.
Crem bone:	183 g; mature adult. Burnt flint and charcoal noted probably derived from pyre, suggesting perfunctory collection of remains.
Grave furniture:	'Iron' noted may be from a container.
Grave goods:	Pottery: *(not illustrated)*. Fragmentary shell-tempered (Fabric 59) cinerary urn, top ploughed off.

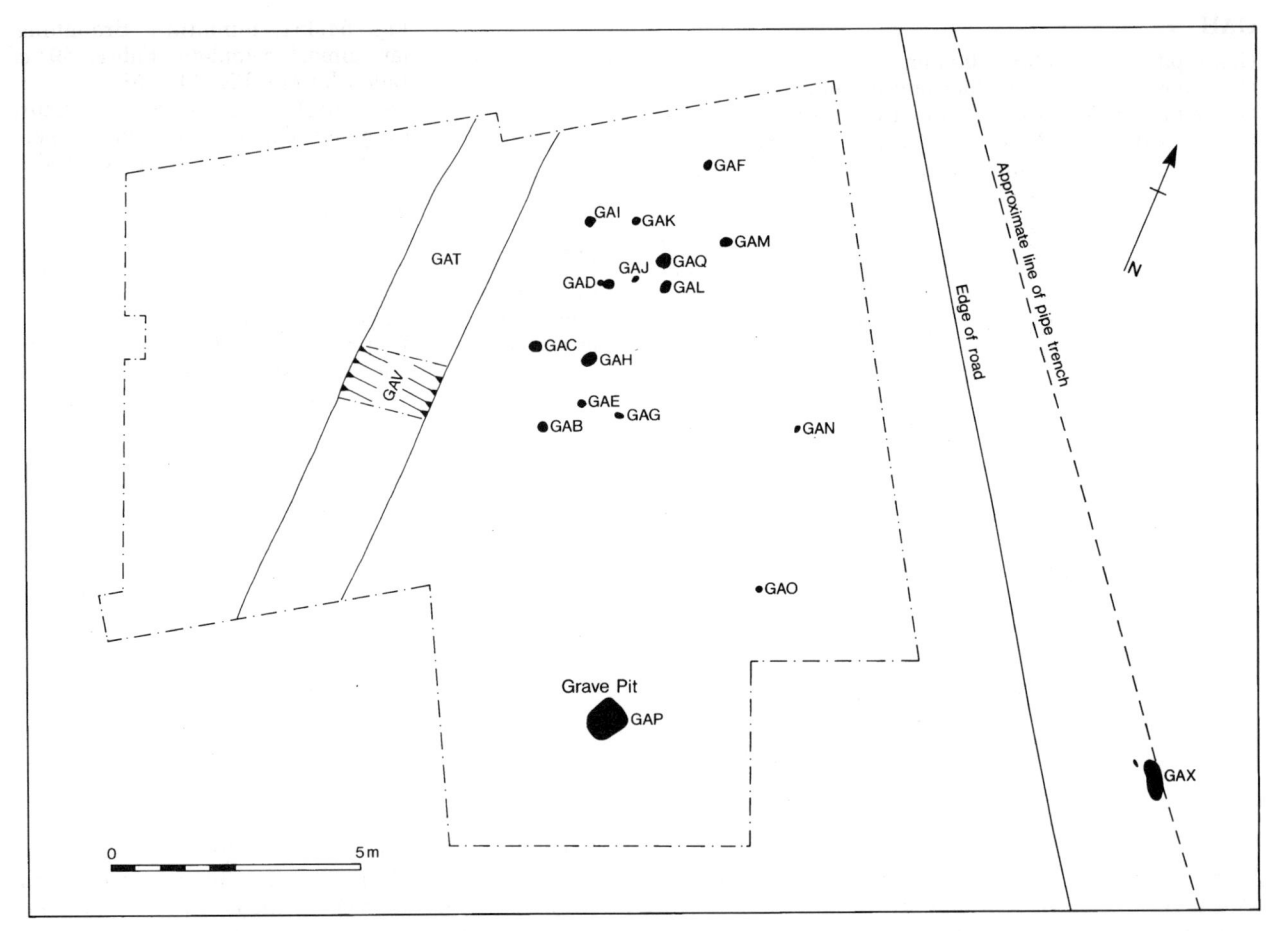

Figure 15   Cemetery; overall plan.

Date: probably Flavian to early second century.

GAC
Grave pit: 320 × 130 mm.
Crem bone: 612 g; mature adult. Burnt flint and charcoal noted probably derived from pyre, suggesting perfunctory collection of remains.
Grave goods: Pottery: *(not illustrated)*. Fragmentary shell-tempered (Fabric 57) cinerary urn, top ploughed off. Samian: CG 18/31 or 31, Hadrianic–Antonine.
Date: Probably Hadrianic–Antonine.

GAD
Grave pit: 320 × 100 mm.
Crem bone: 443 g; older/mature adult. Charcoal from the deposit is probably spent fuel ash from the pyre.
Grave goods: Pottery: *(not illustrated)*. Verulamium Region ware (Fabric 20A) bowl, used as a cinerary urn. Plough-damaged. Also present, sherds of an early shell-tempered jar (Fabric 57), and a vessel of uncertain form in a misc. oxidised fabric (Fabric 19).
Date: Probably Hadrianic–Antonine.

GAE
Grave pit: 200 × 100 mm.
Crem bone: 183 g *(sic)*; adult. Burnt flint and charcoal noted, probably from the pyre.
Grave goods: Pottery: *(not illustrated)*. Coarse reduced ware (Fabric 40) cinerary urn, top ploughed off. Also, body sherds of a vessel of uncertain form in misc. oxidised ware (Fabric 19). Samian: CG 31, Antonine; also an uncertain open form, dish or bowl, early–mid Antonine.
Date: Antonine?

GAF
Grave pit: 220 × 100 mm.
Crem bone: 292 g; adult. Charcoal from the deposit probably from the pyre.
Grave goods: Pottery: *(not illustrated)*. Fragmentary bead-rimmed jar, plough-damaged, used as cinerary urn. Also, sherd of a ring-necked flagon in VRW (Fabric 20a).
Date: Probably second century.

GAG
Grave pit: 120 × 40 mm.
Crem bone: 25 g; subadult/adult. Burnt flint.
Grave goods: Pottery: *(not illustrated)*. Verulamium region ware jar (Fabric 20A) used as a cinerary urn? Samian: CG 18/31 or 31, Hadrianic–Antonine.
Date: Antonine to late Antonine.

GAH
Grave pit: 300 × 200 mm.
Crem bone: 52 g; older/mature adult.
Grave furniture: Iron, possibly from casket?
Grave goods: Pottery: *(not illustrated)*. Early shell-tempered jar (Fabric 59), probably used as a cinerary urn. Plough-damaged: lower body only. Also sherds of unidentifiable vessels in Fabrics 26 (×2), 39, and 56 (one each). Possibly accidental in grave fill.
Samian: CG 18/31, Antonine. Four joining sherds. CG 33, Antonine, also two other samian chips, CG, Antonine.
Date: Mid to later second century?

GAI
Grave pit: 240 × 60 mm.
Crem bone: 120 g; adult. Burnt flint and charcoal found, probably gathered up from pyre at time of collection.
Grave goods: Pottery: Fig. 54.348. Largely complete shell-tempered bead rimmed jar (Fabric 57) probably used as cinerary urn. Also fifteen very abraded sherds, all Fabric 54.
Samian: sherd of CG 18/31, Hadrianic. Sherd from the same vessel in Grave GAK. Date: Hadrianic to early Antonine.

GAJ
Grave pit: 80 × 20 mm *(sic)*.
Crem bone: 37 g; i) infant; ii) adult? Burnt flint, probably from beneath pyre.
Grave furniture: Iron reported, possibly from casket.
Grave goods: Pottery: *(not illustrated)*. Base and lower body of a jar (Fabric 52), used as a cinerary urn.
Date: Probably Flavian to second century.

GAK
Grave pit: 130 × 140 mm.
Crem bone: None recovered.
Grave goods: Pottery: *(not illustrated)*. Base and lower body of jar (Fabric 52), presumably once used as a cinerary urn. Samian: sherd of CG 18/31, Hadrianic; joins one found in Grave GAI.
Date: Probably Hadrianic–Antonine.

GAL
Grave pit: 210 × 130 mm.
Crem bone: 773 g; adult ?female. Much burnt flint in the deposit, also charcoal.
Grave furniture: iron possibly from casket.
Grave goods: Pottery: *(not illustrated)*. Base and lower walls (upper part ploughed off) of a jar in early shell-tempered fabric (Fabric 57).
Bone: ?bird bone noted in cremated bone. Probable offering.
Date: Later first to second centuries.

GAM
Grave pit: 200 × 230 mm.
Crem bone: None recovered.
Grave goods: Pottery: Fig. 54.350; 'Braughing' jar, almost complete, Fabric ?33, *cf* Baldock (Stead and Rigby 1989, Fig. 150.663)
Fig. 54.351; miniature 'Braughing' jar, almost complete, Fabric 49, *cf* Baldock (*ibid,* Fig. 143.558).
Samian: CG 33, Antonine, almost complete. The potters' stamp, if there ever was one, is entirely eroded away.
Date: Antonine.

GAN
Grave pit: 240 × 40 mm.
Crem bone: None recovered.
Grave goods: Pottery: *(not illustrated)*. Very abraded sherds from a shell-tempered vessel (Fabric 57), possibly a cinerary urn.
Fig. 54.349; rim sherd from a bead-rimmed dish, Fabric 11.
Date: Hadrianic, or Antonine.

GAO
Grave pit: 180 × 50 mm.
Crem bone: 9 g (a single vault fragment); juvenile/adult?
Grave goods: Pottery: *(not illustrated)*. Eleven sherds noted from two unidentified vessels (Fabrics 4 and 19).
Date: Later first to second century.

GAP
'Grave pit': 610 × 770 × 100 mm.
This feature was a shallow sub-rectangular pit with a ?lining of carbonised wood. While it contained no grave goods or bone (the only find was a chip of ?prehistoric pottery which was not kept), similar features recovered from other sites have proved to be burials and it is likely that this feature is also that of a cremation burial.
Date: Probably later first or second century.

GAQ
Grave pit: 150 × 20 mm.
Crem bone: 325 g; adult, poss female. Charcoal, possibly fuel ash from pyre.
Grave furniture: Iron, perhaps from casket or box.
Grave goods: Pottery: *(not illustrated)*. Sherds of an uncertain form (perhaps a cinerary urn) in Fabric 54. Also present, sherds of a flagon (Fabric 19).
Samian: CG 18/31, Hadrianic. Nine joining fragments.
Date: Early to mid second century.

GAS
Grave pit: Dimensions too uncertain to record.
Crem bone: No bone survived.
Grave goods: Pottery: fragmentary 'Braughing' jar (Fabric 52) used as a cinerary urn. Hadrianic–Antonine (*cf* Stead and Rigby 1989, Fig. 150.663). Also two sherds from a closed form, probably a flagon.
Samian: CG 18/31 (Montans), c.115–45. The surviving letters of the stamp, ...]C[...]O, suggest the work of Felicio iii.
Date: Early to mid second century.

GAX
Grave pit: 350 × 750 × 250 mm.

Crem bone: No report.
Furniture: Single iron nail found associated with the calcined bones in bottom of the grave pit.
Probably not associated with furniture.
Grave goods: Glass: Drinking cup or *'modiolus'* (Isings form 27) in amber-coloured glass. Date probably Flavian. For a discussion of this important piece, only the second to be recognised from Great Britain, see **Glass 1**.
Pottery: *(not illustrated)*. Three abraded sherds of a vessel in Fabric 34.
Samian: i) SG 18, nearly complete, in pieces, early Flavian.
ii) SG 27(g?), stamped IVII or II II, Neronian–early Flavian.
iii) 36, almost complete, narrow flange without barbotine, Neronian–early Flavian.
Date: Flavian–Trajanic.

NOTE: This feature had been disturbed during the construction of the estate road and doubts had been expressed about whether the finds above were legitimately associated, specifically that the burial containing the glass *modiolus* was later disturbed by the insertion of a second cremation burial which contained two samian dishes and a cup. However, the finds are virtually all contemporary, suggesting that the second interment must have followed the first with considerable speed. Furthermore, the excavation sketch shows a perfectly coherent grave plan. There are no grounds for doubting that the deposit represents a single burial. Its precise configuration was hard to elucidate under salvage conditions. The find of a sherd of the *modiolus* beneath one of the Samian vessels plainly indicates that this precious glass vessel had been broken before interment.

GAY

Grave pit: 200 mm dia. Depth not stated.
Grave goods: Pottery: *(not illustrated)*. Lower body and base of a jar in Fabric 19, probably used as a cinerary urn. Most of the upper part ploughed away.
Date: First to second century.

GAZ

Grave pit: 190 mm dia. Depth not stated. Exposed during road construction.
Grave goods: Pottery: Body and base sherds from two vessels (forms not stated) in Fabrics 17 and 39.
Samian: Eight fragments, some joining, one slightly burnt. CG. Mid to late Antonine.
Date: Probably later second century.

GBA

Grave pit: 850 × 850 mm approx. (pit edge very indistinct).
Crem bone: No weight given. Older/mature adult, possibly male. Burnt flint and charcoal probably from the pyre. The bone was unurned.
Grave furniture: Copper alloy: Five 'lion-headed' studs, two almost complete, also miscellaneous fittings, perhaps from a lock plate. There was 'associated, corroded iron' (presumably a lock and attendant lock plate) but this was not recovered in the 'rushed' excavation conditions. For a detailed description, see **CuAlloy 62**. In addition to the above, 'numerous' iron objects were reported as having been found. These were very badly decayed, and appear not to have been recovered.
Grave goods: Pottery: *(not illustrated)*. 33 sherds from a beaker (*cf* Marsh 1978, type 11) in a fine eggshell-like fabric (Fabric 24). Remains of a flagon also noted.
Samian: Curle 15, CG, almost complete in large pieces. The dish is badly eroded, but appears to be unstamped. Hadrianic or early Antonine.
Glass: Melted fragment, found among the cremated bone (**Glass 23**).
Date: Early to mid second century.

GBF

?Grave pit 400 × 100 mm.
Crem bone: Older infant/young adult. Fragments of cranial vault.
Grave goods: *(not illustrated)*. Urned deposit submitted for examination.

GBH

Grave pit(s) 600 × 500 mm.

It appears that two or three cremations were found in this area. The records are sparse, but imply a multiple interment.

Crem bone: GBH 2: Primary mature/older adult, ?female. Burnt flint, probably from the pyre. Found in the ?primary vessel'.
GBH 4: Secondary, older adult, Burnt flint and charcoal, probably from the pyre. Found in the 'secondary' vessel.
GBH 6: Tertiary, older infant. Charcoal, probably from the pyre.
Grave goods: The *Cremated Human Bone* report describes all of the burials as urned, and three vessels are identified as from this immediate area.
Pottery: i) Fig. 54.353; Fabric 37. Round-bodied beaker with short, everted rim. Narrow groove around girth. Medium grey. Similar to Baldock No 354. First century. GBE 1.
ii) Fig. 54.354: Fabric 33. Small bowl with a bead rim. Dark brown-ochre surfaces. Slightly abraded. GBE 1. R.EVE 0.05.
iii) Fig. 54.355: Fabric 37. Shallow curved dish. Parallel grooves under rim. Medium grey. GBE 1. R.EVE 0.13.

NOTE: The records are very vague. All three pottery vessels are endorsed GBE 1, suggesting the contents of a burial. However, GBE is described as 'redeposited clay'. No reference exists in the relevant record to pottery vessels. It seems probable that the marking is a misreading of GBH. This explanation is not without objections, but the matter must remain unsettled.

GBI
Grave pit: 150 × 20 mm.
Crem bone: Weight not given. Adult. Burnt flint and charcoal, probably from the pyre.
Grave goods: Pottery: Fig. 54.352: Fabric 17. Small, shallow flanged bowl. Fine, pale orange-red ware. All surfaces completely worn away. Very friable. R.EVE 0.85.

The Development of the Roman Cemetery in Periods III–IV

With the exception of GAX (about which there is some doubt), no burials could with certainty be assigned to Period III, *ie* AD 43–*c*.125. Possible candidates, however, comprise Burials GAB, GAJ, GAK, GAL, GAY, GBF, GBH. Of these, GAJ, GAK, GAL, GAY and GBF each contained the remains of only one vessel each and cannot really be dated at all closely.

Most of the burials are datable to the Hadrianic–Antonine periods, or shortly after. While this concentration of dates in the middle of the second century may simply be a reflection of the larger quantities of samian available at this time, a substantial continuation of burials at the site after the end of the second century would have produced recognisably later pottery and inhumation burials, which become common in the third century. On ceramic grounds GAZ may be identified as among the latest of the burials. It seems clear that the cemetery went out of use some time around 200, but whether or not it was superceded by a later cemetery nearby is not known. Winder (*Animal Bone*) noted the bones of neonates or young children in Contexts EBH 1–2 and EBT 1. The interment without full rites of newborn and infants is a phenomenon widely encountered in Roman Britain, and is best known, perhaps, from Hambleden, Bucks (Keith *in* Cocks 1921), where the bodies of ninety-seven infants were found in the courtyard of a farmstead.

The cemetery at Chells produced little in the way of luxury goods: it is notable that virtually none of them contained objects of adornment such as beads, brooches, or other material, and that only one contained what might be termed a luxury item, namely the glass *modiolus* or drinking cup from GAX (**Glass 1**). As at Great Dunmow and Skeleton Green, two more-or-less contemporary cemeteries, pottery grave goods of some value were provided wherever possible. Samian appears to have been provided, if not as a matter of course, then in more instances than not (*eg* in GAC; GAE; GAG; GAH, GAI; GAM; GAQ, GAS), and over half the samian recovered from the site (by estimated vessel equivalence – EVE) came from the cemetery. It was also in the burials rather than on the settlement that some of the other fine wares were found, for example a cup in a local egg-shell ware (Fabric 24) from GBA, and flagon sherds in fine white fabric (Fabric 26) in GAH. Most of the cremations in the surviving burials appear to have been placed in cinerary urns made in shell-tempered pottery (an exception appears to be GAX), but this is perhaps deceptive, as some shallow scrapes containing unurned cremations, particularly if they lacked other grave goods, may have been missed at the time of the excavation.

Heavy plough damage makes it difficult to be clear about details of grave pit construction. However, while it did not produce any cremated bone or other items to prove it, wood-lined Pit GAP was probably a burial. This little burial chamber, with its parallels at such sites as Stebbing (unpub.) and Little Waltham (Drury 1978), is a rather more workaday version of the larger mausolea discovered at Stanway and at Verulamium (Dunnett 1992). A useful addition to the small number of 'casket burials' discovered in Essex and Hertfordshire is GBA, which contained a probable casket with a iron lock-plate, decorated with five 'lion-headed' studs (**CuAlloy 62**). The iron fragments noted in GAB, GAC, GAH, GAL, GAQ, GBA and GBI may be the remains of rather simpler nailed boxes rather than formal caskets. However, none were reported on as being obviously remnants of boxes, and the plough damage was so serious that in most cases it is unlikely that any survived.

Ploughing had truncated many of the burials: the grave pits of GAB, GAD, GAE, GAF; GAG; GAI, GAJ, GAN, GAO, GAQ, GBF, GBI survived only to a depth of 100 mm or less. As well as damaging or displacing grave goods in these interments, ploughing had also removed the upper parts of the cinerary urns in GAB, GAC, GAH, GAJ, GAK and GAL. Yet, despite the fact that many of the remaining objects has been heavily damaged, crushed, or largely ploughed away, it is possible to recognise in a number of these burials the 'classic' configuration of grave goods encountered in many cremation cemeteries, namely a jar, which usually functioned as the cinerary urn, a dish, and a flagon and its concomitant drinking vessel (Table 10).

Also observable was evidence of funerary ritual: while destruction by ploughing makes certainty on this point difficult, it is probable that the references to 'nearly' complete samian vessels in a number of the burials indicates the practice of removing sherds from certain categories of vessel used as grave goods before interment. This phenomenon, observed at a number of cemeteries in the south and east of Great Britain, for example Skeleton Green (Partridge 1981) and Great Dunmow (Going and Ford 1988), was also practised at Chells, while some of the pottery vessels represented in the graves only by single sherds, for example the flagon from grave GAF, may have been placed in the burial itself, or in its backfill, as symbolic fragments.

Other signs of burial ritual were noted. In the cremated material from GAL was a bird bone, almost certainly from an offering to the pyre, and a possible animal bone was noted among the bone from GBH 2. Most events associated with the funeral, however, were very fugitive and have left no archaeological traces. Some indication of the collecting policy exercised over the remains of the dead can be gained from the fact that GAB, GAC, GAE, GAI, GAL, GBA, GBF, two of the three burials in the GBH complex and GBI produced burnt flint, while others produced charcoal ?fuel ash, presumably derived from the pyre. It is clear that the bone was not carefully sorted after the cremation, but that the remains were probably scooped up and heaped into the urn along with the pyre remnants and stones beneath. From time to time objects which had been placed in the pyre were also included: for example, a heat-scorched samian sherd came from GAZ and a melted glass fragment came from GBA. If the dead of Chells were burned on a single pyre-site, as appears likely, there is no guarantee that these offerings were intended for these burials at all.

Discussion

The excavation did not reveal a very dense scatter of prehistoric features, and in Areas 2 and 3 very few were identified as dating to the prehistoric period. It is possible, however, that there were more early features in Area 1, including the isolated Hollows EB, JV and TV as well as the pre-trackway Gullies DQ and DG. These form no coherent pattern and are not closely datable, and it is unwise to speculate further on their significance in view of the fact that a full feature plan was not recovered from this part of the site.

The earliest morphologically intelligible landscape features excavated appear to date to about the time of the Roman conquest. They include a pair of cranked parallel ditches [ABL, ABM] c.80–90 m long, aligned approximately east–west. This feature, which is identified as a length of unmetalled track or droveway, continued westwards beyond the edge of the excavated area, and a cropmark plot suggests that it terminated 20–30 m west of the excavation edge (Fig. 4a). The southern side-ditch appears to be discontinuous towards its west end, suggesting, if it is not ploughed out here or just misplotted, that it might open out into a parcel of land. A few metres to the north of the northern trackway ditch was Well CAB, which is probably of post-Conqest date.

There is no clear indication of any ditched field system which can be associated demonstrably with Trackway ABL/ABM, although it may have briefly formed the south side of the quadrilateral Enclosure ECR, which appears to have been constructed in the later first century (Fig. 4b). It seems more probable, however, that in its original shape the enclosure was trapezoidal, with Ditch ECT forming its south-eastern corner, and that the track simply went out of use when the enclosure, c.80 × 80 m, was apparently built across it. The trackway ditch fills certainly contain material indicating that they were allowed to silt up after this time. A number of small gullies and isolated features may be associated with this putative first-century enclosure. In Area 3 these include two shallow, quarry-like features (EAW and EAN) which may have been constructed to serve as ponds, providing an alternative water source to that supplied by Well CAB (Fig. 8) which, to judge by the material from the lower shaft fills, appears to have gone out of use in the late first or early second century. In Area 1 a substantially greater density of features was observed.

During the early second century Enclosure ECR appears to have been substantially extended to the east by the addition of another trapezoidal ditched enclosure [ECM] of rather greater dimensions, c.120 × 100 m. As is evident from the plan (Fig. 4b) rather little of the interior of this complex was excavated – certainly too little to elucidate its development with much confidence. Soon after this putative extension was created the site water supply appears to have been substantially remodelled. Area 3 features EAN and EAW, being cut into more or less sandy subsoils, can never have served as particularly effective ponds, and seem to have been gone out of use fairly rapidly. Instead, a third clay-lined feature [EAA] appears to have been dug, also in Area 3. This feature had only a brief existence, being backfilled during the Antonine period. A layer of metalling [ABR] which was spread west of the well at or a little before this time suggests that it was envisaged that Well CAB might be brought back into commission, but in the event both EAA and the well shaft were backfilled with material including substantial assemblages of pottery and, in the case of EAA, worked bone. At the time of its final closure the well may have been the site of a ritual involving deposition, and possible sacrifice, of several animals, including three domestic dogs.

Both water sources were now superceded by a pond [GK] which was cut astride Ditch JJ, the old west boundary of Enclosure ECR. This pattern of pond is characteristic in areas where common watering-holes are provided for animals which are otherwise kept separated.

From the later Antonine period onwards, while domestic detritus such as pottery is still found in some quantities on the site, more definite signs of occupation as opposed to agricultural activity become remarkably scanty. Features in Area 1 and its vicinity are best interpreted as essentially agricultural: none seem to be parts of structures. Indeed, the clearest evidence for settlement is rather equivocally provided by the cemetery, which had been established on the northern part of the site, a little to the north of the possible replacement droveway, which during the second century and after appears to have formed the northern edge of the extended field allotment. The cemetery probably came into existence in the middle of the first century AD (the earliest recorded burial [GAX] is datable to the Flavian period), and appears to have been most densely used during the middle decades of the second century.

The history and morphological development of the site during the later Roman era (ie in Period V), is more difficult to elucidate (Fig. 5a). After the second century the density of features and the degree of activity on the site appear to level off considerably. The latest cremation burials [GAG, GAH] appear to be of Antonine to later Antonine date, and there are no inhumations recorded from the cemetery, which suggests that it had gone out of use by the third century, possibly when the settlement focus shifted elsewhere. In Area 3 the only clear indication of post-second century activity is the concealment within Pit EAN of a coin hoard in about 261, which in itself suggests that the area had become a somewhat secluded place. In Area 1 the old enclosure boundary Ditch JJ, which had been cut by Pond GF, appears to have largely silted up by this time, for one of the few later third-century deposits of material identified on the site came from what, in the words of its excavator, was now a rather 'ragged hollow' on the same course [JK]. Elsewhere, earth starts to accumulate over the area of metalling [ABR] close to Well CAB, while Pond GF is beginning to mire up.

However, sporadic activity probably continued in Area 2, where the south-east corner of the enlarged field system appears to have been delineated by a pair of ditches [DCE–DCF, and to their west DAU], forming a sub-enclosure measuring c.60 × 20 m (Fig. 5a). Within this enclosure, which may have been hedged, a circular gully c.16 m in diameter [DAA] enclosed a corn drier constructed of flint, tile and chalk blocks [JF]. During the first part of its life (Period V.1) the drier flue faced north, but subsequently the structure was totally rebuilt with the flue facing southwards. Dating evidence for the construction of the two driers is scanty, but it is likely that the structures belonged to the later third to fourth century, and the fourth century, respectively. In Area 1 a sequence of sump-like gullies [eg CE/GM] were cut through the earth overlying Raft ABR, flowing initially into the slumping weathering cone of Well CAB, and later on round it to the north. To the east of these gullies a series of gully-like hollows [ABQ] may have drained eastwards in the direction of Pond GK. A number of other features close to this gully complex may belong to the period, but none of them appear to be associated with any kind of structure. During the fourth century these probable drainage gullies appear to have been replaced by a series of penannular gullies, similar to DAA in the eastern part of the site. The earliest of these was ABV, subsequently recut as FZ. As noted in the main body of the report, the dating of these features is problematical, since most of the associated finds appear to be residual, but from ABQ was recovered a later third to fourth-century coin (**Coin 302**) which, if it is not intrusive, puts the whole sequence into the later third to fourth centuries.

Activity appears to continue into the later fourth century, and is attested by the comparative commonness of Period XIV (364–388) coinage (*Coin Report*). Pond GK was refurbished and relined with chalk at about this time, as one of its consolidation levels [KA] produced a coin of Valentinian, and while they produced little in the way of useful dating evidence, it seems probable that new internal boundaries were also erected, for example a series of postholes (not planned) on the alignment of the old Ditch JJ/JK is interpreted as a fence line, and in Area 3 a clear posthole alignment on the same axis [ECL] is probably also contemporary with it.

Later in the fourth century this site activity is followed by a series of deposits which suggest that the site suffered a substantial setback to its fortunes. Pond GK, the latest penannular gully FZ, and the weathering cone of Well CAB were all largely backfilled with contemporaneous debris including much pottery, animal bone and a variety of artefacts. The pond upper fills also contained fragments of millstone grit quern, burned in a fire which may also have destroyed the later corn drier. None of the coins from these deposits – in aggregate a fairly substantial assemblage – date to after 388 (*ie* to Coin period XV), suggesting that this backfilling episode may be datable to the 370s. While some site activity does appear to post-date this period, this is restricted to a few isolated pits [*eg* XV, XR, and XT]; there is little evidence of consolidation or reconstruction. No attempt appears to have been made to clear the pond out or to rebuild the corn drier, and while the latest pottery includes material which stylistically may be described as very late Roman, it seems probable that by the end of the fourth century the site was effectively abandoned.

Between the end of the Roman era and the Saxo-Norman period the site appears to have been unoccupied, and the next archaeologically recognisably features are assignable to the medieval and post-medieval periods. Of these the most significant is the c.11 m-diameter Hollow MR, which clearly cuts Roman Pond GK (Fig. 5b), and is itself clearly also a medieval or post-medieval pond. Pit QL in Area 1 produced a medieval iron spur.

The site in its setting

Figure 2 shows the present knowledge of Romano-British settlement in the immediate vicinity of Chells. Most of the sites under consideration here came to light as a result of chance finds of objects such as pottery and coins, while others have been revealed by aerial photography. However, very few have been the subject of archaeological exploration: in addition to those at Chells, excavations have only been carried out at Purwell Mill (Ninesprings) villa (Fox 1923; VCH 1914, 170), at Great Wymondley (*SMR 0034*; Westell 1937/9, 11*ff*) and some distance to the south-east at Wymondley Bury (VCH 1914, 170–1). As all these excavations took place a long time ago, what follows is inevitably interim and to some degree speculative.

More definite evidence of buildings was revealed by excavations at Ninesprings villa, while debris including mortared masonry, tile debris including fragments of *tegulae* and *imbrices*, and *tesserae*, all indicating the former presence of more Romanised structures, came from Weston, just over 3 km north of Chells. Whether or not these structures qualify the sites as those of 'villas' or not is at the moment unclear, particularly as the definition of villa (literally translated from the Latin as *farm*) permits a fairly wide interpretation.

Further settlement evidence comes from the records of burials found in the area. For the most part data are restricted to brief reports of finds, usually cremation burials, from a number of places in the vicinity. Two have been reported from Brox Dell, Stevenage (*TEHAS* 1954, 63), while a single burial, perhaps in a nailed box, was found at Coreys Mill in 1841 (VCH 1914, 171), and the remains of burials were noted at Great Wymondley (VCH 1914, 170). However, the most important burials of Roman date known from this area are the 'Six Hills', the row of *tumuli* sited alongside the Roman road (Margary 220) at Stevenage (Fowler 1891; Jessup 1936), clearly the burying ground of a local community of some substance. Somewhere in the vicinity of these mounds, probably on the south-west facing slopes to the north-east, is clearly a settlement site of some importance and, probably, ostentation. In this context, it is of some interest to note the existence of a mound in Box Wood (*SMR 0458*). Its date is unknown, but there is no reason why it cannot be Roman.

Evidence from elsewhere in the vicinity is considerably more patchy, but hints of settlement at Wymondley and Wymondley Bury suggest that the pattern is probably repeated on the flanks of streams feeding the northwards flowing Ivel, while less certain evidence from further to the south, *eg* from Aston, Datchworth, and Broadwater, implies that further settlement, almost certainly agricultural, existed in the vicinity. The evidence, such as it is, suggests settlement densities were slightly greater in the river valleys than on the boulder clays of the boulder clay plateau. To the east of the site, finds at a number of locations on the valley slopes and the floodplain of the river Beane demonstrate that the valley was under fairly intensive settlement, with cropmark and other evidence at, for example, Church End Common, Walkern, Robins Hall (*SMR 2923*), and Great Collens Wood, suggesting probable farm holdings strung out at fairly regular intervals along the valley. Judging by the items which have been reported to Stevenage Museum, there is a bias in favour of some types of find: the more recognisable 'antiquities', such as Roman coins and samian, have a significantly higher chance of being recognised and reported than, for example, coarse wares, glass, and metal finds such as iron, the age of which is seldom immediately clear. Better reporting of more routine finds, or systematic archaeological work, will certainly produce evidence for greater settlement densities on the heavier soils.

This is certainly the pattern which emerges where intensive archaeological work is carried out in similar terrain. To the north-east, in the Saffron Walden – Great Chesterford area of Essex, an ambitious fieldwalking project carried out by T. Williamson (1984; 1987) found substantial numbers of sites on the heavier soils. This picture is mirrored further south, for example in the area of Stansted airport and, east of that, close to Great Dunmow (Going 1987, 86–8 and Fig. 61).

The ancestry of this pattern is of interest. While there are flints from Chells, the lack of settlement evidence, in particular of pre–middle Iron Age *ceramic* material on the site, mirrors the pattern at, for example, the similarly-sited 'Airport Catering site' at Stansted in Essex (Brown *in* Havis, in prep.), corroborating the suggestion that while the valleys were opened for settlement rather earlier, clearance of the heavier if more agriculturally rewarding plateau soils did not commence in earnest until rather later, towards the middle of the first millennium BC. The cropmark evidence, both from Chells itself and from other sites in the vicinity, suggests that during the Roman period the landscape consisted of a network of gores and unmetalled tracks, linking uneven blocks and ranks of more-or-less irregularly-shaped fields assarted, perhaps piecemeal, from the already diminished wildwoods, which may have been cleared from all but the heaviest clays of the Hornbeam and Hanslope association (*Plant Remains*) by the later Roman era.

In sum, it is safe to conclude that, like many other farms in East Anglia at the time, the settlement of which the Chells site forms a significant part may have practised a mixed farming economy in which the growing of cereals, particularly spelt, played a significant role. Animal husbandry always played a substantial part, which may have increased towards the end of the Roman era, but as the later Roman data at Chells comes from what appear to be somewhat untypical contexts it is best not to generalise from them.

Of the size and location of the land holdings here it is fruitless to speculate. We do not have a clear idea of how many holdings existed in the vicinity, and without this data, and given our lack of any information about their period of occupancy, we can say nothing of their likely size or their relationships with one another. The elucidation of theoretical territories, while sometimes useful as a guide to the possible siting of additional settlements, requires rather more data than we have. On this point, of particular interest is Applebaum's (1972) landscape analysis of the area west of the Margary 220 road, centering on the site at Great Wymondley. The landscape surrounding this site, including the Ninesprings villa, was claimed to exhibit traces of an extensive *limitatio* or planned land allotment of the Roman period (*ibid*, Fig. 10). However, the claim lacks conviction. While wholesale land allotment is known in parts of the Empire (and indeed, small areas are known in Britain) it is more characteristic now to see the landscape of this area as having evolved piecemeal, never quite losing its former character.

The Finds

Coins

Mark Corney

A total of 302 Roman coins and two British coins were submitted for examination. Of this assemblage, forty-seven Roman coins were illegible, although all were of AE3 or AE4 module, indicative of a date in the *c.*260–400 bracket. A detailed list of the coins from the site appears in Table 2. From the intrinsic numismatic viewpoint there are few surprises, although the *semis* of Nero (**Coin 4**) is of note.

The breakdown of the coins by period is given in the accompanying histogram (Fig. 16), the periods used being those adopted by Curnow (1974; 1990) to allow ease of cross-reference with other Hertfordshire assemblages. The total for Period I includes the two British issues and the *denarius* of Mark Anthony (**Coin 3**).

223 of the coins (86.7% of the definable total) date from after 259, with notable peaks for Periods IX (32.2%), XIIb (18.7%) and XIV (19.5%). A note of caution should be added to the totals for Periods VIII and IX, both of which contain coins which, on the basis of their location, condition and reverse type, should be considered as strays from the hoard excavated in 1988 (*The Coin Hoard*). For Period VIII these total nine pieces, and in Period IX as many as thirty-four coins could derive from the hoard. The coins considered as strays are listed below:

Period VIII: 23–26, 28, 29, 45–47.
Period IX: 36, 48–53, 56–82.

Despite the dangers in interpreting the numismatic evidence in isolation from the other archaeological data, certain observations can be made. The presence of six first-century coins (including two British issues) indicate activity during the early Roman period, and the nine coins of second-century date are sufficient to attest continued use of the site. The greatest periods of coin loss occur in the third and fourth centuries, a standard pattern for lowland Romano-British settlements (Reece 1972). Notable peaks occur in Periods IX (20.05% excluding probable hoard strays), XIIb (18.7%) and XIV (19.5%). These patterns of coin loss most likely represent periods of considerable economic activity, with a marked peak in the later fourth century, as evidenced by the Period XIV figures. This last figure contrasts markedly with the loss patterns in the Verulamium area (Curnow 1990), but is in close accord with the Period XIV totals from the Orchard site of the settlement at Cow Roast (Curnow 1990; Reece 1982).

Period XV sees a dramatic downturn in the loss rate, only 2.3% of the total assemblage, perhaps marking a change in the economic fortunes of the site, or a shift away from a coin-using society, reflecting the decrease in the money supply at the end of the fourth century.

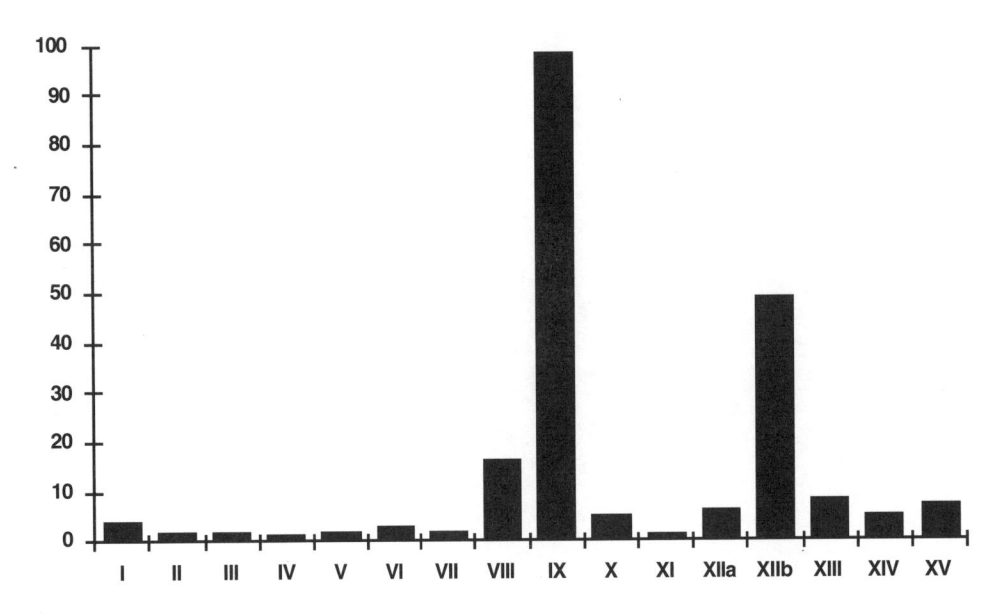

Figure 16   Histogram showing the pattern of coin loss from the site (coin periods after Curnow 1974).

TABLE 1: Catalogue of Iron Age and Roman coins (excluding hoard).

No.	Issuer	Type	Denom	Ref	Date	Mint	Wt (g)	SFNo	Cont.
IRON AGE:									
1	Cunobelin	Obv: [CVNOBE]LINVS REX Rev: TASC, bull pawing at ground, right.	Bronze	Mack 246	c.AD10–40	Cam.	1.87	5	EAW3
2	Uncertain	Uncertain	Bronze	?Mack 260	c.AD10–40	–	1.68	22	DAC 1
REPUBLICAN:									
3	Mark Anthony	Legionary eagle	Den.	RRC 1231	32–31 BC	–	–	1	CAA
IMPERIAL:									
4	Nero	CER QUINC ROM CON	Semis	RIC2: 338	54–68	–	–	33	CAA
5	Domitian	illeg.	Sest.	–	81–96	–	–	211	CAA
6	Domitian	illeg.	As	–	81–96	–	–	8	DG
7	Trajan	illeg.	Dup.	–	98–117	–	–	1	EBB 1
8	Trajan	illeg.	Dup.	–	98–117	–	–	4	EBB 2
9	Hadrian	illeg.	As/Dup.	–	117–138	–	–	31	CAA
10	Antoninus Pius	Vesta	Den.	RIC3: 229a	138–161	–	–	70	CAA
11	Antoninus Pius	Libertas	Sest.	RIC3: 916a	138–161	–	–	72	CAA
12	Marcus Aurelius	Providentia	Sest.	RIC3: 923	161–180	–	–	7	CE 4
13	Faustina II	illeg.	As/Dup.	–	161–175	–	–	1	QX 1
14	Faustina II	Salus	As	RIC3: 1671	161–175	–	–	58	CAA
15	illeg.	illeg.	As/Dup	–	2nd cent.	–	–	151	CAA
16	Septimius Severus	Vota Suscepta	Den.	RIC4: 211	193–211	–	–	140	CAA
17	Elagabalus	Cos III	Den.	RIC4: 32	218–222	–	–	1	AA
18	Severus Alexander	illeg.	Den.	–	222–235	–	–	169	CAA
19	Severus Alexander	Virtus	Den.	RIC4: 182	222–235	–	–	157	CAA
20	Severus Alexander	Mars	Den.	–	222–235	–	–	193	CAA
21	Gordian III	Fides	AR Ant.	RIC5: 1	238–244	–	–	180	CAA
22	Gordian III	Aequitas	AR Ant.	RIC5: 34	238–244	–	–	2	EAJ 1
23	Trebonianus Gallus	Libertas	AR Ant.	RIC5: 92	251–253	–	–	216	CAA
24	Valerian	Apollo	AR Ant.	RIC5: 74	253–260	–	–	219	CAA
25	Valerian	Fides	AR Ant.	RIC5: 89	253–260	–	–	43	CAA
26	Valerian	Sol	AR Ant.	RIC5: 12	253–260	–	–	59	CAA
27	Valerian	Sol	AR Ant.	RIC5: 12	253–260	–	–	29	CAB 1
28	Valerian	Victoria	AR Ant.	RIC5: 127	253–260	–	–	1	HZ
29	Valerian	Deo Volkano	AR Ant.	RIC5: 5	253–260	–	–	199	CAA
30	Gallienus	Aequitas	Ant.	RIC5: 159	253–268	–	–	32	CAA
31	Gallienus	Deo Marti	Ant.	RIC5: 10	253–268	–	–	179	CAA
32	Gallienus	Libero P Cons Aug	Ant.	RIC5: 230	253–268	–	–	1	XS
33	Gallienus	Leg I Adi	Ant.	RIC5: 315	253–268	–	–	28	CAB 1
34	Gallienus	Salus	Ant.	RIC5: 397	253–268	–	–	190	CAA
35	Gallienus	Vict. Germania	Ant.	RIC5: 44	253–268	–	–	15	DAC 1
36	Gallienus	Vict. Germania	Ant.	RIC5: 44	253–268	–	–	62	CAA
37	Gallienus	Apollini Cons	Ant.	RIC5: 163	253–268	–	–	142	CAA
38	Gallienus	illeg.	Ant.	–	253–268	–	–	220	CAA
39	Gallienus	illeg.	Ant.	–	253–268	–	–	24	DAC 1
40	Salonina	Juno Regina	Ant.	RIC5: 13	253–268	–	–	167	CAA
41	Salonina	Juno Regina	Ant.	RIC5: 13	253–268	–	–	18	DAC 1
42	Salonina	Pietas	Ant.	RIC5: 22	253–268	–	–	42	CAA
43	Salonina	illeg.	Ant.	–	253–268	–	–	221	CAA
44	Valerian II	Iovi Crescenti	Ant.	RIC5: 3	253–c.255	–	–	1	DAD1
45	Valerian II	Consecratio	Ant.	RIC5: 9	253–c.255	–	–	46	CAA
46	Valerian II	Consecratio	Ant.	RIC5: 9	253–c.255	–	–	138	CAA
47	Valerian II	illeg.	Ant.	–	253–c.255	–	–	208	CAA
48	Postumus	Fides Equit.	Ant.	RIC5: 59	259–268	–	–	181	CAA
49	Postumus	Herc. Devsoniensi	Ant.	RIC5: 64	259–268	–	–	185	CAA
50	Postumus	Herc. Devsoniensi	Ant.	RIC5: 64	259–268	–	–	26	CAA
51	Postumus	Herc. Devsoniensi	Ant.	RIC5: 64	259–268	–	–	205	CAA
52	Postumus	Herc. Devsoniensi	Ant.	RIC5: 64	259–268	–	–	57	CAA
53	Postumus	Herc. Pacifero	Ant.	RIC5: 67	259–268	–	–	60	CAA
54	Postumus	Laetitia	Ant.	RIC5: 73	259–268	–	–	12	DAC 1
55	Postumus	PM TRP COS II PP	Ant.	RIC5: 54	259–268	–	–	11	DAC 1
56	Postumus	PM TRP COS II PP	Ant.	RIC5: 54	259–268	–	–	182	CAA
57	Postumus	PM TRP COS II PP	Ant.	RIC5: 54	259–268	–	–	69	CAA
58	Postumus	PM TRP COS II PP	Ant.	RIC5: 54	259–268	–	–	147	CAA
59	Postumus	PM TRP COS II PP	Ant.	RIC5: 54	259–268	–	–	201	CAA
60	Postumus	PM TRP COS II PP	Ant.	RIC5: 54	259–268	–	–	17	CAA
61	Postumus	PM TRP COS II PP	Ant.	RIC5: 54	259–268	–	–	202	CAA
62	Postumus	PM TRP COS II PP	Ant.	RIC5: 54	259–268	–	–	178	CAA
63	Postumus	Miner. Fautr.	Ant.	RIC5: 74	259–268	–	–	144	CAA
64	Postumus	Miner. Fautr.	Ant.	RIC5: 74	259–268	–	–	165	CAA
65	Postumus	Miner. Fautr.	Ant.	RIC5: 74	259–268	–	–	47	CAA
66	Postumus	Miner. Fautr.	Ant.	RIC5: 74	259–268	–	–	197	CAA
67	Postumus	Miner. Fautr.	Ant.	RIC5: 74	259–268	–	–	172	CAA
68	Postumus	Miner. Fautr.	Ant.	RIC5: 74	259–268	–	–	188	CAA
69	Postumus	Neptuno Reduci	Ant.	RIC5: 76	259–268	–	–	170	CAA
70	Postumus	Neptuno Reduci	Ant.	RIC5: 76	259–268	–	–	45	CAA
71	Postumus	Salus Aug	Ant.	RIC5: 85	259–268	–	–	159	CAA
72	Postumus	Victoria Aug	Ant.	RIC5: 89	259–268	–	–	103	CAA

No.	Issuer	Type	Denom	Ref	Date	Mint	Wt (g)	SFNo	Cont.
73	Postumus	Victoria Aug	Ant.	RIC5: 89	259–268	–	–	107	CAA
74	Postumus	Victoria Aug	Ant.	RIC5: 89	259–268	–	–	54	CAA
75	Postumus	Victoria Aug	Ant.	RIC5: 89	259–268	–	–	104	CAA
76	Postumus	Victoria Aug	Ant.	RIC5: 89	259–268	–	–	183	CAA
77	Postumus	Victoria Aug	Ant.	RIC5: 89	259–268	–	–	189	CAA
78	Postumus	Victoria Aug	Ant.	RIC5: 89	259–268	–	–	187	CAA
79	Postumus	Virtus Aug	Ant.	RIC5: 93	259–268	–	–	184	CAA
80	Postumus	Virtus Aug	Ant.	RIC5: 93	259–268	–	–	186	CAA
81	Postumus	Virtus Aug	Ant.	RIC5: 93	259–268	–	–	12	DH
82	Postumus	illeg.	Ant.	–	259–268	–	–	152	CAA
83	Victorinus	Invictus	Ant.	RIC5: 114	268–270	–	–	5	JK 1
84	Victorinus	Salus	Ant.	RIC5: 71	268–270	–	–	24	CAB 3
85	Victorinus	Salus	Ant.	RIC5: 71	268–270	–	–	114	CAA
86	Victorinus	Providentia	Ant.	RIC5: 61	268–270	–	–	156	CAA
87	Victorinus	Providentia	Ant.	RIC5: 61	268–270	–	–	224	CAA
88	Victorinus	illeg.	Ant.	–	268–270	–	–	8	FZ 1
89	Tetricus I	Pax	Ant.	RIC5: 100	270–273	–	–	28	CAA
90	Tetricus I	Pax	Ant.	RIC5: 100	270–273	–	–	19	CAA
91	Tetricus I	Salus	Ant.	RIC5: 126	270–273	–	–	105	CAA
92	Tetricus I	Victoria	Ant.	RIC5: 140	270–273	–	–	117	CAA
93	Tetricus I	Virtus	Ant.	RIC5: 148	270–273	–	–	137	CAA
94	Tetricus I	illeg.	Ant.	–	270–273	–	–	110	CAA
95	Tetricus II	Pietas Augustor	Ant.	RIC5: 259	270–273	–	–	67	CAA
96	Tetricus II	Pietas Augustor	Ant.	RIC5: 259	270–273	–	–	20	DAC 1
97	Tetricus II	Princ Iuvent.	Ant.	RIC5: 260	270–273	–	–	109	CAA
98	Gallic	illeg.	Ant.	–	c.268–273	–	–	1	DAA1
99	Irregular radiate	illeg.	Ant.	–	c.268–275	–	–	22	FZ 3
100	Irregular radiate	illeg.	Ant.	–	c.268–275	–	–	14	CAA
101	Irregular radiate	illeg.	Ant.	–	c.268–275	–	–	26	ES 2
102	Irregular radiate	illeg.	Ant.	–	c.268–275	–	–	16	CAA
103	Irregular radiate	illeg.	Ant.	–	c.268–275	–	–	2	EAB 1
104	Irregular radiate	illeg.	Ant.	–	c.268–275	–	–	1	CV
105	Irregular radiate	illeg.	Ant.	–	c.268–275	–	–	9	EK 2
106	Irregular radiate	illeg.	Ant.	–	c.268–275	–	–	1	LC 1
107	Irregular radiate	illeg.	Ant.	–	c.268–275	–	–	60	GK
108	Irregular radiate	illeg.	Ant.	–	c.268–275	–	–	2	CAB 3
109	Irregular radiate	illeg.	Ant.	–	c.268–275	–	–	5	CAB 2
110	Irregular radiate	illeg.	Ant.	–	c.268–275	–	–	112	CAA
111	Irregular radiate	illeg.	Ant.	–	c.268–275	–	–	113	CAA
112	Irregular radiate	illeg.	Ant.	–	c.268–275	–	–	53	CAA
113	Irregular radiate	illeg.	Ant.	–	c.268–275	–	–	71	CAA
114	Irregular radiate	illeg.	Ant.	–	c.268–275	–	–	148	CAA
115	Irregular radiate	illeg.	Ant.	–	c.268–275	–	–	17	DAC 1
116	Irregular radiate	illeg.	Ant.	–	c.268–275	–	–	21	DAC 1
117	Irregular radiate	illeg.	Ant.	–	c.268–275	–	–	26	DAC 1
118	Claudius II	Genius Exerci	AE Ant.	RIC5: 48	268–270	–	–	44	CAA
119	Claudius II	Securitas	AE Ant.	–	268–270	–	–	33	FZ 13
120	Claudius II	Felicitas	AE Ant.	RIC5: 32	268–270	–	–	1	CE 4
121	Claudius II	Salus	AE Ant.	RIC5: 98	268–270	–	–	48	CAA
122	Claudius II	Ubertas	AE Ant.	RIC5: 274	268–270	–	–	1	LB
123	Claudius II	Ubertas	AE Ant.	RIC5: 274	268–270	–	–	1	GF 1
124	Claudius II	Spes	AE Ant.	RIC5: 102	268–270	–	–	2	XT 1
125	Claudius II	illeg.	AE Ant.	–	268–270	–	–	149	CAA
126	Claudius II	illeg.	AE Ant.	–	268–270	–	–	163	CAA
127	Claudius II	illeg.	AE Ant.	–	268–270	–	–	36	CAA
128	Claudius II	Consecratio (posthumous)	AE Ant.	RIC5: 266	c. 270+	–	–	12	CAA
129	Claudius II	Consecratio (posthumous)	AE Ant.	RIC5: 261	c. 270+	–	–	63	CE 8
130	Irregular Claudius II	Consecratio (posthumous)	AE Ant.	as RIC5: 261	c. 270+	–	–	154	CAA
131	Claudius II	Laetitia	AE Ant.	as RIC5: 277	c. 270+	–	–	3	CV
132	Carausius	Pax	AE Ant.	RIC5:	287–293	–	–	4	TA 1
133	Carausius	Provid Aug	AE Ant.	RIC5:	287–293	–	–	30	FZ 16
134	Carausius	illeg	AE Ant.	RIC5:	287–293	–	–	56	CAA
135	Carausius	illeg	AE Ant.	RIC5:	287–293	–	–	1	EAC 1
136	Allectus	Laetitia	AE Ant.	RIC5: 22	293–296	–	–	1	DF
137	Constantius I	Genio Populi Romani	AE1	–	305–306	Lyons	–	10	FZ 2
138	Constantine I	Victoriae Laetae Princ Perp	AE3	RIC7: 213	319–320	Trier	–	15	CAA
139	Constantine I	Beata Tranquillitas	AE3	RIC7: 369	320–324	Trier	–	145	CAA
140	Constantine II	Beat. Tranqlitas	AE3	RIC7: 258	320–324	Lyons	–	209	CAA
141	Constantine I	Providentiae Augg	AE3	as HK1: 12	324–330	illeg.	–	8	EK 2
142	Constantine I	Gloria Exercitus (2 standards)	AE3	HK1: 367	330–335	Arles	–	10	CV
143	Constantine I	Gloria Exercitus (2 standards)	AE3	HK1: 378	330–335	Arles	–	102	CAA
144	Constantine I	Gloria Exercitus (2 standards)	AE3	HK1: 197	330–335	Lyons	–	105	GK
145	Constantine I	Gloria Exercitus (2 standards)	AE3	HK1: 60	330–335	Trier	–	41	CAA
146	Constantine II	Gloria Exercitus (2 standards)	AE3	HK1: 56	330–335	Trier	–	55	CAA
147	Constantine II	Gloria Exercitus (2 standards)	AE3	HK1: 181	330–335	Lyons	–	115	CAA
148	Constantine II	Gloria Exercitus (2 standards)	AE3	HK1: 57	330–335	Trier	–	18	CAA
149	Constantine I	Gloria Exercitus (2 standards)	AE3	–	330–335	illeg.	–	4	DG
150	Constantine I	Gloria Exercitus (2 standards)	AE3	–	330–335	illeg.	–	2	RC 1
151	Constantine II	Gloria Exercitus (2 standards)	AE3	–	330–335	illeg.	–	191	CAA

No.	Issuer	Type	Denom	Ref	Date	Mint	Wt (g)	SFNo	Cont.
152	Constantine II	Gloria Exercitus (2 standards)	AE3	–	330–335	illeg.	–	14	FZ 3
153	H. of Constantine	Victoriae Laetae Princ Perp	AE3	–	319–320	illeg.	–	3	CAA
154	Constantine II	Gloria Exercitus (1 standard)	AE3/4	–	335–337	illeg.	–	155	CAA
155	Constantius II	Gloria Exercitus (1 standard)	AE3/4	–	335–337	illeg.	–	27	CAA
156	Constantius II	Gloria Exercitus (1 standard)	AE4	–	335–337	illeg.	–	19	DAC 1
157	Constantius II	Gloria Exercitus (1 standard)	AE4	–	335–337	illeg.	–	30	CAA
158	Urbs Roma	Wolf and Twins	AE3/4	HK1: 58	330–335	Trier	–	145	GK 11
159	Urbs Roma	Wolf and Twins	AE3/4	HK1: 200	330–335	Lyons	–	68	CAA
160	Urbs Roma	Wolf and Twins	AE3/4	HK1: 184	330–335	Lyons	–	111	CAA
161	Urbs Roma	Wolf and Twins	AE3/4	–	330–337	illeg.	–	146	CAA
162	Urbs Roma	Wolf and Twins	AE3/4	–	330–337	illeg.	–	164	CAA
163	Urbs Roma	Wolf and Twins	AE3/4	–	330–337	illeg.	–	1	EG 1
164	Constantinopolis	Victory on Prow	AE3/4	HK1: 59	330–335	Trier	–	14	EE 1
165	Constantinopolis	Victory on Prow	AE3/4	HK1: 59	330–335	Trier	–	34	CAA
166	Constantinopolis	Victory on Prow	AE3/4	HK1: 71	330–335	Trier	–	113	GK 2
167	Constantinopolis	Victory on Prow	irreg.	–	330–337	illeg.	–	66	CAA
168	Theodora	Pietas Romana	AE4	HK1: 120	337–341	Trier	–	13	DBB 4
169	Theodora	Pietas Romana	AE4	–	337–341	illeg.	–	162	CAA
170	H. of Constantine	Gloria Exercitus (1 standard)	AE4	–	335–341	illeg.	–	2	DAC 1
171	H. of Constantine	Gloria Exercitus (1 standard)	AE4	–	335–341	illeg.	–	56	GK
172	H. of Constantine	Gloria Exercitus (1 standard)	AE4	–	335–341	illeg.	–	95	GK 1
173	H. of Constantine	Gloria Exercitus (1 standard)	AE4	–	335–341	illeg.	–	10	DG
174	H. of Constantine	Gloria Exercitus (1 standard)	AE4	–	335–341	illeg.	–	5	LC 1
175	H. of Constantine	Gloria Exercitus (1 standard)	AE4	–	335–341	illeg.	–	35	CAA
176	H. of Constantine	Gloria Exercitus (1 standard)	AE4	–	335–341	illeg.	–	101	CAA
177	H. of Constantine	Gloria Exercitus (1 standard)	AE4	–	335–341	illeg.	–	10	CAA
178	H. of Constantine	Gloria Exercitus (1 standard)	AE4	–	335–341	illeg.	–	29	DAC 1
179	Constantius II	Victoriae DD Augg Q NN	AE4	HK1: 147	341–348	Trier	–	13	DAC 1
180	Constantius II	Victoriae DD Augg Q NN	AE4	–	341–348	illeg.	–	5	DBB 1
181	Constans	Victoriae DD Augg Q NN	AE4	HK1: 158	341–348	Trier	–	65	CAA
182	Constans	Victoriae DD Augg Q NN	AE4	as HK1: 148/50	341–348	Trier	–	13	CE 4
183	Constans	Victoriae DD Augg Q NN	AE4	HK1: 261	341–348	Lyons	–	223	CAA
184	H. of Constantine	Victoriae DD Augg Q NN	AE4	–	341–348	illeg.	–	65	CE 8
185	H. of Constantine	Victoriae DD Augg Q NN	AE4	–	341–348	illeg.	–	25	DAC 1
186	H. of Constantine	Victoriae DD Augg Q NN	AE4	–	341–348	illeg.	–	64	CE 8
187	H. of Constantine	Victoriae DD Augg Q NN	AE4	–	341–348	illeg.	–	5	CD 1
188	H. of Constantine	Victoriae DD Augg Q NN	AE4	–	341–348	illeg.	–	26	FZ 15
189	H. of Constantine	Victoriae DD Augg Q NN	AE4	–	341–348	illeg.	–	168	CAA
190	H. of Constantine	Victoriae DD Augg Q NN	AE4	–	341–348	illeg.	–	50	CAA
191	Constans	Fel Temp Reparatio (1)	AE2	HK2: 41	348–350	Trier	–	127	GK 10
192	Constans	Fel Temp Reparatio (phoenix)	AE3	–	348–350	illeg.	–	24	CAA
193	H. of Constantine	Fel Temp Reparatio (FH)	AE3	–	348–354	illeg.	–	12	RC 1
194	irreg.	Fel Temp Reparatio (FH)	AE3	–	c.348–354	illeg.	–	32	DAC 1
195	H. of Constantine	Spes Reipublicae	AE4	–	355–361	illeg.	–	71	GK
196	Constantius II	Fel Temp Reparatio (FH)	AE3	HK2: 455	353–360	Arles	–	160	CAA
197	Constantius II	Fel Temp Reparatio (FH)	AE3	–	353–360	illeg.	–	150	CAA
198	Magnentius	Victoriae DD NN Aug et Caess	AE2	as HK2: 5	350–353	illeg.	–	152	GK 1
199	Magnentius	Gloria Romanorum	AE2	as HK2: 3	350–353	irreg.	–	1	CD 1
200	Julian	Votis V Multis X	Siliqua	–	361–363	Lyons	–	3	RY 1
201	Valentinian I	Gloria Romanorum	AE3	as HK2: 1323	364–375	Siscia	–	21	DAC 1
202	Valentinian I	Gloria Romanorum	AE3	–	364–375	Lyons/Arles?	–	54	GK
203	Valens	Gloria Romanorum	AE3	HK2: 1428	364–378	Siscia	–	14	DAC 1
204	Valens	Gloria Romanorum	AE3	–	364–378	illeg.	–	225	CAA
205	Valens	Gloria Romanorum	AE3	–	364–378	Arles	–	1	VP 1
206	H. of Valentinian	Gloria Romanorum	AE3	–	364–378	illeg.	–	141	CAA
207	H. of Valentinian	Gloria Romanorum	AE3	–	364–378	illeg.	–	37	CAA
208	H. of Valentinian	Gloria Romanorum	AE3	–	364–378	illeg.	–	108	CAA
209	H. of Valentinian	Gloria Romanorum	AE3	–	364–378	illeg.	–	6	CAA
210	H. of Valentinian	Gloria Romanorum	AE3	–	364–378	illeg.	–	206	CAA
211	Valentinian I	Securitas Reipublicae	AE3	–	364–375	illeg.	–	108	GK
212	Valentinian I	Securitas Reipublicae	AE3	–	364–375	illeg.	–	106	CAA
213	Valens	Securitas Reipublicae	AE3	as HK2: 478	364–378	Arles?	–	129	GK 10
214	Valens	Securitas Reipublicae	AE3	HK2: 1395	364–378	Siscia	–	8	CAA
215	Valens	Securitas Reipublicae	AE3	–	364–378	illeg.	–	7	CAA
216	Valens	Securitas Reipublicae	AE3	–	364–378	illeg.	–	4	CAA
217	Valens	Securitas Reipublicae	AE3	–	364–378	illeg.	–	11	CAA
218	Valens	Securitas Reipublicae	AE3	–	364–378	illeg.	–	153	CAA
219	Valens	Securitas Reipublicae	AE3	–	364–378	illeg.	–	139	CAA
220	Valens	Securitas Reipublicae	AE3	–	364–378	illeg.	–	76	GK
221	Gratian	Gloria Romanorum	AE3	–	364–378	illeg.	–	138	GK 9
222	Gratian	Securitas Reipublicae	AE3	–	364–378	illeg.	–	52	CAA
223	H. of Valentinian	Securitas Reipublicae	AE3	–	364–378	Arles	–	73	GK
224	H. of Valentinian	Securitas Reipublicae	AE3	–	364–378	Arles	–	3	CG 1
225	H. of Valentinian	Securitas Reipublicae	AE3	–	364–378	Siscia	–	9	RC 1
226	H. of Valentinian	Securitas Reipublicae	AE3	–	364–378	illeg.	–	2	CG 1
227	H. of Valentinian	Securitas Reipublicae	AE3	–	364–378	illeg.	–	8	CG 1
228	H. of Valentinian	Securitas Reipublicae	AE3	–	364–378	illeg.	–	2	DG
229	H. of Valentinian	Securitas Reipublicae	AE3	–	364–378	illeg.	–	–	–
230	H. of Valentinian	Securitas Reipublicae	AE3	–	364–378	illeg.	–	72	GK

No.	Issuer	Type	Denom	Ref	Date	Mint	Wt (g)	SFNo	Cont.
231	H. of Valentinian	Securitas Reipublicae	AE3	–	364–378	illeg.	–	7	CG 1
232	H. of Valentinian	Securitas Reipublicae	AE3	–	364–378	illeg.	–	107	GK
233	H. of Valentinian	Securitas Reipublicae	AE3	–	364–378	illeg.	–	5	CG 1
234	H. of Valentinian	Securitas Reipublicae	AE3	–	364–378	illeg.	–	68	GK
235	H. of Valentinian	Securitas Reipublicae	AE3	–	364–378	illeg.	–	18	GK 1
236	H. of Valentinian	Securitas Reipublicae	AE3	–	364–378	illeg.	–	88	GK 1
237	H. of Valentinian	Securitas Reipublicae	AE3	–	364–378	illeg.	–	23	DAC 1
238	H. of Valentinian	Securitas Reipublicae	AE3	–	364–378	illeg.	–	16	DAC 1
239	H. of Valentinian	Securitas Reipublicae	AE3	–	364–378	illeg.	–	136	CAA
240	H. of Valentinian	Securitas Reipublicae	AE3	–	364–378	illeg.	–	9	CAA
241	H. of Valentinian	Securitas Reipublicae	AE3	–	364–378	illeg.	–	171	CAA
242	H. of Valentinian	Securitas Reipublicae	AE3	–	364–378	illeg.	–	63	CAA
243	H. of Valentinian	Securitas Reipublicae	AE3	–	364–378	illeg.	–	9	CG 1
244	Gratian	Gloria Novi Saeculi	AE3	as HK2: 517	367–378	Lyons/Arles?	–	11	RC 1
245	Gratian	Gloria Novi Saeculi	AE3	as HK2: 517	367–378	illeg.	–	5	RC 1
246	Gratian	Gloria Novi Saeculi	AE3	as HK2: 517	367–378	illeg.	–	1	DG
247	Gratian	Gloria Novi Saeculi	AE3	as HK2: 517	367–378	illeg.	–	30	DAC 1
248	Gratian	Gloria Novi Saeculi	AE3	as HK2: 517	367–378	illeg.	–	1	KA 1
249	Gratian	Gloria Novi Saeculi	AE3	as HK2: 517	367–378	illeg.	–	13	CAA
250	Gratian	Gloria Novi Saeculi	AE3	as HK2: 517	367–378	illeg.	–	4	CG 1
251	Theodosius	Victoria Augg	AE4	HK2: 565	388–395	Arles	–	20	CAA
252	H. of Theodosius	Victoria Augg	AE4	–	388–402	illeg.	–	1	DB
253	H. of Theodosius	Victoria Augg	AE4	–	388–402	illeg.	–	2	XV 1
254	H. of Theodosius	Victoria Augg	AE4	–	388–402	illeg.	–	3*	CD 1
255	H. of Theodosius	Victoria Augg	AE4	–	388–402	illeg.	–	135	CAA
256	H. of Theodosius	Victoria Augg	AE4	–	388–402	illeg.	–	31	DAC 1
257	H. of Theodosius	Salus Reipublicae	AE4	–	388–402	illeg.	–	21	CAA
258	illeg.	illeg	AE3/4	–	late 3rd–late 4th	illeg.	–	4	DBB 1
259	illeg.	illeg	AE3/4	–	late 3rd–late 4th	illeg.	–	39	CAA
260	illeg.	illeg	AE3/4	–	late 3rd–late 4th	illeg.	–	158	CAA
261	illeg.	illeg	AE3/4	–	late 3rd–late 4th	illeg.	–	51	CAA
262	illeg.	illeg	AE3/4	–	late 3rd–late 4th	illeg.	–	99	CAA
263	illeg.	illeg	AE3/4	–	late 3rd–late 4th	illeg.	–	143	CAA
264	illeg.	illeg	AE3/4	–	late 3rd–late 4th	illeg.	–	22	CAA
265	illeg.	illeg	AE3/4	–	late 3rd–late 4th	illeg.	–	5	CAA
266	illeg.	illeg	AE3/4	–	late 3rd–late 4th	illeg.	–	40	CAA
267	illeg.	illeg	AE3/4	–	late 3rd–late 4th	illeg.	–	29	CAA
268	illeg.	illeg	AE3/4	–	late 3rd–late 4th	illeg.	–	23	CAA
269	illeg.	illeg	AE3/4	–	late 3rd–late 4th	illeg.	–	38	CAA
270	illeg.	illeg	AE3/4	–	late 3rd–late 4th	illeg.	–	25	CAA
271	illeg.	illeg	AE3/4	–	late 3rd–late 4th	illeg.	–	27	DAC 1
272	illeg.	illeg	AE3/4	–	late 3rd–late 4th	illeg.	–	1	KF 1
273	illeg.	illeg	AE3/4	–	late 3rd–late 4th	illeg.	–	106	GK
274	illeg.	illeg	AE3/4	–	late 3rd–late 4th	illeg.	–	8	DH
275	illeg.	illeg	AE3/4	–	late 3rd–late 4th	illeg.	–	4	LC 1
276	illeg.	illeg	AE3/4	–	late 3rd–late 4th	illeg.	–	4	RC
277	illeg.	illeg	AE3/4	–	late 3rd–late 4th	illeg.	–	9	MR 1
278	illeg.	illeg	AE3/4	–	late 3rd–late 4th	illeg.	–	10	RC 1
279	illeg.	illeg	AE3/4	–	late 3rd–late 4th	illeg.	–	6	RC 1
280	illeg.	illeg	AE3/4	–	late 3rd–late 4th	illeg.	–	15	DH
281	illeg.	illeg	AE3/4	–	late 3rd–late 4th	illeg.	–	33	GK 1
282	illeg.	illeg	AE3/4	–	late 3rd–late 4th	illeg.	–	75	GK
283	illeg.	illeg	AE3/4	–	late 3rd–late 4th	illeg.	–	59	GK
284	illeg.	illeg	AE3/4	–	late 3rd–late 4th	illeg.	–	93	GK
285	illeg.	illeg	AE3/4	–	late 3rd–late 4th	illeg.	–	84	GK
286	illeg.	illeg	AE3/4	–	late 3rd–late 4th	illeg.	–	3	DG
287	illeg.	illeg	AE3/4	–	late 3rd–late 4th	illeg.	–	41	GK
288	illeg.	illeg	AE3/4	–	late 3rd–late 4th	illeg.	–	9	GH
289	illeg.	illeg	AE3/4	–	late 3rd–late 4th	illeg.	–	6	LC 1
290	illeg.	illeg	AE3/4	–	late 3rd–late 4th	illeg.	–	7	HR 1
291	illeg.	illeg	AE3/4	–	late 3rd–late 4th	illeg.	–	2	LB
292	illeg.	illeg	AE3/4	–	late 3rd–late 4th	illeg.	–	3	LB
293	illeg.	illeg	AE3/4	–	late 3rd–late 4th	illeg.	–	68	CE 8
294	illeg.	illeg	AE3/4	–	late 3rd–late 4th	illeg.	–	1	KC 1
295	illeg.	illeg	AE3/4	–	late 3rd–late 4th	illeg.	–	1	RL 1
296	illeg.	illeg	AE3/4	–	late 3rd–late 4th	illeg.	–	83	GK
297	illeg.	illeg	AE3/4	–	late 3rd–late 4th	illeg.	–	3	XY 1
298	illeg.	illeg	AE3/4	–	late 3rd–late 4th	illeg.	–	85	GK
299	illeg.	illeg	AE3/4	–	late 3rd–late 4th	illeg.	–	10	CG 1
300	illeg.	illeg	AE3/4	–	late 3rd–late 4th	illeg.	–	2	CD 2
301	illeg.	illeg	AE3/4	–	late 3rd–late 4th	illeg.	–	11	CG 1
302	illeg.	illeg	AE3/4	–	late 3rd–late 4th	illeg.	–	2	TL 1
303	illeg.	illeg	AE3/4	–	late 3rd–late 4th	illeg.	–	1	CS
304	illeg.	illeg	AE3/4	–	late 3rd–late 4th	illeg.	–	6	CG 1

REFERENCES:
RRC: Sydenham E.A., 1952 *Roman Republican Coinage* (London).
RIC: Mattingly, H., Sydenham, EA., Sutherland, C.H.V and Carson, R.A.G, 1923ff *Roman Imperial Coinage*, vols 1–9 (London).
HK1,2: Carson, R.A.G., Hill, PV and Kent, J.P.C., 1972 *Late Roman Bronze Coinage, AD 324–498*, 2 vols (London).

Coin Hoard
Roger Bland

Background

As has been noted in the *Introduction*, this hoard of 2579 third-century silver *denarii* and *antoniniani* was found in the first evaluation trench cut by the Trust at Chells in 1986. The following report has already been published in much greater detail elsewhere (Bland and Burnett 1988): the following edited version, included here for completeness' sake, deals with the hoard's date of deposition, and various aspects of interest within it. Coin numbers referred to below are taken from the hoard catalogue in the above publication. Readers are also referred to Mark Corney's report on the main coin assemblage from the site, which identifies additional coins that may have belonged with the hoard. The bulk of the hoard has been deposited with Stevenage Museum, though 129 coins were donated to the British Museum.

Date of Burial and Composition

The latest coins in the hoard (Table 2) are seven specimens of the MONETA AVG type of Postumus (Elmer 336), which may be dated to 263 (Besly and Bland 1983, 48–49. This, therefore is the *terminus ante quem* for its date of deposition is, therefore, 263. This appears to have been the first hoard to have been published from Britain that closes at this precise date, although there are a number of parallels from the Continent. When we compare the present find with others that were buried at about this time, whether in Britain or abroad, it is clear that the Chells hoard has an abnormally high proportion of *denarii* of the period 198–238. The evidence of the other finds, of which Dorchester is perhaps the clearest British example, shows that the great majority of *denarii* had disappeared from circulation before the end of the joint reign of Valerian and Gallienus in 260 (Bland forthcoming). The fact that fifteen per cent of the Chells hoard are *denarii* suggests that it was a 'savings hoard', put together over a period of perhaps ten to twenty years. Certainly the earlier coins in the hoard show a great variation in their amount of wear, perhaps implying that they were removed from circulation at different times. Coin hoards of the early years of Postumus's reign have been discussed most recently by Lallemand (1986).

Table 3, which is based on Lallemand's, compares the composition of hoards that close with coins of the second and third issues of Postumus (262–263); for comparison I have added the Dorchester hoard which terminates a little earlier, in about 257, and also the Creil I and Rocquencourt hoards, published since Lallemand's paper. The pattern is not as clear as it could be, but only two other finds apart from Chells have significant quantities of *denarii*, Vannes and Rouvroy, and of these only Rouvroy offers a statistically significant sample. It seems reasonable to suggest that these hoards also were gradually saved over the years, whereas the remaining finds are more likely to have been put together in a much shorter space of time from the pool of coins in circulation in the early years of Postumus's reign.

The Eastern Coinage of Elagabalus

This presents a number of problems as yet unresolved. While the coins with IMP ANTONINVS PIVS FEL AVG obverses are clearly from an eastern mint, presumably Antioch, those with the legend IMP ANTONINVS AVG are less straightforward. Some authorities would divide coins with this legend between Rome and another mint (*eg* Carson and Hill in their revision of *BMC* V, and Thirion, *Le monnayage d'Elagabale*), while others (*eg* Pink in *NZ* 1934, 11–17) assign them all to a secondary mint, perhaps at Nicomedia. In the catalogue, I have followed the latter course.

Severus Alexander

Coin 151 (Plate 9), dated TR P VII (227–228), has a reverse type showing Mars standing left, holding a shield in his left hand and a spear in his right, which is scarcely recorded for Alexander at all. Cohen 338 records a specimen with this reverse type from Copenhagen with the long obverse legend IMP C M AVR SEV ALEXAND AVG, but Carson was unable to find this coin when he was writing *BMC* VI. It is now possible to confirm the existence of this type with the obverse IMP SEV ALEXAND AVG in this coin from the Chells hoard which is clearly genuine.

Pacatian

The hoard contained the first specimen of Pacatian's coinage to have been found in Britain. Since Pacatian's usurpation took place in Pannonia and Moesia, and his coins were probably struck at the mint of *Viminacium*, it is not particularly surprising that it is only now that one of his coins has been found in this country. One was apparently discovered in a small hoard from Amiens in northern France in 1890 (Evans 1890), while the Collection Raymond in Toulouse contains no fewer than two specimens of his coinage: there must be a suspicion that these too might have a local provenance. The great majority of these coins that have provenances come from the area of the Balkans and the Danube basin. Altogether, some seventy-five coins of Pacatian are known today (Szaivert 1983; Bland and Amandry 1992) with the obverse legends IMP TI CL MAR PACATIANVS PF AVG (and variants PF AV, PF IN, F P A, P AVG and P AV), and IMP TI CL MAR PACATIANVS AVG. Five reverse types are known; CONCORDIA MILITVM, FIDES MILITVM (and FIDE MILITVM), FORTVNA REDVX, PAX AETERNA and ROMAE AETER AN MILL ET PRIMO. Of these PAX AETERNA is the most common, accounting for thirty-eight specimens. The Chells piece has the reverse FORTVNA REDVX, attested from eleven other coins, two of which (BM R0549 and Vienna Inv. 18244) have the same obverse legend, IMP TI CL MAR PACATIANVS AVG. The Chells piece shares its obverse die with the British Museum coin and its reverse die with the coin sold at Glendening, London, on 3rd December 1929 (Nordheim-Anderson), no. 477.

Valerian and Gallienus

Present in the hoard were 969 coins of the joint reign of Valerian and Gallienus, of which 581 (60%) come from the mint of Gaul. This high proportion of Gallic coins is typical of hoards which end during Postumus's reign, and is in sharp contrast to the proportions of these coins in the *Cunetio* hoard, which closed in 274, where out of 10,559 coins of Valerian and Gallienus only 646 (6.1%) were minted in Gaul (Besley and Bland 1983). It seems that the Gallic coinage of Valerian and his family was removed from circulation before the issues of his other mints, principally Rome. This is either, perhaps, because Postumus made a systematic attempt to remove the joint reign coinage from circulation and most of the coins that he was able to get hold of naturally enough came from the local mint, or it could be because the Gallic coins were, on average, finer than those of the other mints, and thus were the first to disappear from circulation (Le Gentilhomme 1962).

There were two unpublished hybrids of this reign: Coin 420, a coin of Valerian from Rome with Salonina's reverse IVNO REGINA, and Coin 522, a radiate in the name of Valerian II from the mint of Gaul with the reverse PIETAS AVG, sacrificial implements, which belongs to Saloninus (Plate 9).

Saloninus as Augustus

The hoard contained no less than three coins (Plate 9) of Saloninus as Augustus (no previous find had contained more than one), although given the presence of 581 coins of the mint of Gaul this is not as surprising as it might first seem. The most recent publication of the coins of Saloninus as Augustus (Gilljam 1987) gives details of thirty-one pieces, whereas Shiel (1979) was able to list only fifteen. Since most of the sixteen extra pieces have either come from recent hoards or have appeared in trade within the last decade, one is left wondering whether coins in the name of Saloninus as Augustus are not considerably more common than has traditionally been assumed. It may be that they were often not recognised in the past, being mistaken for the normal coinage of Saloninus as Caesar, to which they are very similar. Only since Shiel's publication has made this coinage better known have they started to be recognised more frequently. Further evidence of the size of this coinage is provided by the fact that none of the three coins in the hoard shares an obverse die; it is harder to be certain about the reverses, but they too seem to be different. Of the thirty coins available for study, there seem to be as many as fourteen obverse dies.

The Coinage of Salonina from Rome

From the central Empire the hoard ended with ten coins of the sole reign of Gallienus; five from Rome and five from Milan, all of them from the earliest issues of the reign. The Milan coins, which were all in the name of Gallienus, included four examples of the legionary series, the first of the reign, and one piece from the series immediately following it. Of the coins minted at Rome, only one was of Gallienus (a coin of his second series), and the rest were of Salonina. Each of these had a different reverse; two had types that have always been attributed to the first and second series of the sole reign (VENVS GENETRIX from *officina* VI and VESTA, standing left, from an uncertain *officina*), while the other two had types (VESTA, seated left, from *Officina* Q, and PVDICITIA, seated left, from *officina* VI) that were normally attributed to the fourth series, which uses exclusively seated reverse types. However, in the publication of the *Cunetio* hoard (*op. cit.*, 26), it was suggested that these two seated types should in fact be included in the coinage of the first and second series, and this hoard offers strong support for this theory, closing as it does well before the fourth series from the mint of Rome.

The Irregular Coins

There were seventy-three contemporary imitations (2.8%), of which two were plated *denarii*, one a very curious and distinctive forgery of Trajan Decius. Four were copies of Valerian and Gallienus, and the remaining sixty-six coins were all copies of Postumus. The high proportion of imitations of Postumus, sixty-six to 564 official issues, or 11.7%, compares quite closely with the proportion in the *Cunetio* hoard (1259 to 12991, or 9.7%), and demonstrates that the great rash of third-century copying in Britain and Gaul had its origins at the beginning of the reign of Postumus. Possibly his coins were chosen by forgers because they had a premium over the contemporary coinage of Gallienus as a result of their higher silver content. Another notable feature of these imitations of Postumus is that they copy the latest coins in the hoard, those from the second series and the MONETA AVG type from the third series. Evidently the forgers were imitating the most recent official issues as soon as they came into circulation (Gricourt and Hollard 1987).

A number of die-links were noticed among these imitations of Postumus, and they are noted in the catalogue (Bland 1988, 71–72). Of particular interest are Coins 626–634 (Plate 9), a group of twenty-seven coins from four obverse and five reverse dies, one of these reverse dies (MINER FAVTR) occurring on nineteen coins. All the obverse dies at least, and possibly the reverses as well, appear to come from the hand of the same engraver. It would be tempting to speculate that these coins were the product of a local workshop; otherwise why should so many die-linked coins have remained together? However, two coins from this group of dies were found in the *Cunetio* hoard, and another in the hoard from Rocquencourt in northern France (Holland 1986), so although it seems probable that these forgeries were made in Britain rather than Gaul, any further precision is impossible.

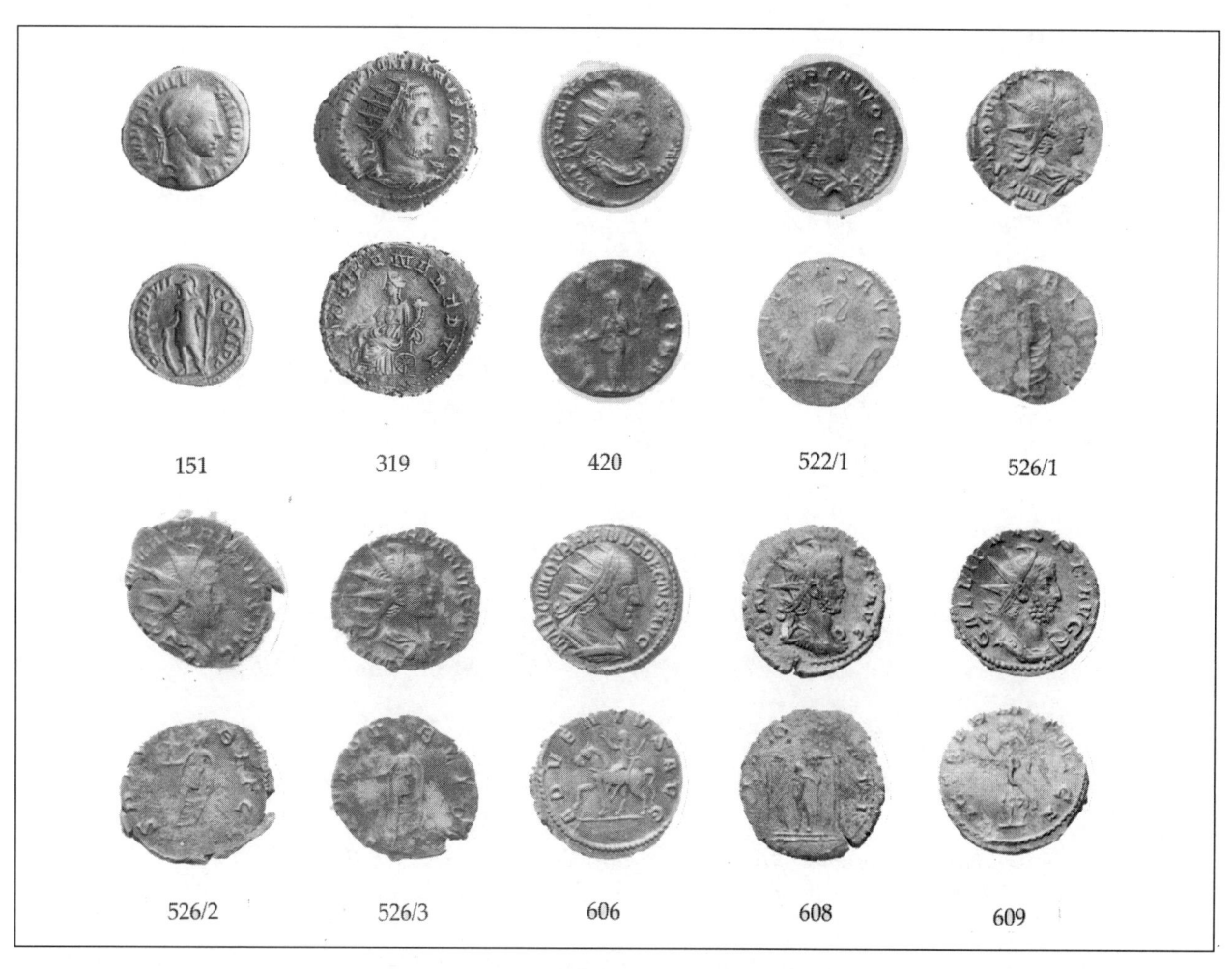

Plate 9A   *A selection of coins from the hoard, discussed in the report:*
151   Severus Alexander (AD 222–35), base silver denarius.
319   Pacatian (AD 249), base silver radiate.
420   Valerian I (AD 253–60), base silver radiate.
522/1   Valerian II (AD 255–8), base silver radiate, posthumus issue.
526/1–3   Saloninus as Augustus (AD 260), base silver radiates.
606   Contemporary forgery of base silver radiate of Trajan Decius (AD 249–51).
608–609   Contemporary forgeries of base silver radiates of Gallienus (joint reign, AD 253–60).

(British Museum)

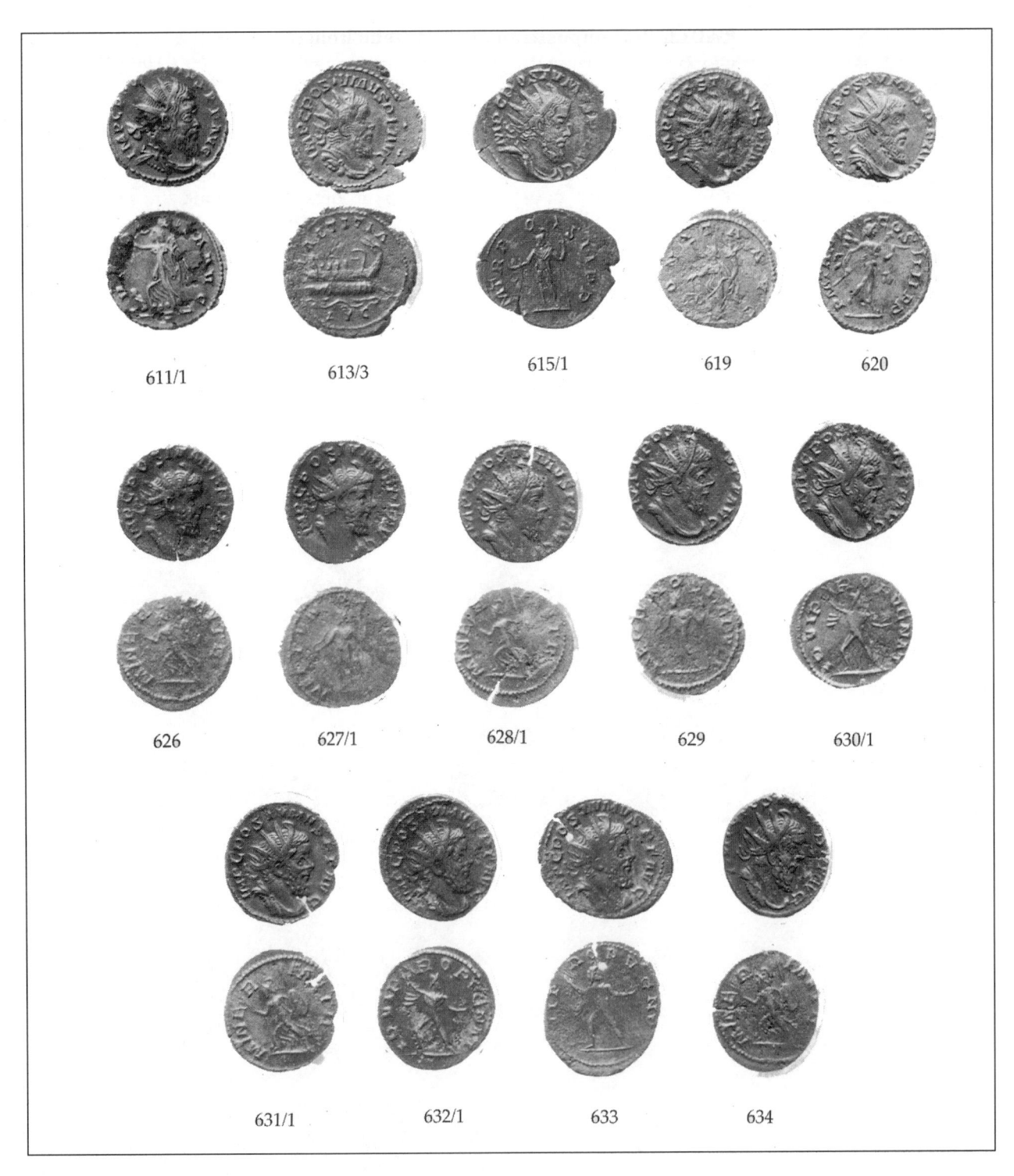

Plate 9B
*611–63   Contemporary forgeries of base silver radiates of Postumus (AD 260–9)
(nos 626–34 are from the die-linked group, possibly made locally).*

(British Museum)

TABLE 2: Composition of the Chells hoard.

Issuer	Date	Rome Den	Rad	Gaul	Milan	Balkan	Eastern Den	Rad	Total
Septimius Severus	193–211	16	–	–	–	–	2	–	18
Julia Domna		5	–	–	–	–	–	–	5
Caracalla	197–217	9	1	–	–	–	–	–	10
Plautilla		1	–	–	–	–	–	–	1
Macrinus	217–218	3	–	–	–	–	–	–	3
Elagabalus	218–222	82	5	–	–	–	7	–	94
Julia Soaemias		10	–	–	–	–	–	–	10
Julia Maesa		27	1	–	–	–	–	–	28
Julia Paula		3	–	–	–	–	–	–	3
Aquilia Severa		1	–	–	–	–	–	–	1
Severus Alexander	222–235	164	–	–	–	–	4	–	168
Julia Mamaea		30	–	–	–	–	–	–	30
Orbiana		1	–	–	–	–	–	–	1
Maximinus	235–238	13	–	–	–	–	–	–	13
Balbinus	238	1	–	–	–	–	–	–	1
Pupienus		–	1	–	–	–	–	–	1
Gordian III	238–244	6	173	–	–	–	–	25	204
Philip I	244–249	–	108	–	–	–	–	1	109
Otacilia Severa		–	23	–	–	–	–	–	23
Philip II		–	28	–	–	–	–	1	29
Pacatian	249	–	–	–	–	1	–	–	1
Trajan Decius	249–251	–	51	–	–	–	–	1	52
Divus Trajan		–	2	–	–	–	–	–	2
Etruscilla		–	18	–	–	–	–	–	18
Etruscus		–	7	–	–	–	–	–	7
Hostilian		–	1	–	–	–	–	–	1
Trebonianus Gallus	251–253	–	59	–	–	–	–	10	69
Volusian		–	49	–	–	–	–	1	50
Aemilian	253	–	11	–	–	–	–	–	11
Valerian I	253–260	–	164	87	–	18	–	7	276
Gallienus		–	93	221	1	11	–	1	327
Mariniana		–	7	–	–	–	–	–	7
Salonina		–	59	109	1	8	–	1	178
Valerian II		–	12	99	–	4	–	–	115
Saloninus		–	1	62	–	–	–	–	63
Saloninus (Augustus)	260	–	–	3	–	–	–	–	3
Gallienus	260–268	–	1	–	5	–	–	–	6
Salonina		–	4	–	–	–	–	–	4
Postumus	260–269	–	–	564	–	–	–	–	564
		372	**1251**	**1145**	**7**	**42**	**13**	**61**	**2506**

IRREGULAR ISSUES:
Julia Soaemias	1
Severus Alexander	1
Trajan Decius	1
Valerian	1
Gallienus (joint reign)	3
Postumus	66
	2579

TABLE 3: Comparison of the Chells hoard with other contemporary hoards.

I	Before 238 No	%	Gordian–Philip No	%	Decius–Aemilian No	%	Valerian & Gallienus No	%	Postumus No	%
Dorchester[1]	234	1.1	15882	76.5	3774	18.2	858	4.1	–	–
Schwarzenacker[2]	58	1.2	2970	61.7	1151	23.9	606	12.6	26	0.5
Bras[3]	2	1.8	21	19.5	20	18.5	3	2.8	62	67.4
Noyers[4]	7	1.6	246	56.7	56	12.9	16	3.7	109	25.1
Belsele[5]	33	2.2	878	57.5	251	16.5	292	19.1	72	4.7
Wallers[6]	–	–	15	10.3	9	6.2	29	20.0	92	63.5
Basecles[7]	1	0.2	54	11.0	42	8.6	121	24.7	271	55.4
Rocquencourt[8]	34	0.7	1130	23.0	581	11.8	1004	20.4	2164	44.0
Creil[9]	9	0.9	589	59.6	185	18.7	201	20.3	4	0.4
Leerbeek[10]	8	6.3	80	63.0	10	7.9	13	10.2	16	12.6
Rouvroy[11]	81	11.9	223	32.8	69	10.2	112	16.5	194	28.6
Vannes[12]	14	12.5	28	25.0	20	17.9	33	29.5	17	15.2
CHELLS	**389**	**15.1**	**366**	**14.2**	**211**	**8.2**	**983**	**38.1**	**630**	**24.4**

References:

1. Mattingly 1939
2. Kienast 1962
3. Lallemand 1986
4. Fabre and Mainjonet 1953
5. van Naeman 1892–93
6. Freudenberg 1867
7. Thirion 1966
8. Hollard 1986
9. Amandry et al 1985
10. Cumont 1898–1907
11. Fabre and Mainjonet 1954: 1958
12. Brenot 1963

Brooches
(Fig. 17)

Mark Corney

La Tène III

1   60 mm in length and badly fragmented. The piece had either a three or four-coil spring (the state of preservation precludes certainty on the point) and had an external chord. The upper and lower bow sections are separated by a boss comprising five prominent transverse mouldings. This latter feature being a stylistic remnant of the collar by which the bow on the La Tène II brooch was closed. Below the boss the bow is triangular in section, decorated with fine vertical grooves and displays some recurve towards the foot. The catchplate is triangular and pierced by at least three circular perforations.
EAW 1/1: *Chalk spread sealing West III quarry/pit EAW. Later first century AD.*

This form of the La Tène III, with the moulded boss, is seen by Stead (1976) as a type-fossil for the Welwyn phase of his Aylesford culture, and is dated to the second half of the first century BC. The well-defined moulding, external chord and pierced catchplate point to an early date within the overall range for the type.

Colchester

2   47 mm in length. The spring has four coils and the chord is held by a short, forward-facing hook. The wings are short and the octagonal-section bow has a pronounced high peak, a typologically early trait. The lower bow and the catchplate are missing.
SJ/1: *gully fill.*

3   56 mm in length. The spring has eight coil and retains a copper alloy axial bar. The hook securing the chord is long and the wings are comparatively short, although corrosion makes their true dimensions difficult to assess. The bow is plain and curves gently to the catchplate, enough of which survives to suggest that it was perforated, although the character of this is now impossible to ascertain.
EC/1: *pit fill.*

4   60 mm in length. The spring, hook, pin and catchplate are missing. Despite a degree of corrosion, enough of the wings survive to demonstrate that they were short and probably plain. The roughly hexagonal-section bow has a central groove with traces of a punched ornament in its lower half.
CAA/177: *unstratified.*

5   39 mm in length. The spring comprises eight coils and the chord is held by a long hook. The wings are ornamented with vertical grooves, whilst the circular bow is plain. Too little of the catchplate survives to demonstrate whether it was perforated.
BBB 2/2: *Area 3, Pit EAN. Later first to early second century.*

The Colchester series appears at the beginning of the first century AD, continued in production down to c.AD 40, and tends to dominate early to mid first-century assemblages in eastern Britain. Usage survives the Roman conquest, but it has largely passed from currency by AD 60. Its popularity in the pre-conquest period is attested by the numbers recovered from the type-site, *Camulodunum* (Colchester: Hawkes and Hull 1947), and the King Harry Lane cemetery (Stead and Rigby 1989).

There are many typological variants of the type, such as the form of the spring, bow and catchplate. Of the Chells examples, **Brooch 2** is particularly noteworthy because of the high peak to the bow and the short hook securing the chord. Such traits should place this piece in the earlier part of the Colchester development. For a recent detailed discussion of the type, particularly relevant to Hertfordshire assemblages, see Olivier (1988, 42–44).

Langton Down

6   Uppermost part only. Much of the spring case is missing and only a small portion of the upper bow survives, although enough is preserved to show that this was richly reeded. The type is well-represented on pre-conquest sites in southern Britain, (Verulamium, King Harry Lane: Stead and Rigby 1989; Silchester: Corney forthcoming), with a *floruit* c.AD 10–40. The form has largely passed from currency by c.AD 50.
GJ/3: *unstratified.*

Thistle

7   48 mm in length. Typologically the form is related to the Langton Down, the spring being encased and having a reeded bow. The obvious difference is the large circular plaque occupying the middle section of the bow which, in the Chells example, is richly moulded. The *floruit* is the same as that for the Langton Down, and it is well represented at the King Harry Lane cemetery (Stead and Rigby 1989, 93–4).
EAA 1/1: *Area 3, pit fill. Mid second century.*

Nauheim Derivative

8   31 mm in length. The brooch has a three-coil spring, an internal chord and a flat-section plain bow which tapers to a point. This form has a long currency in southern Britain, with many regional variations from the pre-conquest period to the late first century AD. The Chells brooch probably falls into the middle of this long sequence. For a fuller discussion relevant to the Hertfordshire series, see Olivier (1988, 36–8).
EBR 1/1: *gully fill.*

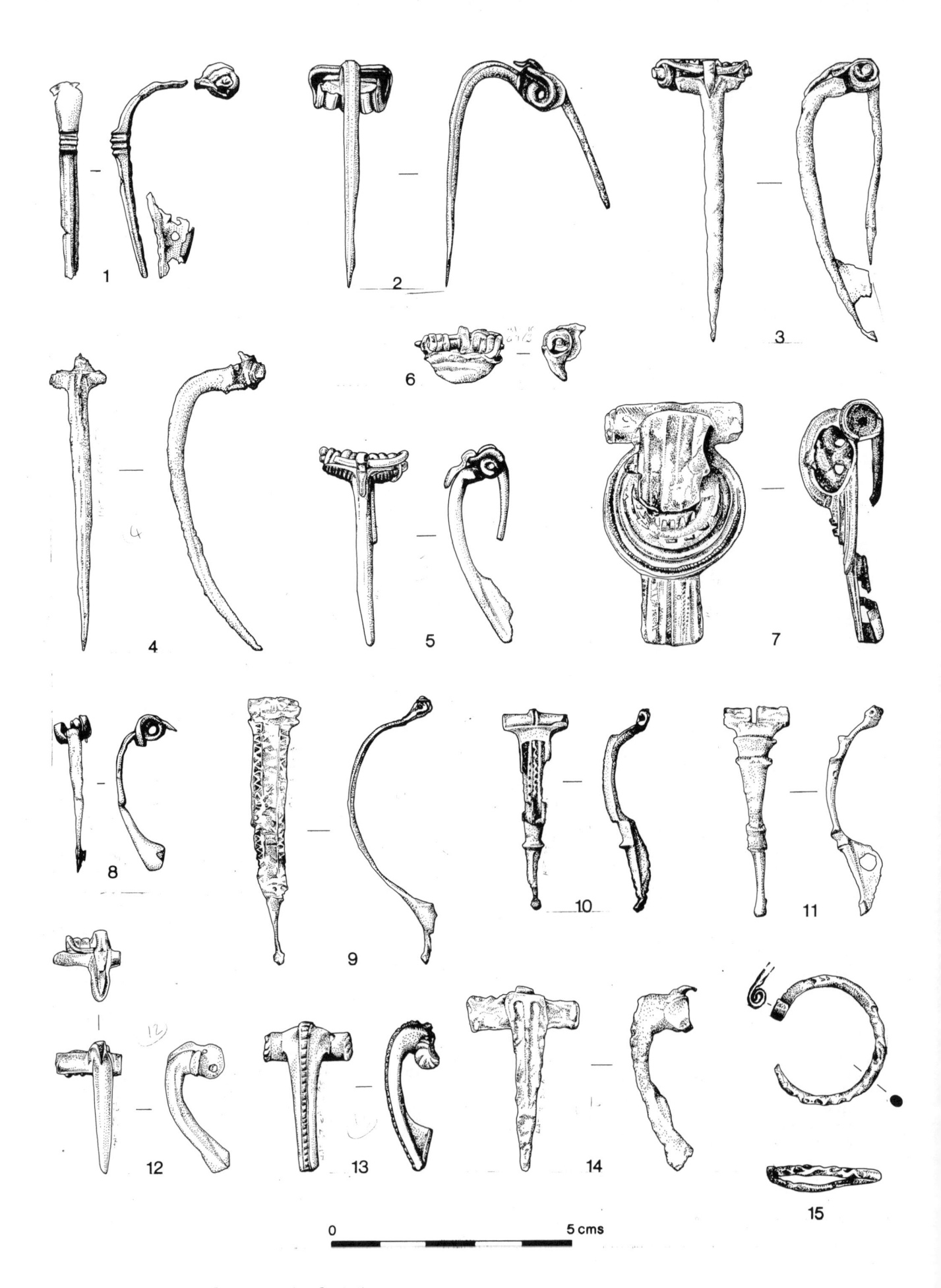

Figure 17   Brooches, 1–15 (scale 1:1).

Aucissa

9 The pin (missing) was hinged and held by the rolled-over head of the bow. Decoration on the bow is confined to either edge, and can be paralleled on examples from *Camulodunum* (Hawkes and Hull 1947, pl. XCVI, Fig. 116, grave 158 no. 2). The brooch is not 'signed', and the bow foot terminates in a small knob. The type is close approaching the end of its currency when it appears in Britain. Originating in the Augustan period, the Aucissa is largely an introduction of the Roman Army in AD 43, although some are pre-Conquest imports (Mackreth *in* Partridge 1981). The type should be passing from use in the Neronian period.
DG/5: *unstratified*

Hod Hill

10 40 mm in length. Typologically related to the Aucissa series, the Hod Hill was most likely introduced with the Roman army in AD 43, there being, to date, no proven pre-conquest examples from Britain.
EAN 3: *Area 3, Pit EAN. Later first to early second century.*

The type occurs in a wide variety of forms, with the Chells piece being a quite restrained example, having a raised longitudinal moulding on the upper bow, with a single plain transverse moulding on the lower element. The catchplate is triangular and solid. The piece retains traces of silvering or tinning. The rarity of the Hod Hill series north of the Humber demonstrates a British *floruit* during the Claudio–Neronian period.

11 41 mm in length. The tapering bow is decorated with four transverse mouldings and has a small terminal knob. The triangular catchplate has a circular perforation. For dating, see comments for **10**.
GBE 2: *gully fill.*

Colchester Derivative

12 27 mm in length. T-shaped two-piece brooch, where the spring and chord are affixed to the body by passing the chord through a hook. This example has a plain bow, and is of quite small proportions.
EAW 2/2: *Chalk spread sealing Area 3 quarry/pit EAW. Later first century AD.*

13 30 mm in length. The spring and the pin were affixed in the same fashion as **12**. The bow and wings are ornamented with simple grooving and the catchplate is solid. The spring, pin and hook are missing, allowing what may be traces of solder to be seen on the rear face of the wings. This device is used to increase the security of the fixing of the spring component to the main brooch body (Olivier *in* Potter and Trow 1988, 46).
CAB 1/35: *Area 1, well weathering cone. Later fourth century onwards.*

14 37 mm in length. The wings and upper bow are decorated with strong vertical mouldings. The spring is missing but was secured by a rear-facing hook and the closed ends of the wings, in the 'Polden Hill' fashion. The lower bow is corroded and the catch plate is missing.
DG/9: *unstratified.*

The Colchester derivative emerges in the decade prior to AD 43 and develops during the second half of the first century AD (Mackreth 1988, 45–6). Of the three examples from Chells, 12 and 13 would fit best in the AD 45–65 bracket, with 14 being the latest piece, of probable Flavian date. The form is popular throughout the later first century, and can occur in deposits running into the second century.

Penannular

15 Penannular brooch of Fowler's type C, with simple rolled back terminals (Fowler 1960). The broad range for the type spans the first century BC to the third century AD, with a *floruit* indicated for the first century AD.
GK/43: *Area 1, pond upper fills. Later fourth century onwards*

Discussion

The Chells assemblage is predominantly pre-Flavian, with a strong pre-conquest bias. The earliest piece is 1, of later first-century BC date, whilst 2–8 represent the first half of the first century AD. Of the brooches considered to be post-AD 43 in date, only 14 and possibly 15 are likely to be later than *c.*AD 70. Despite the small number of brooches recovered, the range of types represented compares well with other larger assemblages recently published from Hertfordshire, namely Baldock (Stead and Rigby 1986), and Puckeridge-Braughing (Potter and Trow 1988).

Copper-Alloy Objects
(Figs 18–20)

Angela Wardle

Summary

The copper alloy from the site covers a limited range of personal and domestic material, typical of rural civilian sites dating from the first to the fourth centuries, with a few items of particular interest and quality.

One of the best preserved objects from the site is a very fine steelyard (**46**). The Romans used both the equal armed balance (*libra*) and the steelyard (*statera*), in which both the point of balance and the weighed object are close to one end of the beam and a weight is moved along the graduated arm. Of interest also is a fragment of a miniature stand (**47**) from the fourth-century fill of the pond, an object perhaps used as a votive offering or cult object.

Items of personal adornment include the variety of brooches, bracelets, rings, earrings and hairpins, expected in a civilian context, but there is nothing of outstanding quality. Two of the bracelets are of a distinctive first-century type (**1, 2**), while the remaining fifteen are of cable or strip designs, some highly decorative, usual in the third and fourth centuries. Seven come from Pond GK, which also yielded a wide range of artefacts, including an openwork buckle plate of fourth-century date (**32**). There is only one identifiable finger-ring, but two earrings, one of the well-known plaited type (**19**), often found in fourth-century contexts (Allason-Jones 1989, 7). The hairpins are of standard Roman types. Of the ten examples, three come from the second-century feature EAA in Area 3, which also produced toilet implements from a matching set (**36, 37**). There is a small range of other cosmetic or pharmaceutical implements, *ligulae* and double-ended spoons or scoops, also a fragment of a cosmetic grinder of a type confined to Roman Britain (**45**). The mirror (**34**), discussed by Dr Lloyd Morgan, is a comparatively rare find and adds to the steadily increasing evidence of the distribution of these desirable and exotic goods.

There are few items that can be described unequivocally as 'domestic'; one needle (**48**), one spoon (**49**) and three fragments which may be from vessels, all too incomplete for certainty. It is possible that items in everyday use, such as spoons, and indeed needles, were made from cheaper materials, bone and wood for example, perhaps reflecting an overall poverty of the assemblage. There is a noticeable lack of items such as locks and keys, which were of course also made of iron. No objects are decorated with enamel, but much of the assemblage dates from the late Roman period, when enamelling was not as common as in the second century.

The site produced a limited range of mounts used for leather and wood, mostly unstratified, and fittings. Among the latter were a group of five lion-headed studs (**62**), found in association with Cremation GBA, indicating that at least one burial was placed in a wooden casket. Such studs frequently adorn the lock plates of such boxes (Borrill in Partridge 1978, 315–16). Apart from these there are a few studs, rivets and tacks that could have been used for sundry wooden objects, including furniture. In addition, there are various unidentifiable fragments of miscellaneous sheeting, strip and plate typically found on all Roman sites, used for example as reinforcements for wooden objects. Most are from undated contexts. Two areas of the site produced notable concentrations of copper-alloy objects. Feature EAA yielded a group of personal items including hairpins and toilet instruments. From fourth-century contexts in Pond GK came a wider range of material, much of it clearly of a late date, including several bracelets, the miniature stand and miscellaneous fragments.

Catalogue

The archive contains full details of fragments, mostly unstratified, which are not illustrated or described here.

Objects of personal ornament and dress

(Copper-alloy brooches are catalogued and discussed by Corney (above), and the iron brooches are noted by Saunders (below). Objects designated 'NI' are not illustrated.

BRACELETS
Seventeen fragments were found, chiefly of types dating to the third/fourth centuries, although two distinctive examples (**1–2**) are of earlier date. There are six cable bracelets made from twisted strands of wire showing variations common on other sites, as for example Colchester (Crummy 1981, 39, Fig. 41). The two strands of **5** are clearly of different alloys, giving a decorative two-colour effect. **4**, made from a single strand twisted back on itself, retains a typical fastening loop, while **3** has a hook. One bracelet of distinctive but well-known type has a crenellated outer edge, and there are six strip bracelets, some with elaborate decoration.

Eight bracelets come from the fourth-century fills of Pond GK, which is consistent with the date of the types. The others were found to the north of the site, with one (**3**) from the top fill of the well.

Early bracelets

1   NI. Surviving length 19 mm; width, 17 mm. Fragment of wide strip bracelet, flattened, with ribbing on outer surface and central punched design, similar to examples from Colchester (Crummy 1982, 38, Fig. 40, no. 1586) and Baldock (Stead and Rigby 1986, 126, fig 52, 163–6), where they were found in first-century contexts.
    JF/1: *Unstratified; cleaning.*

2   Surviving length approx 60 mm; width 18 mm. Wide strip with ribbed decoration running lengthwise. Poorly preserved, one edge fragmentary and distorted.
    CAA/217: *Unstratified.*

Cable bracelets

3   Surviving length 45 mm. Three-strand cable bracelet. One end is almost complete, with traces of the fastening hook.
    CAB 3/21: *Area 1, well weathering cone deposit, fourth century onwards.*

4   Surviving length 45 mm; width 3 mm. Two-strand cable bracelet made from one strand of wire, folded and twisted around itself forming a loop at the one surviving terminal.
    TA 1/3: *Area 1, relining of Pond GF, probably early to mid fourth century.*

5   Surviving length 39 mm; width 4 mm. Two-strand cable bracelet made from two alloys which are of different colours. Fragment from one end, near the terminal. The practice of using different metals for a decorative effect was common.
    RC 2/16: *Area 1, pit, later fourth century.*

6   Surviving lengths 27 mm; 30 mm. Two fragments of three-strand cable, very fine.
    GK 7/132: *Area 1, pond upper fills. Mid fourth century onwards.*

7   Surviving length 21 mm. Fragmentary terminal with fastening hook; trace of cable.
    TL 1/3: *Area 1, gully. Fourth century.*

Plain wire bracelets

8   NI. Surviving length 52 mm; thickness 2 mm. Wire with rectangular section, twisted, possibly from a bracelet.
    GK 10/142: *Area 1, pond upper fills. Mid fourth century onwards.*

9   NI. Surviving length 19 mm. Fragment with oval cross-section, probably part of a plain armlet.
    GK 6/134: *Area 1, pond upper fills. Mid fourth century onwards.*

10 AAJ 2/1: *Area 1, gully. Fourth century.*

Strip bracelets

11 Surviving length 43 mm, width 2 mm. Fragment of bracelet made from a narrow strip with notched outer edge, set at right angles to the wrist; *cf* example from Baldock, (Stead and Rigby 1986, 126, Fig. 52, no. 168).
    GK 1/28: *Area 1, pond upper fills. Mid fourth century onwards.*

12 Complete. Diameter *c.*40 mm. Narrow strip bracelet with continuous dot-and-circle punched decoration and hook fastening. The terminal hook survives and a fastening hole near the other end.
    CH 1/1: *Period IV–V layer.*

13 Surviving diameter 47 mm, width 8 mm. Flat strip bracelet with distinctively shaped edges, elaborately decorated with broad zig-zag lines, punched dots, and dot-and-circle motifs. Two zones of concentric dots and circles are near the terminal. Fourth century.
    GK 2/111: *Area 1, pond upper fills. Mid fourth century onwards*

14 Surviving length 55 mm, width 4 mm. Fragment of strip bracelet with zones of vertical ribbed decoration, interspaced with punched concentric circles.
    GK 1/34: *Area 1, pond upper fills. Mid fourth century onwards.*

15 NI. Surviving length 42 mm. Fragment of strip bracelet near a terminal. There is some indistinct decoration on the outer face and possible carving on the edge.
    CA/1: *unstratified.*

16 NI. Surviving length 7 mm. Fragment of undecorated strip.
    GB 2/2: *Area 1, penannular Gully ABP. Mid fourth century onwards*

17 NI. Surviving length 23 mm, width 2 mm. Fragment of narrow strip bracelet with diagonal line of incised decoration.
    GK/63: *Area 1, pond upper fills. Mid fourth century onwards.*

FINGER-RING

18 Surviving length 15 mm, width of bezel 11 mm. Bezel only with setting for an oval stone, now missing.
    XQ 1/1: *gully, unphased.*

EARRINGS

19 Almost complete. Length 15 mm, width 12 mm, thickness 3 mm. Four-strand plait made from fine wire, bent into a circle, incomplete. Allason-Jones' Type 8 (1989, 7). Both finger-rings and earrings are made from plaited wire, but the width of a four-strand plait makes it more likely to be an earring. The type is generally found in fourth-century contexts *(ibid)*.
    TZ 1/1: *Area 1, Gully ABO. Mid fourth century onwards.*

20 NI. Surviving length 18 mm. Part of a very fine ring with D-shaped section. Possibly a finger-ring or earring of Allason-Jones' Type 1 (1989, 2) but too fragmentary for certainty.
    EBB 2/3: *subrectangular feature.*

HAIRPINS

The ten copper-alloy hairpins are of standard Roman types, found in large numbers in southern England. Three come from the second-century feature EAA, and one is from the well.

21 Surviving length 61 mm. Cool Group 3 (1991), elaborately turned head, a terminal knob surmounting

baluster-and-cordon decoration. The tapering circular-sectioned shank is fractured.
EAA 4/25: *Area 3, mid second century.*

22 Complete, length 104 mm. Slender hairpin with triple-beaded decoration on the head.
EAA 2/16: *Area 3, mid second century.*

23 Complete, length 103 mm. Cool Group 2 (1991), slender hairpin with conical head over one groove. Similar to **27**, below.
DAX 1/3: *pit.*

24 Complete, length 110 mm approx. Slender hairpin. The cylindrical head has lattice decoration over a groove.
EAZ 1/1: *ditch junction.*

25 Almost complete, length 47 mm approx. Hairpin with spherical head, over groove and cordon decoration. The slender shank is now bent.
CAA/121: *unstratified.*

26 NI. Hairpin as **23**, with slender conical head. Length 97 mm, complete.
EAA/2/2: *Area 3, mid second century.*

27 NI. Length 92 mm, complete. Very slender hairpin with conical head over a groove, with small terminal knob. Similar to **23**.
CAA/203: *unstratified.*

28 NI. Length 41 mm, fragmentary. Spherical head, somewhat angular on the upper part, with flattened top. The shaft is very slender. Found with coin hoard deposited *c.*AD 263 (report above).
EAQ 1/1: *Area 3, pit.*

29, 30 NI. Shaft fragments.
CAB 2/3: *Area 1, well weathering cone deposit, fourth century onwards.*
EAJ 1/1: *layer.*

BELT FITTINGS

31 NI. Buckle, surviving length 26 mm. Fragment of D-shaped frame, D-shaped in section.
HR 1/2: *cleaning.*

32 Buckle plate, surviving length 27 mm, width 44 mm. Fragment of heavy openwork plate with carved decoration along one complete edge, and two rivet holes. Part of a late Roman buckle, Hawkes and Dunning (1961) Type IIa, generally found in fourth and fifth-century contexts, as at Richborough (Cunliffe 1968, pl xxxv, 103). A highly decorated complete example from Colchester is illustrated by Hawkes and Dunning (1961, Fig. 17e) and, in a more local context, a fragment of plate similar to the present example was found at Luton in an Anglo-Saxon cemetery (Hawkes and Dunning 1968, Fig. 19 bis, no. 25).
GK 11/148: *Area 1, pond upper fills. Later fourth century onwards* .

33 Strap-end, surviving length 27 mm, width 17 mm. Amphora-type strap-end, taking the form of a stylised amphora with an oval body and openwork decoration at the incomplete neck. The face has punched decoration around the edges. This type, which was hinged with a small butt, occurs at various Romano-British sites, including Richborough (Bushe-Fox 1949, pl. xxvi, 112,113; Cunliffe 1968, pl. xxxvii, 119) and Lankhills, where it is discussed by Clarke (1979, 281, Fig. 36, nos 26, 489). Continental and British parallels suggest a date in the mid fourth century.
LG/1: *unstratified.*

Items of Personal Use

MIRROR

I am indebted to Dr Glenys Lloyd Morgan for the following report:

34 The mirror, which is incomplete, consists of four fragments, two of which make up the only surviving corner of a rectangular shaped mirror, and two further fragments from the interior, one of which has been damaged by oyster-shell corrosion products. The fragments consist of:
1–2: dimensions 32 × 39.5 mm; thickness 1.3 mm.
3: internal fragment 11.7 × 14.6 mm; thickness 0.8 mm.
4: internal fragment 7.8 × 9.4 mm.

The surviving edges are bevelled on the slightly convex finished side, and have a slightly bowed outline, a not uncommon feature of this type of mirror. The underside has the usual unfinished, slightly pitted-looking surface which is characteristic not only of these simple rectangular mirrors but also of the equally well-known small disc mirrors.
GM 1/2: *gully.*

Although it has been suggested that some rectangular mirrors may have come into use during the late Hellenistic period in the Mediterranean area, it is not until the first century AD that they are found in any quantity within the provinces of the Roman Empire (Lloyd-Morgan 1981), and occasionally outside the official frontiers. One (124 × 150 mm) example was found amongst the hoard of family silver in the House of the Menander at Pompeii (Maiuri 1932, 452; now Naples Mus. Acc. No. 4709). Another badly damaged piece (70 × 76 mm) came from a grave in St Pancras Cemetery, Chichester, dated to *c.*AD 80–100 (Down and Rule 1971, 97, Fig. 5.21), while a further item was found during excavations at Usk. It was said by the excavator, Prof. W.H. Manning, to have come from a pre-Flavian context (*ref.* Usk 67 II).

Many mirror types of Roman manufacture were made of a rather brittle copper alloy, containing a high percentage of tin. It was probably for protection, as well as ease of handling, that these pieces were framed or boxed, as witnessed by surviving traces of wood on one or both sides of some mirrors (Ward 1911, 263).

At the time of writing, about eighty rectangular mirrors in varying degrees of completeness or preservation are known to the writer, of which nine come from the old Vice-County of Hertfordshire. Two small fragments from excavations at Braughing have now been published (Potter and Trow 1988, 66–7, nos 111–112). Three somewhat better preserved examples came to light during work at St Stephen's cemetery, St Albans, in 1985 (unpub). Two other mirrors came from earlier excavations within the Roman city; one in 1931, the other during work in 1960 (unpub). A third set of three fragments was found during the Park Street villa excavations in Rubbish Pit I (O'Neill 1947, 65–6). Curiously, the published report describes the find as a circular mirror, though two corners are represented by two of the fragments; the third piece is also from an edge.

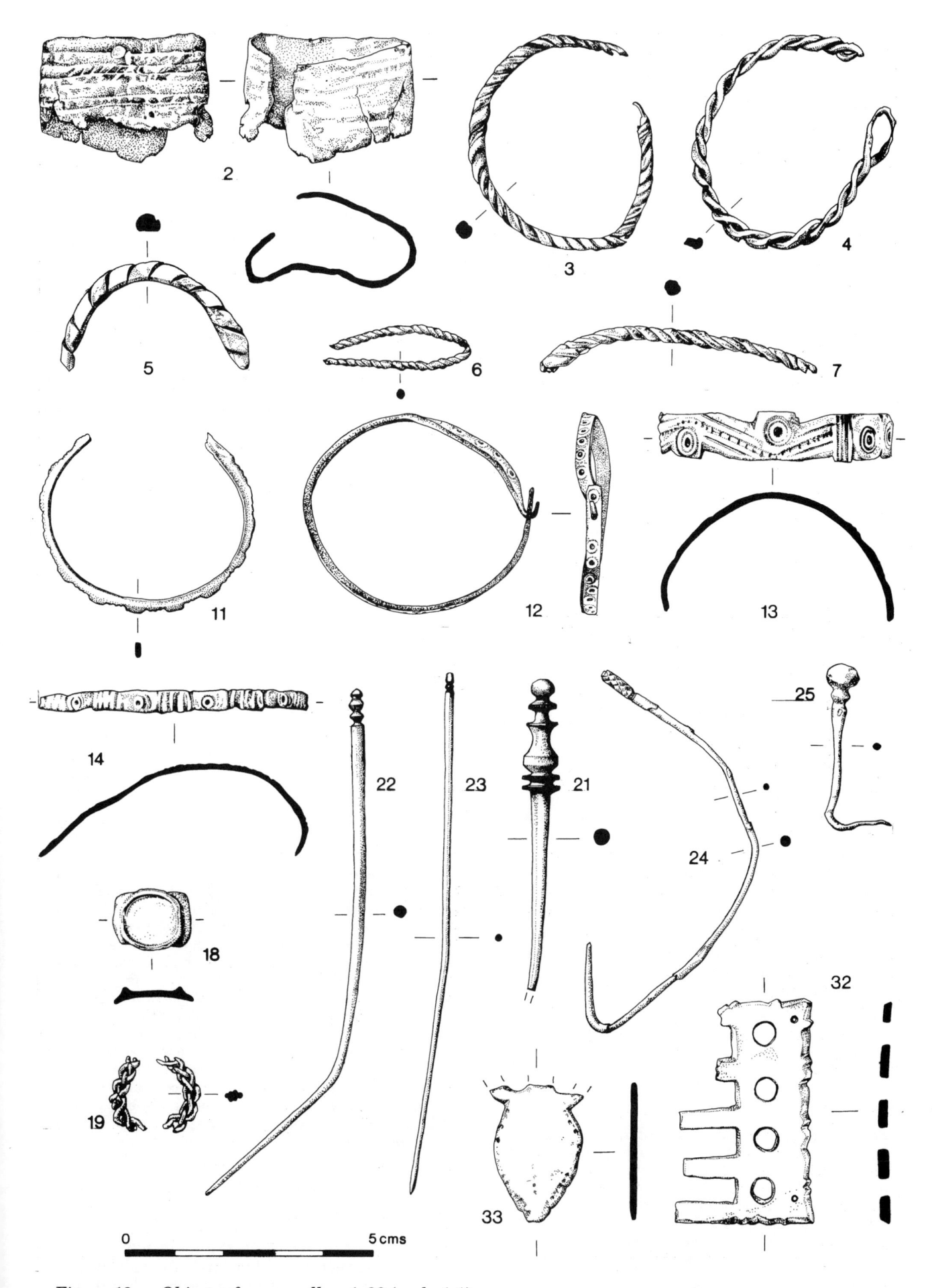

Figure 18   Objects of copper alloy, 1–33 (scale 1:1).

57

Cosmetic Implements

Cosmetic sets comprising nail cleaners, tweezers and small spoons or scoops are frequent finds on Romano-British sites, together with *ligulae*, toilet spoons, or spatulas that may have had general cosmetic or medicinal functions. Several items are represented here, two of them from Feature EAA perhaps belonging to the same set.

NAIL CLEANERS

35 Almost complete, length 49 mm. Leaf-shaped nail cleaner with a series of cuts or indentations on the handle. The points are missing.
EAA 11/1: *Area 3, mid second century.*

36 Almost complete, length 42 mm. Nail-cleaner with incised line decoration along edges of the leaf-shaped blade and a suspension loop at right angles to the plane of the blade; Crummy Type 2a, late first and second century (Crummy 1981, 58, Fig. 62, no. 1874). One point is missing. Probably part of same set as **37,** below.
EAA 2/19: *Area 3, mid second century.*

TWEEZERS

37 Complete, length 41 mm. Tweezers made from folded strip with incised line decoration along the edges. Possibly part of same set as **36**.
EAA 2/18: *Area 3, mid second century.*

COSMETIC IMPLEMENT?

38 Two fragments, one with expanding rectangular shank terminating in a hook, the other a tapering shank with trace of a suspension ring. Possibly cosmetic implements; precise identification uncertain.
GK/58: *Area 1, pond, upper fills. Later fourth century onwards*!

LIGULAE

The only complete example is of a type made throughout the Roman period. Such spoons had a variety of uses – cosmetic, pharmaceutical and surgical – but would have been used generally for scooping cosmetics or medicaments from small containers. A good selection can be seen in the report on the finds from Baldock (Stead and Rigby 1986, 132, Fig. 56).

39 Surviving length 113 mm (bent). Ligula with plain circular-sectioned handle and flat circular spoon set at a slight angle (fractured).
GBD/2: *gully fill*

40, 41 NI. Handles.
ES 2/34: *Area 1, well weathering cone. Mid fourth century onwards.*
CAA/76: *unstratified.*

SCOOPS/SPATULAS

Scoops and spatulas, distinguished by their long narrow spoons, were frequently double-ended with an olivary probe at the other end which, suitably wrapped, could also be used as a swab. Like single-ended spoons they could be used for general toilet purposes, but also had a surgical function (Jackson 1986,129, Fig. 30; 1990,17, Fig. 4, nos 11,15). One complete scoop-probe (*cyathiscomele*) and fragments of two others were found.

42 Complete. Length (bent)134 mm. Cosmetic or surgical instrument with long narrow spoon and olivary probe. The fine ribbed handle has a decorative cordon above the spoon.
CAA/207: *unstratified.*

43 Surviving length 58 mm. Handle and part of the oval scoop, the handle decorated at the junction with three cordons and a baluster. The incomplete end may have had a probe.
GK 2/110: *Area 1, pond, upper fills. Later fourth century onwards.*

44 NI. Olivary probe, with part of the handle. Insufficient remaining to determine if this was a double-ended instrument. Length 39 mm.
CAA/212: *unstratified.*

COSMETIC GRINDER

45 Surviving length 32 mm, width 9 mm. About half the scoop remains, with the terminal knob at the lower end. The object, which is probably of the end-loop type (Jackson 1985) is U-shaped in section with the scoop following the same profile, and there are casting marks on the underside.
CAA/196: *unstratified.*

About one hundred of these objects, some highly decorative with zoomorphic terminals and enamelling, as at Baldock (Stead and Rigby 1986, 136, Fig. 60, no. 377), have been found in southern Britain, sometimes in association with small curved rods. They are discussed in detail by Jackson (1985). Originally thought to have been amulets based on the form of a distinctive type of horse-harness, it has now been suggested that the objects were used as mixing or grinding troughs for cosmetics or medicines, the associated curved rods being pestles. It is possible that the crescent shape may have had amuletic significance, as may the zoomorphic symbols. The type is known only in Britain, and there are other local examples from St Albans, *Magiovinium* (Bletchley), Hitchin and Baldock (Jackson 1985, nos 1, 6, 21, 32, 53, 73).

STEELYARD

46 Steelyard (*statera*). Complete; length 123 mm, distances from *fulcra* to end hole 7 mm and 17 mm. The beam has a circular section with an oval stop at one end, and is flattened at the other to form a plate with three suspension loops, one on each side and one at the end. Graduations are marked on each side, with an average interval of 13 mm on the upper scale and 3 mm on the lower. There are no weight marks. The object to be weighed would hang from the hole at the end of the plate. The steelyard arm was suspended from one of the other holes by means of hooks, now missing. The hole nearer the end was used for heavier objects, the other for lighter articles, and the corresponding scale was used for each position. The arm would have been used with a weight, typically of bi-conical or conical form, as **Lead 2**, but sometimes more elaborately fashioned, for example in the form of a human bust.
CV/4: *unstratified.*

There is a very close parallel to the Chells steelyard from Verulamium (Goodburn *in* Frere 1984, 57, Fig. 23.210), which is slightly larger. On this example the ratio between the markings and the distance between the *fulcra* and the end holes is 1:3, suggesting that both scales were calibrated in the same units. The principle is also clearly

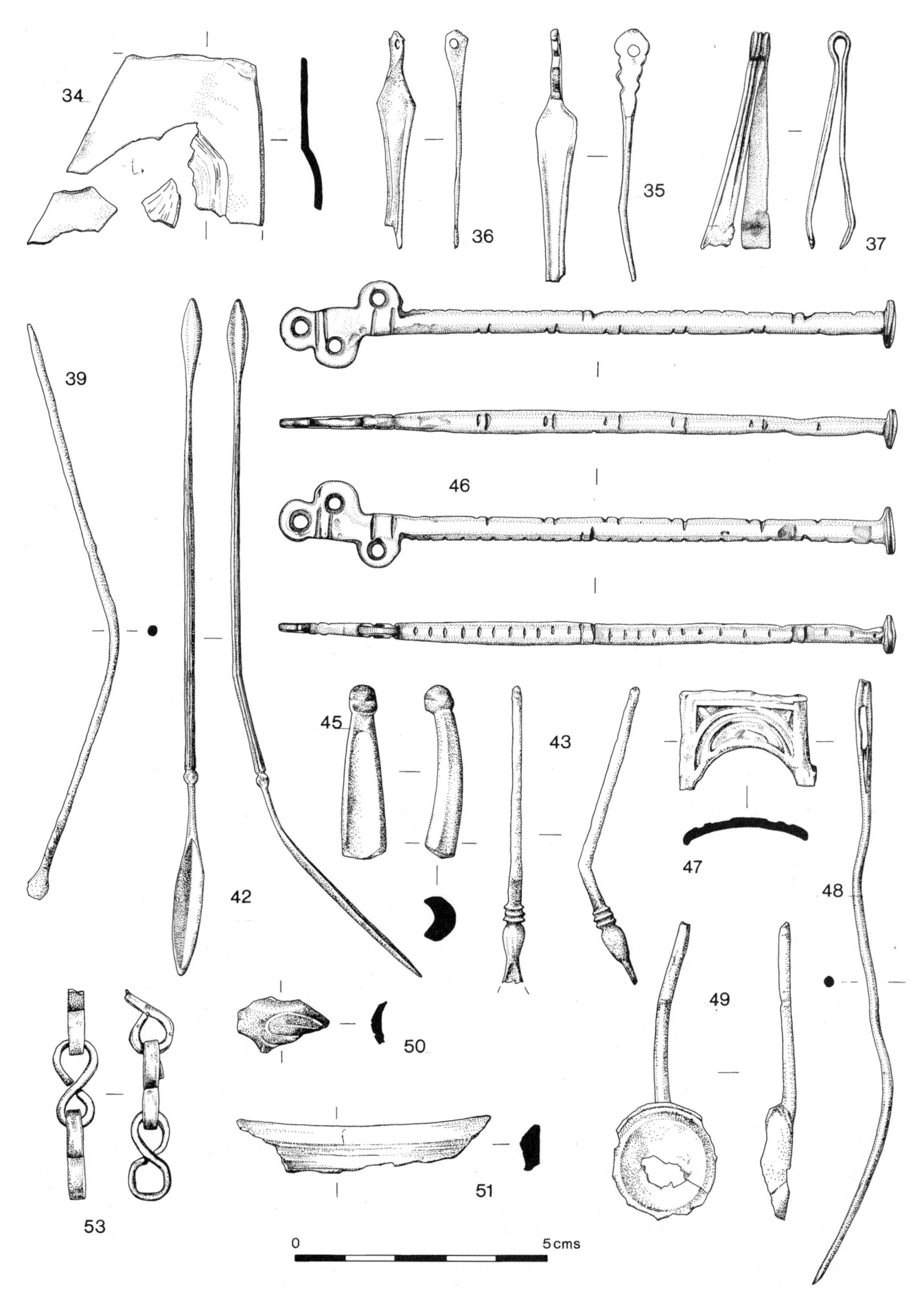

Figure 19 Objects of copper alloy, 34–53 (scale 1:1).

demonstrated by an example from Austin Friars, London (Wheeler 1930, 86, Fig. 23).

MINIATURE OR VOTIVE OBJECT

47   Surviving length 26 mm; width 18 mm. Cast miniature stand, one side only, with relief decoration, similar to examples from South Shields (Allason-Jones and Miket 1984, 92, 31–3). The latter have two tiers and are enamelled. There is apparently no trace of enamelling on the Chells example, but the decorative cells may have originally have held enamel in a champlevé technique. Model stands, perhaps representing furniture, are discussed with other votive and cult objects by Green (1978, 33 and pl. 129a,b).
GK/36: *Area 1, pond upper fills. Later fourth century onwards.*

Domestic Items

NEEDLE

48   Complete, length 112 mm. Needle with a squared head and a long rectangular eye set into a groove, a type found on many Romano-British sites.
TA 1/9: *Area 1, pond relining. Fourth century.*

SPOON

49   Surviving length 58 mm, length of bowl 23 mm. Spoon with a round bowl and thin circular-sectioned handle which continues as a 'rat-tail' under the bowl. The form is that of the *cochleae* common in the first and second centuries (Goodburn *in* Frere 1984, 40 Fig. 15.120–1) but, unusually, the bowl has a small flange. The object, which is of a very heavy alloy, has white metal plating, probably tin.
CAD 1/1: *Period III posthole.*

VESSELS

50   Indeterminate fragment, length 18 mm. Sheet worked into a slightly convex shape with an incised pattern on the exterior surface, possibly from a vessel or figurine.
CAB 1/30: *Area 1, well weathering cone. Mid fourth century onwards.*

51   Surviving length 50 mm. Fragment of cast copper alloy, with flat underside and bevelled upper edge, and tool marks on the upper face. Possibly a vessel rim.
CAA/124: *unstratified.*

52   NI. Indeterminate; length 38 mm, width 20 mm. Fragment of sheeting, perhaps scrap, with white-metal plating on the inside. Possibly from a vessel.
GK/74: *Area 1, pond, upper fills. Later fourth century onwards.*

CHAIN

53   Indeterminate. Length 47 mm, width 3 mm, length of link 18 mm. Heavy chain comprising two and a half links, each made from a narrow strip bent into a figure of eight. It may have had a domestic function, as it is too heavy for jewellery.

GK/57: *Area 1, pond, upper fills. Later fourth century onwards.*

MOUNTS

54   Indeterminate; length 32 mm. Fragment of circular mount with raised central boss, the flange decorated with punched dots in triangular zones. The outer surface is silvered (XRF). No edge is complete.
CAA/122: *unstratified.*

55   Surviving length 35 mm, diameter (approx) 40 mm. Fragment of disc with a hollowed centre and two concentric rings on the upper surface. Turning marks are clearly visible on the reverse side.
CAA/75: *unstratified.*

56   Complete. Length 17 mm, width 11 mm. Mount used for leather or wood, made from copper-alloy sheeting with triple segmented ends. Three ribs run across the centre at right angles forming a bow, and a small rivet is driven through the centre.
CAA/195: *unstratified.*

57–61   NI. Miscellaneous mounts.
DG/6: *unstratified.*
JE 1/1: *soil spread.*
CAA/123: *unstratified.*
GK/64: *Area 1, pond upper fills. Later fourth century onwards.*
MR 1/10: *Area 1 pond, post-medieval?*

FITTINGS – STUDS, TACKS, NAILS

These various fittings, typical of finds on all Romano-British sites, include nails, studs, a double-spiked loop and a ring.

62   Five lion-headed studs (three illustrated), length c.13 mm, two almost complete, the heads cast in high relief. Such studs are frequently found on the lock plates of casket burials, as at Skeleton Green (Borrill *in* Partridge 1978, 315–16). Unidentified miscellaneous fragments of copper alloy, probably box fittings, were also found.
GBA/1: *Cemetery, cremation, early to mid second century.*

63   Stud, complete. Length 34 mm, width of head 10 mm. Stud with spherical head, which is roughly soldered to the shank. Probably used as a furniture or box fitting.
CAA/120: *unstratified.*

64, 65   NI. Studs, unstratified.
CAA/176: GN 1/1.

66   Nail or tack, complete. Length 47 mm, width (of head) 16 mm. Made from a single sheet of metal with wrapped shank and folded head, *cf* Baldock (Stead and Rigby 1986, 135, Fig. 58.347) in a third to fourth-century context.
CAA/118: *unstratified.*

In addition to the above objects, a number of fragments of copper-alloy sheeting, plate and strip were recovered, as well as several objects and fragments of post-Roman date. These have been omitted from the final report, but are detailed in the site archive.

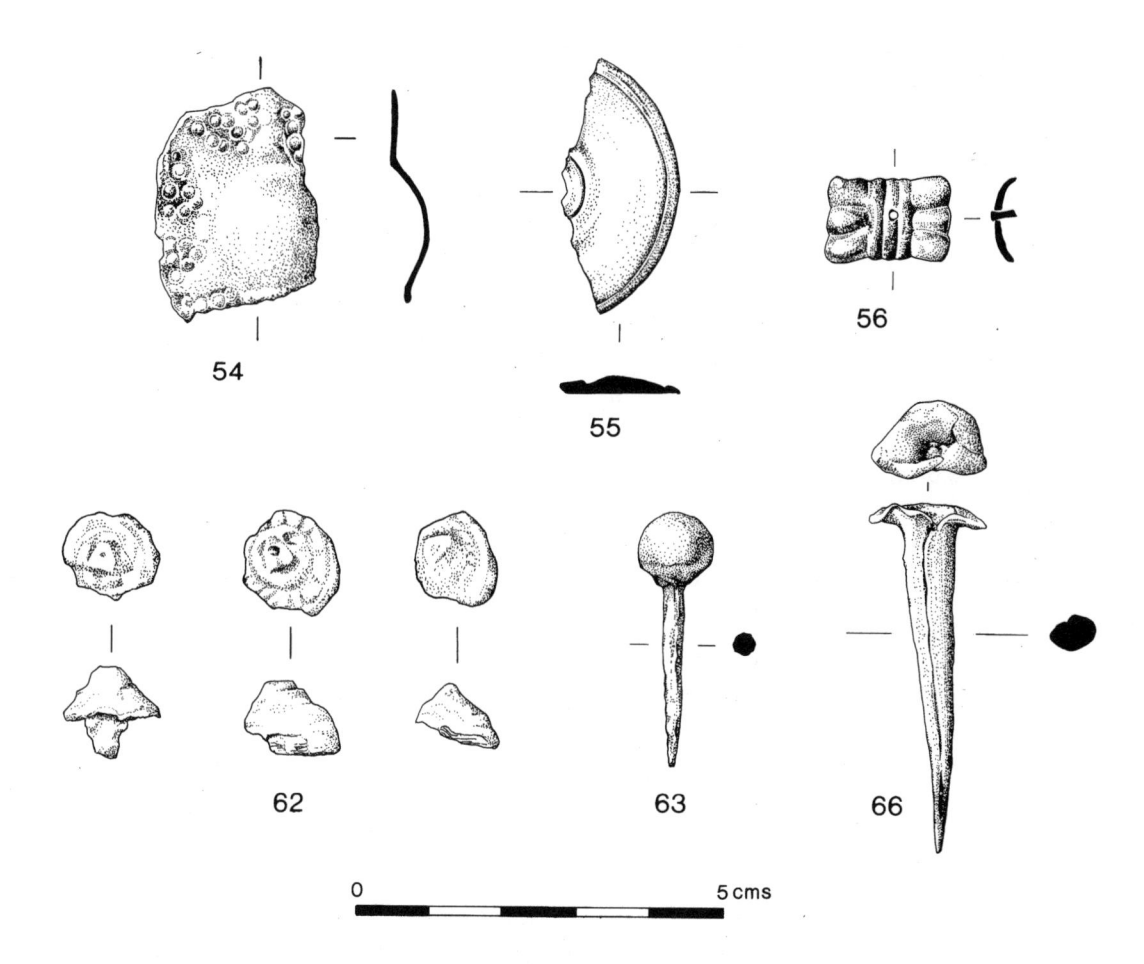

Figure 20   Objects of copper alloy, 54–66 (scale 1:1).

Iron Objects

(Figs 21–24)

Chris Saunders

Objects designated 'NI' are not illustrated.

Agricultural implements

1. Small tanged reaping or pruning hook, the tip of the blade at right angles to the rest of the blade. Such small hooks may have been used for lopping leaves or for pruning rather than reaping cereals (*cf* Rees 1979)
CAA/198: *unstratified.*

2. An open socket, almost certainly from a pruning hook.
GK 7/130: *Area 1, pond upper fills, fourth century.*

3. Fragmentary rivetted socket, possibly from a reaping hook.
FZ 7/12: *Area 1, gully, fourth century.*

For two possible blade fragments, see **24** and **25**.

4. Spud with spatulate blade and socket for attaching a handle. Such tools could be used for weeding or other purposes.
RD 1/4: *Area 1, cobbles west of Pit RC. Second century or later.*

5. Split socket with a tang at the wider end; both ends incomplete. This is part of an object like Manning 1972, fig 61.17, there identified as a bar share for a plough. However, these objects are much lighter than certain plough shares, and must have performed some other function (Manning 1985, 43).
JK 1/9: *Area 1, gully over Ditch JJ. Later third century.*

6. Ox goad.
JK 1/3: *Area 1, gully over Ditch JJ. Later third century.*

7. Probably an ox goad with the *stimulus* missing.
SH 1/1: *fill of posthole.*

For a possible iron pitchfork tip see **36**.

Transport

8. Part of the head of a looped, spatulate-headed linch pin used to retain the wheel on the axle of a cart. A common Roman form, *cf.* Manning 1972, fig 64.33–5.
BBB/6: *Area 3, Pit EAN. Later first to early second century.*

9. Part of a prick spur, the prick now bent (Short 1959).
QC 1/1: *fill of gully.*

10. The side wing from a hipposandal, a form of temporary horseshoe.
EAA 2/42: *Area 3, mid second century.*

11. As **10**.
FC 1/6: *Area 3, gully. Fourth century.*

Rings like **41** and **42** could have been used in harnesses, but other functions are possible.

Tools

12. NI. Probably a small chisel; perhaps a blacksmith's set.
CAB 3/22: *Area 1, well weathering cone. Later fourth century.*

13. Square-sectioned bar ending in a fragmentary socket at one end, the other thickened. Probably a hammer, although not of usual Roman form. Hammers with sockets at one end are normally set-hammers, a blacksmith's tool which is struck with a heavier hammer. The metal around the socket, although now broken and incomplete, seems very thin for such a tool.
CAB 2/4: *Area 1, well weathering cone. Later fourth century.*

14. Perhaps a chisel, although the condition of the object precludes certainty.
GK/62: *Area 1, the pond., upper fills, fourth century onwards.*

15. Tool with square-sectioned tang and circular-sectioned shaft. This is either an awl, tanged for a handle, or a punch. Both are leatherworkers tools. In its present condition the point of the tool is rounded, suggesting the latter function.
RC 2/15: *Area 1, pit, later fourth century.*

Knives and cleavers

16. Socketed cleaver with a triangular blade. An example of Manning's type 4 (1985).
CAB 11/37: *Area 1, well shaft filling. Mid second century.*

17. Socketed knife with a 'split socket' and a triangular blade. A socketed version of Manning's type 11 (1985).
TA 1/8: *Area 1, Pond GK relining, fourth century.*

18. Knife with a twisted handle ending in a 'shepherds crook' loop. The blade is fragmentary. A knife from Wroxeter (Atkinson 1942, pl. 58.B158) had a similar loop, in this case holding a loose ring: the handle is not twisted, but like the present example has a blade, the back of which continues the line of the handle. Other knives with twisted handles have blades of more spatulate form. Manning's type 11b (1985).
GK/52: *Area 1, pond upper filling. Later fourth century.*

19. Tanged knife with a small, incomplete, triangular blade. Manning's type 13 (1985).
GK 5/119: *Area 1, pond upper filling. Fourth century onwards.*

20. Tanged knife with a parallel-sided blade, the tip missing.
GK 2/114: *Area 1, pond upper filling. Fourth century onwards.*

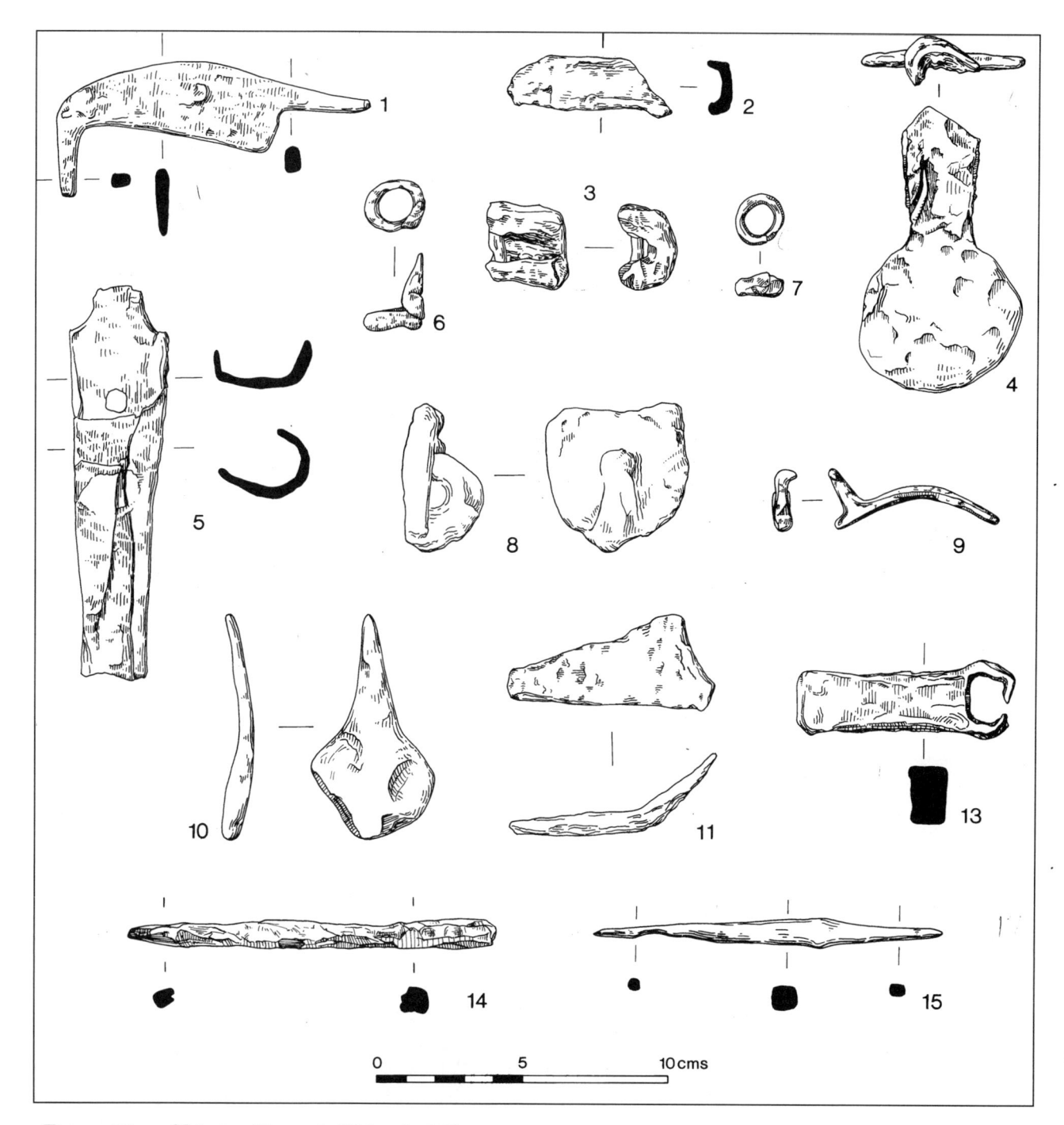

Figure 21   Objects of iron, 1–15 (scale 1:2).

21 Fragment of a blade and tang.
    GK/35: *Area 1, pond upper filling. Fourth century onwards.*

22, 23   Blade tips of two knives.
    GK/53; GK/104: *Area 1, pond top filling. Fourth century onwards.*

24, 25   Two blade tips, from knife or reaping hook.
    GK 14/154; FZ 3/19: *Area 1, pond upper filling. Fourth century onwards.*
    FZ/3: *Area 1, gully. Mid fourth century onwards.*

26 Possible knife.
    GK 11/141: *Area 1, pond upper filling. Fourth century.*

Personal items

27 Part of the bow and catchplate of a bow brooch.
    HR 1/3: *Area 1, clearing west of pond GK. Unphased.*

28 Fragmentary hinged brooch-pin.
    DH/4: *cleaning.*

29 Stylus, Manning's type 3 (1985).
    CAB 3/41: *Area 1, well weathering cone. Later fourth century.*

-   Cluster of hobnails, probably from a sandal or shoe.
    CAB 6: *Area 1, well shaft filling. Mid second century.*

See also **44** for a possible boot cleat.

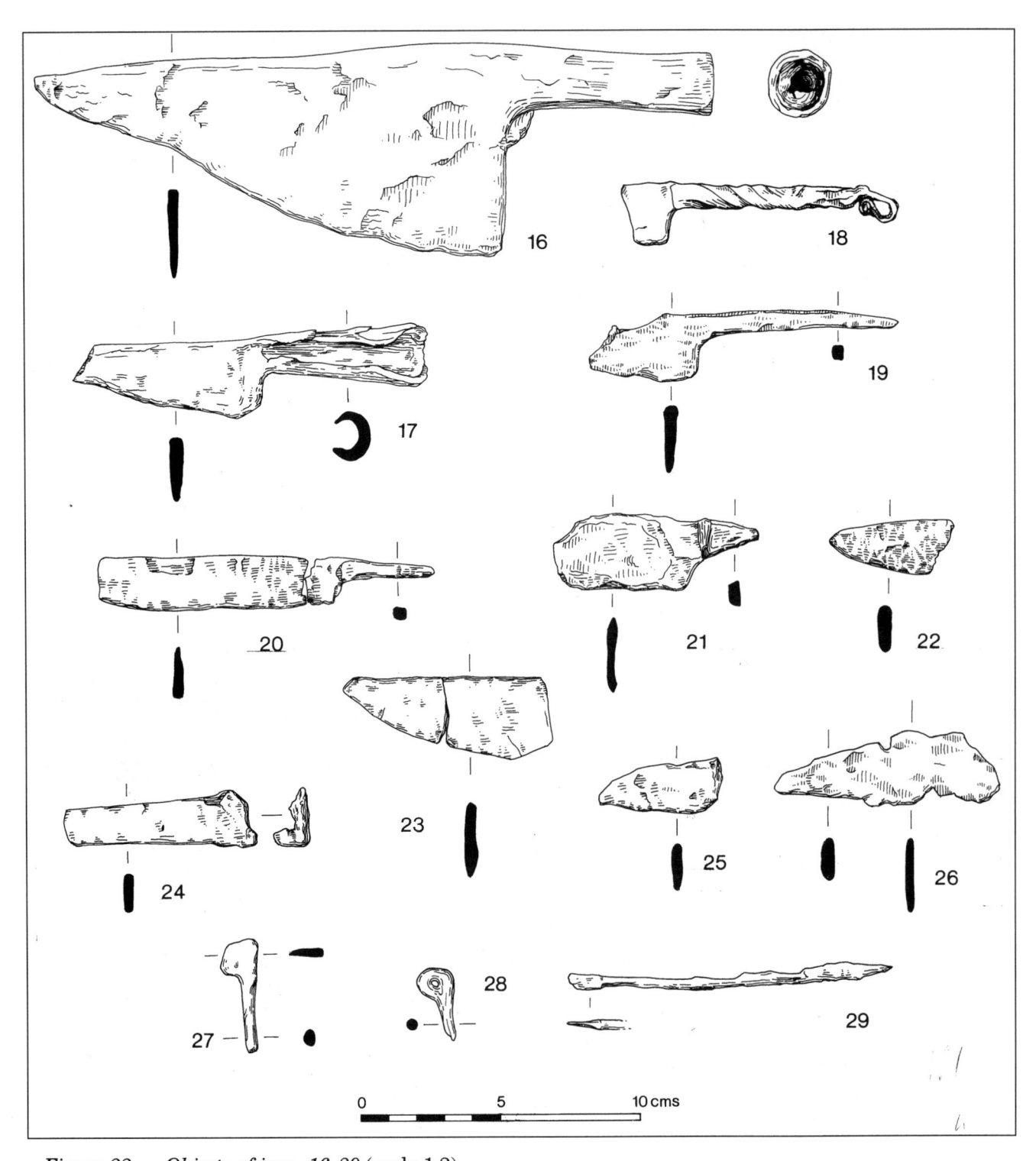

Figure 22   Objects of iron, 16–29 (scale 1:2).

Domestic Objects

30 Part of a fleshhook, the one remaining prong now bent. The stem appears to be twisted, as is usual with this class of object. Fleshhooks of this form came into use in the later pre-Roman Iron Age, and were also used in the Middle Ages. Sometimes the fleshhook formed the handle of a ladle, so combining in one the two essential implements used with cauldrons. It is possible that the present piece was part of such a ladle.
GK 2/115: *Area 1, pond upper filling. Fourth century.*

31 Curved needle with an elongated eye, the tip of which is missing. The curve is slightly angular, but this may be intentional. Modern curved needles are used in upholstery.
GK 1/90: *Area 1, pond upper filling. Fourth century.*

32 Parts of a pin or needle; the taper towards the fine point and a slight flattening at the broken end suggest in fact that this is a needle broken at the eye.
JK 1/10: *Area 1, gully over Ditch JJ. Later third century.*

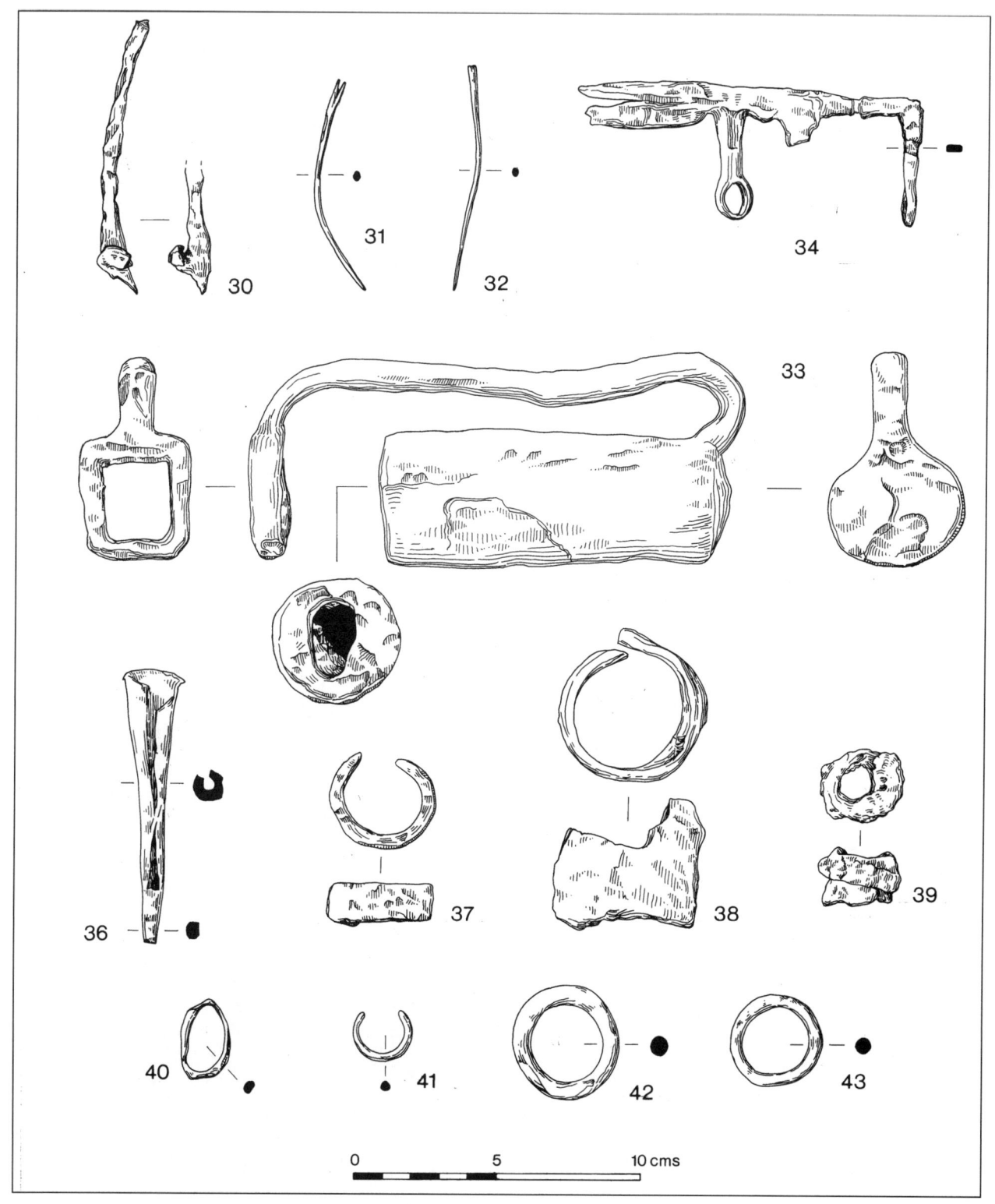

Figure 23   Objects of iron, 30–43 (scale 1:2).

Iron needles are by no means as common as those of copper alloy or bone, but this may result from survival and not be a true reflection of their original frequency.

Locks and keys

33 Well-preserved case of a barb-spring padlock. A common Roman form.

CAB 3/25: *Area 1, well weathering cone. Later fourth century.*

34 Part of a more complex barb-spring padlock which will have had two bolts.
FZ 3/18: *Area 1, gully. Mid to later fourth century.*

35 NI. The lower part of a barb-spring padlock key. The bit is incomplete. Such a key would have been used with a lock like **33**.
GK: *Area 1, well weathering cone. Later fourth century.*

Miscellaneous non-structural

FERRULES

36 Conical ferrule with a split socket; the point is of square section. Such ferrules were used to tip spear butts or staves, but Manning , discussing an example from Verulamium (1972, Fig. 69.120), points to their use in recent times as tips for pitch-forks.
FZ 15/29: *Area 1, gully. Mid fourth century onwards.*

37 'Collar' ferrule made from a rectangular bar.
EBI 1/1: *ditch fill.*

38 A similar example to **37**, but heavier.
EAA 2/23: *Area 3, mid second century.*

39 A spiral ferrule. This might be an ox goad (*see* **6, 7**), but is of heavier form than the normal goad.
EAA 301/4: *Area 3, mid second century.*

CHAIN

40 Small oval chain link, twisted about the long axis.
CAA/73: *unstratified.*

41 Small ring (incomplete), circular cross-section.
CAA/91: *unstratified.*

42 Complete ring, of circular cross-section.
XY 1/2: *Area 1 stone spread. Unphased.*

43 As **42**.
XY 1/5: *Area 1 stone spread. Unphased.*

Structural ironwork

44 Loop from a drop hinge.
RG 1/1: *Area 1, layer. Unphased.*

Probable hinges or hinge components came from the pond fill (GK 6) and also from GE 1.

45 Cleat: may have been used in the soles of boots or perhaps in some cases for fastening wood.
JK 1/2: *Area 1, gully over Ditch JJ. Later third century.*

46 Part of a large joiner's dog, used for fastening timbers.
CAB 3/26: *Area 1, well weathering cone. Later fourth century.*

Smaller examples came from EAU 1; EAA 2, EV 1, and GA.

47, 48 NI. These two objects and another twenty similar seem to be some form of holdfast. They are not the tang and broken blade of a tool, as the thin portion has frequently been hammered.
CD 1/7; GK 9/143: *unstratified.*

49 Clamps like this with 'anchor-shaped' leads were probably used to hold in place a semi-circular-sectioned timber.
TB 1/2: *depression.*

50 Conical-headed rivet.
DAC 1/33: *cleaning.*

51, 52 Two large square-headed rivets.
EAA 2/28: *Area 3, mid second century.*
EB 4: *hollow, unphased.*

53 Double-sided loop. Bar with tapering spiked arms, folded over at the head to form a loop.

54 Double-spiked loop fragment.

50 Flat-headed staple.

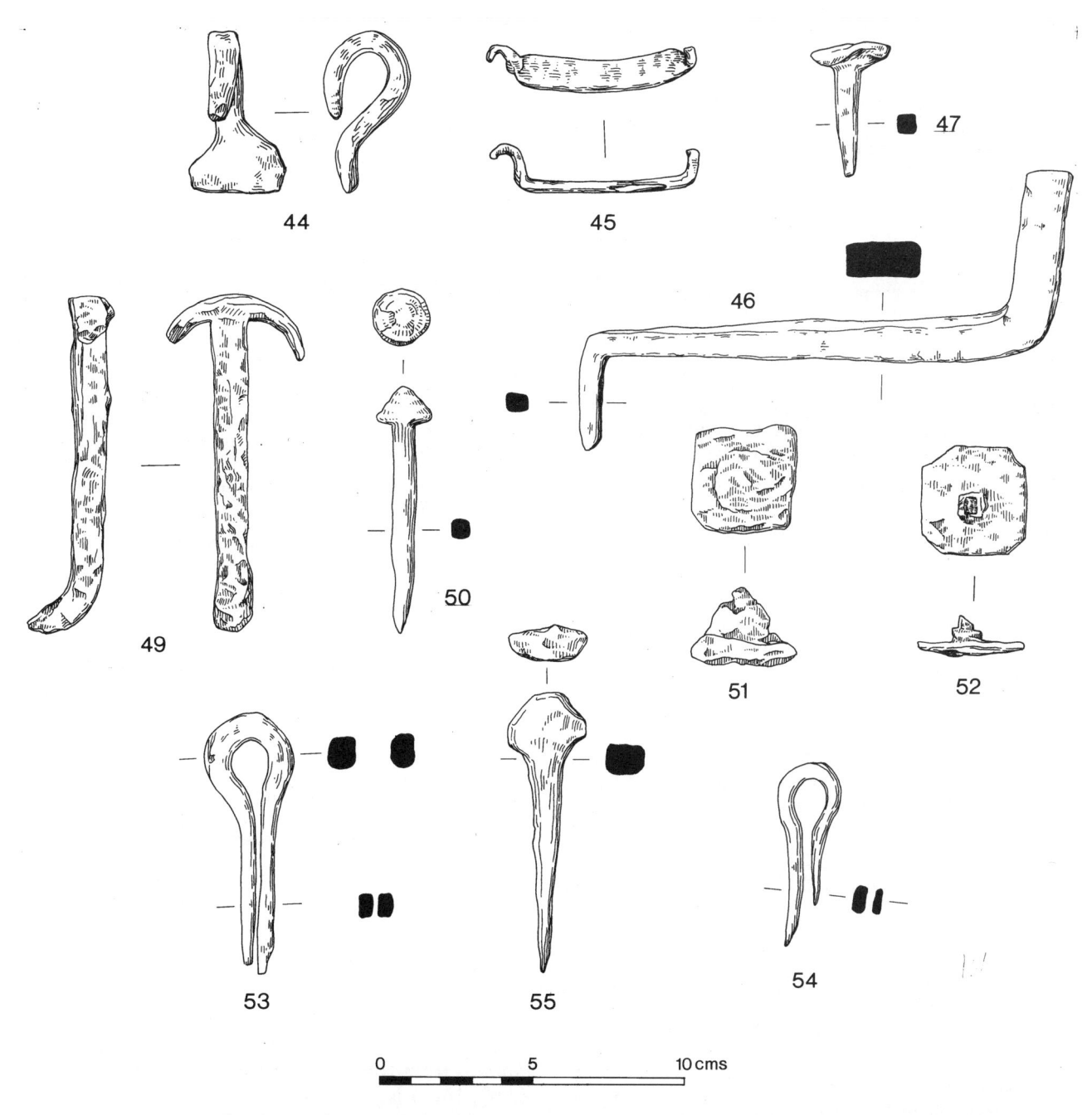

Figure 24   Objects of iron, 44–55 (scale 1:2).

Lead Objects
(Fig. 25)

Julia Green

Summary

The site produced forty-six objects or fragments of lead, of which forty-three came from the 1989 excavations. The greater number reflects the use of metal detectors in 1989, and although several of the objects are of post-Roman date this is a useful addition to the total assemblage. The range of material includes quantities of undated waste and scrap, commonly found on Roman sites, and also weights of several types, patches or plugs for ceramic repair and a post-medieval cloth seal (**30**). Most of the finds were unstratified. Objects designated 'NI' are not illustrated.

Weights

With few exceptions, all come from unstratified contexts. Seven of the sixteen weights identified are of familiar Roman types. All are damaged or corroded to some extent, and the their weights stated below are therefore no more than approximations of their original Roman values.

1 Complete. Length 34 mm, diameter 12 mm, weight *c.*26 g. Cylindrical line weight with convex sides and central hole.
CAA/81: *unstratified.*

2 Almost complete. Length 53 mm, diameter 40 mm (base), weight *c.*325 g. Conical steelyard weight with fragment of iron suspension loop.
CAA/200: *unstratified.*

3 Complete. Length 11 mm, diameter 20 mm, weight *c.*20 g. Line weight with circular base, domed top, and central suspension hole. Very crudely shaped.
CA/89: *unstratified.*

4, 5 NI. Similar to **3**, weight 25 g.
CAA/86; CAA/174: *unstratified.*

6 NI. Almost complete. Length 13 mm, diameter 26 mm, weight *c.*30 g. Pan weight, originally conical with a circular base, the upper part damaged or clipped.
CAA/84: *unstratified.*

7 NI. Similar to **6**. Approximate weight 25 g.
CAA/87: *unstratified.*

8 Complete. Length 25 mm, thickness 4 mm. Line or net weight. Flat disc with suspension hole set off-centre.
CAA/210: *unstratified.*

9 NI. Perforated fragment, possibly a weight.
GK/69: *Area 1, pond. Fourth century.*

10 NI. Pan weight? Weight *c.*100 g.
CAA/133: *Unstratified.*

11 NI. Cylindrical, post-medieval or modern.
CAA/173: *Unstratified.*

12 NI. Rectangular, probably modern.
CAA/85: *Unstratified.*

13 NI. Circular, post-medieval.
CAA/215: *Unstratified.*

14 NI. Circular, flat, modern.
CAA/90: *Unstratified.*

15 NI. Circular line weight, probably modern.
CAA/88: *Unstratified.*

16 NI. Flat plate, possibly a weight, ?modern.
CAA/95: *Unstratified.*

17 NI. Rectangular weight, *c.*20 g.
CAA/127: *Unstratified.*

18 NI. Possible pierced sheet weight.
CAA/130: *Unstratified.*

Sling-shot

19 Complete. Biconical, length 32 mm, diameter (maximum) 18 mm. Similar lead sling-shot *(glandes)* have been recorded at Windridge Farm, St Albans (Greep 1987).
DAC 1/5: *unstratified.*

Plugs or patches

The site produced eleven plugs or patches used in the repair of ceramic vessels. These are frequent finds on Romano-British sites with many examples from Hertfordshire, *eg.* Dicket Mead (Rook 1987, 152, Fig. 61.5).

20 Surviving. Length 33 mm. Two plates joined by a central neck, one flat and one domed.
DAC 1/7: *unstratified.*

21–29 NI. Other plugs or patches came from DAC 1 (SF nos 6, 8), CAB 6 (SF 14), and unstratified (SF nos 2, 80, 129, 134, 213, and 218).

Cloth seal

30 Complete. Length 30 mm. Two-disc cloth seal marked 'IK'. Geoff Egan (Museum of London) has identified it as a clothier's or weaver's seal, probably of eighteenth or early nineteenth-century date.
CAA/222: *unstratified.*

Miscellaneous objects and fragments

Several identifiable objects were found (listed below) together with numerous fragments of sheeting of indeterminate function, probably waste or scrap. One piece of uncertain date (**34**) is decorated.

31 NI. Ferrule, post-medieval.
CAA/132: *unstratified*.

32 NI. Rivet.
CAA/194: *unstratified*.

33 NI. Plate
QC 1/3: *unstratified*.

34 Indeterminate. Surviving length 35 mm. Sheet with moulded relief decoration, possibly ribbing and a floral motif, too fragmentary for identification.
QC 1/3: *unstratified*.

Other fragments of lead, mostly sheet, are recorded in the site archive.

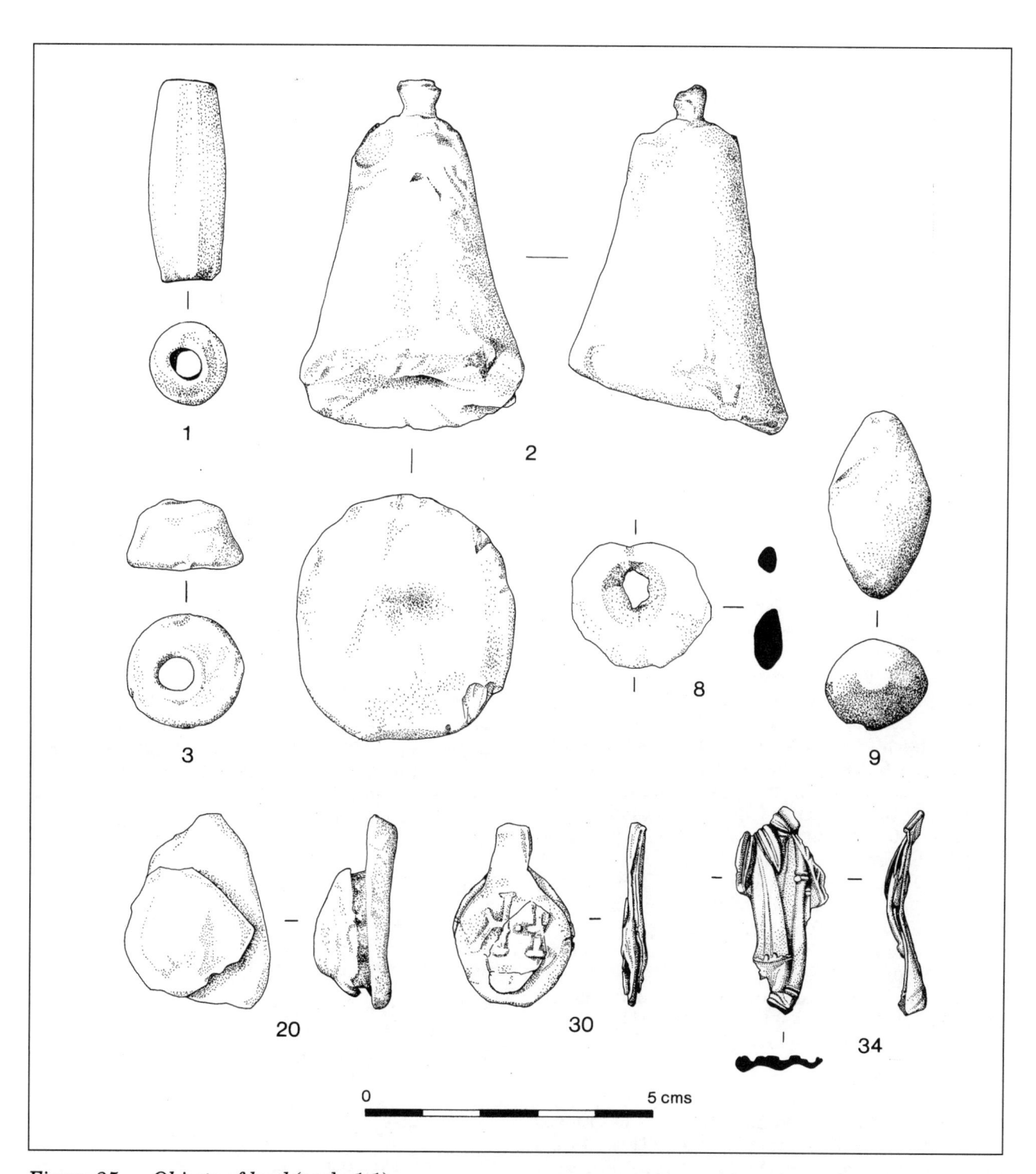

Figure 25   Objects of lead (scale 1:1).

Objects of Bone and Antler
(Figs 26, 27)

Stephen Greep

Summary

The excavations at Chells produced a small but interesting assemblage. The material spans the Roman period, although there is a surprisingly strong assemblage of earlier material, principally from Feature EAA (**3–13**, **21** and **22**). The waste products (**1–2**) demonstrate bone and antler working on site, but there is no indication as to which types were being produced. On the whole, the quality of workmanship is consistently high – unusually so for a rural site – and is best paralleled on sites of a higher social status such as villas (*eg.* Neal, Wardle and Hunn 1990, figs 140–1). For the size of assemblage there are no noticeable omissions except, perhaps, items normally associated with gaming (*eg.* gaming counters and dice), though these are uncommon finds on rural sites, and textile production, which one would normally expect to recover on such a site.

Objects designated 'NI' are not illustrated.

Waste Products

1 NI. Small section of red deer antler tine, sawn at one end. 29 mm long.
   KN1/2: *unphased, but probably fourth century.*

2 NI. Small fragment of knife-cut bone. 46 mm long.
   GK/38: *mid fourth century.*

Hair Pins

Bone and antler hairpins may be divided into two basic types relating to hair styles and, in terms of typology, the form of stem and decorative elements. Hairpins with tapering stems (Type A) are broadly dateable to the earlier Roman period (*c.*AD 40–200/250), and those with swelling stems (Type B) to the later Roman period (*c.*AD 150/200–400+). In this respect the Chells pins conform, the eleven examples from Feature EAA (early second century) forming an interesting assemblage. These are all of the commonest earlier Roman form, Type A2, being deposited at a period just before hair styles and hairpin forms were changing.

For a fuller discussion of the types listed below and their chronology see Greep 1995, 1113–1121.

Type A2.2

Pins with a conical head above a series of grooves or collars and with a tapering stem. These forms are the most common early Roman type recovered in Roman Britain (*eg* Greep 1995, 1116–1117).

3 Single collar. 90 mm long, complete.
   EAA 2/10: *Area 3, early second century.*

4 Single collar. 71 mm long, broken.
   EAA 2/4: *Area 3, early second century.*

5 Single collar. 113 mm long, complete.
   EAA 2/3: *Area 3, early second century.*

6 Single collar. 58 mm long, broken.
   EAA 3/6: *Area 3, early second century.*

7 Single collar. 88 mm long, complete.
   EAA 2/5: *Area 3, early second century.*

8 Single collar. 45 mm long, broken.
   EAA 16/52: *Area 3, early second century.*

9 Single collar. 63 mm long, broken.
   EAA 8/26: *Area 3, early second century.*

10 Single collar. 55 mm long, broken
   EAA 2/40: *Area 3, early second century.*

11 Single collar. 64 mm long, broken.
   EAA 2/48: *Area 3, early second century.*

12 Single collar. 86 mm long, broken.
   EAA 14/50: *Area 3, early second century.*

13 Single collar. 67 mm long, broken.
   EAA 14/51: *Area 3, early second century.*

14 Double collar. 32 mm long, broken. Residual in this context.
   JK 1/12: *early to mid fourth century.*

15 Irregular example with a single collar but crudely carved with an unevenly worked, highly polished, stem. 81 mm long, complete. Possibly residual in this context.
   CAB 3/20: *early to mid fourth century.*

Type A pin stems were recovered from the following contexts: GK 1/164, RC 1/14, FZ 3/16, CE 8/46, EAA 2/13 and 49, EAA 16/53. It should be noted that some of these finds could have formed parts of needles rather than hairpins.

Type B1

Hairpins with a rounded head and a swelling stem. These are the most common form of late Roman hairpin (*eg* Greep 1995, 1117–1118).

16 96 mm long, complete.
   ES 4/54: *early to mid fourth century.*

17 60 mm long, broken.
   ES 2/33: *early to mid fourth century.*

18 94 mm long, complete.
   CAB 3/6: *early to mid fourth century.*

19 66 mm long, complete.
   CAB 3/9: *early to mid fourth century.*

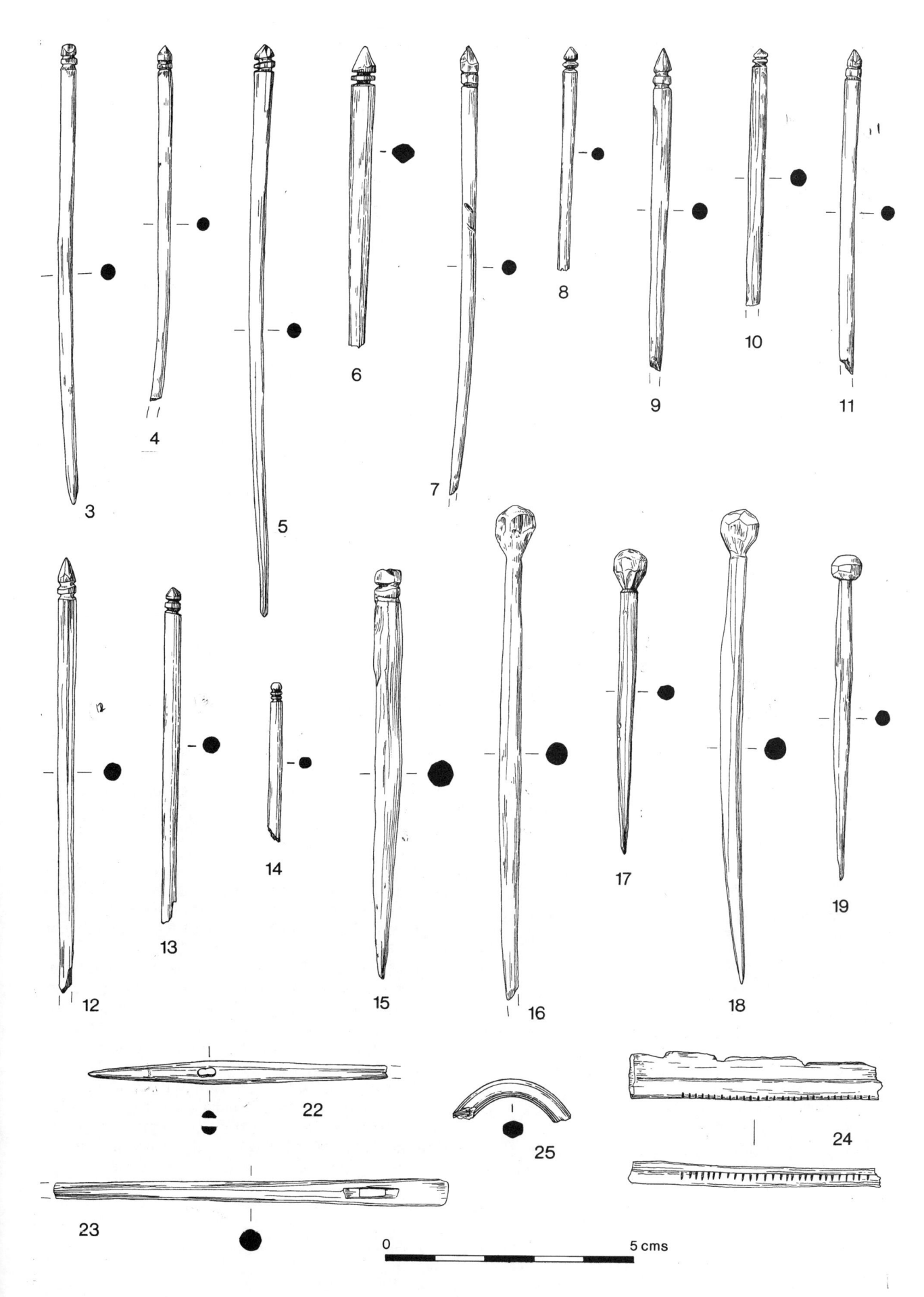

Figure 26 Objects of bone and antler, 3–25 (scale 1:1).

71

Other Type B

20 NI. Hairpin with a facetted head and a swelling stem. 84 mm long, complete.
    CAB 3/15: *early to mid fourth century.*

Two other Type B pin stems were recovered from the well weathering cone [CAB 3/32 and ES 8/1]. Stems of uncertain type were recovered from CAB 3/34, and Context EAA 3/7.

Needles

Bone needles are divisible on the form of the eye and treatment of the head, though there does not seem to be any chronological distinctions between the various forms, as most continue throughout the Roman period. For a discussion of the function and typology of bone and antler needles see Greep 1995, 1122–1125).

21 NI. Needle with a head broken across the eye but with traces of a single round eye (Type 1). 82 mm long.
    EAA 2/14: *early second century.*

22 Type 2.2 needle, with a figure-of-eight perforated eye and a pointed head. 61 mm long, broken.
    EAA 8/24: *early second century.*

23 Type 3.1 needle with a rectangular eye. 79 mm long, broken.
    ES 4/46: *early to mid fourth century.*

Other Roman Objects

24 Fragment from the retaining plate of a double-sided composite comb, apparently undecorated although too little survives to be certain. The remaining edge demonstrates cuts for a series of fine teeth, and there is evidence for at least three rivets, unusually closely spaced. 51 mm long, broken. The date of this example is uncertain, although the profile of the retaining plate suggests a late Roman (fourth-century) rather than a post-Roman date, which is confirmed by its context.
    GK/8: *mid fourth century.*

25 Fragment of a bone finger-ring, 23 mm diameter, of oval section. Although rare finds (eg Greep 1986, Fig. 73.7; Greep 1995, Fig. 503.1010), simple finger-rings of this form are not datable within the Roman period.
    FY/18: *unphased.*

26 Stem fragment, possibly from a spindle, although too little remains to be certain. An alternative suggestion is that this is a fragment from a type B hairpin (above), although it appears to be too large in section for such a function. 73 mm long, broken.
    ES 8/61: *early to mid fourth century.*

27 Fragment similar to **3**. 75 mm long, broken. An irregular wear pattern around the mid-point of the swelling suggests use as a spindle rather than as a hairpin.
    CAB 1/10: *Well weathering cone. Late fourth century onwards.*

28 Small knife handle of waisted oval section, 66 mm long, complete but cracked. Traces of an iron tang *in situ*.
    GM 1/1: *mid fourth century.*

This is an example of a small but well-known and important group of early Roman handles (Greep 1982, Fig. 3.8–11) which usually hafted a fine slender blade, the tang being held in place by an unusual winged clip at the upper end. There are a number of closely dated examples of this form from the continent (*eg.* Greep 1982, 99; Petru 1972, grave 267), where the dating is consistently first century. The current example is, therefore, presumably residual in this context.

29 Slender bone knife handle decorated with a series of weak, hand-cut collars and a band of trellis decoration at either end. Iron tang remaining in situ throughout. 84 mm long, complete. Although a simply ornamented form, trellis-decorated single-piece handles are commonly a late Roman type (*eg.* Neal, Wardle and Hunn 1990, Fig. 141.974).
    CAB 1/8: *early to mid fourth century.*

30 Tip of a red deer antler tine sawn at the upper end, below which there is a knife-cut notch. There are traces of the central tissue having been hollowed, the tine has split and broken opposite the notch on the reverse surface. There are strong horizontal wear marks on all surfaces, although most prominently on the front surface below the notch. 57 mm long.
    FY/6: *unphased.*

This belongs to a small and diverse group of notched and perforated antler tines. The surface may be left completely unworked (*eg.* Verulamium Museum, unpub., acc. no. 78.166) or partially or completely polished (*eg.* Colchester Museum, unpub., acc. no. 1099.31). The central tissue may be untouched (Verulamium Museum, *ibid.*), removed completely (Caerwent, Newport Museum) or, as on the Chells example, hollowed for only a short distance. The size varies considerably from the tips of tines, as at Chells, to larger sections (*eg.* Johnson 1972, Fig. 17.1).

The function of these objects is somewhat uncertain. They are normally termed 'cheek-pieces' (*eg.* Roes 1960; Gallup 1973, *Abb.* 7–8) or whistles (Carrington 1865–6, 209), while Curle (1911, 314) thought that the example from Newstead might have been 'for twisting a light rope so as to tighten it'. The considerable variation within the broad group clearly suggests a series of functions. The strong wear patterns on the Chells piece suggests that a series of microwear analysis and experimentation may well provide further ideas.

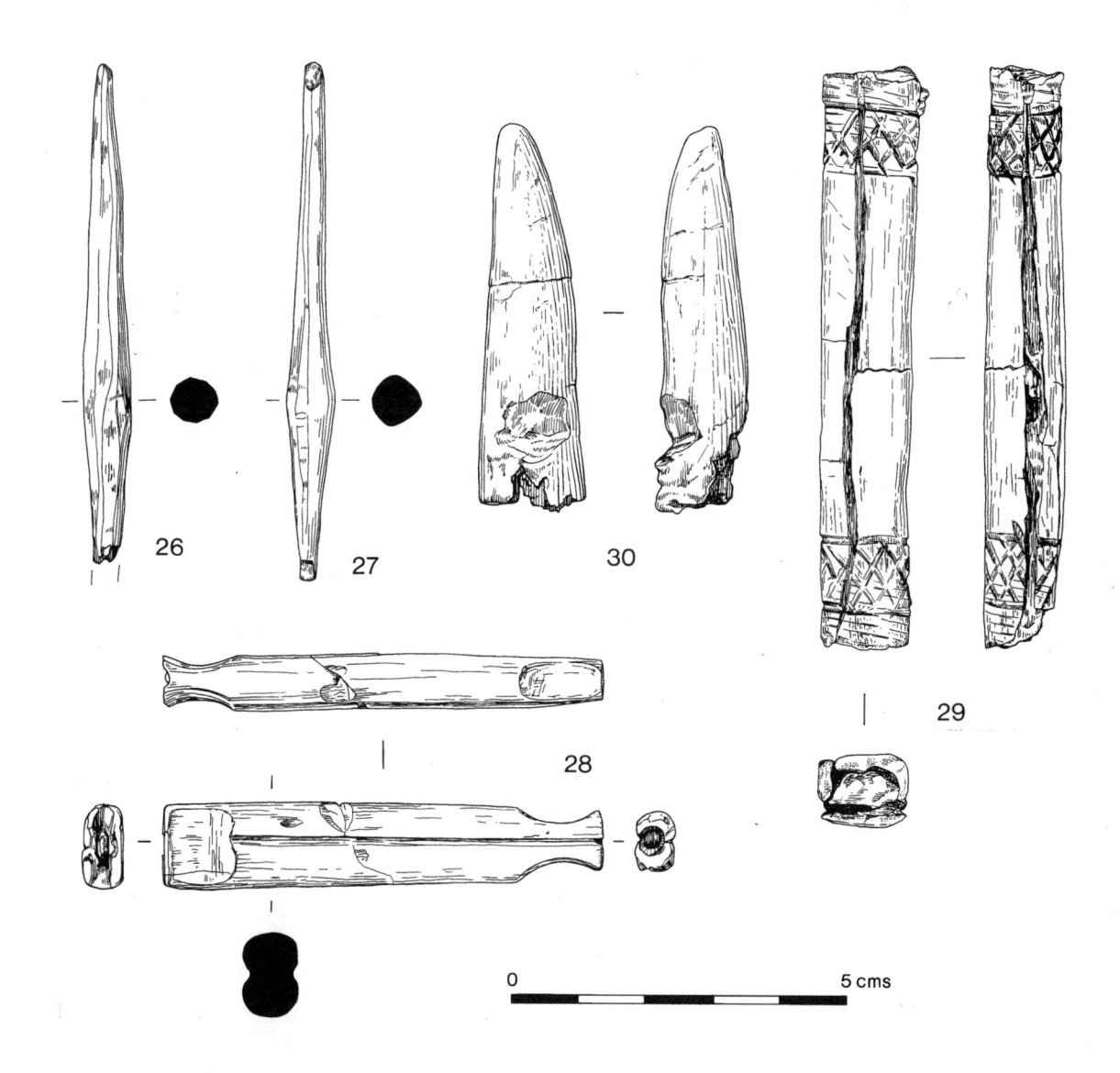

Figure 27   Objects of bone and antler, 26–30 (scale 1:1).

73

Roman Glass
(Figs 28, 29)

Jennifer Price and Sally Cottam

Summary

The excavations at Chells produced a total of 122 fragments of Roman glass, 117 from vessels, dating from the first to the fourth centuries, two from window panes and three from objects. Most of the glass was in good condition, with very few pieces showing signs of weathering.

Seventy-three strongly coloured fragments were of first or possibly second-century date. Sixty-one unweathered deep brown fragments came from a single vessel, a tall one-handled cup (1), found in association with samian dating to the Neronian–early Flavian period in Cremation GAX. This had a horizontal stepped rim with a tubular edge turned up, out and down, a deep cylindrical body, pushed-in base-ring and concave base, and a small curved ribbon handle with a central groove applied to the upper body and attached below the rim. This type of vessel is frequently known as a *modiolus* or measuring cup (Isings 1957, form 37; Kern 1963; Haevernick 1981). *Modioli* made in strongly coloured or blue/green glass have been found in many parts of the Roman world, though they are concentrated in the Western provinces. They are generally dated to the third quarter of the first century AD. A number of examples are known from the north-west provinces. These include two vessels in blue and green glass from Nijmegen (Haevernick 1981, 372 no. 86 & 373 no. 94), a blue vessel with a white rim and handle from Cologne (Fremersdorf 1958, 34, *tafel* 43), an amber/brown vessel from Nida-Hedderheim (Welker 1974, 27–30, pl. 20.1), two vessels from Belgium, one light green from Berlingen (Haevernick 1981, 370.3), the other emerald green from Vervoz (Vanderhoeven 1961, 33.32, pl. VII), and two from northern France, an emerald green vessel from Lille (Vanderhoeven 1961, 33.31 pl. VII) and a brown/yellow example from Reims (Haevernick 1981, 373.99).

The Boxfield Farm *modiolus* is only the second or possibly third example of which a substantial amount has survived, to be recognised in Britain. A nearly complete *modiolus*, lacking only the handle, was found in a pit in Exeter (*JRS* 1953, 124, pl. XXIII), and is also associated with material dated to the Neronian to early Flavian period. This vessel, in blue/green glass, is very similar in form to the Chells vessel, having a vertical tubular rim, tall cylindrical body and tubular pushed-in base ring, though the body is decorated with narrow vertical ribs. A blue/green rim fragment of very similar form, but with a smaller diameter, is known from Kingsholm, Gloucester, (Price and Cool 1985, 50, no. 48, Fig. 19 [illustrated upside down]).

Another nearly complete example, which does not now survive, may have been found in a burial at Bartlow Hills with grave goods including two cylindrical bottles and a coin of Hadrian. The vessel had disintegrated, and it is difficult to make a positive identification on the basis of the illustration (Gage 1834, 7, pl. III, Fig. 8). A strongly everted rim is quite frequently found on vessels of this form, although several different types of rim edge have been noted. The rim can be turned out with a fire-rounded edge as on a green *modiolus* from the former USSR (Haevernick 1981, 371, no. 43, *Abb.* 3f), or turned out and up to form a step, with a fire-rounded rim edge as on the example from Berlingen. A horizontal figure-of-eight fold forming a tubular band is sometimes present below the rim, as on a blue/green *modiolus* from Pompeii (Haevernick 1981, 370, no. 14, *Abb.* 3e). Tubular rim edges similar to this example are less common, and it is notable that two other examples from Roman Britain, those from Exeter and Kingsholm, Gloucester, have similar edges. The body is often plain, as on this vessel and the very similar yellow/brown example lacking a rim, from Nida-Heddernheim, or ribbed, as on the blue/green vessel from Exeter and on a *modiolus* from Palestrina (Haevernick 1981, 374, no. 104, *Abb.* 3a) which has vertical ribs pinched together at intervals. Some were decorated with horizontal wheel-cut lines, as on a blue/green *modiolus* from Pompeii (Haevernick 1981, 370, no. 16, *Abb.* 3 g). Similar cups are also known in metal and terra sigillata, and both metal and glass examples were found at Pompeii. The typically out-splayed rim is particularly wide on the cup from Boxfield Farm and suggests that this was not a drinking vessel, nor does it seem likely that a vessel of this quality and fragility was used as a measuring cup.

Nine pale yellow/brown fragments come from two ribbed vessels (**2, 3**). 2 is probably a conical jug with a concave base (Isings 1957, form 55), although only part of the body and base have survived. The type is frequently found on first and early second-century sites in the north-western provinces, and most of the fragments from this example came from contexts of this period. Similar ribbed jugs have come from burials at Winchester (Harden 1967), and Radnage, Bucks. (Skilbeck 1923, Fig. 2 c). The jug from Radnage, which is also yellow brown, was associated with samian dated to the Flavian period, as was the dark blue jug from Winchester. Some ribbed and plain jugs in yellow/brown and yellow/green glass, with either simple concave bases, or carinated with an open base ring and concave base, have been found in Antonine contexts at Towcester (Price 1980, 66, no. 8) Felmongers, Harlow (Price 1987, 193, Fig. 3.20) and Alcester (Price and Cottam 1994, Fig. 104.9).

Two fragments in pale yellow/green glass (**4, 5**) have shallow spiral ribs, and appear to come from a vessel similar to the pale green jug from Turriff, Aberdeenshire (Thorpe 1933–4). The formation of the ribs on **5** seems to indicate a change in direction, similar to that on a yellow/brown globular jug from Enfield (Price 1977, 155, pl. 8.2), although very little of the vessel now survives. The second yellow/brown ribbed vessel (**3**), a globular jar, is represented by four fragments, two of which come from first to second-century contexts. Globular ribbed jars (Isings 1957, form 67c) are also common on first and early second-century sites in Britain and elsewhere in the north-western Empire. Several vessels of this form in both strongly coloured and blue/green glass have been found at Verulamium, mostly in contexts dating to the second half of the first century and first half of the second century (Charlesworth 1972, 204–5 pl. ix.1–7, Fig. 76.25–6; Charlesworth 1984, 166, nos 246–252, Fig. 67.105–6). A blue/green ribbed jar was found at the Lunt fort in contexts ranging from AD.60–140 (Charlesworth 1975, 39, pl. 10a.5) and a further example, also blue/green, was found at Richborough in a pit dating to AD 80–120 (Bushe-Fox 1932, 84, pl. XV.57).

The last strongly coloured fragment (**6**) comes from a flat base with a slight kick towards the centre. This unusual piece has a circular wheel-cut line and abraded band on the underside of the base, and may come from a cylindrical vessel, possibly a bowl or a bottle, though parallels have not been found.

One polychrome fragment (**7**) was found, a colourless body fragment with an unmarvered opaque blue trail with faint diagonal scoring marks. Although the piece was much too small for the identification of the vessel form to be possible, it clearly belonged to a vessel with snake-thread decoration. Glass of this kind is found in large quantities in the Rhineland, and was probably manufactured in or near Cologne in the later second and early third century (Fremersdorf 1959). Fragments with blue, yellow, white or colourless snake-thread trailed decoration are quite frequent finds in Roman Britain. At Whitton, South Glamorgan, six fragments from a colourless cylindrical vessel are decorated with opaque white and blue trails (Price 1981, 154–5), and at Carlisle three fragments with blue scored and plain trails were found in post second-century contexts (Price 1990, 169, Fig. 160.17a & b). **8** comes from the body of a straight sided colourless cup, decorated with at least one horizontal wheel-cut line. Cups of this type are frequently found in second-century contexts in Roman Britain.

Several examples were found in an Antonine pit at Felmongers, Harlow, dated 150–170 (Price 1987, 189–91, Fig. 2.8–11), and a nearly complete cup came from another Antonine pit at Alcester (Price and Cottam 1994, 224, Fig. 104.11).

Examples are also known from second and early third-century contexts at Verulamium (Charlesworth 1984, 155, nos 93–4, Fig. 63, nos 45–6). One convex body fragment with pinched-up decoration (**9**) may have come from a cup, a bowl or possibly a flask. This method of decoration is found on cups and bowls usually dated to the third century, and is sometimes associated with abraded bands. Although only one projection is visible on this fragment, vessels with projections arranged between pinched-up ribs are known, as on a colourless bowl from Sparsholt villa, near Winchester (*pers. comm.* Denise Allen), and a bowl found at the mid third-century cemetery at Brougham, Cumbria (Price and Cool 1989, 3), and in combination with lugs as seen on examples from Braintree, Essex (Drury 1976, 37, Fig. 19.6), and Chichester (Down 1979, 163, Fig. 56.5).

Blue/green tableware is not well represented at Chells. Only one fragment (**10**) was noted, from the rim of a tubular-rimmed bowl. Tubular rimmed bowls were produced in strongly coloured and blue/green glass, sometimes decorated with ribbing, and are quite common on first and second-century sites in Roman Britain. At Long Melford a dark blue bowl was found in association with Neronian samian (Avent and Howlett 1980, 246, Fig. 41) and a complete blue/green example from Richborough was found in a pit dated to AD 70–100 (Bushe-Fox 1932, 85, pl. XV.63). At least three examples, two blue/green, were found in the Antonine pit at Felmongers, Harlow (Price 1987, 188, Fig. 1.4–6), and numerous tubular rimmed bowls, many from later first to mid second-century contexts were found at Verulamium (Charlesworth 1972, 199, nos 1–18, Fig. 74 nos 6–11).

Nineteen fragments came from cylindrical and prismatic blue/green bottles. Blue/green bottles were common throughout the Roman world in the later first and second centuries, being used for the transport of liquid and semi-liquid substances, and in some cases they have a secondary use as cinerary vessels. The rim, neck, shoulder and handle of cylindrical and prismatic bottles are formed in the same manner, the rim being folded out, in, then flattened, and the handle, usually reeded, being applied to the shoulder of the vessel below the rim.

Cylindrical bottles (Isings 1957, form 51), were made in two principal shapes, being either tall and narrow or short and wide. They were in widespread use during the later first and early years of the second century, being particularly common in the Flavian period. At the fort of Inchtuthil, occupied from about AD 83–86, at least six cylindrical bottles of the narrow and tall variety were found (Price 1985, 307). Five fragments (**12**) come from an unusually thin-walled bottle, made from very bubbly glass. This variety of cylindrical bottle has not often been noted in the north-west provinces, although similar square bottles were found at Harlow (Price 1987, 197–8, Fig. 4.33–34) and elsewhere in Britain in first and second-century contexts. Square bottles (Isings 1957, form 50), by far the most common form of prismatic bottle, were produced at the same time as the cylindrical bottles already mentioned, and continued in use throughout the second century.

Prismatic bottles, like cylindrical bottles, were made in a variety of sizes. They were nearly always mould-blown, and these almost invariably have a raised basal design. A small corner pellet, part of a larger base design, can be seen on **13**. The commonest designs are concentric circles, which often have corners supported by pellets, as at Fishbourne (Harden and Price 1971, 364, Fig. 143.101) and Verulamium (Charlesworth 1972, 200, no. 3, Fig. 75.14).

There was a relatively high proportion of late Roman glass from Chells. Discounting the cremation vessel (**1**), late glass amounted to over 20% of the total number of vessel fragments. All the late Roman glass was bubbly, and several of the body fragments were decorated with abraded lines. Most of the fragments were too small for the form of the vessel to be recognised. **15** comes from a straight-sided cup or beaker, decorated with horizontal abraded lines. These vessels are frequently found on late third and fourth-century sites in Roman Britain. The rim was cracked-off, as on examples from Silchester (Boon 1974, 232, Fig. 36.8), Alchester Road, Towcester, (Price and Cool 1983, Fig. 47.30, 31), and the late Roman cemetery at Lankhills, Winchester (Harden 1979, 213, Fig. 27.382, 391, 530 & 634).

18, which has a fire rounded rim, also comes from a cup or beaker of mid fourth-century or later date. Fourth-century vessels with fire-rounded rims are not as common as those with cracked-off rims, although an increasing number of examples are known from late Roman sites in Britain, including Alchester Road, Towcester (Price and Cool 1983, 117, Fig. 47.40–44) and Burgh Castle (Harden 1983, 83, Fig. 37.85, 87–89). The decorated body fragments, (**16, 17**) are too small to be identified confidently, but they may come from small convex cups or bowls. These are frequently found on late Roman sites, and examples are known from Lankhills cemetery, decorated with abraded bands (Harden 1979, 213, Fig. 27.62 & 385), and from Alchester Road, decorated with abraded bands on their own, or in combination with trails (Price and Cool 1983, Fig. 46.11–21). The base fragment (**19**) could come from a variety of late Roman vessels. At Lankhills, a jug (Isings 1957, form 120b) shows this form of base (Harden 1979, 217.310), and at Burgh Castle it can be seen on both bowls and beakers (Harden 1983, 81–83, Fig. 37.81, 82, 88 & 89).

Only two fragments of window glass were found. Both were blue/green, of the matt/glossy cast variety dating to the first to third centuries, and found in close proximity, probably coming from the same pane. One edge of both fragments showed signs of grozing, indicating the shaping of the pane to fit a particular space. Fragments of cast window glass with evidence of grozing are known from the bath house at Garden Hill, Hartfield, Sussex (Harden 1974, 280) and elsewhere in Roman Britain.

Three glass objects were found; two beads and a twisted rod, probably a hairpin. The green cylinder bead (**20**) belongs to a class of blue and green beads of various lengths found throughout the immediate pre-Roman and Roman periods and beyond, becoming particularly common after the third century (Guido 1978, 95b Fig. 57.4, 5). Similar beads have been found in late Roman contexts at Porchester, Hampshire, and from the late Roman site at Little Chester, Derby (Guido 1978, 209). The dark blue bead (**21**) is a larger example of a type found in Roman Britain from the first century onwards, becoming more common in the late Roman period (Guido 1978, 97a, Fig. 37.12). Six similar beads were found in probable third and fourth-century contexts at Barnsley Park, Cirencester (Guido 1978, 219). **22**, a small, slightly tapering twisted rod in pale green glass, probably comes from a hairpin. Glass hairpins are quite commonly found on Romano-British sites, but are difficult to date closely. The head of this pin is missing, but a similar pale green twisted hairpin from Verulamium has a rounded head (Charlesworth 1972, 215 no. 3, Fig. 79.76), and pale green examples with both rounded and ring heads are known from a post-AD 320 burial at Butt Road, Colchester (Crummy 1983, 28, Fig. 25.461–464). Finally, three fragments of melted blue/green glass were found, one of which (**23**) came from Cremation GBA 9. All the fragments were badly distorted, and reconstruction of the vessel forms was impossible.

Catalogue

Abbreviations:
BD   Base diameter
BT   Base thickness
Dim.   Dimensions
PH   Present height
RD   Rim diameter
WT   Wall thickness

Objects designated 'NI' are not illustrated.

Blown Vessels

COLOURED

1   61 rim, handle, body and base fragments, many joining, of a deep cup. Brown. Wide-stepped, vertical tubular rim, edge folded up, out and down. Almost straight-sided cylindrical body, tapering in slightly to tubular pushed-in base ring. Concave base. Curved ribbon handle with two ribs, applied to upper body and attached below rim. Base edge slightly worn. Large circular pontil-mark around edge of base. No visible weathering. Height 132 mm; RD 120 mm; BD 90 mm; WT 1.5 mm; Dia. of pontil mark 70–72 mm.
GAX 4/61: *later first-century burial.*

2   6 fragments from the body and base of a conical jug. Yellow/brown. Straight-sided body expanding out to rounded edge of slightly concave base. Parts of at least two vertical narrow ribs. Light cloudy weathering; small bubbles. PH 49 mm; WT 2 mm.
BBB 1/1–2; BBB 2/3–4; EAN 1; EAN 3: *Area 3, Pit EAN. Later first to second century.*

3   4 fragments, rim and body of globular jar. Yellow/brown. Irregular tubular rim, folded out and down. Convex curved body with parts of at least two vertical narrow ribs. Patchy weathering on inside surface, light scratching on outside surface. Occasional bubbles. PH 44 mm; WT 2 mm.
BBB 1/2, 5; EAJ 1/1: *Area 3, Pit EAN. Later first to second century.*

4   Body fragment. Yellow green. Parts of three shallow diagonal ribs. Elongated bubbles. Dim. 19 × 15.5 mm; WT 2 mm.
HX 1/1: *fill of hollow.*

5   Body fragment. Yellow/green. Slight evidence for shallow diagonal ribs with change of angle. Elongated bubbles. Dim. 23 × 22 mm; WT 2 mm.
EAW 2: *Area 3, Pit EAW. ?Later first century AD.*

6   Base fragment. Brown/yellow. Curved base edge, flat base, slightly concave towards centre. Circular wheel-cut line on underside. Circular abraded band towards centre at concavity. Base edge worn. Dia. c.150 mm; BT 5–6 mm.
KZ 1/1: *unstratified.*

COLOURLESS

7   NI. Small body fragment. Slightly convex. Curved opaque blue unmarvered trail. Dim. 8 × 6.5 mm; WT 1.5 mm.
GA/8: *unstratified.*

8   Body fragment, cylindrical cup. Slightly everted rim, edge missing. Straight-sided body. Broad horizontal wheel-cut line within abraded band on upper body. PH 19 mm; WT 1.5 mm.
TB 1/1: *fill of hollow.*

9   Body fragment, cup? Convex curved body. One pinched-up projecting point. Light weathering. Bubbly. Dim. 26 × 33 mm; WT 1 m.
ES 2/43: *Area 1, Well CAB weathering cone. Later fourth century.*

Also two undecorated colourless body fragments: GK/100, JG 1/1.

BLUE/GREEN GLASS

10 NI. Rim fragment, bowl? Part of vertical tubular rim, edge bent out and down. Trace of upper body. Dim. 11 × 7.5 mm; WT 1 mm.
GK/39: *Area 1, pond upper fill. Later fourth century onwards.*

BOTTLES

11 Rim and neck fragment. Rim bent out up and in and flattened. Trace of cylindrical neck. PH 14.5 mm; RD 70 mm.
CH 1/2: *loam layer. Third to fourth centuries.*

Also one shoulder fragment from ES, and one reeded handle fragment from QT 1/1.

12 NI. Five fragments from the shoulder, body and base of a thin-walled cylindrical bottle. Curved shoulder, straight-sided body, slightly convex base. Light scratching on base. Very bubbly. PH 38 mm; WT 1–1.5 mm.
EAA 2/3: *Area 3, mid second century.*

Also 5 cylindrical body fragments: EAA 2, KG 1/1 (3 frags), PY 3.

13 NI. Body and base fragment of square or rectangular bottle. Part of one straight side. Edge of base, with trace of moulded decoration close to corner, perhaps pellet. Occasional bubbles. PH 51 mm; WT 4–5 mm.
ES 2/39: *Area 1, Well CAB weathering cone. Later fourth century.*

14 Five fragments of prismatic bottle, handle and body, joined. Lower and small section of upper part of angular reeded handle applied to shoulder. Fifteen ribs pulled out into points on shoulder. Part of straight-sided upper body. PH 72 mm; WT 5 mm; width of handle 52.5 mm.
ES 4/56: *Area 1, Well CAB weathering cone. Later fourth century.*

Also 3 prismatic body fragments: CT 1, FZ 15/27c, JK 1.

Late Roman Glass

15 NI. Body fragment of truncated conical beaker. Pale yellow/colourless. Curving rim, edge missing. Straight-sided body tapering in. Horizontal band of two abraded lines on body. Small specks and bubbles. PH 37 mm; WT 1 mm.
FZ 5/11: *Area 1 gully, post mid fourth century.*

16 NI. Body fragment, colourless. Straight-sided body. Horizontal abraded band. Small specks and bubbles. PH 18 mm; WT 1 mm.
KA 1/3: *Area of flint cobbling.*

17 NI. Two body fragments, joining. Slightly convex body. Horizontal lightly abraded band. Elongated bubbles. Dim. 17 × 16 mm; WT 1 mm.
FZ 3/13: *Area 1 gully, post mid fourth century.*

Also five undecorated colourless body fragments: FZ/34, GK 6/126, RD 1/2, TB 1/3.

18 Rim fragment, cup? Yellow/green. Out-turned fire-rounded rim. Straight-sided upper body. Small specks and bubbles. PH 14.5 mm; RD 72 mm; WT 1 mm.
PZ 1: *unstratified.*

Also one yellow/green body fragment from Pond GK (SF98).

19 NI. Base fragment. Cup? Pale green. Tubular base ring. PH 6 mm.
GK/51: *Area 1, pond upper fill. Fourth century onwards.*

Window Glass

Matt/glossy cast panes (not illustrated)

–   Blue/green. Max dim. 20 × 17 × 3 mm.
ES 4/48: *Area 1, Well CAB weathering cone. Later fourth century.*

–   Blue/green. One edge grozed. Max. dim. 20 × 16 × 3 mm.
ES 4/49: *Area 1, Well CAB weathering cone. Later fourth century.*

Objects

20 Tubular bead, green. Weathered surface. ED 4.5 mm; DP 2 mm; Height 20 mm.
EBH 1/1: *?Pit.*

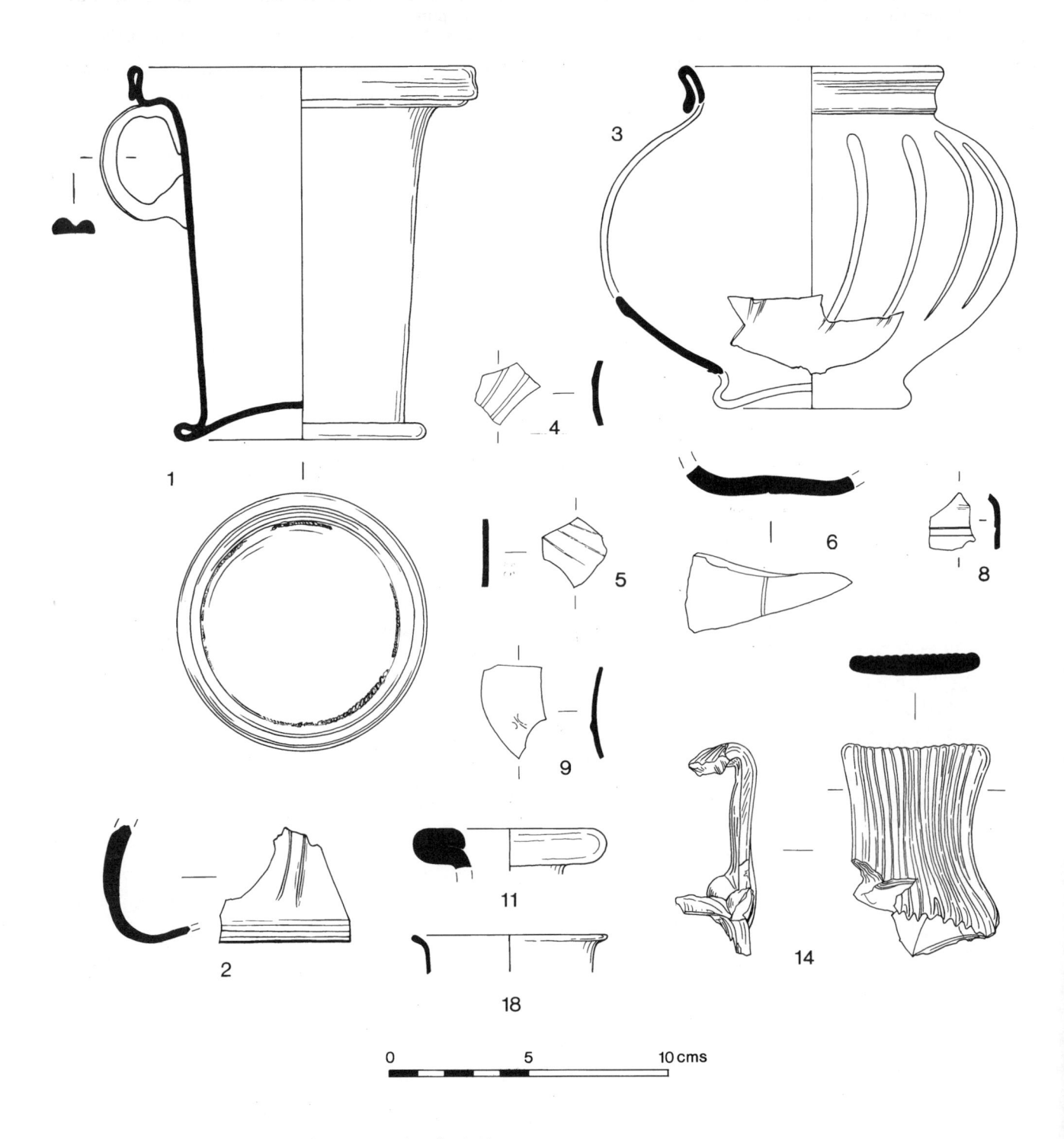

Figure 28 *The Roman glass, 1–18* (scale 1:2).

21 Small dark blue biconical bead. ED 6 mm; DP 1 mm; Height 2.5 mm.
DBB 1/11: *Area 2, fill of cess pit. Later fourth century?*

22 Fragment of hairpin, pale green. Solid circular-section rod. Left-hand twist, tapering in. Broken at both ends. PH 29 mm; Dia. 4–5 mm.
GK 1/92: *Area 1, pond upper fills. Later fourth century onwards.*

23 NI. Badly melted fragment. Blue/green. Dim. 21 × 17 mm.
GBA 9 *(Cemetery). Hadrianic–Antonine burial.*

Two other melted fragments came from EAC 1 (yellow/green) and GK 1 (blue/green).

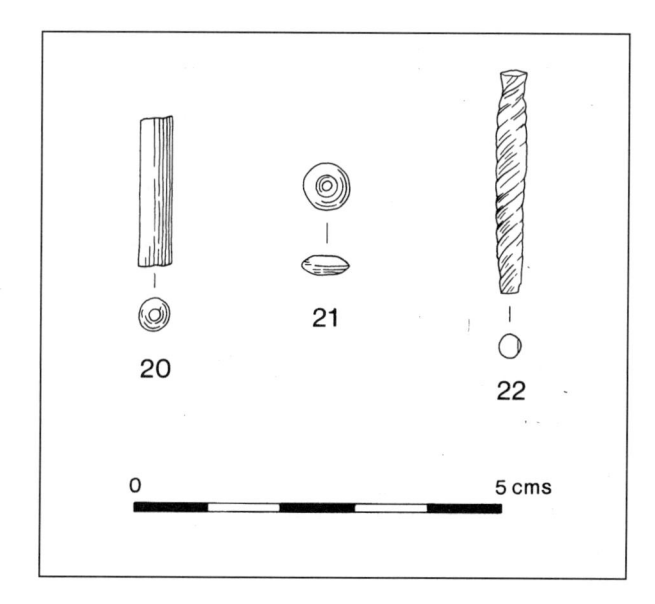

Figure 29   The Roman glass, 20–22 (scale 1:1).

Objects Of Shale
(Fig. 30)

Julia Green

Bracelets

1. Fragment, internal diameter about 40 mm, thickness 6 mm, height 5.5 mm. Similar to an example from Verulamium (Frere 1972, Fig. 57.222).
   CG 1/1: *black loam, later fourth century.*

2. Fragment, internal diameter about 70 mm, thickness 6.5 mm, height 9 mm. Pronounced ridge where the core has been removed. No parallels found.
   FZ 3/39: *Area 1, gully. Later fourth century.*

3. Fragment, internal diameter about 65 mm, thickness 4.5 mm, height 7.5 mm. Similar to an example from Silchester (Lawson 1976, Fig. 4.31).
   GK 3/183: *Area 1, pond filling. Later fourth century.*

4. Fragment, internal diameter about 55 mm, thickness 7 mm, height 7.5 mm. Similar to an example from Verulamium (Frere 1972, Fig. 57.224).
   AAM 1/1: *pit. Fourth century.*

5. Fragment, internal diameter about 70 mm, thickness 6 mm, height 7 mm. Similar to an example from Silchester (Lawson 1975, Fig. 4.26c).
   DAE 1/1: *Area 3, segment of Ditch DAA. Probably fourth century.*

Beads

6. Length 13 mm, diameter 8 mm. Fragment of a long cylinder bead with circular section. Undecorated. Pierced twice transversally, each piercing being drilled from both sides. The ends show lathe centering marks. *cf* an example from Colchester (Crummy 1983, Fig. 36.974). Possibly post-Roman.
   EC 1/18: *Area 1, Well CAB weathering cone. Later fourth century, but not sealed.*

7. Length 18 mm, width 15 mm, height 4 mm. Plano-convex spacer bead, pierced twice lengthways. Similar to Crummy 1983, Fig. 36.1447.
   FC 2/3: *semicircular gully.*

Spindle whorls

8. Diameter 30.5 mm, thickness 14.5 mm, diameter of perforation 7 mm. Biconical in section. Undecorated, lathe manufactured. Similar to an example from Bancroft, Milton Keynes (Zeepvat 1987, Fig. 46.186).
   GK 2: *Area 1, pond filling. Later fourth century.*

9. Fragment. Diameter 32.5 mm, thickness 13 mm, diameter of perforation 5.5 mm. Similar to **8**.
   AAK 1/1: *later fourth century.*

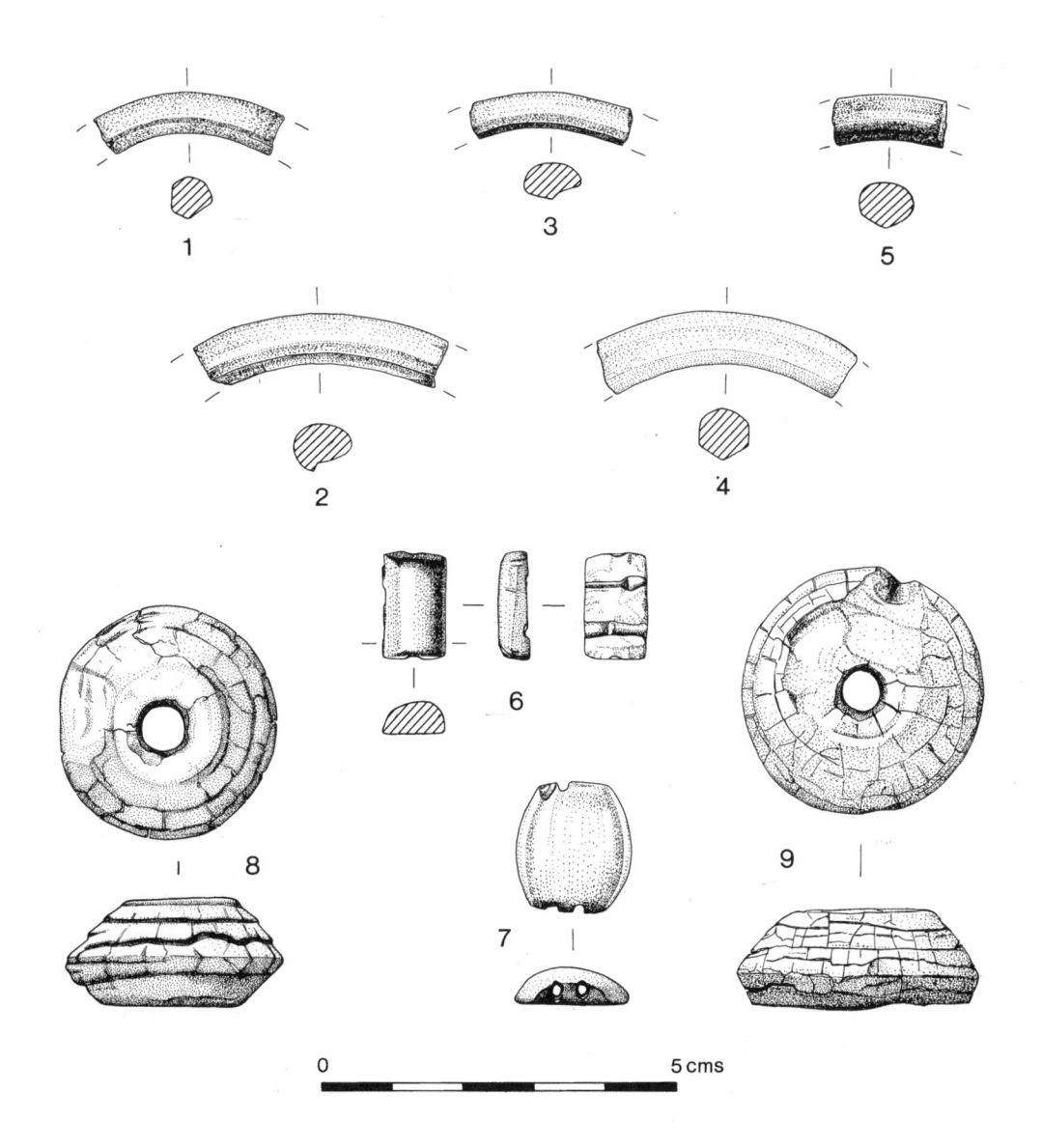

Figure 30   Objects of shale (scale 1:1).

Quernstones and Honestones

David Williams

Rotary Quernstones

Some seventy quernstone fragments have been examined in the hand-specimen, together with one honestone. The principal objectives of the study were the geological identification and possible geographical provenance of the samples. Despite the number of Mayen lava and Millstone Grit fragments present, few of the pieces could be reassembled, and so in many cases it is difficult to identify from which part of the quern a particular stone came from, or indeed estimate how many separate quernstones might be represented in total. The local Hertfordshire Puddingstone is also present, but only in a small way. Bearing this in mind, the quern assemblage from Chells is particularly interesting, because it illustrates nicely the variety of imported long distance quernstones that were available to what other categories of evidence suggest was a fairly modest Romano-British rural settlement. The condition of the fragments, however, was such that none were thought to merit illustration. Individual finds are noted in the *Dating Evidence* sections in the excavation text, cross-referenced to a list in Table 4. A full description and context list is preserved in the site archive.

MAYEN LAVA

This is a grey, fairly coarse vesicular lava, in which it is possible to observe sparse dark coloured phenocrysts of pyroxene. Due to the small size and irregular shape of the majority of the thirty fragments of lava noted, it is difficult to say with any degree of confidence how many separate quernstones may be represented here. One small sample of lava was thin-sectioned and studied under the petrological microscope. This revealed frequent grains of green and colourless clinopyroxene, mainly augite, set in a groundmass of small lath-shaped crystals of andesine/labradorite felspar, opacite, leucite and some xenomorphic nepheline. The rock can be classified as a nepheline-tephrite, and is a type of volcanic rock which is commonly found in the lavas of the Mayen and Niedermendig area of the Eifel Hills of Germany. This region was well-known as a producer of quernstones in Roman and Saxon times, and in Britain many examples of these lava quernstones have been recovered from sites of both periods (Parkhouse 1976; Kars 1980; Peacock 1980). The Chells lava fragments are identical to Mayen quernstones seen by the writer, both in the hand specimen and thin section, and can be ascribed an origin to this part of Germany. According to Peacock (1980), this type of quern is most common in Britain during the first two centuries AD.

MILLSTONE GRIT

The following fifty-four quernstone fragments are pinkish-grey to buff in colour, and uneven in grain size, ranging from medium to fairly coarse-grained. In the hand-specimen, the rock can be seen to contain mostly angular grains of quartz with some quartzite, felspar, lithics and occasional mica. In thin section, the inclusions can often be seen cemented by a thin boundary of ferruginous or opaque material. These stones can almost certainly be identified as Millstone Grit, and probably originated from either the Derbyshire/Yorkshire area or, perhaps less likely, the west of the country, from Devon, the Mendips or South Wales. As far as one can tell, all the shaped fragments are from the normal flat Roman quernstone types.

HERTFORDSHIRE PUDDINGSTONE

One of the main outcrops of the distinctive flint conglomerate known as Hertfordshire Puddingstone is at Radlett, some 24 km to the south of Chells. Given the fairly close proximity of this common source of quernstone material, it is at first glance somewhat surprising that only two smallish quern fragments of Hertfordshire Puddingstone have been recovered from the site. At nearby Baldock, some one third of the querns were made from this rock (Stead and Rigby 1986), though at King Harry Lane, Verulamium, they were absent from the site (Stead and Rigby 1989). A possible chronological explanation for this variation in local distribution has been put forward by Stead (ibid.), who suggests that the end of production of Hertfordshire Puddingstone querns may coincide with the start of the occupation at King Harry Lane of c.AD 70, since Baldock is thought to have begun somewhat earlier, around the middle of the first century BC. However, it is clear that Hertfordshire Puddingstone querns were in circulation long after this date (King 1986).

Honestone

1 NI. Small fragment of a honestone, rectangular in section, 35 mm long and 30 mm thick, broken at both ends. Similar kind of stone as **66** and **67** (Table 18).
RC 1/24: *Area 1, pit. Late fourth century onwards.*

TABLE 4: Catalogue of quernstone and millstone fragments.

No.	Context	Description
MAYEN LAVA:		
1	CG 1/13	Small irregular fragment.
2	CS 4	Three small irregular fragments.
3	ES 2/62	Larger piece with a flat working surface.
4	GF 6/21	Three small irregular fragments.
5	GK 4/169	Nine small irregular fragments.
6	GK 6/171	Larger irregular piece.
7	GK 5/185	Three small irregular fragments.
8	GK 15/180	Three small irregular fragments.
9	KL 1/1	Small irregular fragment.
10	RY 1/6	Small irregular fragment.
11	TX 1/2	Slightly larger piece with a flat working surface.
12	ZS 13	Larger shaped piece, possibly from a top stone, with radial tooling lines on the working surface.
13	TA 1/10	a) Small irregular fragment.
		b) Medium–sized piece from a lower stone.
MILLSTONE GRIT:		
14	HG 1/3	Medium-sized shaped piece.
15	GK 10/176	Small shaped piece.
16	CD 1/10	Small shaped piece.
17	GK 1/166	Small shaped piece.
18	GK 6/173	Small shaped piece.
19	GK 10/177	Small irregular fragment.
20	GK 3/168	Medium-sized shaped piece.
21	RG 1/2	Medium-sized shaped piece.
22	AAJ 1/3	Medium sized shaped piece.
23	CD 1/9	Medium-sized shaped piece.
24	CS 3	Medium-sized shaped piece.
25	YN 1/4	Medium-sized piece with a flat working surface.
26	RY 1/5	Small fragment with radial tooling lines on a flat working surface.
27	YN 1/3	Medium-sized shaped piece.
28	YH 1/2	Medium-sized shaped piece.
29	GK 14/157	Medium-sized piece with radial tooling lines on a flat working surface.
30	GK 2/167	Medium-sized piece with radial tooling lines on a flat working surface.
31	XV 1/1	Medium-sized piece with radial tooling lines on a flat working surface.
32	GK 10/175	Medium-sized piece with radial tooling lines on a flat working surface.
33	YF 1/1	a) Small irregular fragment.
		b) A large, thick fragment with radial tooling lines on a flat working surface.
34	HG 2/4	Two medium-sized pieces.
35	RC 1/23	Small shaped piece.
36	FZ 16/37	Small shaped piece.
37	GK 10/178	Small shaped piece.
38	EC 1/32	Small irregular fragment.
39	SY 1/1	Medium-sized shaped piece.
40	EC 1/31	Medium-sized irregular fragment.
41	EC 1/33	Joins with **40**.
42	GF 6/22	Medium-sized piece from an ?upper stone.
43	EP 1/1	Small irregular fragment.
44	YN 1/2	Small irregular fragment.
45	WA 1/2	Medium-sized shaped piece from an ?upper stone.
46	EV 2/5	Large fragment with one flat working surface.
47	TJ 1/3	Thick piece with radial tooling lines on a flat working surface.
48	EBA 1/1	Thick irregular piece with ?radial tooling lines on a flat working surface.
49	GF 6/18	Large shaped piece with signs of radial tooling lines on one small flat area.
50	ZF 1/1	Thick piece showing part of the central hole.
51	TX 4/1	Large thick fragment of an upper stone in three joining pieces, showing radial tooling lines on a flat working surface.
52	KA 1/9	Thick piece showing part of the central hole.
53	RY 1/4	Thick piece showing radial tooling lines on a flat working surface.
54	CAA 37/223	Very thick fragment with one flat working surface.
55	ZS 1/2	Medium-sized piece from an ?upper stone.
56	EAQ 1/1	Medium-sized piece with a flat working surface.
57	VR 1/1	Medium-sized piece with a flat working surface.
58	CAB 3/40	Medium-sized shaped piece.
59	MD 1/1	Medium-sized shaped piece.
60	FZ 21/38	Small irregular fragment.
61	CG 1/12	Medium-sized piece with a flat working surface. ?Burnt Millstone Grit.
62	FZ 2/35	Small piece with a flat working surface. ?Burnt Millstone Grit.
63	GF 20/23	Part of a ?rubbing stone. ?Burnt Millstone Grit.
HERTFORDSHIRE PUDDINGSTONE:		
64	GK 6/172	Medium-sized irregular fragment.
65	MM 3/1	Medium-sized piece with one flat working surface. Medium grained and wellcemented sandstone. Tertiary, and possibly from the Reading Beds.
66	KA 1/8	Very thick piece of ?lower stone showing part of the central groove.
67	CAA 37/222	Medium-sized piece with a flat working surface. Greensand.
68	GK 11/179	Small irregular fragment of Greensand. Uncertain origin.

Samian
(Figs 31, 32)

Brenda Dickinson

Summary

The samian from this site divides into two distinct groups. One consists of sherds with fabrics and glazes relatively intact, but with many small and rather battered pieces among them. The other is comprised of a number of complete or substantially complete vessels, some of which are severely eroded.

The total number of vessels represented is not large, and it is clear that the proportion of decorated to plain samian on the site was always extremely low. This is not unusual on relatively unromanised sites in Britain, especially in areas such as the Fenland.

The evidence of the samian suggests that the first activity on the site was pre-Flavian; it is difficult to be more precise than this. There are only a few recognisably pre-Flavian forms, such as Drag. 24 and Ritterling 1, and only one piece is specifically Claudio–Neronian. The rest, dated by fabrics and glazes, seem to be Neronian.

Samian was supplied to the site continuously to the end of the second century or beyond, the greatest quantities being used in the Hadrianic and, particularly, Antonine periods.

The first-century ware is all from La Graufesenque. Most of the central Gaulish ware, with the exception of the Trajanic material and a few Hadrianic–Antonine pieces, comes from Lezoux. The rest is from Les Martres-de-Veyre. The later East Gaulish ware is mostly from Rheinzabern, with perhaps a few Trier vessels and one piece which may be Argonne ware and Antonine.

According to the number of individually-identified vessels, the collection divides thus: South Gaulish ware 30% (including two second-century Montans pieces); Trajanic and Trajanic/Hadrianic ware from Les Martres-de-Veyre 8%; Antonine ware from Les Martres 2%; Lezoux 63%; East Gaulish 4%. The proportions of East Gaulish and early Les Martres ware are rather lower than usual for Britain as a whole.

Worthy of note are two pieces of second-century Montans ware. This was exported to Britain in small quantities in the period c.110–145, and tends to be found mainly around London, in the West Midlands, and in the vicinity of the Antonine Wall in Scotland. The two vessels on this site were presumably distributed from London.

Although most of the East Gaulish ware belongs to the end of the second century or later, there is a dish from Blickweiler which will not be later than the middle of the second century. Why it should be on the site at all is not clear, since Blickweiler ware scarcely features in Britain. One other East Gaulish piece may be from an Argonne factory, and is almost certainly Antonine.

A number of sherds have fabrics and glazes matching Hadrianic–Antonine samian from Les Martres-de-Veyre, of the kind produced by Suobnus for plain ware and Cettus for decorated ware. Plain samian of this date from Les Martres is not particularly common in Britain, so it is possible that all the pots were part of a single consignment.

The more complete vessels from the site do not form a homogeneous group, but range in date from the pre-Flavian to the Antonine period. Three, from the first-century Burial GAX, have had their surfaces completely removed by chemical or mechanical erosion. The vessels from Burials GAH, GAK, GAI, GAM, GAQ, GAS, GAW, which are substantially complete, are in a similar state. Another, from a second-century burial, is in better condition, but shows some signs of erosion.

The vessels in the early to mid-Antonine group from the well [CAB 11] have not been subject to erosion, but all were broken in antiquity, and all their footrings show some signs of wear, and therefore must have been buried in different soil conditions from GAX and GBA. The question of whether these vessels, like the coarse wares found with them, were deposited whole in the well, were broken by the pressure of the filling, or were dumped after accidental damage while in use, is considered in more detail by Waugh (*Roman Coarse Pottery*).

Catalogue

Decorated ware

1   Form 30, SG. The ring-tongued ovolo is on two bowls of this form in an early-Flavian context at York, but is almost certainly pre-Flavian in origin. The plant between the arcades occurs on Form 29s with internal stamps of potters such as Felix i (Knorr 1919, *Taf*.32, 7), Pass(i)enus and Rufinus iii. c.55–70.
    DP 1: *fill of pit/posthole.*

2   Form 29, SG. The lower zone includes one or more zones, the one below the cordon consisting of straight gadroons. c.55–80.
    TA 2: *lining of pond.*

3   Form 37, CG. Probably by Sacer ii or an associate, with a vine scroll and spindle tendril. c.125–145.
    TB 1: *fill of pit/hollow.*

4   Form 37, CG. A panelled bowl, with a dolphin to right (O.2385?). Part of a mould signature

survives, inscribed upside-down below the decoration before firing. A striated spindle was used by both Cassius i and X-5; cf a signed Cassius bowl from Strasbourg (Stanfield and Simpson 1990, pl. 174.5). However, the initial letter of the signature seems to be a G rather than a C and, in any case, Cassius is not known to have placed his signatures upside-down. No other candidate springs to mind, but the date of the bowl is not in doubt. c.130–150.
KP 1: *stone spread*.

5   Form 37, CG. The ovolo (Rogers B144) was used at Lezoux by members of a group of potters which included Cerialis ii and Cinnamus ii. c.135–170.
ES 3: *fill of pit*.

6   Form 37, CG. The T-tongued ovolo (Rogers B206) and a wavy line are on a signed bowl of Mercator ii from Arbury Road, Cambridge (Stanfield and Simpson 1958/90, Fig. 51.1), and on one in the style of Paullus iv from Lezoux (*ibid*, Fig. 50). Both these bowls are closer to the Cerialis ii – Cinnamus ii style than to that of the potters normally associated with the ovolo, such as Quintilianus i and Paternus v. The vine leaf in both parts of the scroll (Rogers H51) and the bird (D.1038 = O.2315) were also used by Cinnamus and some of his associates. c.135–170.
AAJ 2: *soil spread*.

7   Form 37, CG. A small bowl, complete (in pieces) and with a slightly worn footring. The ovolo (Rogers B107), astragaloid borders and general layout are typical of Albucius ii. He also regularly used the Venus (D.204 = O.338), bird (D.1011 = O.2324), leaf (Rogers J146) and column (Rogers P3, partly impressed). However, the warriors (D.120 = O.191 and a larger version of D.116 = O.189) are not known for him. The other figure type, a Cupid, is not recorded by Déchelette or Oswald, but is on a stamped Albucius bowl from Wymyslowo, Poland (Stanfield and Simpson 1990, pl. 172.5), which has a rim-stamp of Osbimanus. c.150–180.
CAB 11/5: *Area 1, fill of well*.

8   Form 37, CG. Two joining fragments of a panelled bowl, with a single festoon containing a hare (O.2057A?) between partly-impressed leaves (Rogers J146). All the details are on a bowl from Corbridge in the style of Albucius ii (Stanfield and Simpson 1958/90, pl. 122.25). c.150–180.
QX 1: *fill of gully*.

9   Form 37, CG. Ovolo (Rogers B147) and zig-zag border (Rogers A26) used at Lezoux by Servus iv (Stanfield and Simpson's 'Servus 2'). c.160–200.
JK 1: *fill of pit*.

10   Form 37, EG. A stamped mould of Primiti(v)us from Rheinzabern (Ricken 1948, *Taf*. 196.6F) has the same layout, with the same boxer (Ricken-Fischer 1963, M191c), medallions and candelabrum (*ibid*, O160b?), with acanthus (*ibid*, P145) attached, upside-down. A hare (*ibid*, T165) is on a stamped Form 30 mould (Ricken 1948, *Taf*. 190.6F). c.180–240.
FZ 5: *fill of gully*.

11   Form 37, EG. The decoration is perhaps similar to that of **10**, with the same medallion and acanthus, but apparently from a different bowl. c. 180–240.
TJ 3: *gully of Building ABQ*.

Potters' stamps

(a) and (b) indicate:
(a) a stamp attested at the pottery in question.
(b) potter, but not the particular stamp, attested at the pottery in question.
Ligatured letters are underlined.

1   Form 33, stamped [CRAC]VNA·F: Cracuna of Lezoux (a), Die 2a. This occurs at forts on Hadrian's Wall and in Antonine Scotland. It is also in a pit of the 150s at Alcester (Hartley, Pengelly and Dickinson 1994, 109, S131), and in period IIB at Verulamium (before 140; Hartley 1972, S69). c.130–160.
KJ 1/1: *soil spread*.

2   Form 33, stamped DVꟼPIVSF: Duppius of Lezoux (b), Die 1b. A stamp noted in period IID (post-150) at Verulamium (Hartley 1972, S115), and in a pit of the 150s at Alcester (Hartley, Pengelly and Dickinson 1994, 109, S135–6). It was used on Forms 27 and 80. c.150–180.
DAC 1/3: *unstratified*.

3   Form 18/31, grooved footring, stamped [G]ABRILLI·M: Gabrillus i of Central Gaul, Die 2b (Holwerda 1923, *Afb*.68.74). The pale fabric and brownish glaze are reminiscent of the Hadrianic–Antonine range at Lezoux. Seven of the twelve examples noted so far come from Rhineland forts, and all are on either Forms 18/31, 18/31R or 27. The form of this dish suggests early to mid-Antonine date.
CAB 13/49: *fill of well shaft*.

4   Form 31, stamped [GEM]INI·: Geminus vi of Lezoux (b), Die 7a. This stamp is known only on Forms 31, 33 and 38, but M.F-Geminus, who was probably the same man, stamped his collars of the late Antonine mortarium, Form 45. c.160–200.
CAB 2/50: *upper fill of well*.

5   Dish (Form 15/17 or 18, etc), stamped MACCARVSF: Maccarus of La Graufesenque (a), Die 30a. Maccarus began work under Tiberius, but this is one of his latest stamps. There are three examples from the Burghöfe Geschirrdepot of AD 69 (Ulbert 1959, no. 72), and it also occurs at the Nijmegen fortress. He can scarcely have been at work in the Flavian period, however. c.AD 50–65.
EAA/37: *fill of feature*.

6   Form 27 g, stamped OFMOE: Modestus i of La Graufesenque (b), Die 8a. One of the potter's later stamps, featuring several times in Flavian contexts and apparently not used on any pre-Flavian forms. c.AD 60–70.
EAA/40: *fill of feature*.

7   Form 18/31, stamped PATE[RCLVSF]: Paterclus ii of Les Martres-de-Veyre (a), Die 12a (Terrisse 1968, pl. LIII). Stamps from this die, used on dishes, and from a broken version, used on cups, occur in the London Second Fire groups. The associated forms are typically Trajanic. c.100–120.
MM 4: *fill of ditch*.

8   Form 33, stamped REBVRRIOF: Reburrus ii of Lezoux (a), Die 4 m. Complete, in large pieces, with shallow, triangular footring, slightly worn. The stamp occurs in a mid-Antonine group at Lezoux and was used on a wide range of forms including 15/31, 18/31, 27, 38 and 79. c.150–170.
CAB 11/46: *fill of well shaft*.

9   Form 31, stamped R[E]DITI·M: Reditus of Lezoux (a), Die 3a (Vanderhoeven 1975, 589). Almost complete, in pieces, with slightly worn footring. The stamp is known from Camelon, and was used on Forms 18/31 and 18/31R. Stamps from other dies occur in the Rhineland, where Lezoux ware is scarce after c.150. His range will be c.135–160, in view of a stamp from the Saalburg Erdkastell (before 139), but this piece is likely to be c.140–160.
CAB 11/43: *fill of well shaft.*

10 Form 33, Central Gaulish, complete with worn footring. The stamp, RVFVS·F◄, belongs to Rufus iv, who almost certainly worked at Lezoux. This, his only stamp, occurs on Form 18/31, and at Corbridge. Early Antonine.
CAB 11/39: *fill of well shaft.*

11 Form 31, slightly worn footring, substantially complete, stamped SECVNDVS·F: Secundus v of Lezoux (a), Die 4a. The die for this stamp was used on both plain and decorated samian, the latter connected stylistically with Cinnamus ii. The plain forms include 18/31 and 18/31R, and the stamp occurs in Antonine I at Birrens (Wild 1975, 143.5), and in a pit of c.150–160 at Alcester (Hartley, Pengelly and Dickinson 1994, 110, S154). This particular dish is typologically early Antonine, and is unlikely to be much later than 150.
CAB 11/45: *fill of well shaft.*

12 Form 27, stamped SEVERI·🐾: Severus iv of Central Gaul, Die 1a. No other examples of this stamp have been noted. The orangy fabric and glaze are reminiscent of the Hadrianic–Antonine wares of Les Martres-de-Veyre, where similar palm branches were used. c.130–160.
EAA 2: *fill of feature.*

13 Form 31, about half-complete and with slightly worn footring, stamped [TITV]S·FEC+: Titus ii of Lezoux (b), Die 10a (Juhász 1935, no. 318). Titus's stamps occur at Mumrills, in a pit of the 150s at Alcester, and in a group of burnt samian of the 170s from Tác (Hungary). His forms include 31R, 38 and, with this particular stamp, 18/31 and 18/31R. c.150–170.
CAB 11/48: *fill of well shaft.*

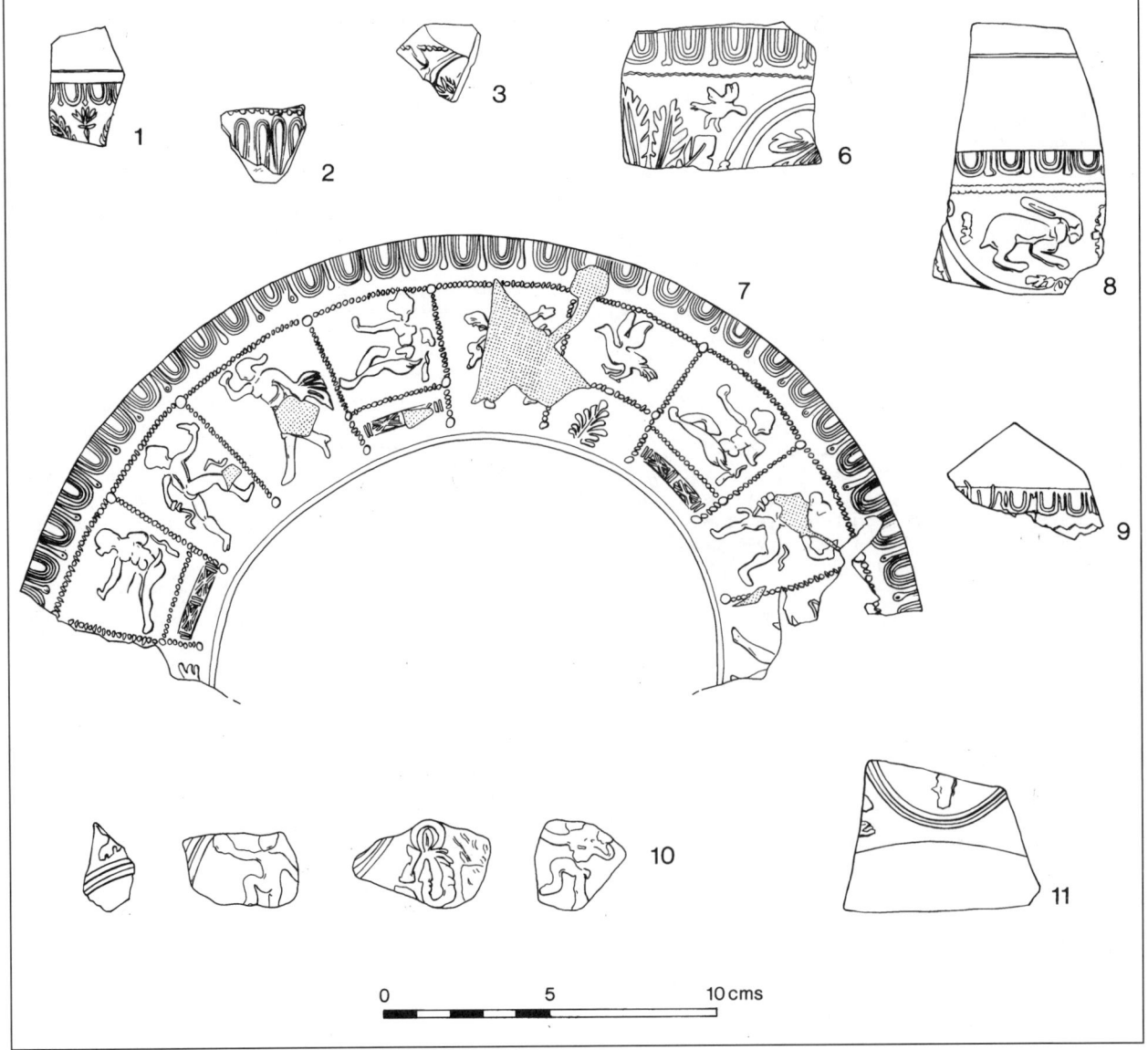

Figure 31   Decorated samian (scale 1:2).

14 Form 18/31R, stamped ITOCCAFECIT/: Tocca of Blickweiler (a), Die 9a (Knorr and Sprater 1927, 110, 28e). An itinerant potter of this name worked in East Gaul, but there is no evidence that this die was used anywhere but Blickweiler. The stamp occurs at the Saalburg Erdkastell, before 139. Blickweiler ware is not common in Britain: only two stamps from this die have been noted here, from London and Colchester. c.125–150.
CAB 11/51: *fill of well shaft.*

15 Form 31 or 31R, stamped [VITLL]I⌒K in guidelines: Vitalis ix of East Gaul, Die 2a. It is not clear where this potter worked. There are four examples of this stamp from the Trier kilns, but it has also been noted at Rheinzabern (Ludowici 1905, 85, 505). The distribution does not help and there is not much dating evidence, but one stamp from Niederbieber should belong to the late second or first half of the third century.
XY 1/1: *stone spread.*

16 Form 27(g?), stamped IVII or IILI, South Gaulish. Neronian or early Flavian.
GAX 1: *Cremation burial.*

17 Form 18/31, South Gaulish, from the second-century kilns at Montans. The surviving letters of this stamp, ...C...O, suggest the work of Felicio iii. c.115–145.
GAS 1: *Cremation burial.*

18 Form 18/31, Central Gaulish, probably stamped SEX[.. Antonine.
RS 1: *fill of depression.*

19 Form 31, Central Gaulish. The stamp in the centre of the base seems to be a leaf, in low relief. Hadrianic–Antonine.
GX 1: *unstratified.*

20 Form 33, stamped S[.. or ..]S, Central Gaulish. Antonine.
JK: *fill of pit.*

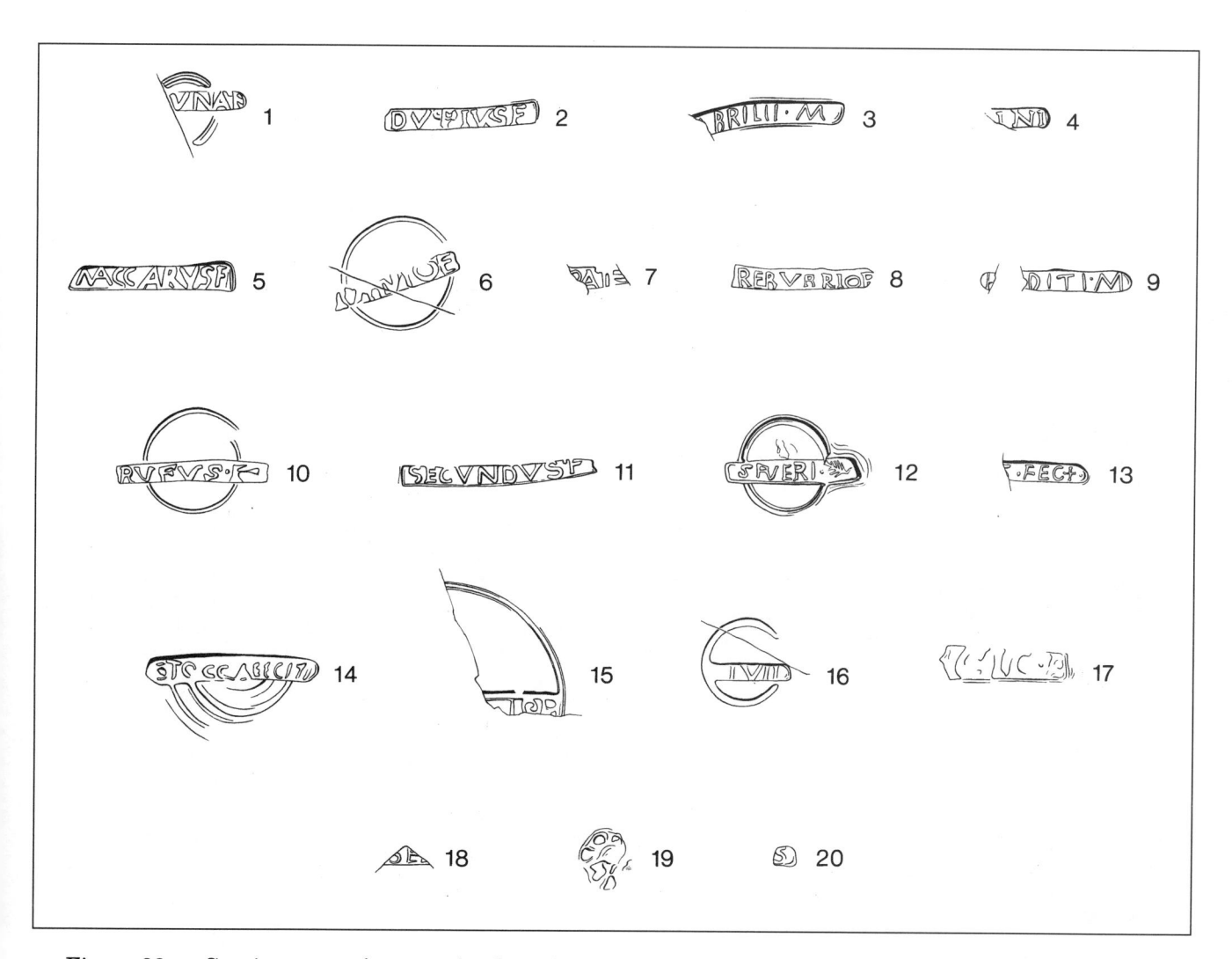

Figure 32   Samian potters' stamps (scale 1:1).

Roman Coarse Pottery
Karen Waugh

Introduction

The site was badly plough-damaged, and the ground surface and upper layers of many features had been destroyed, so that useful stratigraphy only survived in a few deep features and areas which often had no direct stratigraphical relationship. With few lengthy stratigraphical sequences surviving, the elucidation of the site development rested to a large degree on finds dating.

The objectives of the pottery analysis programme were;

a) to provide a date range for activity on the site, and
b) to explain the chronological make-up and build-up of deposits within features from a ceramic point of view.

In the *Dating Evidence* sections within the excavation report a list of all fabrics occurring within each feature is given with summaries of the dating evidence from the specialist coin and samian reports. This is referenced to the *Catalogue* (below), where the reader will find a brief description of the context producing the material, or the catalogue number of an illustrated parallel (in brackets, indicated by an asterisk). In the few instances where the form is not included in the catalogue, a published parallel is cited.

Table 8 sets out the site and ceramic phase to which the pottery assemblage from each feature belongs. For some features the nature of the pottery, either in condition or amount, means that a precise date cannot be given. In these cases, the phase in the table offers a possible *terminus post quem* for ceramic deposition. All stratigraphically phased features have been included in Table 8 and the *Discussion*. Table 8 and the *Catalogue* also include other features that remain unphased stratigraphically, but whose ceramic deposits are datable.

The site assemblage, therefore, was examined:

1) to assist in the clarification of the site's structural history and development;
2) to assess by looking at patterns of supply and usage of pottery on the site through time, something of its socio-economic status;
3) to assess the cemetery pottery in terms of its dating potential and ritual significance.

Methodology

The initial recording of the pottery was by context. Pro-forma sheets were used to record the fabric, sherd count, weight (in grammes), general class of vessel (flagon, jar, bowl, dish etc., based on Millett 1979), extent (presence of rim, base, sherd, handle etc), condition, decoration, dimensions and 'estimated vessel equivalence' of the rim (hereafter referred to as R.EVE: Orton 1975). Base EVE for bases was also recorded, but not used in any further calculations.

An estimated date range, based on the pot types present, was given for each context. Feature codes and ceramic phase information was also added to the sheet. The pottery was divided into five ceramic phases (Table 5). The fifth ceramic phase was again subdivided into three as follows:

5.1: assemblages of probable early to mid fourth-century date.
5.2: at least 350/360, possibly as late as 400+, due to the relatively abundant presence of later fabrics, *ie* shell-tempered wares, Oxfordshire colour-coat and later Hadham wares.
5: of fourth-century date, but the small size of the assemblage does not allow for greater precision.

TABLE 5: Ceramic phases and their dates.

Ceramic phase	Date range	Structural period
–	undiagnostic	uncertain
1	c.55/60–75/80	III
2	c.80–120/130	III
3	c.130–180/200	IV
4	c.200–260/275	V
5.1	c.275/300–350	V
5.2	c.350–400+	V
5	c.300–400+	V

The information formed the basis of a computerised database to enable computerised calculation of the results. The paper archive and computer database are retained in the site archive, together with a fabric series.

As many of the vessel forms were duplicated at Verulamium (Wilson 1972, 1983, 1984) and on other sites in the region, such as Baldock (Rigby 1986), no site form typology was devised. However, one example at least of each diagnostic form is illustrated in the catalogue, as far as possible.

Because of their small size and the high level of abrasion quite a large percentage of the sherds could not be classified beyond general "flagon, jar, bowl" categories. During processing a five-point alphabetical scale, set out below, was used to help classify the condition of each pottery assemblage:

A Complete or almost complete pots that were still functional at the time of their discard or deposition.

B Large sherds, still in good condition, with fresh or clean breaks; usually with profiles or at least a considerable proportion of the vessel remaining.

C Moderately-sized sherds still in fairly good condition, with clean breaks and often with joins; diagnostic sherds, *ie* rim fragments, are often present in these assemblages.

D A moderate to large quantity of small, mostly abraded sherds, showing no obvious joins. Rim sherds may remain, but on the whole sherds are rarely diagnostic. These groups often proved to be residual or redeposited, *ie* formed by the process of secondary dumping, or comprising deposits disturbed by ploughing.

E A small quantity of usually very abraded and often 'battered' sherds, similar to D. These sherds are undiagnostic and, in general, of no help in dating the context.

Such a classification proved particularly useful when determining the factors controlling the nature and make-up of a deposit (Table 8).

All the pottery assemblages from stratified contexts on the site were quantified to give an overall picture of total fabric and form occurrence across the site and in the cemetery. In total, 33,559 sherds were processed, weighing 327.634 kg, with a R.EVE of 323.53.

The Fabrics

The fine ware and coarse pottery was divided macroscopically into sixty fabric groups (excluding the samian and the small amount of residual Iron Age flint-tempered sherds). Reference has been made to publications were fabric descriptions are already defined; the remainder of the fabrics are described in detail below. The basic criteria for classification was based on the appearance of the clay matrix and the size frequency and type of inclusions present as well as the surface texture. In some cases, sherds were examined under a ×20 microscope. Colour distinction was also considered; the Munsell soil colour chart was used to give an approximate identification. Table 7 shows the total amount of each fabric from the site.

Fabric Descriptions

All illustrated vessels are listed by their catalogue number below each fabric description. Percentages quoted in each section refer to the fabric weight unless otherwise stated.

GLAZED WARES

Fabric 1. *Romano-British glazed ware (not illustrated)*

Fabric description and discussion: Arthur 1978, 293–355. Only one vessel was represented on the site. This appears to belong to the 'south-east English group' of Romano-British lead-glazed ware, as defined by Arthur (*ibid*, 298–300), which may have been produced at Staines, on the river Thames between *c*.AD 70/80 and the early Hadrianic period. All the sherds were recovered from the backfill of EAA which is essentially of Antonine date; therefore, the beaker may be either slightly residual in context, or have survived unbroken until this period.

Hairpin Beaker: 144.

COLOUR-COATED WARES

Fabric 2. *Rhenish ware: Central Gaulish black colour-coated ware (not illustrated)*

Fabric description: Greene 1972, 4–5; 1978, 18. Often known as 'black samian'. Three fairly abraded fragments from a hemispherical cup were recovered from the fourth-century well deposit (not illustrated). The vessel is obviously residual here as Greene (1978) dates the ware to *c*.150–200. See Greene 1978, Fig. 2.3, no. 7, for a similar vessel; the example from Chells has a narrow band of rouletting above the girth groove.

Fabric 3. *South Gaulish colour-coated ware (not illustrated)*

Fabric description: Greene 1978, 16. This ware has only been recognised in one context (EAJ 1) Three fragments with traces of barbotine hairpin decoration, probably from a cup, were recovered.

Fabric 4. *North Gaulish colour-coated ware*

Fabric description: Anderson 1980, 33–34, Fabric 2. Again, only a few sherds, fifteen in all, were recovered from the site. All sherds are a hard, buff-white ware, with roughcast decoration and a matt, black colour-coat, probably all from the same or similar vessel/s. The date range for such vessels on civilian sites, according to Anderson, is *c*. 80–135/140 or slightly later.

Cornice-rim beaker: 145.

Fabric 5. *Nene Valley colour-coated wares*

Fabric description: Anderson 1980, 38; Howe *et al* 1981, 9. A few fragments from beakers do occur already in Antonine deposits on Chells (*eg* Hunt Cup in TB; cat.no. 208), but otherwise the ware does not appear in any quantity until the late third to fourth centuries. Over 95% of the fabric occurs in fourth-century contexts, and it is the commonest fine ware on the site in the late fourth-century (Ceramic Phase 5.2), although it accounts for only 4% by weight of the total fourth-century assemblage. The majority of the fragments are from the later products of the industry, *eg* flanged bowls, dishes, 'Castor box' lids and white slip-trailed or barbotine-decorated beakers. The sherds have been divided according to the paste colour, as follows:

Fabric 5A: this is the more typical fabric which has an off-white to yellow/white paste and a dark brown to black matt colour-coat.

Disc-mouthed flagon: 272.
Necked jars: 273, 333.
Plain-rimmed beaker: 29.
?Bag beaker: 30.
Everted-rim beaker: 274.
Straight-sided dishes: 277, 278, 334.
Bead-rim, shallow bowl: 31.
Incipient-flanged bowl: 279.
Flanged bowl: 335.

Fabric 5B: the paste ranges from a pinkish-orange red or dark orange-red (2.5YR 5/8–6/8), to a pale orange due to the amount of red ironstone present in the clay. Dark brown to black colour-coat, usually matt but can be quite lustrous.

Pentice-moulded beaker: 27.
Decorated and 'Hunt cup' beakers: 28, 208.
Bead-rim beaker: 200.
Straight-sided dish: 276.
Flanged bowl: 280.
'Castor box' lid: 231.

Fabric 5C: a pale pinkish-white paste, again due to a sparse red ironstone content, and an orangey colour-coat. The fabric has quite a chalky feel; the softness is probably due to the effects of adverse soil conditions.

Hemispherical bowl: 32.

Fabric 6: *Misc. roughcast ware (not illustrated)*

Possibly of Colchester origin? The sherds are from beakers, but are very small, abraded and hard to identify. Only two sherds were recovered from the site, from fourth-century contexts, although an earlier, probably Antonine, date is likely for their manufacture. A hard fine fabric with no visible inclusions; dark reddish-brown core (2.5YR 3/4 – 3/6) and dark grey margins (2.5YR 3/0), with a black, matt, colour-coat over fine, roughcast decoration.

Fabric 7: *Misc. hard-fired colour-coated ware*

Only one small bowl, in good condition, found on the site. The fabric is extremely hard-fired or possibly over-fired. It may well be a late variant of Nene Valley ware, otherwise origin unknown. A very hard red-orange paste (2.5YR 5/8) with no visible inclusions and with a lustrous dark brown colour-coat.

Small bowl: 251.

Fabric 8. *Oxfordshire red colour-coated ware*

Fabric description: Young 1977, 123. Vessels in this ware, unless intrusive, only make an appearance in the latest deposits on Chells (small amounts in Ceramic phase 5.1, but the majority in 5.2). The disruption of the industry's earlier markets in central and southern Britain (Fulford 1979, 125–6) may well have been a reason for its expansion into the Hertfordshire/Essex region after the mid-fourth century. Only a few examples of these late products have been found on Chells.

It seems likely that, in the case of North and East Hertfordshire at least, the Oxfordshire industry could never compete in a market virtually monopolised by the local Hadham industry (Fabrics 9 and 39). The ratio of Hadham red ware to Oxfordshire colour-coat on the site is 11:1 by R.EVE (13:1 by weight; 22:1 by sherd count).

Shallow bowls with bead-rim: 34, 267.
Deep-flanged bowl: 35, 347.
Stamped bowl: 336.
Other bowls: 269, 281, 345, 346.

Fabric 9. *Hadham oxidised red ware*

Fabric description Harden and Green 1978, 170 and 174. Much useful advice on identifying this ware (see also Fabrics 12, 16, 39, 40) and helpful discussion on the development and importance of the industry was given by Chris Going. His corpus of the industry's products and kiln material from Bromley Hall Farm, which includes all the forms occurring on Chells, was constantly referred to during the processing of the site assemblage. However, since it is still unpublished, it has not been quoted in this report.

The oxidised fabric can be dark reddish brown (*c.*5YR 5/6) changing to a bright orange. The best quality examples are hard, orange to orange-red (2.5YR 5/8 – 5YR 6/8) with a burnished colour-coat. Vessels with horizontal brown streaks on the external surfaces are fairly common in the later deposits on Chells. Some sherds do appear in second to third-century contexts, but the vast majority of the fabric (86%) occurs in late fourth-century deposits. Hadham red wares represent 20% of the total fourth-century assemblage on the site. Not illustrated are the fragments of sieve-like vessels found in most contexts dating to Ceramic phase 5.2.

Bottle or flagon: 252.
Two-handled flagon: 209.
Face flagons: 36, 258, 259.
Other flagons: 265, 285, 337.
Frilled-rim jars: 37, 39, 40.
Pedestal base: 38.
Narrow-necked jar: 37.
Necked jars: 41, 228, 290–292.
S-profile jars: 253, 270, 287, 288.
Other jars: 232, 266, 289, 327.
Straight-sided dish: 338.
Dish with moulded rim: 293, 294.
Deep-flanged bowl: 54.
Other bowls: 49, 50, 51, 295, 297.
Mortarium: 339.

Fabric 10. *?Hadham red ware*

This fabric occurs infrequently and only in the latest contexts on Chells (Ceramic phase 5.2). The forms have been identified separately from Fabric 9, since they are not present within the corpus (see reference to Going, above). However, the fabric is in many instances indistinguishable from abraded fragments of Fabric 9, and ought to perhaps be seen as a slightly coarser variant. For this reason, the calculations above for Fabric 9 also include those for Fabric 10. It seems likely that these forms may be late products of the Hadham industry.

Bowls: 311, 312, 328.

MICA-DUSTED WARES

Fabric 11. *Local mica-dusted ware*

Fabric description and discussion: Marsh 1978, 122–3. Only four fragments were recovered from the site; all are produced in the smoother version of the fabric that occurs in London.

Beaker: 207.

WHITE-SLIPPED RED WARES

Fabric 12. *Hadham white slipped ware*

Fabric description and discussion: Going 1987, 5.14. One or two ?intrusive fragments occur in late first or early second-century contexts, and a few ?redeposited sherds have been identified in fourth-century contexts. Most of the sherds occur in Antonine deposits (Ceramic phase 3; 60%), tailing off in the third century (Ceramic phase 4)

Ring-necked flagon: 18
Hemispherical bowl: 157.
Mortarium: 299.

Fabric 13. *Misc. white- or cream-slipped red wares*

Only a few sherds or vessel fragments on the site are assigned to this category. The fabrics probably derive from several sources; judging from the majority of material on the site, they are either local or regional products.

Flagon or tettine: 19.
Tazza: 234.

MISCELLANEOUS SLIPPED RED WARES

Fabric 14. *Fine, slipped red ware (not illustrated)*

Only two small undiagnostic sherds have been recovered from the site; one from a second-century and the other from a late third to fourth-century context (Ceramic phases 3 and 5.1 respectively). The fabric is easily distinguishable from the rest of the red wares since it is a very hard-fired, smooth, dark orangey-red ware (10R 5/8–2.5YR 5/8), slightly micaceous, but otherwise with no visible inclusions. The thin dark red–orange slip on the exterior surface appears slightly marbled and patchy.

RED WARES

Fabric 15. *Red ware with external grey slip:?Hadham origin*

The fabric occurs from the second century (Ceramic phase 3) onwards. It appears to be visually identical to Hadham red ware, Fabric 9 (5YR 6/4), except for very sparse, tiny fragments of buff-coloured grog-tempering. Sherds always have a thin dark grey matt slip on exterior (c. 5Y 4/1). This surface treatment is probably another variant of the Hadham industry (like the brown streaks; see Fabric 9).

S-profile jar: 271.

Fabric 16. *Grit-tempered red ware: ?Hadham origin*

The clay matrix of this fabric is identical to Fabric 9, but includes abundant rounded and sub-angular rose-coloured and translucent quartz, especially on the surfaces. This is not a common fabric, represented only by small jars and bowls occurring primarily in post-mid fourth-century assemblages (88% in Ceramic phase 5.2).

S-profile jars: 256, 308–310.
Flanged bowl: 257.

Fabric 17. *Misc. fine red ware*

This category is a grouping together of all remaining red-orange fabrics with either sparse fine sand or no visible tempering, which are of unidentified but most likely local or regional origin.

S-profile jar: 235.
Hemispherical bowl: 136.

Fabric 18. *Oxidised 'gritty' ware*

A sandy fabric of pale buff-orange colour (5YR 6/8 = core, 10YR 7/4 = surfaces). The surfaces are extremely abrasive or rough, due to the presence of abundant sub-angular and round quartz, $c.0.5$–1.5 mm in diameter, throughout the matrix. Red ironstone frags $c.2.0$–2.5 mm in diameter are also present. So few sherds recovered (Table 7) make it difficult to date. The fabric occurs in the second century (Ceramic phase 3) and may be residual in fourth-century contexts. A local origin is likely.

Jar or bowl: 139.
Reeded-rim bowl: 213.

Fabric 19. *Misc. sandy red wares*

This category is distinct from Fabric 17 in that it groups together all abrasive oxidised red wares with abundant sand and quartz-tempering (0.25–1.5 mm white and brown to rose opaque quartz). Some sherds contain sparse fragments of black iron oxide. Examples of these fabrics seem to occur throughout the sequence at Chells.

Ring-necked flagon: 22.
S-profile jars: 86, 307.
Necked jar: 87.
Flanged bowl: 88.

WHITE WARES

Fabric 20. *Verulamium region wares*

Fabric description: Tyers 1983, 2. The majority of the assemblage could be products of the

Brockley Hill industry, where there is apparently no evidence for pottery production after c.160 (Castle 1973). At Chells the fabric occurs sporadically from c.60, reaching a peak in Ceramic phase 3 (71%, although this still constitutes a small amount; Table 12) but continuing to occur, mostly residually, until the late fourth century. Reduced wares occur only as residual sherds. The total amount of this fabric group on the site is very small, only c.3% (Table 7), suggesting that the industry, whilst extremely well-represented in the south of the county and especially on sites in London, had very little impact on the markets controlling rural North Hertfordshire.

The colour variations of the VR wares appear to be without chronological significance. For processing therefore, distinctions were only made between the paler fabrics and the reduced grey wares;

Fabric 20A. white/buff – pinkish orange granular fabric:

Two-handled flagons: 109, 147.
Disc-mouthed flagon: 146.
Necked jars: 148, 149.
Neckless, round-bodied jar: 150.
Reeded-rim bowls: 152, 212.
Other bowls: 151, 219.
Lid: 156.
Mortaria: 154, 155.

Fabric 20B. Reduced grey ware:

It sometimes proved difficult to determine whether the fabric was not in fact an over-fired example of 20A, rather than genuine reduced grey ware.

Carinated, reeded-rim bowl: 153.

Fabric 21. Oxfordshire white ware

Fabric description: Young 1977,56. Fifty fragments were recovered from the site; all are from mortaria. One or two sherds occur in third or late third to fourth-century contexts; the majority of sherds, however, occur in assemblages deposited after 350 (93%).

Mortaria: 283, 284.

Fabric 22. Nene Valley 'self-coloured' ware

Fabric description: Howe et al 1981, 10. The fabric occurs infrequently from the mid to late third century onwards. The majority of the sherds (89%) are only present in post-350 deposits.

Mortaria: 33, 331, 332.

Fabric 23. Gallo-Belgic white ware (not illustrated)

A very fine hard white ware with no visible inclusions. Only four very abraded sherds of this fabric have been found on the site.

Fabric 24. 'Eggshell' ware (not illustrated)

Fabric description: Marsh 1978, 129. Found only in the cemetery; thirty-three sherds, from the same beaker, were recovered from Grave GBA (Table 10).

Fabric 25. Fine, smooth, buff-white wares

A fine, iron-free, buff-white fabric (10YR 8/2), with no obvious inclusions, probably of regional origin. Diagnostic sherds are from flagons, most notably the complete example from the Antonine well deposit (CAB 10).

Flagon: 21.

Fabric 26. Misc. fine white wares (not illustrated)

Found only in the cemetery (Table 10). Similar to OXIDC iron-free clay very fine quartzite sand fabric. Sparse red iron oxide inclusions and occasional tiny black specks. The sherds, which appear to come from flagons, date to Ceramic phase 3 in the burials.

BUFF WARES

Fabric 27. Colchester buff ware (not illustrated)

Fabric description: Hull 1963, 107–8. Only one worn fragment of a ?wall-sided mortarium was recovered, from a context dated to the mid to late second century.

Fabric 28. Oxfordshire parchment ware

Fabric description: Young 1977, 81. Only fourteen sherds were found on the site. Rim fragments from only one vessel were recovered. The remaining sherds were clearly from the same or a similar vessel, with internal and external red-painted decoration. All the sherds are from post-350 deposits.

Wall-sided bowl: 282.

Fabric 29. Verulamium Region fine ware (not illustrated)

Fabric description: Greene 1978, 109–18. Only one small sherd identified on the site, representing the distinctive pale buff-pink ring-and-dot beaker with white barbotine rings; from a late Flavian context.

Fabric 30. Fine granular ware: ?Verulamium region

A pale buff-yellow ware (10YR 8/3–7/3) which is probably a product of the Verulamium region industry but is much finer, with smoother surfaces compared with Fabric 20 above. Flagon sherds occur sporadically between c.AD 70–160/180 on the site.

Ring-necked flagon: 23.

Fabric 31. Fine buff-pink ware

A fine hard-fired fabric appearing in Ceramic phase 3 contexts, with a buff-pale yellow exterior

(10YR 8/3) and a pinkish interior and core (7.5YR 8/4). The only inclusions are sparse quartzite up to 3 mm in diameter, and sparse dark red iron oxide up to 2 mm in diameter.

Ring-necked flagon: 20.
Bowl: 203.

Fabric 32. *Butt beaker fabric*

Fabric description and discussion: Rigby 1986, 261.5. At Baldock this type of vessel is common in Claudian and Flavian contexts. The single sherd from Chells is in a fourth-century deposit and is therefore residual.

Butt beaker: 202.

EARLY ROMAN SANDY WARES

Fabric 33. *Early sandy wares*

A dark grey-black fabric (2.5Y 3/0–2/0) with coarse abundant quartz sand-tempering and sparse grit inclusions up to 0.5 mm in diameter. Surfaces are usually smoothed or lightly burnished. 15% of sherds come from unphased features, but the majority (57%) date from the mid first to early second century (Ceramic phases 1 and 2). Hereafter, the fabric appears in small quantities in each phase but is residual, certainly after the early to mid second century.

Bead-rim jar: 124.
Lid: 96.

Fabric 34. *Early sand- and grog-tempered wares*

These vessels mark the post-Conquest continuance of late Iron Age 'Belgic' traditions. Many of the forms find parallels on other late Iron Age and early Roman sites in Hertfordshire (see *Catalogue* and Thompson 1982). Most of the vessels are wheel-finished, if initially handmade. The dark grey to ochre-brown fabric (7.5YR 3/0–10YR 3/1–10YR 3/3) is tempered with moderate to abundant amounts of ill-sorted white and opaque quartzite, from <0.5–1.0 mm in diameter; sparse brown grog inclusions measure <2 mm in diameter. The fabric occurs predominantly in mid first to early second-century contexts (Ceramic periods 1 and 2; 70%). Its occurrence declines rapidly thereafter, with only 10% of sherds occurring in Ceramic phase 3, by which time the fabric has been gradually replaced by more Romanised grey wares.

Bead-rim jars: 97, 105, 128, 132.
Narrow-necked jar: 122.
Necked jars: 104, 112, 119, 122, 123, 130, 131, 133, 134, 141.
Other jars: 129, 250.

GREY WARES

Fabric 35. *Romanising grey ware*

Fabric description and discussion: Going 1987, 9.45. This fabric has been identified at Chells by Chris Going. Only a relatively small number of sherds have been recovered, the majority from Ceramic phase 1 (56% by sherd count, 19% by weight, 86% by R.EVE).

Necked jar: 110.

Fabric 36. *Fine grey ware (not illustrated)*

A hard-fired, fine, micaceous grey ware (10YR 6/2–5/2–7.5YR 4/0). Only 38 sherds are known from Chells, occurring infrequently in late first to mid/late second-century contexts. 29% of the sherds are residual, from redeposited mid fourth-century deposits.

Fabric 37. *Misc. sandy grey wares*

This category combines fabrics derived from various sources, including all wares presumably of local origin that do not fit in the other groups. Inclusions vary slightly in size and frequency, but the fabrics are generally quite fine and smooth-surfaced, varying from a brownish-grey to blue-grey. After Hadham ware (Fabric 39) this is the largest category of grey ware on the site. Except for Ceramic phase 5.2 which contained 44% of the sherds, but comprised to some extent redeposited and residual material, the largest number of sherds (25%) occurs in phase 3.

Bottle or narrow-necked jar: 142.
Everted-rim jars: 12, 71, 300.
Necked jars: 14, 15, 173, 174, 175.
Narrow-necked jar: 172.
Other jars: 65, 301, 343.
Biconical beakers: 117, 171.
Folded beaker: 72.
Poppy head beaker: 179.
Other beakers: 113, 137, 180, 181.
Straight-sided dishes: 261, 341.
Gallo-Belgic imitations: 183, 184.
Other dishes: 114, 115, 182, 185, 186, 189, 226.
Incipient flanged bowl: 214.
Bowls: 76, 187, 210, 218.

Fabric 38. *Highgate Wood ware*

Fabric description: Brown and Sheldon 1969, 63–4; SLAEC 1978, 535. This fabric is the Highgate Wood 'C' ware from the north London kilns, in production *c*.AD 60–160. A small number of sherds have been recovered from contexts belonging to Ceramic phases 1 and 2. The main occurrence of the fabric, although always in small amounts, is in the mid second century, including two almost complete poppy-head beakers in the well deposit (Ceramic phase 3: 88% by weight, 100% by R.EVE). It proved difficult to determine the Highgate or Hadham origin of a small assemblage of sherds, especially from earlier contexts, which may indicate a link between the two industries. The treatment of the clay within both industries is certainly very similar.

Poppy head beakers: 10, 11.
Jars: 143, 169.
Bowl: 170.

Fabric 39. Hadham grey ware

For references, see Fabric 9. At its best quality, the fabric is blue-grey in colour, hard-fired and burnished, with black 'specks' or short streaks through the matrix. Other examples of the fabric can appear much more sandy or granular, with paler brownish-grey surfaces (compare with Highgate, Fabric 38). It is difficult to be certain of parallels for the vessels occurring on other sites in the region, since the fabric has only been recognised comparatively recently; in earlier reports, *eg* Verulamium (Wilson 1972, 1983, 1984), the fabric was never separated from the mass of grey wares. At all periods the grey wares made up the biggest part of Hadham industry products (Going, pers. comm.). This is duly represented in the site assemblage from Chells, the grey wares being introduced gradually from the late first to early second century onwards. This is the largest fabric group within the site assemblage (Table 7). The fabric is well-represented in Ceramic phase 3 (37% by weight), the most complete vessels occurring in the Antonine well deposit (*Catalogue*, below). The supply of the products to the site continued until the late fourth century, Ceramic phase 5.2 accounting for 39% of the fabric present on the site, although some of this may be residual. The characteristic forms of the industry, such as Braughing jars, cordoned jars and flanged bowls, are all present on Chells.

Beaker: 159.
Jars: 3–9, 42–48, 140, 158, 160–162, 215, 216, 227, 233, 254, 286.
Straight-sided dishes: 60–62, 255, 296.
Other dishes: 53, 164.
Flanged bowls: 56–59, 163, 167, 168, 298.
Other bowls: 55, 165, 217, 260.

Fabric 40. Grit-tempered grey ware; ?Hadham origin. (not illustrated)

This is a reduced version of Fabric 16, occurring in small numbers throughout all ceramic phases. 55% of the fabric was recovered from contexts of Ceramic phase 5.2. There are no diagnostic forms.

Fabric 41. 'Pimply' grey ware

The fabric is hard-fired and has a fine blue-grey matrix (2.5YR 5/0–4/0) with moderate to abundant rounded white quartz inclusions up to 0.25–0.5 mm in diameter, which give a pimply feel to the surfaces. The assemblage shows clear similarities in fabric and in some of the forms (*eg* rilled jars or 'Braughing jar' types) with Hadham ware (Fabric 39), and may well be another coarser variant of the Hadham industry, or a direct competitor. The fabric most frequently occurs in Ceramic phase 3 (35%).

Rilled jars: 13, 66, 67, 176, 177.
Flanged bowl: 84.
Bowl: 118.

Fabric 42. Black burnished ware I

Fabric description and discussion: Farrar 1973, 86–97; Williams 1977, 163–220. Only a moderate number of sherds have been identified on the site; very few are diagnostic forms, and of these only straight-sided dishes (Gillam 1977, type 329) are represented. Sherds do occur infrequently in contexts from the mid to late second to fourth century; the majority are from Ceramic phase 5.2 (75%).

Straight-sided dish: 64.

Fabric 43. Alice Holt/Farnham ware

Fabric description: Lyne and Jeffries, 1979, 18 Fabric A–B. Only eight sherds from the Surrey kilns are present on the site, all from late fourth-century contexts. The flanged bowl is the only diagnostic form.

Flanged bowl: 63.

Fabric 44. Nene Valley grey ware (not illustrated)

Fabric description: Howe *et al* 1981, 7. Only four sherds have been recovered from the site that are certainly of Nene Valley origin; two from Ceramic phase 5.2 and two from unphased contexts. The fabric has a very fine matrix, medium grey core (5YR 5/1) with pale grey margins (10YR 8/1) and a very dark brown-grey matt self-slip (5YR 2.5/1).

Fabric 45. Grey wares of likely Nene Valley origin

This group of fabrics shows many similarities with Fabric 44, and a similar origin is likely. The pale to medium grey clay matrix is always very fine, but in some cases moderate to abundant rose-coloured quartz gives the surface a pimply feel. All examples have a dark grey colour coat, as Fabric 44. 93% of these sherds occur in fourth-century deposits.

Necked jar: 236.

Fabric 46. Black-surfaced ware

A fine micaceous ware, with sparse red grog inclusions less than 2 mm in diameter and sparse grey–white grog 0.5–2.0 mm in diameter; sparse white rounded quartz. The fabric is a distinctive red/pinkish brown (5YR 5/6) with black surfaces which are often burnished. The fabric occurs sporadically on the site from the mid-second century onwards; most sherds (78%) were recovered from Ceramic phase 5.2.

Straight-sided dishes: 74, 240.
Flanged bowl: 81.

Fabric 47. Unspecified Black-burnished ware 2 (not illustrated)

The fabric varies from a dark brown (5YR 4/3 –3/3) to reddish core (2.5YR 4/6), with dark brown-grey to ochre-brown surfaces, with moderate ill-sorted quartzite less than 5 mm in diameter and sparse ill-sorted inclusions that may be limestone. The surfaces are smoothed and lightly burnished. The provenance of this sherds is not certain, since there are various sources for the production of Black-burnished ware 2. Only forty-three sherds were recovered, suggesting the ware was never in common use on the site, and was only found as residual in fourth-century deposits.

Fabric 48. Hard-fired sand-tempered ware with smoothed surfaces

This fabric, probably of local origin, is characterised by being hard-fired sand-tempered ware with a dark grey (5YR 4/0) to grey-brown core (5YR 4/1), often with narrow red-brown margins (7.5YR 5/4) and medium grey to dark grey surfaces (7.5YR 5/0–4/0). The surfaces are smoothed and often burnished. Inclusions are abundant, well-sorted rounded opaque, rose-coloured and white quartzite approx. 0.5 mm in diameter. The first appearance of the fabric is in Ceramic phase 3 (10% of the fabric), but it occurs most frequently in deposits of Ceramic phase 5.2 (71%).

Jars: 70, 178.
Straight-sided dish: 75, 303, 304, 305.
Other dishes: 73, 188, 241, 242.
Bowls: 16, 77–79, 229, 243, 245, 264, 302
Flanged bowl: 80, 82, 83, 224.
Lid: 85.

Fabric 49. Misc. coarse grey sandy wares

This group of fabrics, varying from dark grey to dark brown in colour, are recognisable from their very abrasive surfaces, due to the presence of abundant quartzite (up to 0.5 mm in dia.) and sparse grit (up to 3 mm in dia.) inclusions. Varies in colour from dark grey to brown to medium grey. The fabric begins to occur from Ceramic phase 2 onwards, 83% occurring in fourth-century deposits, especially post-350.

Jars: 61, 69, 125, 237–239, 342.
Bowl: 211.
Flanged bowl: 246, 344.

Fabric 50. Coarse sandy ware with black surfaces and red core (not illustrated)

Only nineteen abraded sherds occur in fourth-century contexts on the site; most of them may well come from the same vessel. The sherds are thin-walled, hard-fired, with abundant fine quartzite inclusions (0.25–0.5 mm in diam.), giving a pimply feel to the surface. The fabric is uniformly dark reddish-brown (2.5YR 4/6) with black surfaces.

Fabric 51. Uncertain reduced ware (not illustrated)

Only eleven sherds were identified on the site. Its earliest occurrence is in Ceramic phase 3, after which it is only found in fourth-century deposits which appear to consist primarily of redeposited material. The fabric has a fine clay matrix varying from dark grey to buff in colour, due to uncontrolled firing conditions. Inclusions are abundant ill-sorted irregular white and opaque quartzite up to 3 mm in diameter, and sparse red-brown grog fragments. The surfaces are unevenly finished.

GROG-TEMPERED WARES

Fabric 52. Red-brown grog-tempered wares

The fabric has a dark grey (7.5YR 3/0–2/0) to red-brown (5YR 5/6) core and surfaces, with a fine clay matrix containing moderate to abundant ill-sorted grog inclusions; mainly red-brown, but also brown-grey, as well as very sparse crushed shell. Surfaces are smoothed, but tend to be pitted or vesicular. As with Fabric 34, Fabrics 52 and 53 represent a post-conquest continuance of earlier 'Belgic' or native wares in the region (Thompson 1982). The fabric is already present (6%) in Ceramic phase 1, increasing to 18% by the late first to early second century. The greatest quantities (65%) have been retrieved from Ceramic phase 3 contexts. After this period, its occurrence falls off dramatically, occurring as residual material.

Jars: 17, 98, 100, 190–194.

Fabric 53. Black grog-tempered wares

This fabric is much harder-fired than Fabric 52, with a medium grey core (10YR 5/1–7.5YR 4/0), often with narrow red-brown margins (5YR 5/6) and patchy dark grey/ochre to brown surfaces that are usually burnished. Black grog inclusions are usually approx. 0.5–1.0 mm in diameter. The fabric occurs most frequently in first-century contexts (Ceramic phase 1: 44%), continuing into the early second (31%), tailing off to 11% by the mid to late second century.

Cup: 1.
Jars: 2, 99, 101–103, 126.
Dish: 206.

Fabric 54. Grog and grit-tempered wares (not illustrated)

This fabric is similar to Fabric 53 but with abundant, 'gritty' ill-sorted quartzite inclusions, mostly c.0.5 mm in diameter, but up to 2 mm in diameter.

Fabric 55. Coarse reduced storage jar ware

This fabric is relatively hard-fired with a reduced, medium to dark grey (c.10YR 6/1–7.5YR 6/0), coarse open matrix, with abundant large ill-sorted black grog inclusions. Represented by thick-walled storage jar sherds, it occurs almost exclusively (93% by weight) in Antonine contexts (Ceramic phase 3). The sherds could well all be from only one or two vessels.

Storage jar: 89.

Fabric 56. *Coarse oxidised storage jar ware*

This assemblage contains similar forms to Fabric 55 as well as smaller jars, but the fabric is much softer and can feel rather soapy. It is generally an oxidised pink to pale orangey-brown colour (7.5YR 6/6–5YR 5/4), with abundant large ill-sorted orange-buff to reddish-brown grog inclusions. Some sherds also contain black grog. Small quantities of this fabric are present throughout the Roman period, the greatest amount (61%) again occurring in Ceramic phase 3.

Storage jar: 195, 196.

Jars: 111, 205.

SHELL-TEMPERED WARES

Fabric 57. *Early handmade shell-tempered wares*

Fabric description and discussion: Rigby 1986, 261.4. Bonfire-fired. Most of this fabric occurring on the site is reduced, the matrix varying from dark grey/black (5YR 3/1) to a patchy reddish-brown (5YR 5/6–4/6), with a dark grey core. The fabric contains abundant crushed shell tempering (Rigby suggests the presence of fossilised shell in the clay as well as additional tempering). The provenance of these early wares is not known; suitable clay resources do not lie in the immediate vicinity of the site. Some vessels also have sparse inclusions of red-brown grog. The fabric is at its most common in the first to early second century (Ceramic phases 1 and 2) where 81% is present.

Jars: 95, 106–108, 116, 120, 127, 199, 204.

Fabric 58. *Shell-tempered ware*

Fabric description: Rigby 1986, 261.4. The majority of this assemblage appears to be of the same provenance as Fabric 57. This source, however, is uncertain. The fourth-century forms present at Chells are paralleled across southern Britain, and are well-documented for London and Verulamium. Such comparison makes a regional origin, *eg.* the Harrold kilns in Bedfordshire, a likely source. Fabric colour can vary from patchy dark ochre to brown grey, to buff to pinkish brown, depending on the firing conditions. As with Fabric 57, the matrix contains abundant crushed shell. A large percentage of the fabric recovered shows extremely vesicular surfaces (Fabric 58A) where organic material has been burnt out during firing. After products of the Hadham industry (Fabrics 9 and 39), this is the most common fabric on the site, almost 10% of the total site assemblage. Small quantities are present in Ceramic phase 2, its occurrence increases rapidly in Ceramic phases 3 and 4 until the fourth century, where 81% of the fabric is present.

Jars: 90, 91, 220–223, 225, 230, 247–249, 262, 263, 313–320.
Straight-sided dishes: 92, 321, 322, 330.
Flanged bowl: 93, 323–326.

Fabric 59. *Pale red/buff-coloured shell-tempered ware*

This fabric is distinct from Fabric 58, but is again of unknown, although probably regional, origin. The fabric is hard-fired, usually having a grey core (7.5YR 4/0–10YR 4/1) with smoothed pale orange-brown to buff surfaces (10YR 7/4–7.5YR 7/4–6/6). It is tempered with abundant fine crushed shell and sparse quartzite. Apart from a small number of sherds occurring in early second-century contexts (Ceramic phase 2), the fabric is especially prevalent in the Hadrianic–Antonine period. For example, three almost complete large storage jars are present in the well deposit (Ceramic phase 3 contains 77% of this fabric). The remaining sherds occur in late fourth-century deposits, which comprise mainly redeposited earlier material.

Storage jars: 24–26.
Other jars: 197, 198.
Bowl: 138.

OTHER WARES

Fabric 60. *South Spanish amphorae*

Fabric description: Peacock and Williams 1986, 136–139, Class 25. Only Dressel 20 amphorae, from the Guadalquivir region of Baetica, are represented on the site. They were most common in Britain from the late first to early third centuries, and originally contained olive oil. Only body sherds were recovered, from contexts dated to the late first to early second to late fourth centuries (Ceramic phases 2–5.2). The majority of the sherds belong to Ceramic phase 3 (59%).

Fabric 61. *Samian*

This is reported on in detail elsewhere in this volume. The totals in Table 6 refer to the amounts recovered (by weight) for each industry. Percentages given in Table 6 refer to the total amount within each samian assemblage (*ie* Areas 1–3 or cemetery).

THE CERAMIC CONTENT OF THE KEY GROUPS

Analysis of the pottery from all the significant structural features identified in the site report was undertaken to provide the information for the objectives listed above. Important or key groups were studied in detail. These comprised sealed deposits of pottery, and features where fills had apparently been deposited fairly rapidly, and which may indicate the range of pottery types and forms available on the site at certain periods. Only two assemblages fulfilled this classification; (i) the second-century well deposit, and (ii) the fill of Feature EAA, both of which were essentially of Antonine date. As well as these, important fourth-century assemblages came from the weathering cone backfill of Well CAB, the fill of Pond GK, and part of Circular Building ABO.

The first objective of the pottery analysis was to provide a date-range for activity on the site, and second, to elucidate the build-up of deposits within features from a ceramic point of view. Table 8 sets out the structural and ceramic phase to which the pottery assemblage from each feature belongs. For some features, the nature of the pottery means that a precise date cannot be given. In these cases, the phase in the table offers a possible *terminus post quem*.

All stratigraphically phased features have been included in Table 8, the more significant of these being discussed in the *Dating Evidence* sections of the excavation report. Table 8 and the *Catalogue* also include stratigraphically isolated features whose ceramic deposits are nevertheless datable.

For each feature discussed in the *Dating Evidence* sections, the relevant coin and samian evidence has been summarised, and reference made to significant pottery forms and/or fabrics. A list of all fabrics occurring within each feature is also given. All diagnostic forms occurring within each feature are noted by reference either to their own catalogue number, or to that of an illustrated parallel (the latter in brackets, indicated by an asterisk). In the few instances where the form is not included in the catalogue, a published parallel is cited.

The Key Groups

WELL CAB

This feature contained the largest percentage R.EVE on the site (33.92% of the total). By weight, this proved the second largest deposit on the site (18% of the total weight; see also Feature EAA, below). Three separate phases of infilling can be clearly identified (Table 8).

(a) Lowest layers (CAB 16–19): Ceramic period 1

A small assemblage in which most of the sherds represent a range of grog-tempered jars that date to the pre-early Flavian period (Ceramic phase 1). The second-century samian is intrusive, probably having sunk down from deposits above (but see Editor's note, *Period III discussion*). A few sherd links and 'mixing' between the contexts suggests this material belongs to a single-action dumping of rubbish, rather than the gradual silting up of the well bottom.

These sherds are amongst the earliest recovered from the site. It is significant to note that they only come from the lowest layers excavated, and not the lowest deposits in the well since it was never fully excavated. If these sherds are of a period when the well had already fallen into disuse, then the original construction and use of the well as a supply of uncontaminated water could have been considerably earlier, probably pre-conquest. This would imply that the well is one of the earliest, if not the earliest, structural feature excavated on the site.

Fabrics: 35, 52, 53, 54, 56, 61.
Forms: Cat. nos 1, 2.
Samian: Curle 15, Hadrianic-early Antonine (CAB 19).

(b) Middle layers (CAB 6–13): Ceramic period 3

The majority of the vessels come from Context CAB 11, but there are so many sherd links between all the contexts, that this again must be seen as a single-action deposit; all the vessels fit within a date range of 150–180/190. Over 22% of all Ceramic phase 3 material from the site is present in this deposit (22.73% by weight, 22.80% by R.EVE). The percentages of the various fabric groups present are shown in Fig. 33. Fig. 34 indicates the percentages of each form type within the assemblage. The assemblage comprises complete and reconstructable vessels as well as sherds. Most are large, in very good condition, and have clean breaks. Because the exact position of the sherds was not recorded during excavation, it is not possible to state whether the vessels were a) broken before deposition, b) broken on impact when thrown down the well, or c) broken by the pressure of subsequent back-filling. Table 9 attempts to show the minimum number of complete or semi-complete vessels present in the deposit. These results should be treated with caution however, since the exact number of vessels that can be reconstructed into a complete or semi-

TABLE 6: Quantities of samian from the site, by origin.

	Weight(g)		R.EVE	
Areas 1–3:				
South Gaul	748	(14.24%)	0.54	(7.71%)
Martres deVeyre	421	(8.02%)	0.52	(7.43%)
Montans	17	(0.32%)	–	
Central Gaul	3442	(65.55%)	5.79	(82.71%)
Blickweiler	488	(9.30%)	0.15	(2.15%)
East Gaul	135	(2.57%)	–	
The Cemetery:				
South Gaul	617	(31.82%)	1.77	(39.42%)
Central Gaul	1322	(68.18%)	2.72	(60.58%)

TABLE 7: Fabric incidence from stratified contexts on the site (excluding the cemetery).

Fabric No.	Description	Quantity No.	%	Weight (g)	%	R.EVE No.	%
1	Romano-British glazed ware	22	0.07	64	0.02	0.85	0.27
2	Central Gaulish black colour-coated ware	3	0.01	16	0.01	–	–
3	South Gaulish colour-coated ware	3	0.01	22	0.01	–	–
4	North Gaulish colour-coated ware	15	0.05	65	0.02	0.84	0.26
5	Nene Valley colour-coated ware	969	3.16	7453	2.38	7.92	2.52
6	Misc. rough-cast ware	4	0.01	23	0.01	–	–
7	Misc. hard-fired colour-coated ware	2	0.01	52	0.02	0.4	0.13
8	Oxfordshire red colour-coated ware	234	0.76	2515	0.8	2.69	0.86
9	Hadham oxidised red ware }	5231	17.07	31817	10.15	29.24	9.32
10	?Hadham red ware						
11	?Local mica-dusted ware	4	0.01	55	0.02	0.24	0.07
12	Hadham white-slipped ware	86	0.26	814	0.26	1.05	0.33
13	Misc. white- or cream-slipped red wares	21	0.07	299	0.1	8.05	0.36
14	Fine slipped red ware	2	0.01	13	0.01	–	–
15	Red ware with external grey slip: ?Hadham	149	0.49	1466	0.47	0.58	0.18
16	Grit-tempered red ware: ?Hadham	233	0.76	961	0.31	2.8	0.89
17	Misc. fine red ware	68	0.22	595	0.19	1.93	0.61
18	Oxidised 'gritty' ware	39	0.13	320	0.1	0.32	0.1
19	Misc. sandy red wares	1255	4.1	6156	1.96	2.71	0.86
20	Verulamium region/Brockley Hill ware	870	2.83	9981	3.18	9.57	3.05
21	Oxfordshire white ware	50	0.16	2194	0.7	1.48	0.47
22	Nene Valley 'self-coloured' ware	46	0.15	1433	0.46	0.56	0.18
23	Gallo-Belgic white ware	4	0.01	12	<0.01	–	–
24	'Eggshell' ware	(only found in the cemetery)					
25	Fine smooth buff-white ware	2	<0.01	445	0.14	1.0	0.32
26	Misc. fine white wares	(only found in the cemetery)					
27	Colchester buff ware	1	<0.01	39	0.01	0.09	0.03
28	Oxfordshire parchment ware	14	0.05	248	0.08	0.19	0.06
29	Verulamium region fine ware	1	<0.01	1	<0.01	–	–
30	Fine granular ware: ?Verulamium region	36	0.12	643	0.21	2.0	0.64
31	Fine buff-pink ware	10	0.03	136	0.04	1.0	0.32
32	Butt beaker fabric	1	<0.01	5	<0.01	0.15	0.05
33	Early sandy ware	125	0.41	918	0.29	0.87	0.28
34	Early sand- and grog-tempered ware	1069	3.49)	8532	2.72	5.87	1.87
35	Romanising gray wares	165	0.54	1558	0.5	0.84	0.27
36	Fine grey ware	38	0.12	197	0.06	0.5	0.16
37	Misc. sandy grey wares	2793	9.12	23490	7.5	23.57	7.51
38	Highgate Wood 'D' ware	106	0.35	764	0.24	1.26	0.4
39	Hadham grey ware	6648	21.7	57381	18.31	77.05	24.56
40	Grit-tempered grey ware: ?Hadham	125	0.41	1427	0.46	0.28	0.09
41	'Pimply' grey ware	1417	4.62	13881	4.43	43.89	13.99
42	?Black-burnished ware, fabric I	141	0.46	2483	0.79	3.4	1.08
43	Alice Holt/Farnham ware	8	0.03	165	0.05	0.1	0.03
44	Nene Valley grey ware	4	0.01	69	0.02	–	–
45	Grey wares of likely Nene Valley origin.	182	0.59	1109	0.35	1.43	0.46
46	Black-surfaced ware	90	0.29	1529	0.49	2.76	0.87
47	Black-burnished ware, fabric II or imitation	43	0.14	242	0.08	–	–
48	Misc hard-fired grey sand-tempered ware with smoothed surfaces	795	2.59	13285	4.24	15.47	4.93
49	Misc. coarse grey sandy wares	1182	3.86	12197	3.89	6.65	2.12
50	Coarse sandy ware with black surfaces and red core	19	0.06	147	0.05	0.05	0.02
51	Unnamed	11	0.04	111	0.04	–	–
52	Red-brown grog-tempered wares	1081	3.56	15858	5.06	18.66	5.94
53	Black grog-tempered wares	475	1.55	4213	1.34	3.53	1.13
54	Grog- and grit-tempered wares	4	0.01	33	0.01	–	–
55	Coarse reduced storage jar ware	80	0.26	3534	1.13	0.05	0.02
56	Coarse oxidised storage jar ware	530	1.73	15463	4.93	1.27	0.4
57	Early handmade shell-tempered ware	579	1.89	4203	1.34	3.54	1.13
58	Shell-tempered ware	2955	9.65	30232	9.64	23.97	7.64
59	Red/buff-coloured shell-tempered ware	390	1.27	14043	4.48	3.09	0.98
60	South Spanish amphorae	143	0.47	13059	4.17	–	–
61	Samian (all industries)	not counted		5251	1.68	7.0	2.23
62	Residual Iron Age fabrics	54	0.17	162	0.05	–	–
	TOTAL AMOUNTS:	**30637**		**313379**		**313.68**	

Percentages given are of the total site assemblage.

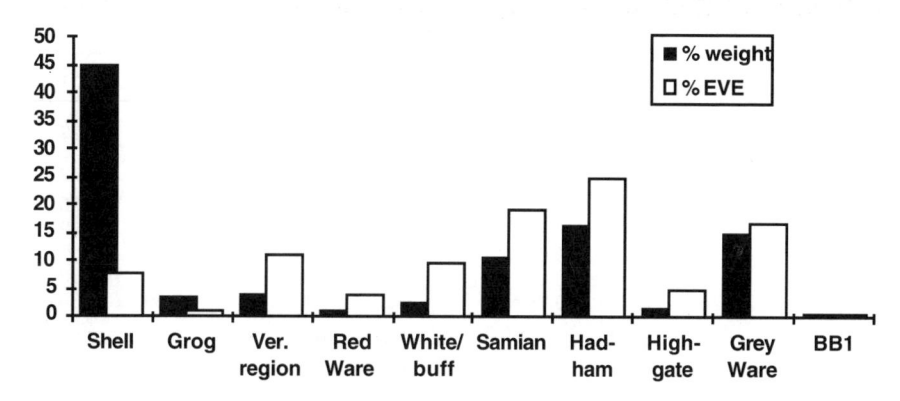

Figure 33   Fabric occurrence by weight percentage and R.EVE, Well CAB, Ceramic phase 3.

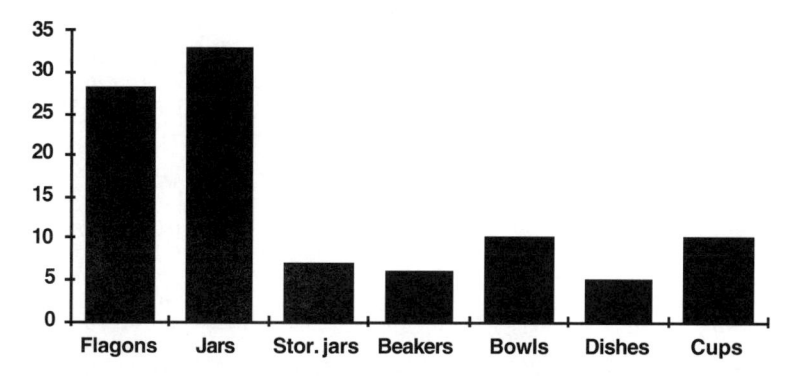

Figure 34   Occurrence of vessel forms, Well CAB, Ceramic phase 3.

complete state is not known. During processing, only the most obvious sherd links were noted, as time did not allow for the detailed analysis of all links between body sherds. For instance, with the ring-necked flagons (**22, 23**), complete bases in the same fabric were recovered, but too few body sherds existed to allow the construction of a more complete profile. Fig. 37 also shows the number of vessel forms present by % R.EVE.

The nature of the deposit: rubbish or ritual?
To be certain that a deposit is characteristic of a ritual shaft as opposed to a rubbish dump made up of domestic debris is extremely difficult (see the discussion on the shafts and pits at Newstead in Ross and Feachem 1976). One of the principal characteristics of votive and sacrificial offerings is that they must be 'removed' from this world and placed where recovery or re-use is not possible. It is a relatively common recorded phenomenon on Celtic sites, where objects were thrown into water or were buried deep in the ground, for instance in pits, shafts and wells. Such ritual practices were disseminated into Roman society, and beyond into the medieval period (see Ross 1968 for a catalogue of such sites). If viewed as a ritual deposit, the condition of the pots suggests that, whilst some were complete and possibly 'new' when deposited, others may have been deliberately broken before inclusion. A few pots show signs of use for cooking purposes, *eg* interior lime-scaling and exterior sooty patches, and thus were clearly not 'new' when deposited. A few vessels have abraded surfaces or worn slip. Most of the samian vessels were broken in antiquity, and the footrings show signs of wear (*Samian Report*). It is quite possible that a certain number of vessels were deliberately selected to be used for the dedication of food, where the age and condition of the pot was of minor importance compared with its contents (which have not survived); *ie* flagons, cups and dishes for eating and drinking, jars for provisions or for more functional use, *eg* cooking, in the after-life. Alternatively, the dedication of the pot itself could be the reason for its inclusion, *ie* the greater value of the vessel, the more significant its part in the ritual. In this case, new and more costly items might be expected to be selected whenever possible. A combination of both these practices could well have been the case here. The well deposit is very similar in content and date-range to that found down the unfinished and unused well-shaft in Building 8, Insula IV at Verulamium (Wheeler 1936, 103), for which a date of 160–90 has been suggested. Wheeler does not discuss the motive behind this deposition. As at Chells, the deposit contained extremely little

TABLE 8: Dating of features discussed in the report.

S.p.	C.p.	Feature and contexts	Weight (g)	R.EVE
		Well		
III	1	CAB 16–19 (D/E)	684	0.27
IV	3	CAB 6–13 (A/B/C)	22907	20.22
V	5.2	ED 1–2; BX 1–2: EB 1–8: CAB 1–5 (C/D)	32671 (18%)	88.29 (34.68%)
		Quarry		
IV	3	EAA; EAA 1–19, 40; EAA 301–305 (B/C)	61470 (19.6%)	55.64 (17.73%)
		Pond		
III	2	TX 1–5 (C/D)	1937	0.2
V	5	TA 4 (D)	93	–
V	5.1	TA 3 (D)	80	–
V	5.2	RA 1; TA 1–2 (D)	1357	0.6
V	5.2	BK 1–15 (C/D)	44103 (15.18%)	35.98 (11.73%)
		WS: clay deposits		
III	1	WS 1–8 (E)	233 (0.07%)	0.16 (0.05%)
		SF: palisade slot		
–	–	SF 1; KR 1; VE 1	100 (0.03%)	–
		ABN: parallel ditch system		
III		*ABL:*		
	1	EN 1 (C/D); DP 1 (C); ML 1–3 (E)	4350	3.32
III		*ABM:*		
	3	MM 1 (B); MM 2 (C); DK 1 (C)	575	0.3
	2	MM 3 (C)	687	0.33
	1	MM 4–6 (C/D)	1195 (2.2%)	1.79 (1.83%)
III		**ECM: ditch**		
	–	DDW 1 (E)	25	–
	5	BAM 2 (C); EAF 1 (C/D)	2168	2.04
	5.1	BAB 3 (D)	1016	0.98
	5.2	BAB 1–2 (D)	2274 (1.75%)	1.25 (1.36%)
III		**ECZ: parallel ditch system**		
	2	*ECP:* EAE 2 (E)	34	–
	2	*ECQ:* EAD 1 (D); EAD 2 (E)	1119 (0.37%)	0.7 (0.22%)
III		**GAT: ditch**		
	2	GAV 2 (E)	132	–
	5.2	GAT (D); GAV 2 (E)	521 (0.21%)	–
III		**ECU: ditch**		
	2	EAV 1 (E)	225	–
	3	EAI 1 (C/D)	366 (0.19%)	0.51 (0.16%)
III		**ECW: ditch**		
	2	EBA 2 (C/D)	265	0.82
	5.2	EBA 1 (D)	336 (0.19%)	0.53 (0.43%)
III		**AAJ: ditch**		
	2	AAJ 3 (E); AAJ 4 (B/C)	3179	1.8
	3	AAJ 2 (D)	466	0.39
	5	AAJ 1 (D)	1109 (1.51%)	0.27 (0.78%)
III+		**JJ: ditch**		
	2	JJ 6–7 (D)	2067	1.38
	3	JJ 1, 2, 5 (E); JJ 3 (C)	183 (0.72%)	0.11 (0.48%)
III		**DDF: curving palisade**		
	–	DDF 1, DDM 1; DDN 1 (E)	79 (0.03%)	–
III		**DDJ: east/west palisade**		
	2/3	DDJ 1 (C/D)	1071 (0.34%)	1.06 (0.34%)
III		**DCE: palisade**		
	–	DCC 1; DCD 1 (E)	57	–
	3/4	DBH 1 (C)	1072 (0.36%)	1.05 (0.33%)
III		**DCF: palisade**		
	–	DCG 1; DDD; DDR (E)	266	0.15

S.p.	C.p.	Feature and contexts	Weight (g)	R.EVE
	2	DCH 1 (C)	50	0.3
	3	DCI 1 (E)	162 (0.15%)	0.11 (0.18%)
III		**ABS: irregular features/structure**		
	5	FH 1 (D)	295	–
	3	KL 1; LR 1; QC 1 (E)	81	0.15
	2	GD 1; LK 1; LM 1; QN 1 (E); LP 1; QM 1 (C/E)	641 (0.32%)	0.72 (0.28%)
III		**EAW: circular feature/raft**		
	1	EAW 1–3 (E)	186 (0.06%)	0.05 (0.02%)
III		**EAN: pit**		
	2	BBB (D); BBB 1–2 (E); EAN 1–2 (C/D); EAN 3 (E)	2836 (0.9%)	2.05 (0.65%)
IV		**ABR: raft/building**		
	2	EV 2; CE 2 (E)	373	0.74
	3	EF 2 (D)	247	0.18
	5	FF 1 (C/D)	985	0.95
	5.1	CE 5 (D)	126 (0.55%)	0.12 (0.63%)
–		**TB: pit**		
	2	TB 2	34	0.16
	3	TB 1	2574 (0.83%)	2.59 (0.88%)
V		**ABQ: circular building**		
	–	TR 1 (E)	427	–
	5.2	TS 1; TJ 1–3; TL 1 (D)	3818 (1.35%)	3.52 (1.12%)
V		**JK: pit**		
	4	JK 1; VJ 1 (C)	7208 (2.3%)	4.51 (1.44%)
V		**EK 2: organic layer**		
	5.2	EK 2 (D)	1134 (0.36%)	1.59 (0.51%)
V		**ABV: ditch**		
	–	FZ 11, 17 (E)	62 (0.02%)	–
V		**ABO: ?circular building**		
	5	TZ 1 (C); TZ 2 (D)	2086	2.83
	5.1	FC 1–3 (C/D)	1994	1.77
	5.2	EG 1; FZ 1–10, 12–16, 18–22 (C/D)	16761 (6.7%)	12.29 (5.38%)
V		**DDX: ?circular building**		
	–	DBI 1; DBM 1; DBO 1; DBR 1; DBT 1; DBU 1; DBV 1 (E)	217	0.05
	5.1	DAB 1 (D); DAZ 1 (C/D)	497 (0.23%)	0.74 (0.25%)
V		**DAA: drainage gully**		
	–	DAA 1 (E)	74 (0.02%)	–
V		**DBB: pit inside DDX**		
	5.2	DBB 1, 4 (C/D)	744 (0.24%)	0.64 (0.2%)
V		**YJ: pit inside DDX**		
	5.1	YJ 1 (E)	49 (0.02%)	0.11 (0.03%)
V		**ABT: posthole alignment**		
	–	VT 1; VG 1 (E)	25	0.08
	1	WF 1 (E)	59	–
	5.2	VA 1 (E)	152 (0.08%)	0.07 (0.08%)
V		**ABU: posthole alignment**		
	1/2	XH 1; ZQ 1; VW 2 (E)	81	0.09
	3	VV 1; VW 1 (E)	263 (0.11%)	0.12 (0.07%)
V		**CE9: gully**		
	–	CAE 2 (E)	8	–
	2	CBI 1; CAE 1; CAI 1; CAJ 1; CAK 1 (E)	395	0.22
	5.2	CE 4; CE 8 (D)	3812 (1.35%)	1.3 (0.48%)
V		**GF: corn drier**		
	3	JA 2–5, 8, 11 (E)	95	0.25

Table 8 (continued)

S.p.	C.p.	Feature and contexts	Weight (g)	R.EVE
	5.2	GF 1 (C); GF 2, 3, 6, 9, 13, 16, 17, 20 (E);JA 1 (C)	2679 (0.9%)	2.38 (0.84%)
V		**ABP: ?circular building**		
	3	VQ 1 (C/E)	71	0.16
	5.2	GB 1–3 (D)	736 (0.26%)	0.54 (0.22%)
V		**DAD: pit**		
	5.1	DAD 1 (E)	122 (0.04%)	0.21 (0.07%)
V		**RC: pit**		
	3	RC 4 (E)	176	0.2

S.p.	C.p.	Feature and contexts	Weight (g)	R.EVE
	5.2	RC 1–3 (D)	8894 (2.9%)	7.09 (2.32%)
V		**WV: pit**		
	2	WV 3 (E)	42	–
	3	WV 1–2 (E)	356 (0.13%)	0.1 (0.03%)
V		**AAF: pit**		
	–	AAF 1 (E)	8 (0.0%)	–
V		**KA: layer**		
	5.2	KA 1 (D)	449 (0.14%)	0.11 (0.04%)

Only those contexts containing pottery have been listed in this table.
Letters in brackets refer to the condition of the sherds (see *Methodology*).
Numbers in brackets refer to the percentage of the site total represented by the feature.
S.p. Structural phase
C.p. Ceramic phase

TABLE 9: Minimum number of vessels within Well CAB (C.p.3)

Vessel type	Complete/almost complete when excavated	Complete/almost complete when reconstructed	Semi-complete when reconstructed	Substantial rim fragments only
COARSE WARE:				
Disc-mouthed flagon	1	–	–	–
Ring-necked flagon	–	–	2	2
Flagon/tettina	1	–	–	–
Narrow-necked jar	–	3	1	1
Everted-rim jar	–	–	1	2
Cordoned jar	–	1	1	–
Straight-sided jar	–	1	–	–
Necked rilled jar	–	1	2	1
Storage jar	–	–	–	1
Poppy-head beaker	–	–	2	1
Round-rim bowl	–	–	1	1
SAMIAN:				
Form Dr 37 or 30	–	1	–	1
Form Dr 42	–	–	1	–
Form Dr 18/31 0r 31	–	–	4	4
Form Dr 33	1	1	–	2

fine ware (the well at Chells actually contains no fine ware except for samian), amongst the large mass of coarse pottery. Several vessel forms are present in both assemblages (*Catalogue*). Again at Verulamium, the deposit was interpreted as being a single action, not a gradual accumulation. Stead and Rigby (1986, 47, 257–259) suggest that the composition of certain pit and shaft fills at Baldock included complete pots which appeared to have been deliberately selected, and which resembled burial groups in the limited range of types represented. These could therefore be seen as evidence for ritual practice. The groups, however, contained more 'decorated and decorative' forms than the well deposit at Chells. The lack of fine wares other than samian in the well reflects the situation on the site as a whole. Fine wares are present within the cemetery, but still only in relatively small amounts in relation to the coarse ware (see below). Rather than ruling out a ritual significance, the lack of presumably costly, fine colour-coated and decorated vessels may simply indicate their unavailability on a fairly low-status site where the inhabitants had fairly minimal resources.

The pottery from the fill of EAA is the only significant assemblage of comparable size and date recovered from the site. No ritual significance has been ascribed by the excavator to this material, which seems to consist purely of domestic debris. The well deposit could be viewed in the same light; even as part of the same 'house-clearing' activity, since the fill of the well and backfilling of Feature EAA could have been contemporaneous. The completeness of certain vessels included in the fill may be explained by their being from out-of-date stock, or merely unused vessels which were no longer needed and were therefore thrown directly onto the rubbish pile, or into the pit.

However, in comparison with the assemblage from EAA there is a marked difference in the percentages of the various fabrics present (compare Figs 33 and 37), most apparent in the case of samian, but also clear when comparing the amount of shelly wares and grog-tempered wares, for example. The variation in the percentages of different vessel types between the two assemblages also contrasts sharply (Figs 34 and 38) with complete or nearly complete vessels occurring almost exclusively in the well. A greater number of 'table ware' vessels, including flagons and cups, are present in the well, as are the large shell-tempered storage jars (Fabric 59). The large quantity of samian present (3.88 R.EVE) only compares in amount with that recovered from the Cemetery (see below; 4.49 R.EVE). This may well be seen as proof of a more selective inclusion of vessels within the well, associated with a specific ritual procedure.

A discussion of the pottery alone is not enough to confirm the ritual or more mundane nature of the deposit in question. Conclusions can only be drawn from the synthetic analysis of all the accompanying finds. Even after a systematic examination of all the evidence, there is still often room for doubt. Wait (1985), in his analysis of ritual and religion in Iron Age Britain, lists twenty-seven characteristics of ritual deposits, including the deliberate layering of material, the deliberate placement of pottery, the presence of complete vessels as well as sherds and the presence of animal bones such as cattle, dog, pig and horse. In contrast, Ross (1968, 79) lists only twelve principal elements, incorporating those above, for civilian sites. Wait goes on to state, however, that none of these characteristics alone, or indeed even a combination of two or three, are sufficient to define a deposit as ritual.

Fabrics: 9, 12, 13, 15, 19, 20A, 25, 30, 31, 37, 38, 39, 41, 42, 48, 49, 52, 58, 59, 61.

Forms: Figs 43, 44, nos 3–26.

Samian: Form Dr.36, first century. Form Dr.18/31, Trajanic–Hadrianic. Form 18/31, Hadrianic-early Antonine (three). Form 18/31, early to mid Antonine. Form Dr.31 (four), 140–160; 150; 150–170 and mid Antonine. Form Dr.18/31R, 125–150. Form Dr.33 (four), Hadrianic–early Antonine; early Antonine, Antonine; 150–170. Form Dr.30 or Dr.37, early to mid Antonine. Form Dr.37, 150–180. Form Dr.42, Hadrianic. Form Curle 15, Hadrianic or early Antonine.

(c) Upper layers (EC 1–2; BX 1 =ES 1; ES 2 =ES 3 =CAB 1 =EE 1 =BX 2; CAB 2–5; ES 4–5, 7–9) Ceramic period 5.2.

Over 32 kg of pottery were recovered from these layers, 23.52% of the total pottery from Ceramic phase 5.2 (51.85% by R.EVE; Table 9). There are enough sherd links between the various layers to suggest that this late material was part of a single-action deposit. Apart from within the uppermost layers (EC) which were subject to later plough damage and comprised as a result small, abraded sherds, the majority of the sherds are in good condition. In some cases quite a large percentage of the vessel remains intact, suggesting that the vessels were thrown down the well immediately they broke, or that a dump from elsewhere was thrown down the well, but only a short time after it had accumulated. The section showing the stratigraphical build-up of the layers (Fig. 8) suggests that a domestic rubbish dump was moved in various stages, either in barrow or bucket loads. It appears that the well shaft, the fill of which had subsided considerably by this time, was deliberately filled in and levelled off. The large number of shell-tempered hook-rim jars and the presence of Oxfordshire colour-coat and late Hadham ware, such as frilled-rim jars, suggests this cannot have taken place before 350/360–400+ (see below for a discussion of fourth-century activity on the site). Fig. 35 indicates the percentage of each fabric present in the assemblage. Of particular note is the rare occurrence of fragments of Alice Holt/Farnham ware (Fabric 43). The samian, Verulamium region products and much of the grog-tempered ware is redeposited residual material. Fig. 36 shows the forms occurring within this deposit, dominated by jars, of which the majority are necked and hooked rim types (79.75%), and bowls, of which most are flanged types (81.84 %).

Coins: CAB 1, 253–268; CAB 2, 268–275; CAB 3, 268–275; EE 1, 330–335; ES 2, 268–275.

Fabrics: 5A, 5B, 5C, 8, 9, 16, 19, 20A, 22, 37, 39, 41, 42, 43, 46, 48, 49, 50, 52, 55, 56, 58, 59, 61.

Forms: Figs 44–46, nos 27–94 (Cat. nos 161, 160, 290, 291, 313, 317, 318*)

Samian: C.G. Hadrianic–Antonine and E.G. Late second to first half of third century. Forms Dr.18/31 and Dr.35/36, S.G. Flavian–Trajanic. Form Dr.27, C.G. Hadrianic–early Antonine. Form Dr.33, C.G. Hadrianic–early Antonine (three), Antonine (three). Form Dr.18/31, C.G. Hadrianic–early Antonine. Form Dr.31 (two), C.G. Antonine and 160–200. Form Dr.30 or Dr.37, C.G. Hadrianic–Antonine. Form Dr.37, C.G. 135–170. Form Curle 11, C.G. Hadrianic–Antonine.

THE DEW POND/QUARRY (EAA, EAA1–19, 40; EAA 301–305) PERIOD 3

Again, the homogenous nature of the assemblage, with many sherd links, suggests it was a single-action dumping of rubbish during the Antonine period. The deposit also contained a quantity of other domestic debris, including a large amount of ash, animal bones – presumably the remains of food – and a number of other more personal objects such as bone hairpins (*Objects of Bone and Antler*). Many of the vessels were represented by large sherds, often in good condition. Over 61 kg of pottery was recovered from the fill, making up the largest amount of pottery from Ceramic phase 3;

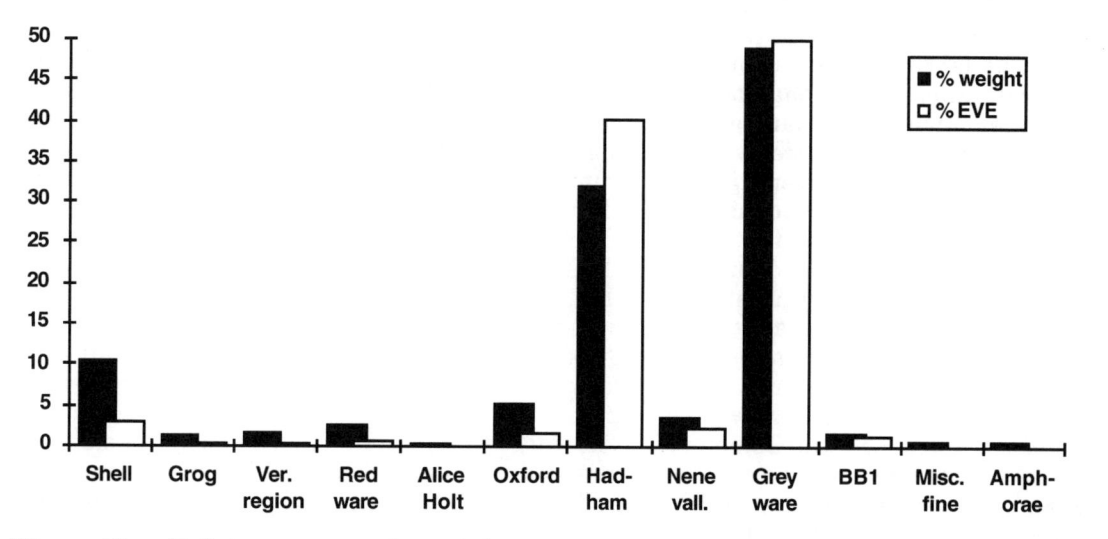

Figure 35   Fabric occurrence by weight percentage and R.EVE, Well CAB, Ceramic phase 5.2.

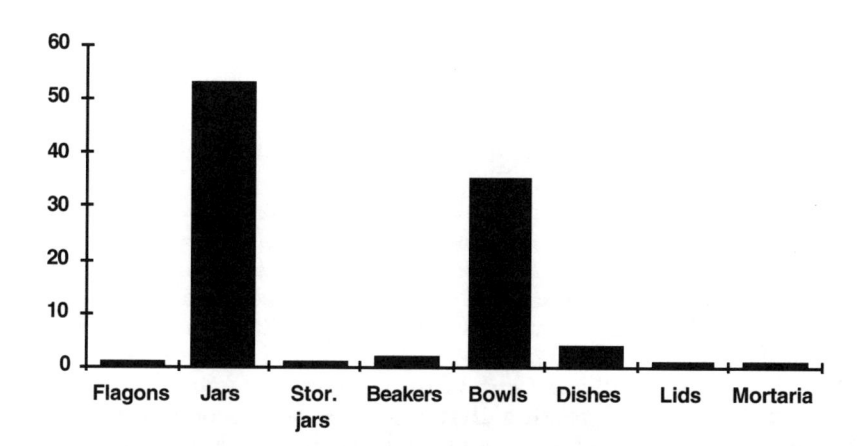

Figure 36   Occurrence of vessel forms, Well CAB, Ceramic phase 5.2.

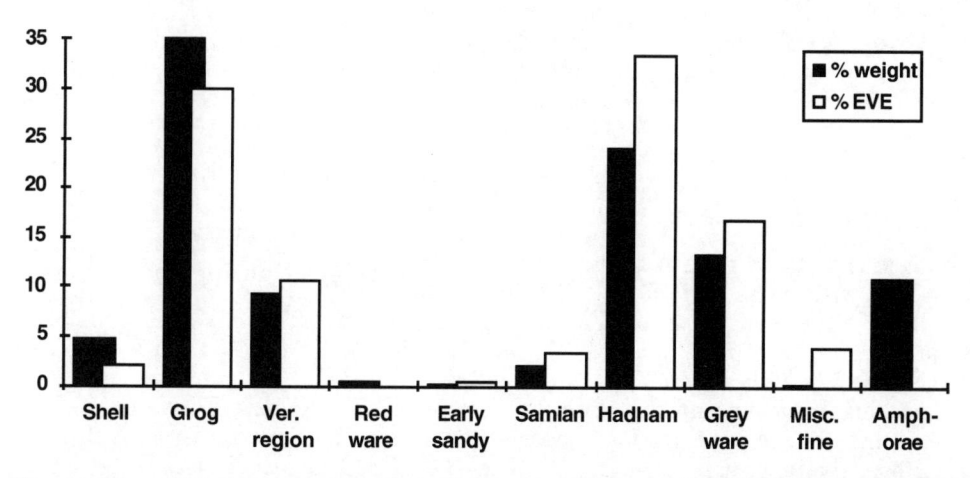

Figure 37   Fabric occurrence by weight percentage and R.EVE, Quarry EAA, Ceramic phase 3.

61% by weight, 62.66% by R.EVE (Table 8). Comparisons have already been made above between this assemblage and that of the well deposit. The pottery from EAA seems more comparable with some of the numerous pit groups from Baldock (Stead and Rigby 1986, 257–259). These contained a relatively wide range of forms, fabrics and sizes, and were regarded by the excavators as being of 'accidental' rather than deliberate selection, ie comprising domestic refuse rather than elements of a votive offering.

Fig. 37 shows the percentage of the various fabrics present in the fill of EAA. The growing dominance of the Hadham industry during this period is apparent. Fig. 38 indicates the percentages of each form type within the assemblage. The percentage of jars present is significantly higher than any other class of vessel. Necked jars account for 56.17% of this total; bead-rim jars in early shell-tempered fabrics (Fabric 57) amount to only 2.61%, indicating the decline in their production and use by the late Hadrianic–Antonine period. The Verulamium region (Fabric 20A) was the only source of mortaria found in EAA. This feature produced the only example of a Romano-British glazed-ware beaker found on the site (Fabric 1, Fig. 48.144).

Fabrics: 1, 4, 5A, 5B, 9, 12, 13, 15, 16, 19, 20A, 33–41, 48, 49, 51–58, 60, 61.

Forms: Figs 48 & 49, nos 144–199.

Samian: Form Ritterling 1, S.G. Neronian. Form Dr.24(?), S.G. Pre-Flavian. Cup, S.G. Neronian – early-Flavian. Cup, S.G. Flavian. Form Dr.30, S.G. Flavian. Form Dr.15/17, S.G. Flavian (two). Form Dr.18, S.G. Flavian. Form Dr.18R, S.G. Flavian. Form Dr.18/31, M. de V. Trajanic; M. de V. Trajanic–Hadrianic; M. de V. Hadrianic–Antonine; C.G. Hadrianic (three). Form Dr.18/31, C.G. Hadrianic–early Antonine (two); C.G. Early to mid Antonine. Form Dr.37, S.G. Flavian; M. de V. Trajanic (two); C.G. Hadrianic–early Antonine. Form Dr.42, M. de V. Trajanic. Form Curle 11, M. de V. Trajanic. Form Curle 15, M. de V. Hadrianic–Antonine. Form Dr.27 g, S.G. 60–70. Form Dr.27, M.de V. Trajanic; M. de V. 130–60: from EAA 2 possibly link with fragment in Pond GK 10; C.G. Hadrianic–Antonine; C.G. early to mid Antonine.

THE POND

The Lining (TX1–5; TA1–4; RA1)

The pottery within the chalk lining of the pond is of a much earlier date than that within the rest of the fill, including early storage jar fragments (Fabric 56) and bead-rim jar fragments of first or early second-century date (Fabric 57). This material is likely to be residual material, incorporated by the disturbance of pre-existing earlier deposits when the pond was dug. Alternatively, it may be early material thrown into the pond when it was still in use (Table 8).

The Fill (GK1–15)

The vast majority of the material in the pond comes from the back-filling deposits, 15.18% by weight of the total pottery from the site (11.73% by R.EVE). The presence of Oxfordshire colour-coat (Fabric 8), late hook-rimmed jars (Fabric 58) and Nene Valley ware (especially Fabrics 5A–C) date the assemblage to post-350/360+, ie Ceramic phase 5.2 (Table 8). 32.72% by weight (21.48% by R.EVE) of all Phase 5.2 material was recovered from this feature. Fig. 40 illustrates the percentages of each fabric recovered. In comparison with the late well deposit and Ditch FZ in ABO (Figs 36 and 42 respectively) the amount of Hadham ware and late shelly ware present in the pond is larger. The amount of misc. grey wares is considerably less. It is unlikely that these variations mean a different date for this fill, but rather reflect the variations within different household assemblages, or the rather haphazard dumping of domestic debris. As in the well deposit, a small amount of late Alice Holt/Farnham ware (fragments from a flanged bowl) and black-burnished wares are present.

Much of the material from the pond fill comprises small, abraded fragments. The upper layers have suffered badly from plough damage. The largest group of pottery (GK+) had been so disturbed that it could not be used within the quantification. Once again, there is evidence of this being a single-action deposit, with numerous sherd links between layers. The coin dates support this, since some of the latest coins occur nearer the bottom of the deposit in GK 9 and 10.

The samian is of particular interest even though it is obviously all residual. There is evidence for links with sherds in ABO, Ditch FZ, and also possibly in Context EAA 2 (below and *Samian* report), suggesting that the same dump or dumps were incorporated in the backfill of different features at different periods. There may well be other links between much of the coarse ware within different assemblages, but time did not allow such cross-site analysis.

Fig. 40 shows the occurrence of vessel forms within the assemblage, showing a marked predominance of jars (19.12% necked, 15.84% hook-rimmed), bowls (6.78% flanged) and dishes (all shallow, straight-sided 'dog dish' types). All the mortaria present are from the Oxfordshire kilns (Fabric 21).

Coins: 367–378; 364–378 (three); 350–353; 348–350; 335–341; 330–335 (two); 287–293; late third to late fourth century.

Fabrics: 5A, 5B, 5C, 8, 9, 12, 15–17, 19, 20A, 21, 22, 28, 36–43, 45–49, 52, 56, 58, 60, 61.

Forms: Figs 52 & 53, nos 272–332 (Cat. nos 25, 28, 32, 56, 61, 153, 160, 161, 164, 215, 216, 225, 231, 242, 244, 245*).

Samian: Form Dr.27, S.G. Pre-Flavian; M. de V. possibly from cup by Severus in EAA 2. Form Dr.27 g, S.G. Pre-Flavian. Form Dr.30 or 37, C.G. Antonine (twice). Form Dr.37, C.G. Antonine (three); E.G. 180–240 (SHL with

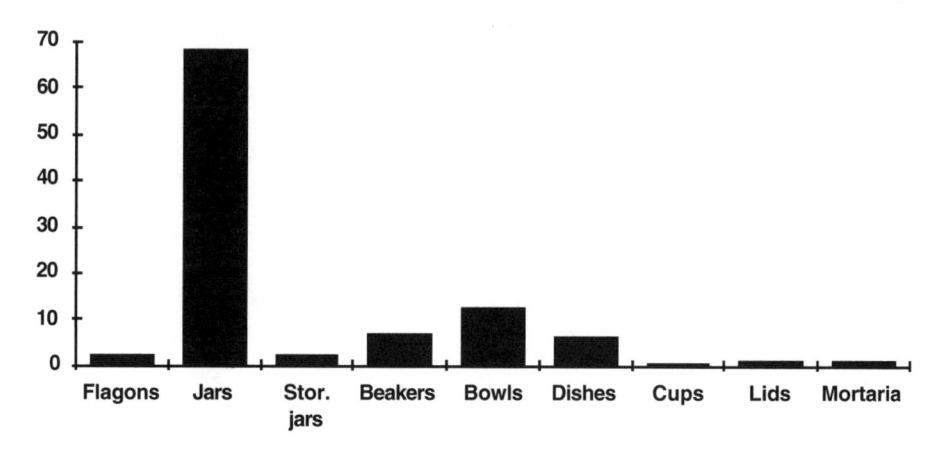

Figure 38   Occurrence of vessel forms, Quarry EAA, Ceramic phase 3.

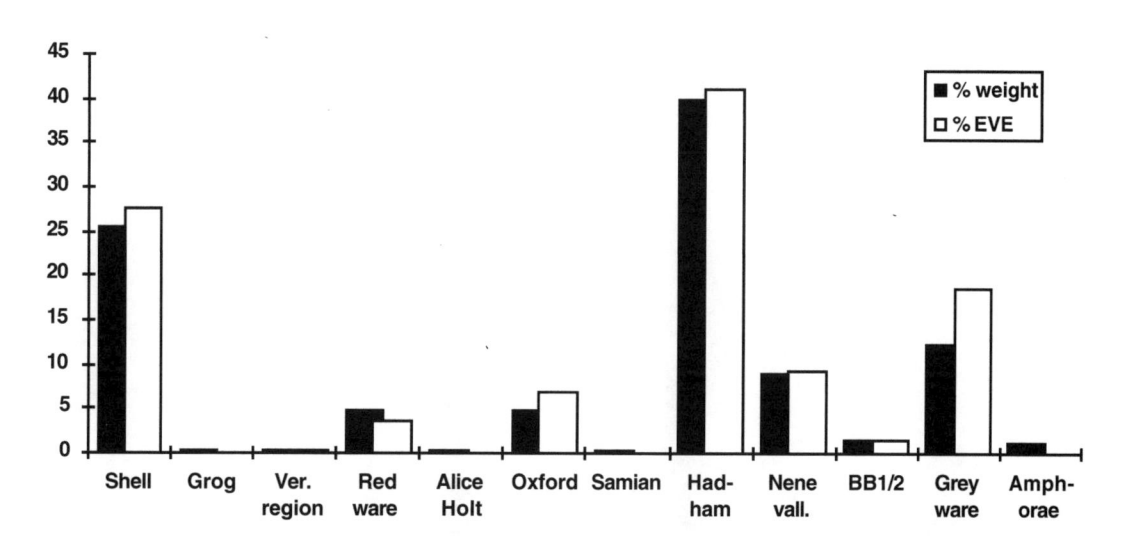

Figure 39   Fabric occurrence by weight percentage and R.EVE, Pond GK, Ceramic phase 5.2.

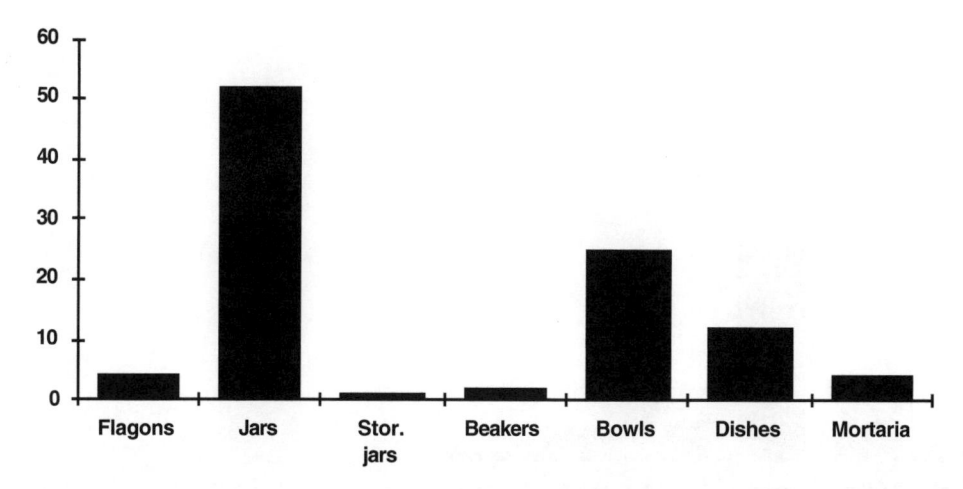

Figure 40   Occurrence of vessel forms, Pond GK, Ceramic phase 5.2.

FZ 5, QR 1). Form Dr.33, E.G. Late second to first half of third century. Dish, C.G. Hadrianic–Antonine. Sherds C.G. and E.G.

CIRCULAR BUILDING ABO

Only sections of the penannular ditch were excavated. Over 77% by weight (79% by R.EVE) of this large ceramic assemblage comes from ditch section FZ. Figs 41 and 42 show the percentage fabric and form composition for this assemblage. The deposit contains second-century material including Samian, but in the main comprises an accumulation of third to fourth-century pottery in fairly good condition. The deposit includes Nene Valley ware (Fabric 5a) and late shell-tempered jars, giving a *terminus post quem* of c.350/360+ (Ceramic phase 5.2). On excavation, eighteen different layers were recognised in the fill. However, close examination of the assemblage shows enough sherd links and mixing throughout the layers to suggest, in this section at least, that the ditch was filled in a single action using domestic rubbish. The coin evidence supports this; fourth-century coins were recovered from the fill (**Coin 137, 152, 188**), with third-century coins appearing towards the top (**Coin 88, 99, 119, 133**).

Much of the material shows signs of having been burnt. The assemblage compares well in its range of forms to that of the pond fill [GK], and as samian fragments in FZ5 and FZ6 come from a vessel recovered from the pond (Fig. 31.10) it is likely that the same dump was used to fill both features. If so, the relatively small number of late shell-tempered jars in FZ and the lack of shell-tempered dishes in comparison with the pond assemblage is coincidental.

Coins: 268–70 (2); 268–275; 287–293; 305–306; 330–335, 330–337; 341–348.
Fabrics: 5a, 5b, 8, 9, 12, 13, 15–17, 19, 20a, 21, 22, 34, 37–42, 45–52, 56, 58, 58a, 60.
Forms: Fig. 51.231–250 (Cat. nos 10, 13, 15, 57–59, 61, 74, 225, 240, 276, 298, 317, 326, 330*).
Bowl Ver. no. 933; Storage jar, Ver. no. 919.
Samian: Cup(?), first century. Cup, Hadrianic–early Antonine; sherd, Flavian or Flavian–Trajanic; sherds, Hadrianic–Antonine; Dr 33, Antonine (two); Dr 33, late second to first half of third century; Dr 31, Antonine (two); Dr 18/31, Trajanic; Dr 18/31, Hadrianic to early Antonine; Dr 37, 180–240 (SHL FZ 5, FZ 6, GK 5, GK 14, QR 1).

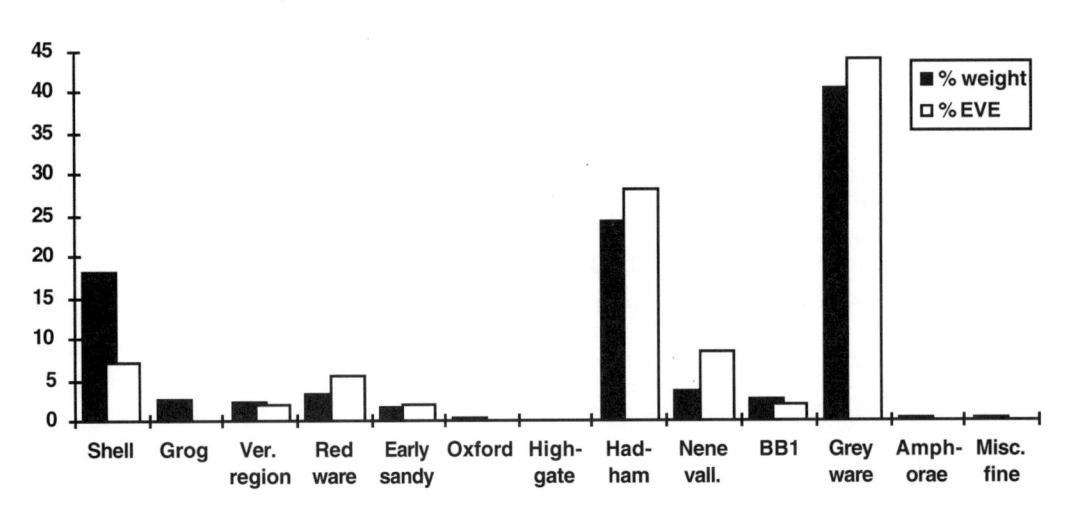

Figure 41   Fabric occurrence by weight percentage and R.EVE, Ditch ABO, Ceramic phase 5.2.

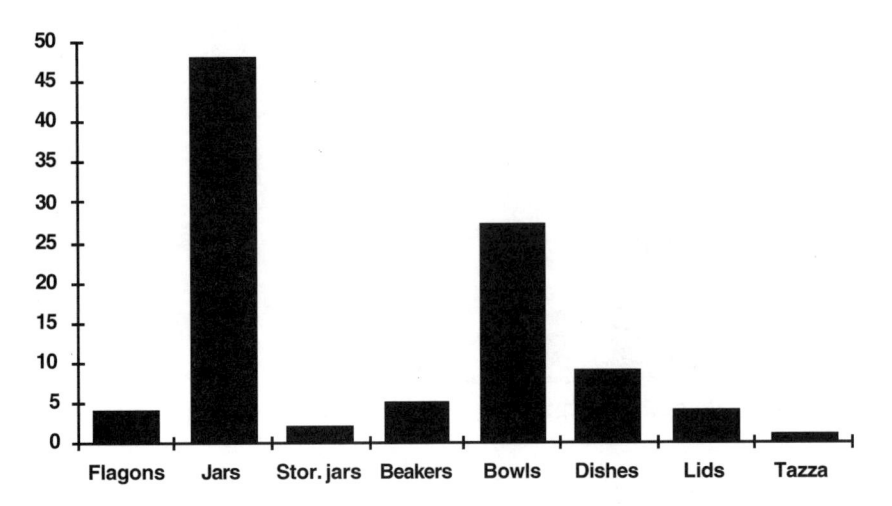

Figure 42   Occurrence of vessel forms, Ditch ABO, Ceramic phase 5.2.

TABLE 10: Fabric incidence from the Cemetery.

Fab. no.	Description	Quantity No.	%	Weight (g)	%	R. EVE No.	%
9	Hadham oxidised red ware	1	0.03	1	0.01	–	–
11	?Local mica-dusted ware	1	0.03	30	0.21	0.35	3.55
17	Misc. fine red ware	11	0.38	212	1.49	1.0	10.15
18	Oxidised 'gritty' ware	2	0.07	7	0.05	–	–
19	Misc. red wares	293	10.03	1205	8.45	0.31	3.15
20	Verulamium region/Brockley Hill ware	120	4.11	699	4.9	–	–
24	Eggshell ware	33	1.13	15	0.11	0.2	2.03
26	Misc. fine white wares	42	1.44	71	0.5	–	–
33	Early sandy ware	413	14.13	2045	14.34	0.7	7.11
34	Early sand- and grog–tempered wares	507	17.35	834	5.85	0.64	6.5
37	Misc. sandy grey wares	168	5.75	252	1.77	0.55	5.58
39	Hadham grey ware	52	1.78	127	0.9	0.08	0.81
40	Grit–tempered grey ware: ?Hadham	21	0.72	322	2.26	–	–
41	'Pimply' grey ware	5	0.17	5	0.04	–	–
48	Misc. hard-fired sand-tempered ware with smoothed surfaces	1	0.03	29	0.20	–	–
49	Misc. coarse sandy wares	24	0.82	293	2.05	0.95	9.64
52	Red-brown grog-tempered wares	178	6.09	1270	8.91	0.06	0.61
53	Black grog-tempered wares	156	5.34	1341	9.4	0.08	0.81
54	Grog and grit-tempered wares	187	6.4	570	4.0	–	–
56	Coarse oxidised storage jar ware	4	0.14	37	0.26	–	–
57	Early handmade shell-tempered ware	528	18.07	1576	11.05	0.44	4.47
58	Shell-tempered ware	109	3.73	574	4.03	–	–
59	Red/buff coloured shell-tempered ware	56	1.92	768	5.39	–	–
61	Samian (all industries)	(not counted)		1939	13.6	4.49	45.59
62	Residual Iron Age fabrics	10	0.34	33	0.23	–	–
	TOTAL AMOUNTS:	**2922**		**14255**		**9.85**	

TABLE 11: Totals of assemblages for each Ceramic phase.

Ceramic phase	Sherd count	Weight (g)	R.EVE
–	1248 (4.07%)	9424 (3.0%)	4.84 (1.54%)
1	1274 (4.16%)	8904 (2.84%)	7.11 (2.27%)
2	1825 (5.96%)	18490 (5.9%)	12.97 (4.13%)
3	6184 (20.18%)	100771 32.17%)	88.8 (28.31%)
4	1408 (4.60%)	12858 (4.1%)	10.77 (3.43%)
5.1	616 (2.01%)	6407 (2.04%)	5.94 (1.9%)
5.2	15960 (52.09%)	138929 (44.34%)	170.26 (54.28%)
5	2122 (6.93%)	17596 (5.61%)	12.99 (4.14%)
TOTALS:	**30637**	**313379**	**313.68**

Numbers in brackets refer to the percentage of the total.
NB: totals and percentages given for sherd count do not include samian.

TABLE 12: Fabric incidence by Ceramic phase.

Fabric no.		Ceramic phase —	1	2	3	4	5.1	5.2	5
1	sherd count	–	–	–	0.36	–	–	–	–
	weight	–	–	–	0.06	–	–	–	–
	R.EVE	–	–	–	0.96	–	–	–	–
2	sherd count	–	–	–	–	–	–	0.02	–
	weight	–	–	–	–	–	–	0.01	–
	R.EVE	–	–	–	–	–	–	–	–
3	sherd count	0.24	–	–	–	–	–	–	–
	weight	0.23	–	–	–	–	–	–	–
	R.EVE	–	–	–	–	–	–	–	–
4	sherd count	–	–	–	0.24	–	–	–	–
	weight	–	–	–	0.06	–	–	–	–
	R.EVE	–	–	–	0.96	–	–	–	–
5	sherd count	1.2	0.16	–	0.74	1.5	4.38	4.93	3.29
	weight	0.38	0.17	–	0.16	0.87	1.87	4.82	1.75
	R.EVE	–	–	–	–	–	–	2.63	3.0
6	sherd count	–	–	–	–	–	–	0.02	–
	weight	–	–	–	–	–	–	0.02	–
	R.EVE	–	–	–	–	–	–	–	–
7	sherd count	–	–	–	–	–	0.16	0.01	–
	weight	–	–	–	–	–	0.7	0.01	–
	R.EVE	–	–	–	–	–	5.89	0.03	–
8	sherd count	0.16	–	0.05	0.05	0.78	0.65	1.22	0.89
	weight	0.12	–	0.05	0.02	0.46	0.29	1.66	0.48
	R.EVE	–	–	–	0.11	0.37	–	1.37	0.85
9/10	sherd count	11.53	–	1.69	1.81	7.38	11.85	27.42	18.42
	weight	6.29	–	0.52	0.56	3.05	7.02	19.68	13.48
	R.EVE	11.15	–	–	0.59	1.21	13.46	14.63	10.16
11	sherd count	–	–	0.11	–	–	–	0.01	–
	weight	–	–	0.21	–	–	–	0.01	–
	R.EVE	–	–	1.85	–	–	–	–	–
12	sherd count	0.32	–	0.05	0.74	0.35	–	0.17	0.09
	weight	0.45	–	0.01	0.49	0.02	–	0.18	0.05
	R.EVE	–	–	–	1.05	–	–	0.07	–
13	sherd count	–	–	–	0.26	–	–	0.03	–
	weight	–	–	–	0.27	–	–	0.02	–
	R.EVE	–	–	–	1.12	–	–	0.07	–
14	sherd count	–	–	–	0.01	–	–	0.01	–
	weight	–	–	–	0.0	–	–	0.01	–
	R.EVE	–	–	–	–	–	–	–	–
15	sherd count	0.48	–	0.11	0.30	0.28	–	0.73	0.04
	weight	0.51	–	0.14	0.28	0.04	–	0.78	0.01
	R.EVE	–	–	–	–	–	–	0.32	–
16	sherd count	0.64	–	–	0.04	–	0.32	1.31	0.47
	weight	0.25	–	–	0.04	–	0.15	0.61	0.23
	R.EVE	–	–	–	–	–	1.85	1.52	–
17	sherd count	0.32	–	0.16	0.03	0.14	0.48	0.33	0.04
	weight	0.08	–	0.11	0.01	0.05	0.18	0.36	0.22
	R.EVE	2.27	–	1.69	–	–	–	0.84	0.84
18	sherd count	0.56	–	–	0.13	–	0.16	0.08	0.47
	weight	0.75	–	–	0.07	–	0.14	0.06	0.46
	R.EVE	6.61	–	–	–	–	–	–	–
19	sherd count	3.52	2.35	5.8	2.44	2.98	2.27	5.16	2.07
	weight	1.55	0.88	2.44	0.88	1.52	1.37	2.93	1.32
	R.EVE	–	–	3.16	0.22	2.69	–	0.93	1.15
20	sherd count	1.68	3.61	2.19	9.55	2.62	0.97	0.56	1.83
	weight	2.16	6.92	1.86	7.02	2.07	0.79	0.77	1.91
	R.EVE	5.16	14.06	1.15	7.9	1.11	3.03	0.48	–
21	sherd count	–	–	0.05	–	0.07	0.48	0.26	0.14
	weight	–	–	0.07	–	0.56	0.78	1.47	0.07
	R.EVE	–	–	–	–	0.93	–	0.77	–

Fabric no.		Ceramic phase –	1	2	3	4	5.1	5.2	5
22	sherd count	0.08	–	–	–	0.14	0.16	0.24	0.18
	weight	0.46	–	–	–	0.06	0.68	0.92	0.35
	R.EVE	–	–	–	–	–	–	0.28	–
23	sherd count	–	0.23	0.05	–	–	–	–	–
	weight	–	0.02	0.05	–	–	–	–	–
	R.EVE	–	–	–	–	–	–	–	–
24		only found in the cemetery							
25	sherd count	–	–	–	0.03	–	–	–	–
	weight	–	–	–	0.44	–	–	–	–
	R.EVE	–	–	–	1.13	–	–	–	–
26		only found in the cemetery							
27	sherd count	–	–	–	0.02	–	–	–	–
	weight	–	–	–	0.04	–	–	–	–
	R.EVE	–	–	–	0.1	–	–	–	–
28	sherd count	–	–	–	–	–	–	0.17	–
	weight	–	–	–	–	–	–	0.08	–
	R.EVE	–	–	–	–	–	–	0.1	–
29	sherd count	–	0.07	–	–	–	–	–	–
	weight	–	0.01	–	–	–	–	–	–
	R.EVE	–	–	–	–	–	–	–	–
30	sherd count	–	–	–	0.56	–	–	0.01	–
	weight	–	–	–	0.62	–	–	0.01	–
	R.EVE	–	–	–	2.25	–	–	–	–
31	sherd count	–	–	–	0.14	–	–	0.01	–
	weight	–	–	–	0.13	–	–	0.0	–
	R.EVE	–	–	–	1.13	–	–	–	–
32	sherd count	–	–	–	–	–	–	0.01	–
	weight	–	–	–	–	–	–	0.0	–
	R.EVE	–	–	–	–	–	–	–	–
33	sherd count	2.0	1.17	2.52	0.19	0.35	–	0.03	0.75
	weight	1.4	2.53	1.61	0.08	0.28	–	0.04	0.48
	R.EVE	3.09	3.37	1.62	0.19	–	–	0.05	–
34	sherd count	2.8	23.39	21.15	1.68	9.23	–	0.27	3.39
	weight	0.68	25.86	19.87	0.79	4.55	–	0.35	3.5
	R.EVE	–	21.23	20.5	1.06	2.6	–	0.18	1.15
35	sherd count	0.24	7.29	–	1.08	–	–	0.01	0.04
	weight	0.19	3.34	–	1.21	–	–	0.01	0.02
	R.EVE	–	10.26	–	0.12	–	–	–	–
36	sherd count	0.08	0.23	0.43	0.19	–	–	0.08	–
	weight	0.22	0.22	0.12	0.07	–	–	0.04	–
	R.EVE	–	–	–	0.56	–	–	–	–
37	sherd count	8.01	1.56	14.63	12.32	10.36	12.5	7.48	10.65
	weight	6.66	1.41	10.17	7.15	8.79	11.83	7.45	7.97
	R.EVE	9.5	6.46	24.05	9.83	15.69	3.36	4.05	13.24
38	sherd count	0.8	0.08	0.22	1.34	–	–	0.02	0.23
	weight	0.36	0.11	0.04	0.67	–	–	0.02	0.08
	R.EVE	–	–	–	1.42	–	–	–	–
39	sherd count	25.64	3.06	12.6	32.4	38.49	27.59	17.85	23.23
	weight	18.31	1.8	6.32	21.16	41.63	24.64	15.92	22.45
	R.EVE	15.08	0.7	8.17	29.23	39.46	0.32	22.91	9.7
40	sherd count	0.8	–	0.16	0.32	0.49	0.32	0.46	0.42
	weight	2.83	–	0.14	0.13	0.65	0.25	0.56	0.67
	R.EVE	–	–	–	–	–	–	0.15	–
41	sherd count	4.32	0.08	0.27	5.37	6.25	9.57	4.9	4.52
	weight	2.88	0.03	0.41	4.85	5.27	6.02	5.04	3.21
	R.EVE	8.47	–	–	4.86	11.04	5.05	20.62	8.69
42	sherd count	0.48	–	0.05	0.24	0.21	0.97	0.63	0.42
	weight	1.29	–	0.05	0.22	0.62	0.61	1.34	0.82
	R.EVE	3.09	–	–	0.29	3.06	–	0.99	3.69
43	sherd count	–	–	–	–	–	–	0.05	–
	weight	–	–	–	–	–	–	0.12	–
	R.EVE	–	–	–	–	–	–	0.05	–

Fabric no.		Ceramic phase –	1	2	3	4	5.1	5.2	5
44	sherd count	0.16	–	–	–	–	–	0.01	–
	weight	0.49	–	–	–	–	–	0.01	–
	R.EVE	–	–	–	–	–	–	–	–
45	sherd count	0.08	0.07	–	0.02	0.07	2.27	0.89	0.99
	weight	0.07	0.09	–	0.02	0.32	1.22	0.58	0.85
	R.EVE	–	–	–	–	1.39	1.01	0.49	2.69
46	sherd count	0.4	–	–	0.17	0.21	0.81	0.36	0.37
	weight	0.37	–	–	0.1	0.63	0.9	0.85	0.35
	R.EVE	–	–	–	–	2.87	–	1.24	1.92
47	sherd count	–	–	0.43	–	–	0.97	0.18	–
	weight	–	–	0.2	–	–	0.6	0.12	–
	R.EVE	–	–	–	–	–	–	–	–
48	sherd count	0.56	–	0.05	1.29	0.57	6.49	3.8	2.45
	weight	1.59	–	0.11	1.28	0.58	19.29	6.81	5.93
	R.EVE	20.66	–	0.38	2.43	–	19.52	5.83	7.54
49	sherd count	5.44	1.02	1.97	1.89	2.55	6.49	4.71	5.65
	weight	4.79	0.89	2.15	0.86	2.57	6.1	5.85	8.76
	R.EVE	2.06	0.84	1.93	0.8	1.57	2.35	1.99	13.0
50	sherd count	0.16	–	–	–	–	0.16	0.1	–
	weight	0.13	–	–	–	–	0.06	0.09	–
	R.EVE	–	–	–	–	–	–	0.03	–
51	sherd count	–	–	–	0.04	–	0.81	0.02	–
	weight	–	–	–	0.04	–	0.51	0.02	–
	R.EVE	–	–	–	–	–	–	–	–
52	sherd count	5.6	6.43	13.48	9.52	2.41	0.48	0.2	1.65
	weight	3.21	11.03	15.95	10.3	2.61	0.46	0.31	2.52
	R.EVE	–	8.72	9.09	18.76	–	–	0.02	1.15
53	sherd count	3.85	19.94	6.52	0.56	0.42	–	0.05	0.23
	weight	4.29	21.0	7.15	0.46	0.34	–	0.04	0.28
	R.EVE	7.64	24.33	7.47	0.38	–	–	–	0.92
54	sherd count	–	0.23	–	0.02	–	–	–	–
	weight	–	0.29	–	0.01	–	–	–	–
	R.EVE	–	–	–	–	–	–	–	–
55	sherd count	0.08	–	–	1.19	0.07	–	0.02	–
	weight	0.17	–	–	3.26	0.13	–	0.15	–
	R.EVE	–	–	–	–	–	–	0.03	–
56	sherd count	4.88	1.88	2.9	3.92	2.48	0.48	0.51	1.27
	weight	12.09	5.72	7.71	9.49	6.1	0.29	0.95	3.69
	R.EVE	–	1.12	1.92	0.71	1.11	–	0.03	0.92
57	sherd count	1.52	26.76	8.16	0.82	0.07	–	0.06	0.37
	weight	0.77	16.83	10.45	0.57	0.06	–	0.02	0.45
	R.EVE	–	8.86	12.02	1.44	–	–	0.04	–
58	sherd count	7.13	–	2.74	3.77	8.45	7.63	13.22	14.51
	weight	5.68	–	1.43	3.69	9.97	8.91	15.45	13.51
	R.EVE	2.89	–	0.77	1.66	12.35	8.92	10.78	9.85
59	sherd count	0.72	–	0.44	2.81	–	–	1.2	0.33
	weight	1.5	–	0.24	10.79	–	–	2.09	0.42
	R.EVE	2.27	–	–	1.87	–	–	0.74	–
60	sherd count	6.41	–	0.66	1.16	0.99	0.32	0.15	0.47
	weight	12.36	–	8.29	7.69	4.91	4.06	0.79	0.44
	R.EVE	–	–	–	–	–	–	–	–
61	sherd count	–	–	–	–	–	–	–	–
	weight	3.32	0.69	1.96	3.74	1.02	0.03	0.39	0.12
	R.EVE	–	–	4.16	6.83	2.6	–	0.08	–
62	sherd count	2.96	0.31	0.27	0.06	–	–	0.02	–
	weight	0.94	0.08	0.14	0.01	–	–	0.01	–
	R.EVE	–	–	–	–	–	–	–	–

NB: sherd count percentages do not include samian.

Catalogue Of The Illustrated Pottery

Publications most frequently cited in the text have been abbreviated as follows: Ver.No. = Wilson, 1972, 1983, 1984. Baldock No. = Rigby, 1986. N.V.No. = Howe *et al* 1981. Young = Young, 1977. Also: SHL = Sherd link. Cp. = ceramic phase. The ceramic phase has only been cited for a feature or context that has not already been discussed above.

WELL CAB
(Figs 43–46)

Lowest layers (CAB 16–19)

Grog-tempered wares

1 Fabric 53: Carinated wide-mouthed cup or bowl with multiple cordons; upper wall may have been more convex. Patchy ochre brown to dark grey surfaces, interior and core; abraded but remains of burnishing. Wheeler 1936, 161, Group B from Prae Wood, Fig. 15.35a–d; dates first half of first to mid first AD. Thompson 1982, category E1–2, or F3–2 which has a pedestal; not known as a post-conquest form. (CAB 18) R.EVE = 0.04 .

2 Fabric 53: Jar. Ochre brown to dark grey surfaces, interior and core. Lightly burnished surface. Rook 1970b, Fig. II.3, first third of first century AD. (CAB 16) R.EVE = 0.08.

Shaft central filling (CAB 6–13)

Hadham reduced wares

3 Fabric 39: narrow-necked jar. Hard; blue-grey; lightly burnished rim and neck. (SHL: CAB 11,13) R.EVE = 0.20.

4 Fabric 39: everted-rim jar. Fabric as **3**; burnished upper body. (CAB 13). R.EVE = 0.22.

5 Fabric 39: narrow-necked jar. Fabric as **3**. Lightly burnished surface. Decoration: burnished lattice in a "herring-bone" form around upper girth. Similar vessel, with different decoration, in Rook 1973, Grange Cemetery No.7, Antonine. (SHL: CAB 7,11) R.EVE = 0.80.

6 Fabric 39?: everted-rim jar. Semi-complete when reconstructed. Hard; medium grey. Decoration: deep band of burnished acute lattice. (SHL: CAB 6,7,9,11,12,13). R.EVE = 0.28. B.EVE = 1.00.

7 Fabric 39: cordoned jar. Complete when sherds reconstructed, except for small section of lower body. Hard; blue-grey with self-slip; burnishing on upper body, extending onto rim interior. Both **7** and **8** are Romanised development of an earlier native type. Same as Baldock No.493; early to mid second century; see also Wheeler 1936, 184 and Fig. 28.18, from well deposit in Building IV.8 at Verulamium; dating 160–190; also Partridge 1977, Fig. 42.6, from Ford Street Cemetery, Braughing; Hadrianic. (CAB 11) R.EVE = 1.00.

8 Fabric 39: cordoned jar. Semi-complete when reconstructed. Similar to **7**, only smaller. (CAB 11) REVE = 0.90. B.EVE = 0.20.

9 Fabric 39: straight-sided jar with folded-over rim. Almost complete except for base when reconstructed. Hard; blue-grey with self-slip; burnishing of exterior surface executed with uneven, downward strokes. Unique on the site. (CAB 11) R.EVE = 0.89. B.EVE = 0.97.

Highgate Wood wares

10 Fabric 38: poppy head beaker. Semi-complete when reconstructed. Medium grey with external white slip over upper body, extending onto rim interior. Decoration: vertical zones of barbotine dots around girth of vessel. Similar to Ver.No.838, dated 145 –70. See also Wheeler 1936, Fig. 27.12 and 13, dated 160–190. (CAB 11,13) R.EVE = 0.16. B.EVE = 0.91.

11 Fabric 38: poppy head beaker. Shorter neck than **10**. Semi-complete when reconstructed. Medium to dark grey with external black slip over upper body, extending onto rim interior. Decoration: vertical zones of barbotine dots. Examples at Verulamium, *eg* Ver.No. 1740, dated 90–130, normal at Verulamium in the second quarter of the second century; at London, *eg* form IIIF.4, dated 100–175 (Hammerson 1988, 207). See also **10** (CAB 11) R.EVE = 0.65. B.EVE = 0.15.

Other coarse grey wares

12 Fabric 37: everted-rim jar. Hard; medium grey surfaces; darker grey core. Traces of black slip on and below rim. Decoration: deep band of burnished acute lattice. Ver.No.614; 125–160 date range. See also Wheeler 1936, Fig. 28.23, dated 160–190. (CAB 11). R.EVE = 0.49.

13 Fabric 41: necked jar. Over half the vessel can be reconstructed. Medium grey; surfaces has been wiped or smoothed unevenly, giving a pimply, slightly rough finish. Potter's fingerprints still visible on lower body/base. Decoration: rilling on shoulder. Similar vessels at Baldock, *eg* No.663, of Hadrianic–Antonine date, and Ver.No.2174, context dated 155/60. (SHL CAB 11,12,13). R.EVE = 0.35. B.EVE = 0.91.

14 Fabric 37: necked jar. Semi-complete when reconstructed. Smaller but similar form to **13**; longer neck. Hard fine fabric; medium grey; surface is unevenly smoothed, giving a sandy abrasive and, in some areas, pitted finish. Traces of lime-scaling on the interior and sooty patches on the exterior surfaces. (SHL CAB 11,13) R.EVE = 0.76. B.EVE = 1.00.

15 Fabric 37: necked jar. Semi-complete when reconstructed. Decoration: narrow zone of rilling on shoulder. Hard; medium to dark grey ware; smoothed surface. (CAB 11). R.EVE = 0.23. B.EVE = 0.55.

16 Fabric 48: bowl with rounded rim. semi-complete when reconstructed. Hard; dark grey core and blackish surfaces; lightly burnished rim top. Underside of base roughly smoothed. Decoration: burnished lattice on a matt background. An imitation of BB2 'pie dish' form. See Ver.No.715, 135–180 date range. At Baldock, the form dates late Antonine, *eg* Baldock No.535. In London the form appears after *c.*140, but is commoner in the later Antonine period, *eg* Hammerson 1988, 208; Southwark form IVH4. For origin of form see

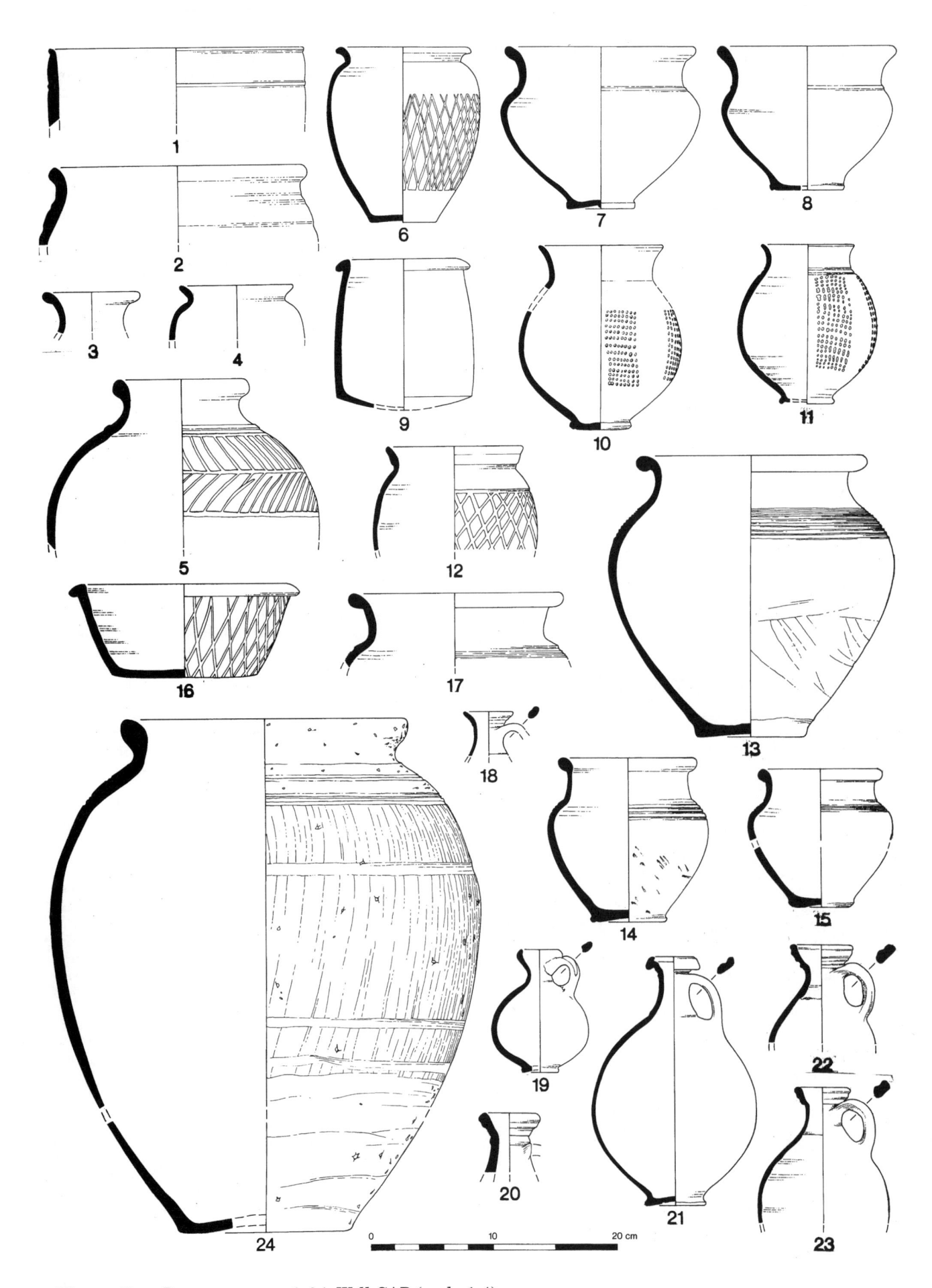

Figure 43 Roman pottery; 1–24, Well CAB (scale 1:4).

Farrar 1973. (SHL CAB 7,11). R.EVE = 0.80. B.EVE = 0.90.

Grog-tempered wares

17 Fabric 52: necked jar; slightly flaring rim. Hard; exterior is patchy buff – ochre brown – grey and lightly burnished. Decoration: narrow zone of rilling on shoulder. Similar form to Baldock No.657; Antonine. (CAB 6). R.EVE = 0.22.

Misc. oxidised wares

18 Fabric 12: ring-necked flagon; badly moulded rings. Bright orange; original overall white slip now very patchy from abrasion. (SHL CAB 11,13). R.EVE = 0.83.

19 Fabric 13: miniature flagon or *tettina*, spout not present. Complete when reconstructed except for one fragment from body. Hard; bright orange, granular; abraded surface with faint traces of white slip remaining. (CAB 11). R.EVE = 1.00. B.EVE = 1.00.

20 Fabric 31: ring-necked flagon; badly moulded rings. Hard, granular; pale buff-yellow surfaces; slurried or self-slipped externally. (SHL CAB 6,11,12). R.EVE = 1.00.

21 Fabric 25: flagon. Complete when excavated: in very good condition. Hard, fine, white ware; smoothed external surface. (CAB 10). R.EVE = 1.00. B.EVE = 1.00.

22 Fabric 19: ring-necked flagon; badly moulded rings. Orange to light brown surfaces. similar types at Verulamium, *eg* Ver.No.559; 135–180 date range. (CAB 11,13). R.EVE = 1.00.

23 Fabric 30: ring-necked flagon, as **22**, but with shallower flaring rim. Hard; buff-yellow core and surfaces; slurried or self-slipped externally. See Ver.No.1940; 140–190 date range. (CAB 11,13). R.EVE = 1.00.

Shell-tempered ware

24 Fabric 59: storage jar. Semi-complete when reconstructed. Hard; patchy buff-pale orange surfaces with grey core; smoothed rim and lower body. Decoration: parallel bands of narrow grooves at shoulder and wider shallow grooves around girth; "furrowed" upper body. Very similar to Ver.No.919, from deposits dating 150–200. (SHL CAB 6,7,11). R.EVE = 0.78. B.EVE = 0.41.

25 Fabric 59: narrow-necked storage jar. Semi-complete when reconstructed. Hard; patchy pale buff-beige surfaces with grey core; smoothed exterior and rim. Decoration: faint rilling around maximum girth. Very similar to Baldock No.675 (except for decoration) which comes from a third-century deposit. (SHL CAB 8,9,11,13). R.EVE = 0.56. B.EVE = 1.00.

26 Fabric 59: narrow-necked storage jar. Same form as **25** except larger, with more extensive rilling. Semi-complete when reconstructed. (CAB 11). R.EVE = 0.40. B.EVE = 0.90.

Upper layers (EC 1–2; BX 1=ES 1; ES 2=ES 3=CAB 1=EE 1=BX 2; CAB 2–5; ES 4–5, 7–9)

Nene Valley wares

27 Fabric 5B: pentice-moulded beaker. Semi-complete when reconstructed, sherds abraded. Bright orange paste; external, dark brown, matt colour coat. Decoration: rounded girth covered in rouletting. N.V.No.56; fourth century. (SHL CAB 1,2,3,BX 1,ES 2,EE 1). R.EVE = 0.55.

28 Fabric 5B: body sherd of decorated beaker, originally with beaded rim. Rather coarse, bright orange paste; dark brown to black colour coat with lustrous sheen. Decoration: white barbotine lattice over the colour coat and rouletting on the shoulder. For a parallel, see Ver.No.1134; from fill dating 310–315. Also similar to Ver.No.1860; date range 280–340. (SHL CAB 3, ES 8).

29 Fabric 5A: straight-sided beaker. Fine white-pale grey paste; dark brown, matt, colour coat. Decoration: white barbotine dots over the colour coat, below a narrow groove. Similar to Ver.No.1808; 250–300 date range. (CAB 3). Rim Dm = 60 mm. R.EVE = 0.07.

30 Fabric 5A: ?bag beaker with cornice-rim. White paste; dark brown, matt, colour coat. (CAB 3). R.EVE = 0.08.

31 Fabric 5A: shallow bowl with bead-rim. Dark brown to black, matt colour-coat. (BX1). R.EVE = 0.15.

32 Fabric 5C: hemispherical bowl. Rather soft, pinkish paste; pale orange colour coat, very abraded. Decoration: white barbotine arcs over colour coat. Similar vessel Baldock No.801; also late Roman. N.V.No.85. (SHL CAB 2, BX 1, ES 2). R.EVE = 0.27.

33 Fabric 22: hammer-head mortarium; ribbed exterior. Hard, white-buff ware. Black trituration grits; slightly worn. Decoration: reddish-brown painted vertical stripes on flange (EC 1). Rim Dm = 230 mm. R.EVE = 0.16.

Oxfordshire wares

34 Fabric 8: shallow bowl with bead-rim. Semi-complete when reconstructed. Darkish orange paste; surface abraded. Young type C45; in production 270–400+. (SHL CAB 1–4, ES 2,4,8, BX 1). R.EVE = 0.97.

35 Fabric 8: flanged bowl; flange and rim burnt. Young type C51.6; in production 240–400+. (ES 8). R.EVE = 0.13.

Hadham wares

36 Fabric 9: face flagon. In good condition; burnished surface. Face in moulded relief; head-dress represented by horizontal, slightly oval-shaped, incisions (CAB 2). R.EVE = 0.35.

37 Fabric 9: narrow-necked jar with a flaring neck and a frilled rim. Hard; fine orange ware, in good condition; burnished exterior. (EE 1). R.EVE = 0.13.

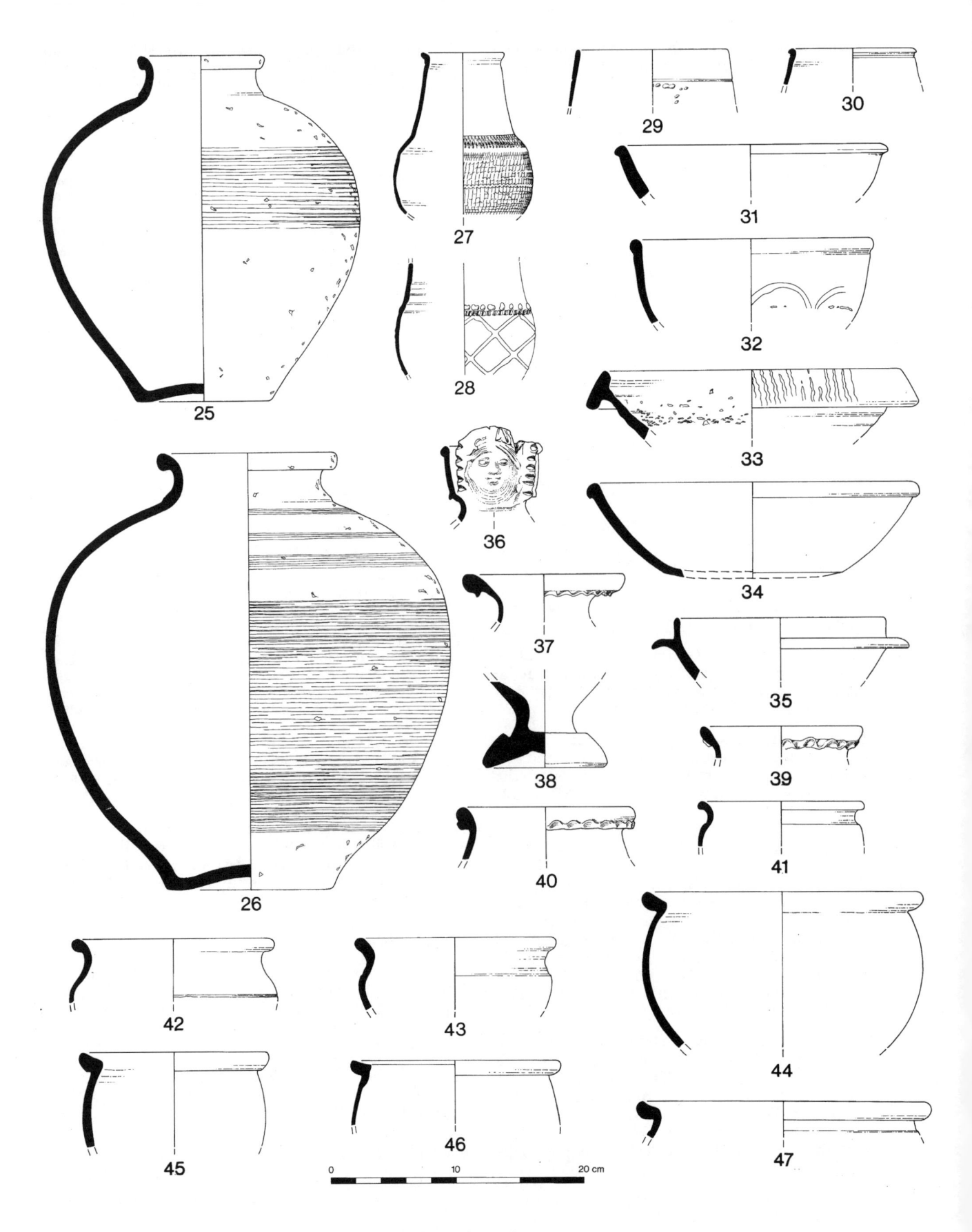

Figure 44   Roman pottery; 25–47, Well CAB (scale 1:4).

38   Fabric 9: pedestal base from a narrow-necked jar. Condition as for **36**. See Rook 1986, Fig. 34.108, dating 220–290 from coins. (CAB 3). B.EVE = 1.00.

39   Fabric 9: jar with frilled rim. Burnished surface. (ES 2). R.EVE = 0.13.

40   Fabric 9: form similar to **39**. Abraded. (SHL ES 2, BX 1). R.EVE = 0.10.

41   Fabric 9: necked jar. Condition as **36**. (ES 8). R.EVE = 0.20.

42   Fabric 39: s-profile jar. Hard; blue-grey; lightly burnished exterior. (SHL CAB 2, BX 1). R.EVE = 0.35.

43   Fabric 39: s-profile jar. Fabric as **42**; surfaces abraded. (CAB 1). R.EVE = 0.07.

44   Fabric 39: round-bodied jar. The body of this vessel is noticeably rounder than other examples on the site. Large sherds, in good condition; fresh breaks. Hard; blue – grey; smoothed exterior with narrow highly burnished zone under rim. Similar vessel Rook 1986, no. 135; dates 220–290 on coins. (SHL CAB 3, ES 8). R.EVE = 0.69.

45   Fabric 39: similar form, although not so rounded, and fabric to **44**. Smoothed exterior. The rim is slightly undercut. (CAB 1). R.EVE = 0.13.

46   Fabric 39: round-bodied jar with lid-seated rim. Internal wall thickened towards the rim. Fabric as **44**. Exterior lightly burnished. (CAB 3). R.EVE = 0.26.

47   Fabric 39: jar with lid-seated rim. Hard; blue-grey; abraded surfaces. (CAB 2). R.EVE = 0.09.

48   Fabric 39: jar with lid-seated rim. Fabric as **46**; light abrasion on surfaces. (ES 4). R.EVE = 0.07.

49   Fabric 9: hemispherical bowl; narrow cordon under rim. Rather soft, bright orange ware; surfaces powdery and abraded. (ES 2). R.EVE = 0.13.

50   Fabric 9: hemispherical bowl; grooves and cordon under rim. Fabric and condition as **49**. (SHL BX 1). R.EVE = 0.06.

51   Fabric 9: hemispherical bowl; grooves and cordon mid-way down wall. Bright orange fabric; lightly burnished surfaces. (SHL ES 2, ES 4). R.EVE = 0.45.

52   Fabric 39: shallow bowl or dish with rounded rim. Hard; blue-grey; burnished rim and upper body. (ES 4). R.EVE = 0.10.

53   Fabric 39: shallow dish with rounded rim. Profile. Hard; light grey core; dark grey burnished surfaces. (CAB 4). R.EVE = 0.10. B.EVE = 0.10.

54   Fabric 9: deep flanged bowl. Hard; bright orange; lightly burnished surfaces. (BX 1). R.EVE = 0.25.

55   Fabric 39: small, round-bodied bowl with short, hooked flange. Medium grey; smoothed surfaces; light burnishing on rim. (BX 1). R.EVE = 0.21.

56   Fabric 39: flanged bowl; straight, up-turned flange. Hard; blue-grey; burnishing on rim and top of flange. (CAB 1). R.EVE = 0.18.

57   Fabric 39: flanged bowl; straight, down-turned flange. Profile. Hard; blue-grey core and dark surfaces; burnished exterior, especially on top of flange. (ES 4). R.EVE = 0.13. B.EVE = 0.05.

58   Fabric 39: flanged bowl; slightly chamfered rim and horizontal flange. Hard; blue-grey; burnished exterior.(SHL CAB 1, CAB 3). R.EVE = 0.06.

59   Fabric 39: flanged bowl; down-turned flange. Hard; medium to dark grey; burnished rim and upper flange. (CAB 3). R.EVE = 0.18.

60   Fabric 39: small, straight-sided dish or 'dog dish'. Profile. Hard, blue-grey; lightly burnished surfaces. (CAB 2). R.EVE = 0.17. B.EVE = 0.15.

61   Fabric 39: larger version of **60**. (SHL CAB 2,3). R.EVE = 0.12.

62   Fabric 39: slightly deeper version of **61**. (ES 1). R.EVE = 0.09.

Alice Holt / Farnham ware

63   Fabric 43: flanged bowl; short, squared flange. Dark grey, ware, abraded; internal white slip extending over rim and flange. Most similar to Lyne and Jeffries 1979, type 5B.9; produced 270–420. (BX 1). R.EVE = 0.10.

Black Burnished ware

64   Fabric 42: straight-sided dish or 'dog dish'. Handmade. Smoothed, lightly burnished exterior; faint uneven rilling under rim. (CAB 1). R.EVE = 0.10.

Other coarse grey wares

65   Fabric 37: s-profile, cordoned jar. Dark grey core and medium grey surfaces; faint, oxidised streaks on exterior around girth; light burnishing on upper body, extending onto interior of rim. (CAB 3). R.EVE = 0.16.

66   Fabric 41: s-profile jar. Dark core and medium grey-brown surfaces; rather pimply finish to surfaces. Decoration: rilling on shoulder. (CAB 1). R.EVE = 0.15.

67   Fabric 41: s-profile jar; squared rim with external groove. Hard; light grey; pimply surfaces. Decoration: grooves around shoulder and girth. (SHL BX 1, ES 2,8, CAB 2, 3). R.EVE = 0.69.

68   Fabric 49: s-profile jar; slightly flaring rim. Hard; grey core and grey-brown surfaces; sandy, abrasive surfaces. (CAB 1). R.EVE = 0.13.

69   Fabric 49: similar form and fabric to **68**; longer neck. (BX 1). R.EVE = 0.16.

70   Fabric 48: neckless jar with moulded, hooked rim. Light grey core and grey-brown surfaces; smoothed interior with narrow burnished band below rim. (CAB 2). R.EVE = 0.11.

71   Fabric 37: small, everted-rim jar. Medium grey; lightly burnished exterior. (ES 7). R.EVE = 0.15.

72   Fabric 37: folded beaker. Parallel cordons under rim. Hard; medium grey core and dark grey, smoothed surfaces. (CAB 3). R.EVE = 0.16.

73   Fabric 48: shallow dish with rounded rim. Profile. Medium grey-brown ware; smoothed surfaces. (CAB 2). R.EVE = 0.08. B.EVE = 0.09.

74   Fabric 46: straight-sided dish. Profile. Patchy pinkish-buff to dark grey-black surfaces and core (?overfired); burnished. Wipe marks on interior

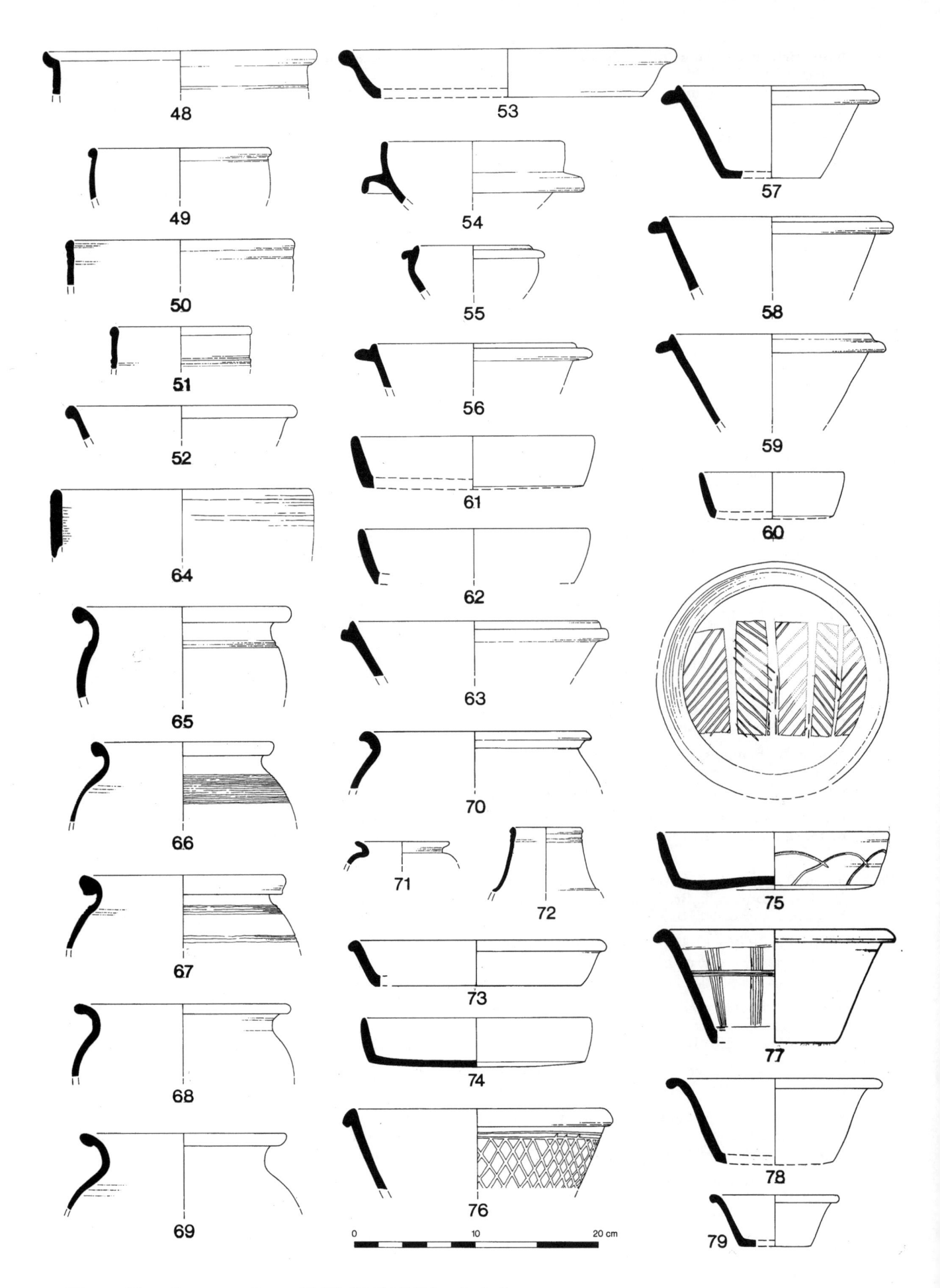

Figure 45   Roman pottery; 48–79, Well CAB (scale 1:4).

116

base. (SHL BX 1, EE 1, ES 2, CAB 2,3). R.EVE = 0.68. B.EVE = 0.34.

75 Fabric 48: straight-sided dish. Complete, except for small part of base, when reconstructed. Hard; dark grey; smoothed, burnished surfaces. Decoration: burnished intersecting arcs on exterior and burnished "herring-bone" design on interior base. Imitation of BB1/2 Gillam 329; 290–340 (Gillam 1977). (CAB 3). R.EVE = 0.80. B.EVE = 1.00.

76 Fabric 37: bowl with folded-over, down-turned rim. Hard; medium grey ware; burnished upper rim. Decoration: burnished acute lattice on matt background. Residual in this context, Ver.No. 2584 has a date range of 145–200. (ES 8). R.EVE = 0.16.

77 Fabric 48: Bowl with out-turned rim; developed 'pie dish' form. Profile. Hard; light grey core and dark grey surfaces; burnishing on upper rim, extending onto interior. Decoration: groups of vertical and horizontal burnished lines on a matt background. Examples of this type of vessel found at Verulamium and Baldock all date to the late third to fourth centuries. (CAB 3). R.EVE = 0.20. B.EVE = 0.11.

78 Fabric 48: similar form to **77**; small with more developed rim and apparently sagging base; uneven surfaces. Profile. Light grey core and dark grey surfaces. The lower half of the exterior wall is burnished whilst the upper body remains rough and rather granular; overall internal burnishing. Sooty patches under the rim. (SHL ES 2, CAB 1,4). R.EVE = 0.55. B.EVE = 0.09.

79 Fabric 48: much smaller version of **77** and **78**. Profile. Dark grey ware with lighter core; smoothed surfaces. (CAB 3). R.EVE = 0.09. B.EVE = 0.20.

80 Fabric 48: straight-sided flanged bowl; short, square flange, set rather low down wall. Abraded. Dark grey-black ware with medium grey core; light burnishing on rim and top of flange. Decoration: burnished rilling over body. (BX 1). R.EVE = 0.37.

81 Fabric 46: flanged bowl with bead-rim; flange slightly undercut. Hard-fired, smooth black surfaces with pinkish core; overall light burnishing. Similar vessels date to the late third to fourth centuries at Verulamium (Ver.No.1437 appears to be similar fabric). (CAB 2). R.EVE = 0.22.

82 Fabric 48: small flanged bowl; short, rounded flange. Almost half of vessel in one piece. Black, burnished surfaces. Sooty patches under flange. (CAB 2). R.EVE = 0.37. B.EVE = 0.50.

83 Fabric 48: flanged bowl with in-turned rim; elongated, straight flange set high up the wall. Dark grey ware with lighter core; smoothed surfaces. R.EVE = 0.33.

84 Fabric 41: rather shallow, convex-sided flanged bowl. Dark grey-brown ware with medium grey core; burnished rim and upper flange and narrow burnished bands around body. Smoothed interior surface. (SHL CAB 1,2). R.EVE = 0.30.

85 Fabric 48: lid with up-turned rim. Semi-complete. Hard-fired, medium grey ware. Smoothed surfaces. Shallow 'ribbing' around boss. (CAB 1). R.EVE = 0.49.

Misc. oxidised wares

86 Fabric 19: s-profile, round-bodied jar. Hard-fired sandy pale orange ware with light grey core. (ES 8). R.EVE = 0.21.

87 Fabric 19: necked jar with 'figure-7' rim. Hard-fired, fine sandy, bright orange ware. Abraded. (BX 1). R.EVE = 0.10.

88 Fabric 19: flanged bowl with bead rim; thickened hooked flange. Abraded. Sandy, dark reddish-orange ware, with medium grey core. (ES 2). R.EVE = 0.11.

Grog-tempered ware

89 Fabric 55: large storage jar with rounded rim. Hard-fired; coarse matrix but smooth surfaces. Similar example at Dicket Mead (Rook 1986, no. 69); unstratified. (ES 2). R.EVE = 0.05.

Shell-tempered ware

90 Fabric 58: jar with hooked, squared rim. Dark brown-black ware; abundant shell-tempering. Worn surfaces. (CAB 3). R.EVE = 0.13.

91 Fabric 58: hooked-rim jar. Black surfaces with greyish-buff core; abundant shell-tempering. Abraded. Ver.No.2194, dated 350–400. (BX 1). R.EVE = 0.06.

92 Fabric 58: convex-sided dish or bowl. Dark brown to black surfaces. Decoration: faint rilling under rim. (BX 1). R.EVE = 0.10.

93 Fabric 58: straight-walled bowl with rim folded-over to form pointed flange (slightly damaged). Dark brown-black surfaces with lighter, buff-coloured core. Abundant shell-tempering, but quite vesicular surface. Late Roman. (ES 8). R.EVE = 0.07.

94 Fabric 58: mortarium; only two fragments of flange remain. Dark reddish-brown ware with dark grey core; abundant shell-tempering. (SHL ES 4, CAB 3). Rim Dm = ?260 mm+.

OTHER CERAMIC PHASE 1 – PHASE 3 MATERIAL
(Figs 46–48)

JT: Chalky Feature (C.p.1)

Shell-tempered ware

95 Fabric 57: bead-rim jar; thickened internal rim. Handmade. Black, smoothed surfaces. R.EVE = 0.09.

PA: Gully

Early Roman sandy ware (C.p.1)

96 Fabric 33: lid. Handmade. Dark grey core; patchy dark-medium brown, uneven surface. Abraded. (PA 1). R.EVE = 0.20.

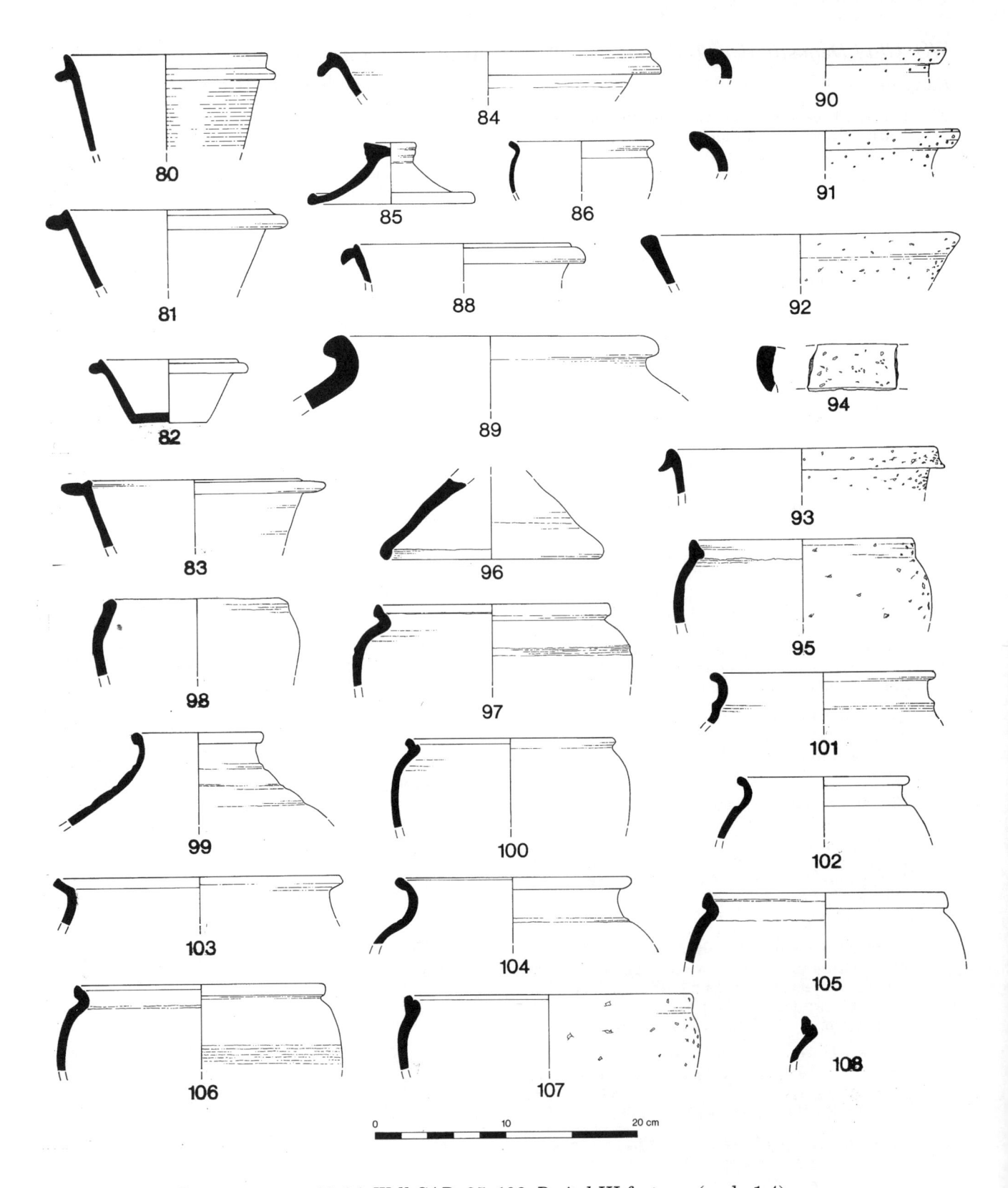

Figure 46 Roman pottery; 80–94, Well CAB: 95–108, Period III features (scale 1:4).

118

WS: Clay Deposits (C.p.1)

Early Roman sandy ware

97 Fabric 34: bead-rim jar with internal lid-seating. Hard; dark brown-black. Decoration: groove around maximum girth. (WS 8). R.EVE = 0.16.

AAL: Pit (C.p.1 or earlier)

Grog-tempered ware

98 Fabric 52: bead-rim jar. Handmade. Fairly coarse matrix. Dark, ochre-brown. Lime-scaling on interior. Possibly residual, *ie* late pre-Roman Iron Age. (AAL 1). R.EVE = 0.20.

ABL: The Northern Ditch (DP 1, EN1, ML 1–3): Upper Layers (DP 1, EN 1)

Grog-tempered wares

99 Fabric 53: ?tall, narrow-necked jar; multiple cordons on neck. Hard; grey core and patchy light buff to brown surfaces; burnished. Long-lived Belgic type, later adopted by Roman potters. Similar vessels; Wheeler 1936, 163 and Fig. 16.46; Group B at Prae Wood, up to mid first AD; Baldock no. 194, pre-Flavian; Ver.No. 2203, residual in late first-century contexts; Thompson 1982, category B3–9. (DP 1). R.EVE = 0.45.

100 Fabric 52: bead-rim jar with internal lid-seating. Dark brown core and patchy black-dark brown surface; burnished. (EN 1). R.EVE = 0.30.

101 Fabric 53: cordoned jar. Hard; medium grey core and grey-brown patchy surfaces; burnished. (EN 1). R.EVE = 0.06.

102 Fabric 53: necked jar. Ware as for **101**; abraded. (EN 1). R.EVE = 0.38.

103 Fabric 53: jar with 'figure 7' rim. Ware as for **101**; burnished. (EN 1). R.EVE = 0.27.

Early Roman sandy wares

104 Fabric 34: necked, cordoned jar. Ware as for **101**; lightly burnished. Similar to Thompson 1982, category D1–2. (DP 1). R.EVE = 0.52.

105 Fabric 34: bead-rim jar with slight internal lid-seating. Ware as for **112**; lightly burnished. (DP 1). R.EVE = 0.07.

Shell-tempered wares

106 Fabric 57: bead-rim jar with internal groove or lid-seating on rim. Patchy reddish-brown to dark brown ware; smoothed surfaces. (DP 1). R.EVE = 0.10.

107 Fabric 57: bead-rim jar with internal groove. Dark brown-grey core; reddish-brown internal surface and dark brown to black (?smokey) external surface; vesicular. (EN 1). R.EVE = 0.34.

108 Fabric 57: jar with moulded bead-rim and internal groove. Ware as for **106**. (DP 1). R.EVE = ?

ABM: The Southern Ditch (DK, MM): Lowest Layer (MM 4), Middle Layer (MM 3)

Verulamium Region ware

109 Fabric 20A: two-handled flagon with slightly flaring neck. Uneven three-ribbed handles. Hard; coarse granular, pinkish ware. Pre or early Flavian. (MM 4). R.EVE = 1.00.

Romanising grey ware

110 Fabric 35: necked, cordoned jar. Hard; dark grey core; dark grey-black surfaces; abraded. (MM 4). R.EVE = 0.58.

Grog-tempered ware

111 Fabric 56: necked jar. Pale pinkish-buff/brown ware; lightly burnished. Decoration: rilling on the shoulder. R.EVE = 0.12.

VM: Linear Feature (C.p.1/2)

Early Roman sandy ware

112 Fabric 34: round-bodied, necked jar. Ware as for **112**; abraded. (VM1). R.EVE = 0.22.

TF: Linear Feature (C.p. 1/2)

Fine grey ware

113 Fabric 37: hard; medium grey core and dark grey exterior; slightly abraded exterior. (TF2). R.EVE = 0.52.

114 Fabric 37: concave-sided dish with folded-over, curved rim. Hard; fine, medium grey ware; slightly abraded exterior. The break is so clean it appears that the base has been deliberately broken or cut off. (TF2). R.EVE = 1.00.

Misc. grey wares

115 Fabric 37: concave-sided dish. Hard; medium grey core and dark grey surface; slightly abraded. R.EVE = 0.17.

Shell-tempered ware

116 Fabric 57: round-bodied jar with moulded rim. Almost all the upper body remains. Dark brown core; orange – brown internal and patchy ochre-brown black external surfaces; patchy abrasion.

EBB: Ditch (EBB 1–2: C.p.1/2)

Fine grey ware

117 Fabric 37: biconical beaker. Hard; fine, medium grey ware; smoothed and lightly burnished. Similar to Baldock No.513; first century to Trajanic, and especially Baldock No. 586; dates up to the Antonine period. Partridge 1977, Cemetery A at Puckeridge, Burial no. 4; Vespasianic date from association with samian. (EBB 2). R.EVE = 0.30.

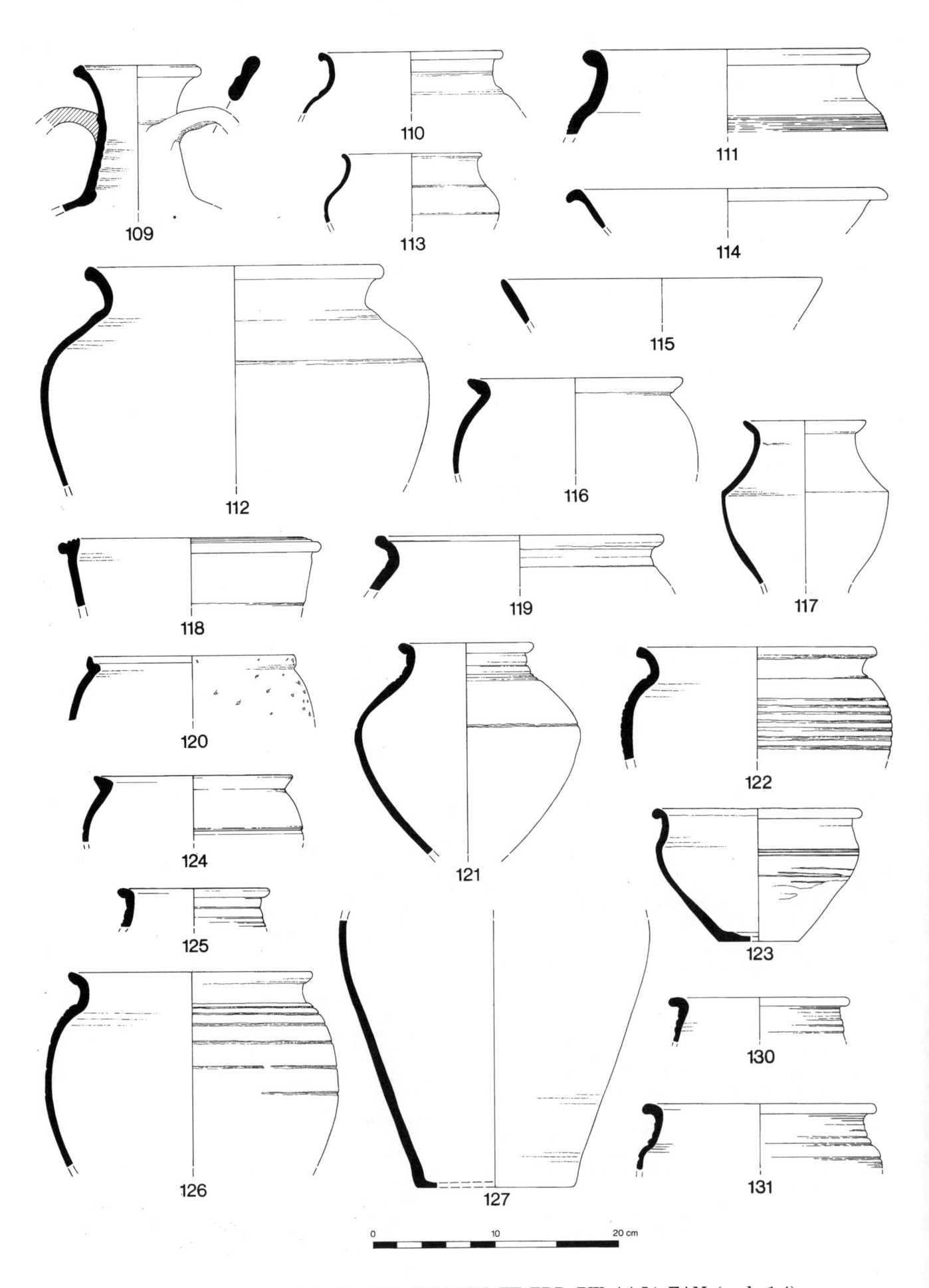

Figure 47   Roman pottery; 109–131, ABL–ABM, VM, TF, EBB, RW, AAJ4, EAN (scale 1:4).

120

Misc. grey ware

118 Fabric 41: bowl with short, squared, reeded-rim. Hard; medium grey; slightly pimply surface. Burnt. (SHL EBB 1, 2). R.EVE = 0.25. RW: Linear Feature (RW 2: *c*.p. ½)

Early Roman sandy ware

119 Fabric 34: short-necked jar with internal groove on rim. Hard; grey-brown core and ochre-brown-dark to brown surfaces; burnished. R.EVE = 0.53.

Shell-tempered ware

120 Fabric 57: bead-rim jar with internal lid-seating. Grey core and patchy dark brown – grey surfaces. R.EVE = 0.22.

AAJ: Ditch. Lowest layers (AAJ 4)

Early Roman sandy wares

121 Fabric 34: narrow-necked jar; moulded neck. Almost a complete profile. Hard; dark grey-brown core; dark brown to ochre brown surfaces; lightly burnished. R.EVE = 0.25.

122 Fabric 34: round-bodied jar with cordon and horizontal rilling. Similar form to **126**. Hard; dark grey-brown core: dark brown to black surface; patchy burnishing, especially on the rim, otherwise abraded. One of the commonest Belgic type at Verulamium, see Wheeler 1936, Fig. 20.61d and e, Group B at Prae Wood; survives into the third quarter of the first century AD; Brickwall Hill (Rook 1970a, Fig. IV.1a, 1c; Partridge 1979, Fig. 15.31, 34, 36; AD40–70. R.EVE = 0.27.

123 Fabric 34: high-shouldered jar. Profile; over a quarter of the vessel remains. Hard; dark grey core; dark brown to black surfaces; abraded. A few sooty patches under the rim. Decoration: grooves around shoulder. R.EVE = 0.19. B.EVE = 0.25.

124 Fabric 33: Jar with triangular bead-rim. Dark grey to black core; black, burnished surfaces. In good condition. Decoration: groove around maximum girth. R.EVE = 0.45.

Misc. grey wares

125 Fabric 49: narrow-necked jar with moulded neck. Very similar form to **121**. Hard; light grey core; medium grey, abrasive surfaces. R.EVE = 0.15.

Grog-tempered wares

126 Fabric 53: see **122**. Almost half the vessel remains. Hard; medium grey core; black, abraded surface. Decoration: uneven grooves around upper body. R.EVE = 0.45.

Shell-tempered ware

127 Fabric 57: base of a large, tall jar; exact form uncertain. Hard; patchy dark orange to dark brown/black surfaces. B.EVE = 0.50.

EAN: Pit (EAN 1–2, BBB)

Early Roman sandy wares

128 Fabric 34: bead-rim jar with internal lid-seating. Dark brown-grey core and ochre-brown surfaces; abraded. (BBB 1). R.EVE = 0.09.

129 Fabric 34: neckless jar. Hard; dark brown-black core and ochre-brown surfaces; burnished. (BBB 1). R.EVE = 0.04.

130 Fabric 34: short-necked, moulded jar. Fabric as **129**; burnished. (EAN 1). R.EVE = 0.15.

131 Fabric 34: short-necked cordoned and grooved jar. Fabric similar to **130**. Similar form to **122**. (EAN 1). R.EVE = 0.26.

EAB: Feature. Lowest layers (EAB 4: C.p.2)

Early Roman sandy ware

132 Fabric 34: jar with squared, bead-rim. Hard; grey-brown core and ochre-brown to dark brown surfaces; burnished. Decoration: grooves around rim and shoulder. R.EVE = 0.32.

133 Fabric 34: round-bodied jar with deep, vertical cordoned neck and groove around shoulder. Fabric as **132**. Thompson 1982, cat. D2–3. R.EVE = 0.11.

134 Fabric 34: cordoned jar with 'figure 7' rim. Fabric as **132**; burnished. R.EVE = 0.19.

135 Fabric ?38: Ovoid beaker with short, sharply everted rim. Hard; blue-grey ware; smoothed surface. R.EVE = 0.32.

ECQ: Ditch (EAD)

Misc. Oxidised Ware

136 Fabric 17: small, hemispherical bowl with a pedestal base. Profile. Hard; bright orange; sandy abrasive surfaces. (EAD 1). R.EVE = 0.41. B.EVE = 0.50.

DCF: Palisade Ditch (DCG, DCH, DCI, DDO, DDR:C.p. 2/3)

Fine grey ware

137 Fabric 37: Beaker with long flaring neck and rounded body. Hard; light grey core with medium grey surfaces; lightly burnished. (DCH 1). R.EVE = 0.30.

Shell-tempered ware

138 Fabric 59: large bowl with folded-over, horizontal rim. Hard; grey core with patchy pinkish-buff to brown surfaces; vesicular. (DCI 1). R.EVE = 0.11.

EAU: Ditch (EAU 1–3: C.p.?3)

Misc. grit-tempered ware

139 Fabric 18: small, high-shouldered jar, with short, everted rim. (EAU 3). R.EVE = 0.11.

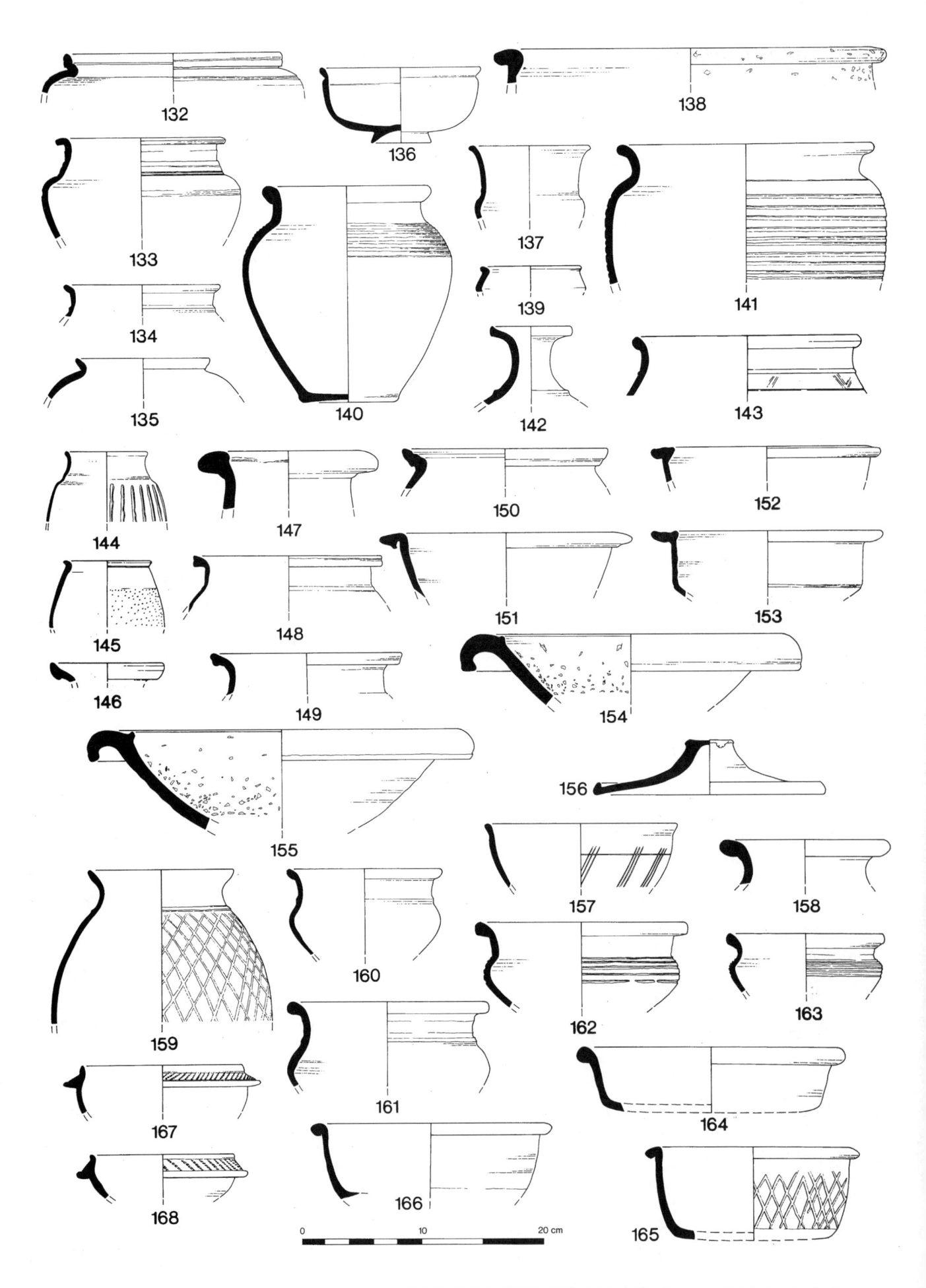

Figure 48   Roman pottery; 132–143, EAB, ECQ, DCF, EAU, DC: 144–165, Quarry EAA (scale 1:4).

DCE: Gully (DBH, DCC, DCD, DDH)

Hadham ware

140 Fabric 39: necked jar. Most of the vessel remains. Blue-grey; lightly burnished rim. Decoration: rilling on the shoulder.(DBH 1). Second to third century. R.EVE = 0.62. B.EVE = 1.00.

Other pottery attributed to features of C.p.2/3

Early Roman sandy wares

141 Fabric 34: necked jar. Similar form and fabric as **122** and **126**; burnished rim and neck. Decoration: uneven parallel grooves around girth. (GP 1). R.EVE = 0.16.

Misc. grey wares

142 Fabric 37: narrow-necked jar or bottle. Hard; medium grey; abraded dark grey-black slip.(SJ 1). R.EVE = 1.00.

Highgate Wood ware

143 Fabric 38: cordoned jar. Medium grey. Decoration: zone of alternating diagonal burnished lines on the shoulder. Late first to first half of second century. (LF 1). R.EVE = 0.16.

THE DEW POND/QUARRY (EAA, EAA 1–19, EAA 40, EAA 301–305)
(Figs 48, 49)

Fine wares

144 Fabric 1: hairpin beaker. Hard, dark reddish-orange paste; dark olive green to yellowish lead glaze, slightly mottled in places. Decoration: under-glaze hairpins in white barbotine. In good condition. This vessel is likely to be residual, as the production of the ware is deemed to have ended by the early Hadrianic period (see above). Alternatively, the vessel may well have had an extended life, possibly as an heirloom, that was only discarded when broken beyond reasonable repair. This vessel is a narrow-bodied variant of the globular beakers produced at Staines (Arthur 1978, Fig. 8.2, esp. No.2.3). (SHL EAA 2,5,13,15). R.EVE = 0.85.

145 Fabric 4: roughcast, probably bag-shaped, beaker with cornice rim. Dark grey-brown, matt colour coat. See Anderson 1980, Fig. 12.4, dated 130/135–160. (SHL EAA 5, 303). R.EVE = 0.37.

Verulamium Region wares

146 Fabric 20A: flagon with flaring neck and disc-like rim. Pinkish-orange granular ware. This type of vessel dates 120–160 in London (IH1). See also Castle 1972, Fig. 3.6, dated AD80+. (EAA 2). R.EVE = 0.26.

147 Fabric 20A: amphora-type flagon, probably two-handled. Hard, finely granular buff ware. Similar to Ver.No.818, from a context dated 155/160. (EAA 19). R.EVE = 0.10.

148 Fabric 20A: necked, cordoned jar; out-turned rim with external groove. (EAA 14). R.EVE = 0.10.

149 Fabric 20A: similar to **148**. Hard, granular pale buff fabric. (EAA 2). R.EVE = 0.30.

150 Fabric 20A: neckless jar with moulded rim; internal grooving. Hard, granular white-buff fabric. Smokey, dark grey exterior rim. Early to mid second century. (EAA 5). R.EVE = 0.22.

151 Fabric 20B: hemispherical bowl with folded-over rim; rim is chamfered and undercut. Hard, dark grey, fine granular fabric. (EAA 16). R.EVE = 0.30.

152 Fabric 20A: bowl with short, squared reeded rim. Hard, medium buff, rather coarse granular fabric. Similar types found in the Antonine fire deposits at Verulamium; Ver.No.929. (EAA 2). R.EVE = 0.12.

153 Fabric 20B: carinated bowl with horizontal reeded rim. Hard, dark grey, granular fabric with paler core. Sooty patches on the interior surface. See Ver.No.671, from a context dated 140–50. (EAA 13). R.EVE = 0.20.

154 Fabric 20A: hooked-flange mortarium. Hard; grey-buff granular fabric. Very worn trituration grits. (EAA 2). See Hartley 1971, 157, Fig. 4, similar to mortaria of Doinus at Brockley Hill and Radlett; Flavian–Trajanic. It is not uncommon for earlier mortaria to be in later layers. R.EVE = 0.16.

155 Fabric 20A: hooked-flange mortarium; see **154**. Hard; white-buff granular fabric. Very worn trituration grits. (EAA 2). R.EVE = 0.16.

156 Fabric 20A: lid. Profile. Upper surface of lid boss badly finished. Hard, fine, pale pinkish-white, granular fabric. (SHL EAA 301, 303). R.EVE = 0.13.

Oxidised slipped wares

157 Fabric 12: hemispherical bowl, possibly with footring base *(not illustrated)*. Bright orange ware with all-over external white slip. Decoration: narrow groove around girth and groups of three, incised, diagonal lines around mid to lower body. (EAA 16). R.EVE = 0.40.

Hadham ware

158 Fabric 39: narrow-necked jar. Hard-fired, blue-grey fabric; lightly burnished exterior and upper rim. (EAA 301). R.EVE = 0.18.

159 Fabric 39: beaker, imitating poppy-head form. Flaring, narrow neck, cordon at shoulder. Decoration: burnished acute lattice.

160 Fabric 39: cordoned jar; similar to **7** and **8**. Large sherds in good condition. Hard-fired blue-grey fabric; lightly burnished exterior. Sooty patches on interior surface. Hadrianic–Antonine. (EAA 2). R.EVE = 0.26.

161 Fabric 39: cordoned jar. Similar to **160** but with more pronounced out-turned rim. (EAA 5). R.EVE = 0.34.

162 Fabric 39: wide-mouthed jar with squat body. Hard-fired, blue-grey fabric; burnished rim and neck. Decoration: rilling on shoulder. Sooty patches on interior and exterior. See Ver.No. 1081; from a context dated 155/160. R.EVE = 0.28.

163 Fabric 39: smaller version of **111**. (EAA 8). See Trow 1988, Fig. 54.144; Flavian to early second-century date. R.EVE = 0.15.

164 Fabric 39: dish with rounded rim. Profile. Hard-fired, blue-grey ware; smoothed surfaces. Lightly burnished rim. (EAA 303). R.EVE = 0.17.

165 Fabric ?39: deep, straight-sided bowl with folded-over rim; slight carination above the base. The majority of exterior surface is oxidised, reddish-orange, whereas the interior is dark grey; medium grey core. Decoration: burnished acute lattice starting c.10–15 mm below rim, ending at carination. (EAA 15). R.EVE = 0.20.

166 Fabric ?39: hemispherical bowl with folded-down rim. Fabric is rather sandier and paler grey than the typical 39. Abraded surfaces. Burnished rim. (EAA 2). R.EVE = 0.15.

167 Fabric 39: round-bodied flanged bowl; up-standing rim and down-turned flange. Medium grey to blue-grey fabric. Decoration: closely-spaced diagonal lines of stabbed dots on upper flange. Similar to Ver.Nos.2383 and 2384; dates for contexts are 110–30 to 170–80 and 145–150 to 155/60 (Antonine fire deposits) respectively. See also Partridge 1977, Fig. 38.3 and Fig. 39.6 and 7, Wickham Hill Nursery, dated 120–140. (EAA 2). R.EVE = 0.18.

168 Fabric 39: smaller version of **167**. Decoration: wide-spaced diagonal lines of stabbed dots on upper flange. Sooty, carbonised patches on the flange and interior surface. (EAA 5). R.EVE = 0.10.

Highgate Wood ware

169 Fabric 38: round-bodied necked jar. Medium to dark grey granular fabric; grey-black slip over exterior surface and interior of rim. Decoration: zone of diagonal burnished lines on the shoulder. Ver.No.608, 130–150; others date 85–160. (EAA 2). R.EVE = 0.18.

170 Fabric 38: shallow, hemispherical bowl with rounded rim. Medium to dark grey fabric. (EAA 2). R.EVE = 0.15.

Misc. grey wares

171 Fabric 37: ?biconical beaker. Similar to **117**. Hard, medium-grey fabric. (EAA 2). R.EVE = 0.26.

172 Fabric 37: narrow-necked jar with short, sharply everted rim. Hard, fine, medium grey; lightly burnished exterior. Decoration: zone of burnished chevron pattern above another with vertical lines, between grooves on shoulder. Romanized adaptation of Belgic forms. (EAA 303). R.EVE = 0.40.
173. Fabric 37: necked jar; long neck with out-curving rim. Hard-fired, fine, medium-grey fabric; burnished to maximum girth. (EAA 2). R.EVE = 0.17.

174 Fabric 37: cordoned jar. Dark grey surfaces and medium grey fabric; sandy surfaces. Decoration: zone of burnished lattice on the shoulder. (EAA 2). R.EVE = 0.50.

175 Fabric 37: cordoned jar; larger version of **123**. Slightly granular fabric, with smoothed black surfaces and dark core. Decoration: zones of alternate burnished diagonal lines on the shoulder. (EAA 2). R.EVE = 0.30.

176 Fabric 41: 'Braughing jar' type; see **162–163**. Almost complete profile. Hard, medium grey fabric; pimply surfaces. Light burnishing on rim and neck. (EAA 2). R.EVE = 0.19.

177 Fabric 41: necked jar with thickened rim. Profile. Hard-fired medium grey fabric; lightly burnished rim and neck. Lower body rather pitted (see **14**). Decoration: rilling on the shoulder. (SHL EAA 14,15). R.EVE = 0.84. B.EVE = 0.56.

178 Fabric 48: large, cordoned, necked jar. Hard-fired, very light grey fabric with medium grey core; rather abrasive surface. (EAA 4). R.EVE = 0.06.

179 Fabric 37: poppy-head beaker. Almost complete profile. Fine medium grey fabric; external overall white slip. Decoration: irregular vertical zones of barbotine dots. R.EVE = 0.07.

180 Fabric 37: ovoid beaker with short, sharply everted rim; cordon on the shoulder. Fine light grey fabric. Decoration: diamond-shaped patterns of barbotine dots. (EAA 2). R.EVE = 0.28.

181 Fabric 37:ovoid beaker with short, everted rim. Fine, pale grey fabric; burnished rim and shoulder. (EAA 303). R.EVE = 0.15.

182 Fabric 37: shallow, concave-sided dish with squared rim. Profile. Hard-fired, medium grey fabric; internal overall white slip, extending over rim. R.EVE = 0.15. B.EVE = 0.25.

183 Fabric 37: moulded platter or dish. Profile. Romanised version of Gallo-Belgic forms. This type of vessel in circulation at least until at least the 160s (Going, pers. comm.). See Baldock No. 533; Antonine. Partridge 1977, Fig. 18.4, from the bath house at Braughing, dated 70–140, and Fig. 19.7, dated 140–250; also Wickham Hill Nursery, Fig. 39.9. (EAA 2). R.EVE = 0.13. B.EVE = 0.12.

184 Fabric 37: A deeper, thick-walled version of **183**. Profile. (EAA 2). R.EVE = 0.20. B.EVE = 0.21.

185 Fabric 37: shallow dish with small triangular rim; carination above the base. Medium grey fabric; smoothed interior and a thin overall white slip. Decoration: burnished lattice from below rim to carination. (EAA 2). R.EVE = 0.21. B.EVE = 0.25.

186 Fabric 37: carinated, shallow dish with folded-over hooked rim; the walls become markedly thinner above the carination. Hard-fired, fine medium grey fabric; white slip over lower exterior body (below carination) and internal base. (EAA 2). R.EVE = 0.11. B.EVE = 0.13.

187 Fabric 37: round-bodied, shallow bowl with folded-over hooked rim; groove under rim. Fine medium grey fabric; dark grey-black core and light grey-buff margins. (EAA 2). R.EVE = 0.17.

188 Fabric 48: shallow dish with elongated, triangular rim. Profile. Medium grey fabric with streaky white slip. (EAA 2). R.EVE = 0.42. B.EVE = 0.29.

189 Fabric 37: shallow, round-bodied dish or platter with exaggerated folded-over rim. Hard, fine, medium-grey fabric; lightly burnished surface. (EAA 6).

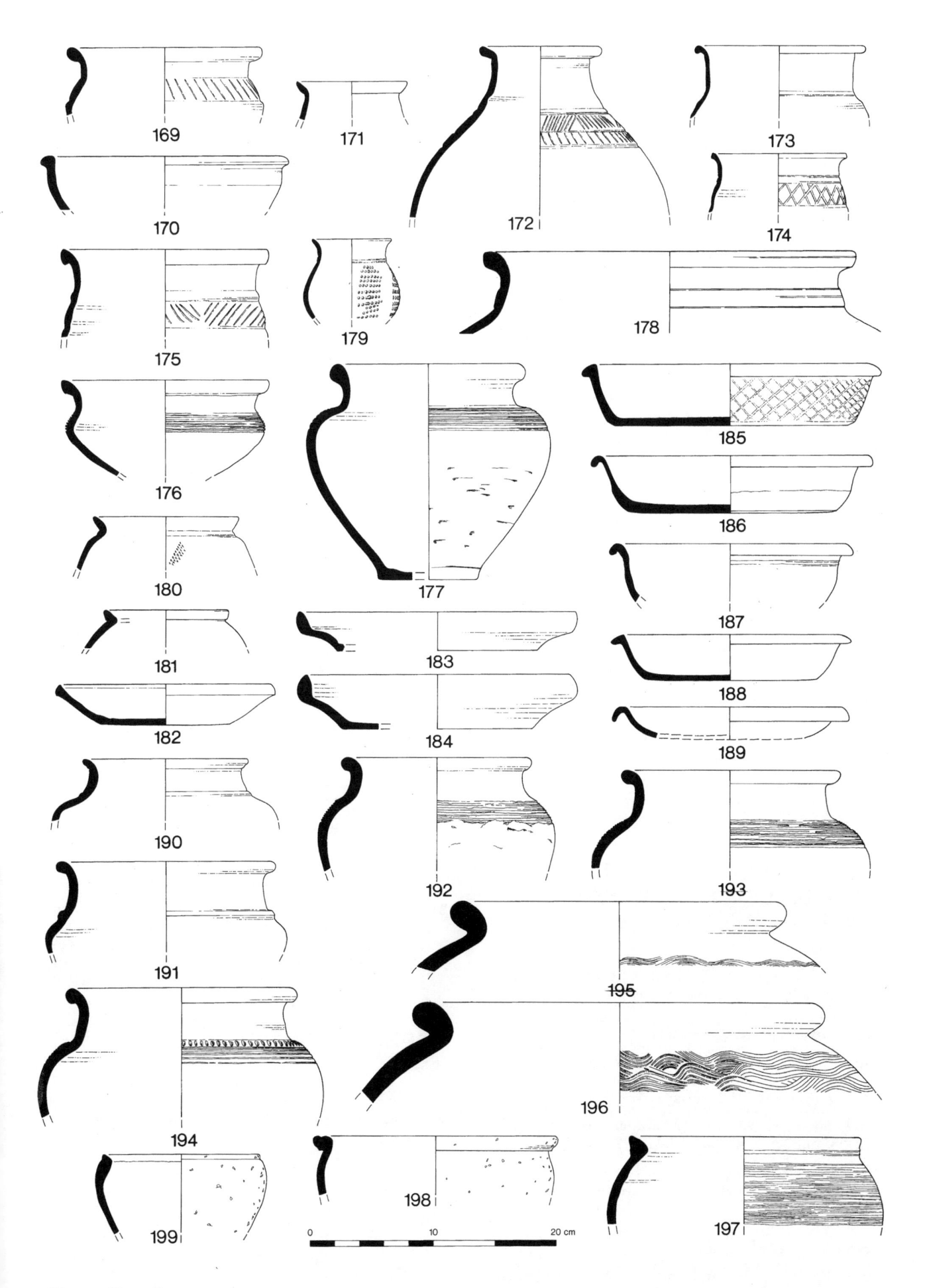

Figure 49 Roman pottery; 169–199, Quarry EAA (scale 1:4).

Grog-tempered wares

190 Fabric 52: cordoned, necked jar with 'figure 7' rim. Dark brown to black burnished exterior. Residual?, probably first century. (EAA 19). R.EVE = 0.22.

191 Fabric 52: cordoned, necked jar. Dark brown, burnished exterior. Sooty patches all over surface. Flavian. (EAA 13). R.EVE = 0.16.

192 Fabric 52: round-bodied jar with rounded rim. Decoration: rilling around shoulder. Coarse matrix; black, unevenly smoothed exterior. (EAA 14). R.EVE = 0.19.

193 Fabric 52: necked jar. Similar to **111**. (EAA 2). R.EVE = 0.20.

194 Fabric 52: necked jar. Dark brown, lightly burnished exterior. Decoration: row of oval stabbed decoration above shoulder rilling. (EAA 2). R.EVE = 0.50.

195 Fabric 56: large storage jar with thickened rolled rim. Smoothed surfaces. Rather soft pinkish-orange fabric. Decoration: wavy combing on shoulder. Both **195** and **196** are Romanised versions of a popular native type, continuing through the Roman period. (EAA 13). R.EVE = 0.08.

196 Fabric 56: larger version of **195**. Smoky grey rim. (EAA 19). R.EVE = 0.14.

Shell-tempered wares

197 Fabric 59: bead-rim jar with straight, internally thickened rim. Hard; light-brown to buff patchy exterior; grey core. Decoration: overall rilling. Similar vessel Baldock 570; Hadrianic–Antonine. (EAA 2). R.EVE = 0.22.

198 Fabric 59: bead-rim jar; groove on upper edge. Hard; grey core; light brown to buff patchy exterior; vesicular. (EAA 2). R.EVE = 0.10

199 Fabric 57: jar with very small bead-rim. Handmade. Residual. Medium brown core; dark brown exterior; unevenly smoothed. Sooty patches. (EAA 3). R.EVE = 0.25.

ABR: FLINT AND CHALK RAFT (CE 2, CE 5, EF, EF 2, EV 2, FE, FF)
(Fig. 50)

Fine wares

200 Fabric 5B: bead-rim beaker. Hard; orange paste; dark brown, matt colour coat. (FF 1). R.EVE = 0.12.

Misc. oxidised wares

201 Fabric 46: flagon with horizontal rim; external groove and internal lid-seating. Hard; dark red fabric with black surfaces. (FF1). R.EVE = 0.12.

202 Fabric 32: butt beaker hard; grey core with yellow – buff surfaces; burnished. (FF 1). R.EVE = 0.15.

203 Fabric 31: bowl or dish with moulded rim. Hard; finely granular pinkish – white fabric. (EF 2). R.EVE = 0.07.

Shell-tempered ware

204 Fabric 57: bead-rim jar with internal thickening and internal groove on rim. Dark brown-grey core with patchy dark brown to reddish-brown surfaces.

Grog-tempered ware

205 Fabric 56: large everted rim storage jar. Rather soft, pinkish – pale orange fabric; burnished. (FF 1). R.EVE = 0.12.

206 Fabric 53: moulded platter or dish; imitation of *terra nigra*. Vessel may have had a shallow footring. Grey core with dark ochre-brown surfaces; burnished.

TB: pit Lower Layer TB 2 (C.p.2); Upper Layer TB 1 (C.p.3)
(Fig. 50)

Mica-dusted ware

207 Fabric 11: folded beaker with short, everted rim. Hard; fine yellow – beige fabric; mica-dusted exterior surface. See March 1978, Fig. 6.9, type 21, of late first to early second-century date. (TB 2). R.EVE = 0.16.

Fine ware

208 Fabric 5B: sherds from a 'Hunt Cup'. Orange paste; dark brown, matt colour-coat. Decoration: elongated under-slip barbotine animal (?deer). Extremely abraded. Probably Antonine to early third-century date. (TB 1)

Hadham ware

209 Fabric 9: large, horizontal-rimmed, two-handled flagon. Medium orange; ?burnished but abraded. See Stevenson 1978, Fig. 1.1 for a parallel from Royston Heath, dated late first century. (TB 1) R.EVE = 0.20.

Misc. grey wares

210 Fabric 37: deep bowl with elongated, triangular rim. Hard; fine, medium-grey fabric; burnished. (TB 1) R.EVE = 0.50.

211 Fabric 49: deep bowl with folded-over, rounded rim; slightly sagging base. Hard; dark grey-brown fabric; sandy, abrasive surfaces. (TB 1) R.EVE = 0.13.

Verulamium Region ware

212 Fabric 20A: bowl with short, squared reeded-rim. The rim has been produced by moulding out of the wall, rather than folding over. Hard, pinkish – orange granular fabric. In London, such forms are uncommon and date to 150-180/200 (Hammerson 1988, 207, IVA8). R.EVE = 0.07.

OTHER POTTERY DATING TO C.p.3
(Fig. 50)

Grit-tempered ware

213 Fabric 18: bowl with down-turned reeded-rim. Hard; pinkish-buff fabric; abrasive, gritty surfaces. (TQ 1). R.EVE = 0.15.

Misc. grey ware

214 Fabric 37: Although this vessel comes from a pit stratigraphically unrelated to other features and is therefore "unphased", this is the only example of this type on the site. Incipient flanges were introduced in the second century, continuing into the third. (EBS 1). R.EVE = 0.11.

JK: PIT (JK 1, VJ 1)
(Fig. 50)

Hadham ware

215 Fabric 39: narrow-necked cordoned jar. Hard; blue-grey; burnished. Good condition. (JK1). R.EVE = 1.00.

216 Fabric 39: necked jar with moulded rim. Blue-grey; burnishing on rim. Decoration: zone of wavy combing between parallel grooves on the shoulder. (JK 1). R.EVE = 0.38.

217 Fabric 39: small, deep bowl with bead-rim. Hard, blue-grey fabric, lightly burnished. (JK 1). R.EVE = 0.07.

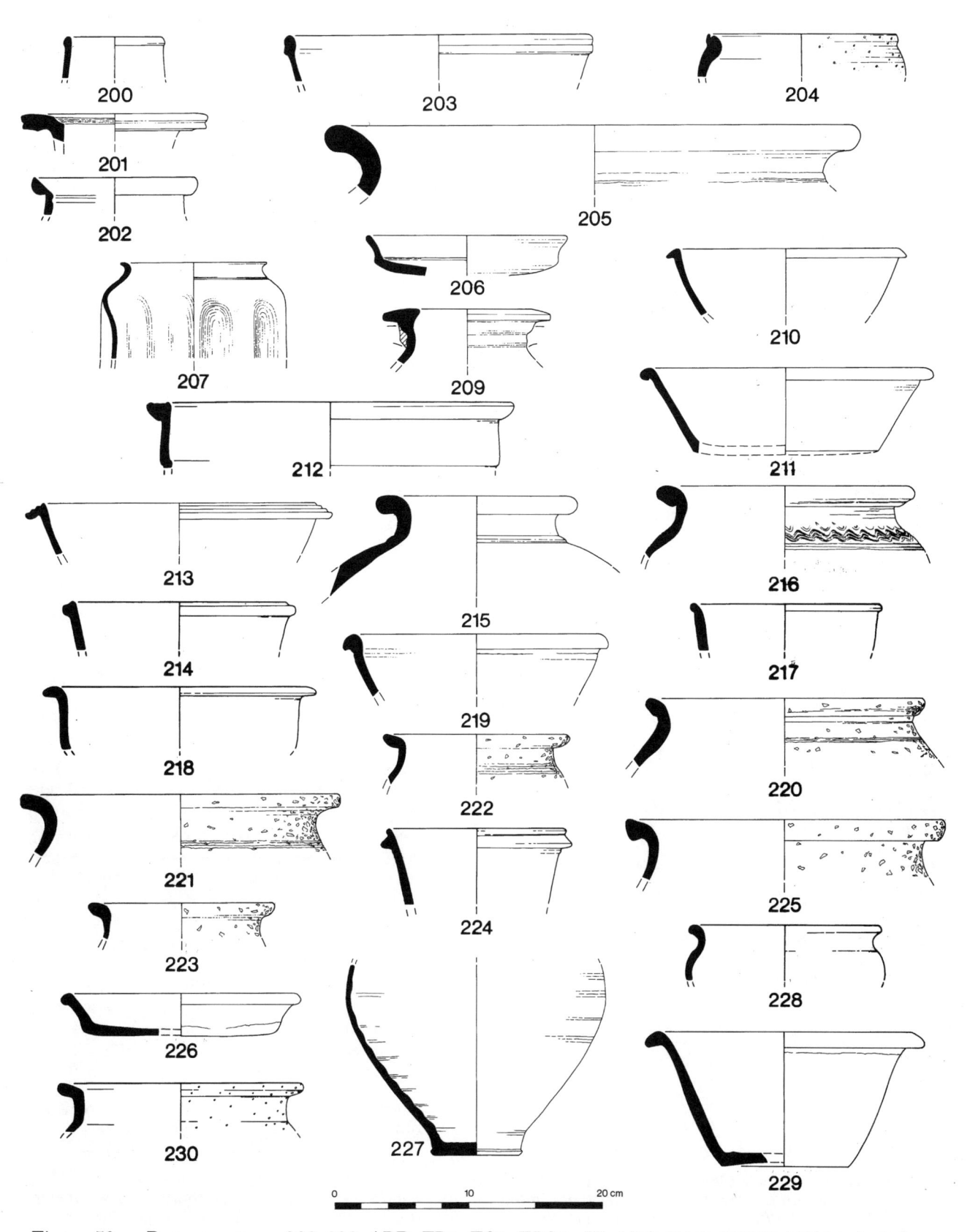

Figure 50 Roman pottery; 200–230, ABR, TB1, TQ1, EBS1, JK, ABQ, EAO, TT/YL/JE (scale 1:4).

Misc. grey ware

218 Fabric 37: deep bowl with out-turned rim. Hard; medium grey core with dark grey surfaces. (JK 1). R.EVE = 0.10.

Verulamium region ware

219 Fabric 20A: deep bowl with thickened hooked rim. Hard; granular pale buff-cream fabric. (JK 1). R.EVE = 0.12.

Shell-tempered ware

220 Fabric 58A: neckless jar with thickened slightly everted rim. Grey core with patchy buff/brown-grey surfaces; vesicular. (JK 1). R.EVE = 0.15.

221 Fabric 58: jar with squared, everted rim. Fabric as **220**. Decoration: zone of rilling on the shoulder. Similar to Baldock No.673, dated third century. (JK 1). R.EVE = 0.57.

222 Fabric 58: small jar with 'figure 7' rim. Fabric as **220**. Decoration: zone of rilling on shoulder. Similar to Baldock No.727, dated to the late third or fourth century. (VJ 1). R.EVE 0.26.

223 Fabric 58: jar with out-turned, squared rim. Fabric as **220**. Similar types at Baldock (Nos. 705, 706); dated mid to late third century. (JK 1). R.EVE = 0.17.

ABQ: GULLIES FOR CIRCULAR BUILDING (= TJ, TL, TR, TS)
(Fig. 50)

Misc. grey ware

224 Fabric 48: straight-sided flanged bowl; short, triangular flange. Hard; medium to dark grey fabric; smoothed surfaces. (SHL TJ 1, TJ 3). R.EVE = 0.21.

Shell-tempered ware

225 Fabric 58: jar with out-turned, squared rim. Fabric as **220**. Similar to Baldock No.753; third to early fourth century. R.EVE = 0.13.

Misc. grey ware

226 Fabric 37: shallow dish with rounded rim. Profile. Medium grey; abraded. (TJ 1). R.EVE = 0.38. B.EVE = 0.40.

OTHER VESSELS DATING TO C.p.4
(Fig. 50)

Hadham ware

227 Fabric 39: only the complete base of the vessel remains. Abraded. (EAO: Coin Hoard vessel).

228 Fabric 9: round-bodied, necked jar. Hard; orange fabric with irregular horizontal brown streaks on exterior; lightly burnished. (TT 1. TT=TK; links with ABQ). R.EVE = 0.65.

Misc. grey ware

229 Fabric 48: deep bowl with folded-over, thickened rim. Profile. Developed form of 'pie dish'. Hard; medium grey fabric; burnished lower body. (YL 1). R.EVE = 0.33. B.EVE = 0.33.

Shell-tempered ware

230 Fabric 58A: necked jar with 'figure 7' rim. Patchy buff-brown fabric with grey core; vesicular. Similar to Baldock No.706; mid to late third century. (GE 1). R.EVE = 0.05.

ABO: PENANNULAR GULLY (FC, EG, TZ, FZ 1–10, 12–16, 18–22)
(Fig. 51)

Fine ware

231 Fabric 5B: 'castor box' lid. White paste; patchy dark brown-orange colour-coat. Decoration: rouletting up to lid boss. N.V.No.89; third to fourth century. Ver.No. 1119; from contexts dated 280–350. (SHL FZ 4, 5). R.EVE = 0.17.

Hadham ware

232 Fabric 9: miniature jar. Bright orange fabric; lightly abraded. (FZ 3). R.EVE = 0.10.

233 Fabric 39: necked jar. Probably originally with cordon at base of neck. Hard; blue grey. (FZ 3). R.EVE = 0.11.

Misc. slipped ware

234 Fabric 13: small *tazze* or incense-cup. Probably had a pedestal base. (FZ 21).

Misc. oxidised ware

235 Fabric 19: s-profile jar with external groove on rim. Sandy, abrasive orange fabric. (FZ 3). R.EVE = 0.25.

Misc. grey wares

236 Fabric 45: s-profile jar with out-turned, thickened rim. Abundant quartz-tempering in a fine, hard matrix; light buff-grey fabric; abraded, grey slip. (TZ 1). R.EVE = 0.20.

237 Fabric 49: s-profile jar with thickened rim. Sandy, abrasive, dark grey-brown. (TZ 1). R.EVE = 0.08.

238 Fabric 49: similar form and fabric to **237**. (FZ 16).

239 Fabric 49: everted-rim jar. Fabric as for **237**. (TZ 1).

240 Fabric 46: straight-sided dish. Profile. Fine, hard; pinkish-orange core with smoothed black surfaces. (FZ 7). R.EVE = 0.14. B.EVE = 0.13.

241 Fabric 48: shallow dish with rounded rim. Dark grey-brown; smoothed surfaces. (SHL FZ 10, 14). R.EVE = 0.25.

242 Fabric 48: straight-sided dish with rounded rim. Profile. Medium grey core with grey-black surfaces; abraded. Similar to Baldock No.809; fourth-century date. (FZ 3). R.EVE = 0.16. A similar vessel was recovered from CD 1.

243 Fabric 48: deep bowl with squared hooked rim. Profile. Dark grey to black; overall burnishing. Decoration: faint narrow rilling on the upper exterior body; burnished design on the interior base. (FZ 14). R.EVE = 0.28. B.EVE = 0.31.

244 Fabric 37: deep bowl with out-curving rim. Medium grey; smoothed. (FZ 7). R.EVE = 0.19.

245 Fabric 48: profile; almost half of vessel remains. Blue-grey; burnished rim. Sherds in good condition; clean breaks. (FC 1). R.EVE = 0.44. B.EVE = 0.40.

246 Fabric 49: flanged bowl; short squared flange. Hard; light grey core and medium grey-brown surfaces; sandy, abrasive. (FZ 4). R.EVE = 0.10.

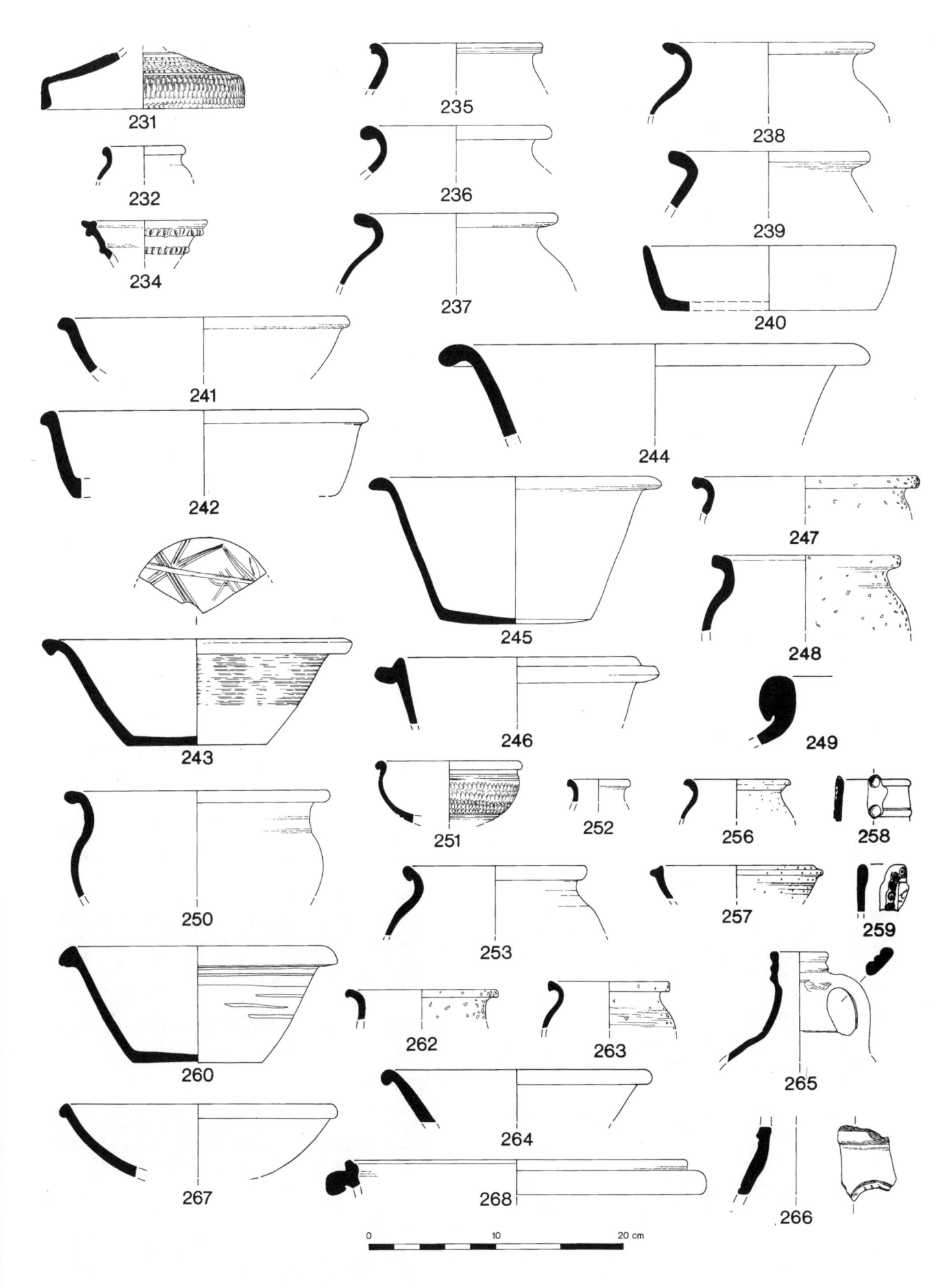

Figure 51   *Roman pottery; 231–268, ABO, DDX, RC, GF, DAD* (scale 1:4).

Shell-tempered ware

247 Fabric 58: s-profile jar. Grey-brown core with patchy grey-buff-brown surfaces; vesicular. (TZ 1). R.EVE = 0.11.

248 Fabric 58: necked jar with 'figure 7' rim. Reddish-brown core with dark brown-black surfaces. Decoration: narrow zone of rilling on the shoulder. (FZ 5). R.EVE = 0.15.

249 Fabric 58A: storage jar with hooked rim. Medium grey core with patchy brown-beige surfaces; vesicular. Decoration: rilling on the shoulder. (FZ 21).

Early Roman sandy ware

250 Fabric 34: s-profile, round-bodied jar. Hard; dark, reddish-brown fabric. Residual. (FZ 10). R.EVE = 0.25.

DDX: CIRCULAR BUILDING (DAB, DAE, DAH, DAJ, DAZ, DBI, DBM, DBO, DBT, DBU, DBV, DAF, DAG, DAI, DBN, DBP, DBQ, DBS, DBR)
(Fig. 51)

Fine ware

251 Fabric 7: small, round-bodied bowl with folded-over hooked rim. Hard; orange paste with dark brown lustrous colour-coat. Decoration: broad zone of rouletting around the body. (DAZ 1). R.EVE = 0.35.

RC: PIT (RC 1–4)
(Fig. 51)

Hadham ware

252 Fabric 9: bottle or flagon. Orange fabric; abraded. (RC 1). R.EVE = 0.15.

253 Fabric 9: s-profile jar with hooked rim. Orange fabric with uneven horizontal brown streaks on surface; abraded. (RC 2). R.EVE = 0.30.

254 Fabric 39: necked jar with parallel cordons at shoulder. Hard; medium grey. (RC2). R.EVE = 0.17.

255 Fabric 39: straight-sided dish. Almost complete profile. Hard; blue-grey. (RC4). R.EVE = 0.06.

Misc. oxidised ware

256 Fabric 16: s-profile jar with moulded rim. Orange fabric with abundant angular quartz. (SHL RC 1, VP 1). R.EVE = 0.25.

257 Fabric 16: small flanged bowl with short, square flange. Fabric as for **256**. (RC 1). R.EVE = 0.07.

GF: CORN DRIER STOKEHOLE (GF 1–3, 6, 13, 16, 17, 20; JA 1–3,5, 8, 11)
(Fig. 51)

Hadham ware

258 Fabric 9: ?face flagon with applied strip, decorated with finger impressions. Bright orange fabric; very worn surfaces. See **36** for similar type of vessel. (GF 1). R.EVE = 0.25.

259 Fabric 9: part of **258**? A fragment of the face; the head-dress is represented by an irregular border of ring-and-dot decoration. (GF 1).

260 Fabric 39: deep bowl with thickened triangular rim. Profile. Hard; blue-grey fabric. Two narrow bands of black slip under the rim; lightly burnished upper rim. (JA 1). R.EVE= 0.42. B.EVE = 0.85.

Misc. grey ware

261 Fabric 37: straight-sided dish. Profile. Medium grey core; almost black surfaces. (GF1). R.EVE = 0.05. B.EVE = 0.21.

Shell-tempered ware

262 Fabric 58: small jar with out-curving, hooked rim. Dark grey core with patchy dark brown-black surfaces. (GF 6). R.EVE = 0.22.

263 Fabric 58: s-profile jar with hooked rim. Grey-brown core with light brown surfaces. Decoration: zone of rilling on the shoulder.

DAD: PIT (DAD 1)
(Fig. 51)

Misc. grey ware

264 Fabric 48: concave-sided bowl with folded-over rim. Light grey core with medium grey surfaces; lightly burnished. R.EVE = 0.11. Spread over corn drier (HG 1–2, YH 1).

Hadham ware

265 Fabric 9: ring-necked flagon. Orange ware; surfaces slightly worn. (YH 1). R.EVE = 1.00.

266 Fabric 9?: unusual form; ?jar with aperture on shoulder. Fabric as for **265**. (HG 1).

Oxfordshire wares

267 Fabric 8: large shallow bowl. Hard; narrow, grey core with reddish-orange surfaces; colour-coat worn and patchy. Young type C.45.3; 270–400+. See **34**. (HG 2). R.EVE = 0.15.

268 Fabric 21: mortarium with upstanding internally-grooved rim and squared hooked flange. Hard; white-buff ware. Young type M.17; 240–300. (HG 1). R.EVE = 0.07.

HB: PIT OVERLYING GF (HB 1: C.p.5.2)
(Fig. 52)

Oxfordshire ware

269 Fabric 8: hemispherical bowl with rounded rim. Hard; dark reddish-orange fabric; very worn. Decoration: zone of rouletting defined by horizontal grooves around the girth. Young type C.84; 350–400+. R.EVE = 0.12.

Hadham ware

270 Fabric 9: round-bodied jar. Hard; orange fabric; burnished. R.EVE = 0.15.

Misc. oxidised ware

271 Fabric 15: s-profile jar with external groove

around rim. Bright orange core; dark grey-black exterior surface (slip?). R.EVE = 0.17.

GK: THE POND
(Figs 52, 53)

Nene Valley wares

272 Fabric 5A: small, disc-mouthed flagon; two-handled. Matt, dark brown-black colour-coat. (GK4). R.EVE = 0.45.

273 Fabric 5A: necked jar. White paste with dark brown, matt colour-coat. (SHL GK 1, 2). R.EVE = 0.19.

274 Fabric 5A: beaker with short, everted rim. Fabric as for **273**. (GK 9). R.EVE = 0.15.

275 Fabric 5A: beaker with short, everted rim. Fabric as for **273**. (GK 14). R.EVE = 0.09.

276 Fabric 5B: small, straight-sided dish. Profile. Pinkish-orange paste with patchy orange to dark brown colour-coat. (GK 5). R.EVE = 0.07. B.EVE = 0.08.

277 Fabric 5A: straight-sided dish. Profile. White paste with dark brown to grey colour-coat. (SHL GK 1, 2). R.EVE = 0.40. B.EVE = 0.30.

278 Fabric 5A: straight-sided dish. Profile. White paste with orange colour-coat. Burnt on one fractured edge; sooty patches. (GK 1). R.EVE = 0.05. B.EVE = 0.17.

279 Fabric 5A: small, incipient flanged bowl. Fabric as for **277**. (GK 2). R.EVE = 0.07.

280 Fabric 5B: flanged bowl; short squared flange. Profile. Fabric as for **277**. (GK 10). R.EVE = 0.09. B.EVE = 0.04.

Oxfordshire wares

281 Fabric 8: carinated bowl with bead-rim. Narrow grey core with reddish-orange surfaces; colour-coat worn away; very abraded. Decoration: rouletting under rim and above carination. Young type C.68.3; 300–400+. (GK 1). R.EVE = 0.10.

282 Fabric 28: wall-sided bowl with moulded rim. Hard; white to pale grey ware. Decoration: red paint on rim as well as a horizontal band around girth. Young type P.24.1; 240–400+. (GK 13). R.EVE = 0.14.

283 Fabric 21: mortarium with upstanding rim and hooked flange. Hard; white-buff ware. Young type M.17; 240–300+. (GK 1). R.EVE = 0.18.

284 Fabric 21: mortarium with upstanding rim and short, down-turned flange. Profile; almost half the vessel remains. Good condition, although most of trituration grits worn away. Young type M.22.8; 240–400+. (GK 14). R.EVE = 0.50. B.EVE = 0.45.

Hadham wares

285 Fabric 9: flagon with moulded rim. Bright orange fabric; rather soft, abraded. (GK 1). R.EVE = 0.15.

286 Fabric 39: narrow-necked jar. Hard; blue-grey ware; burnished rim. (GK 9). R.EVE = 0.25.

287 Fabric 9: small, s-profile jar. Fabric as for **285**. (GK 11). R.EVE = 0.15.

288 Fabric 9: s-profile jar. Hard; bright orange ware with smoothed surfaces; light burnishing on the rim. (GK 10). R.EVE = 0.10.

289 Fabric 9: round-bodied jar with upright cordoned rim. Fabric as for **283**. (GK 1). R.EVE = 0.13.

290 Fabric 9: necked jar with rounded rim. Fabric as for **285**. (GK 1). R.EVE = 0.15.

291 Fabric 9: necked jar with squared rim; almost half the upper body of the vessel remains. Hard; thin grey core with dark orange surfaces; lightly burnished. (GK 10). R.EVE = 0.40.

292 Fabric 9: necked jar with slightly hooked squared rim. Fabric as for **291**; uneven horizontal brown streaks on exterior. (GK 1). R.EVE = 0.42.

293 Fabric 9: dish or platter with moulded rim. Dark orange fabric; slightly burnt. Zone of stabbed decoration on the rim interior. (GK 1) Rim Dm = ?

294 Fabric 9: dish or platter with moulded rim; external groove around rim. Reddish-orange fabric. (GK 1). R.EVE = 0.12.

295 Fabric 9: shallow dish with horizontal rim. Rather coarse dark orange fabric. (GK 1). R.EVE = 0.20.

296 Fabric 39: straight-sided dish. Hard; blue-grey fabric. (GK10). R.EVE = 0.20.

297 Fabric 9: hemispherical bowl. Hard; grey core with orange surfaces; smoothed. (GK 6). R.EVE = 0.07.

298 Fabric 39: flanged bowl. Hard; blue-grey fabric; burnished rim and flange. (GK 2). R.EVE = 0.09.

299 Fabric 12: mortarium with upstanding rim with internal groove; squat slightly hooked flange. Rather coarse bright orange fabric; traces of white slip on rim interior. (GK 6). R.EVE = 0.12.

Misc. grey wares

300 Fabric 37: jar with short, everted rim. Hard; medium-dark grey fabric. (GK 1). R.EVE = 0.16.

301 Fabric 37: small jar or bowl. Medium grey fabric with darker grey exterior surface. (GK 1). R.EVE = 0.14.

302 Fabric 48: deep bowl; rim almost round in section. Hard; medium grey fabric. SHL GK12. (GK6). R.EVE = 0.44.

303 Fabric 48: deep straight-sided dish. Profile. Hard; medium grey surfaces with paler core. SHL GK2 (GK1). R.EVE = 0.25. B.EVE = 0.06.

304 Fabric 48: shallow, straight-sided dish. Profile. Hard; medium grey fabric. (GK15). R.EVE = 0.10. B.EVE = 0.10.

305 Fabric 48: similar to **303**. Hard; medium grey. (GK15). R.EVE = 0.07.

Misc. oxidised wares

306 Fabric 19: necked jar with external groove on rim. Narrow groove around girth. Abraded surfaces. Finely granular, reddish-orange fabric; ?originally slipped. (GK1). R.EVE = 0.15.

307 Fabric 19: s-profile jar; external groove around rim. Bright orange fabric; matt brown streaky exterior. (GK 5). R.EVE = 0.18.

308 Fabric 16: s-profile jar with squared rim. Dark orange fabric with gritty surfaces. (GK 1). R.EVE = 0.07.

309 Fabric 16: s-profile jar with hooked rim. Fabric as for **308**. (GK 1). R.EVE = 0.20.

310 Fabric 16: s-profile jar with squared rim. Fabric as for **308**. (GK 10) R.EVE = 0.15.

311 Fabric 10: carinated wall-sided bowl; squared rim with internal groove or lid-seating. Rather coarse dark orange fabric. (GK 10). R.EVE = 0.13.

312 Fabric 10: small deep bowl with triangular rim. Fabric as for **311**. (GK 1). R.EVE = 0.20.

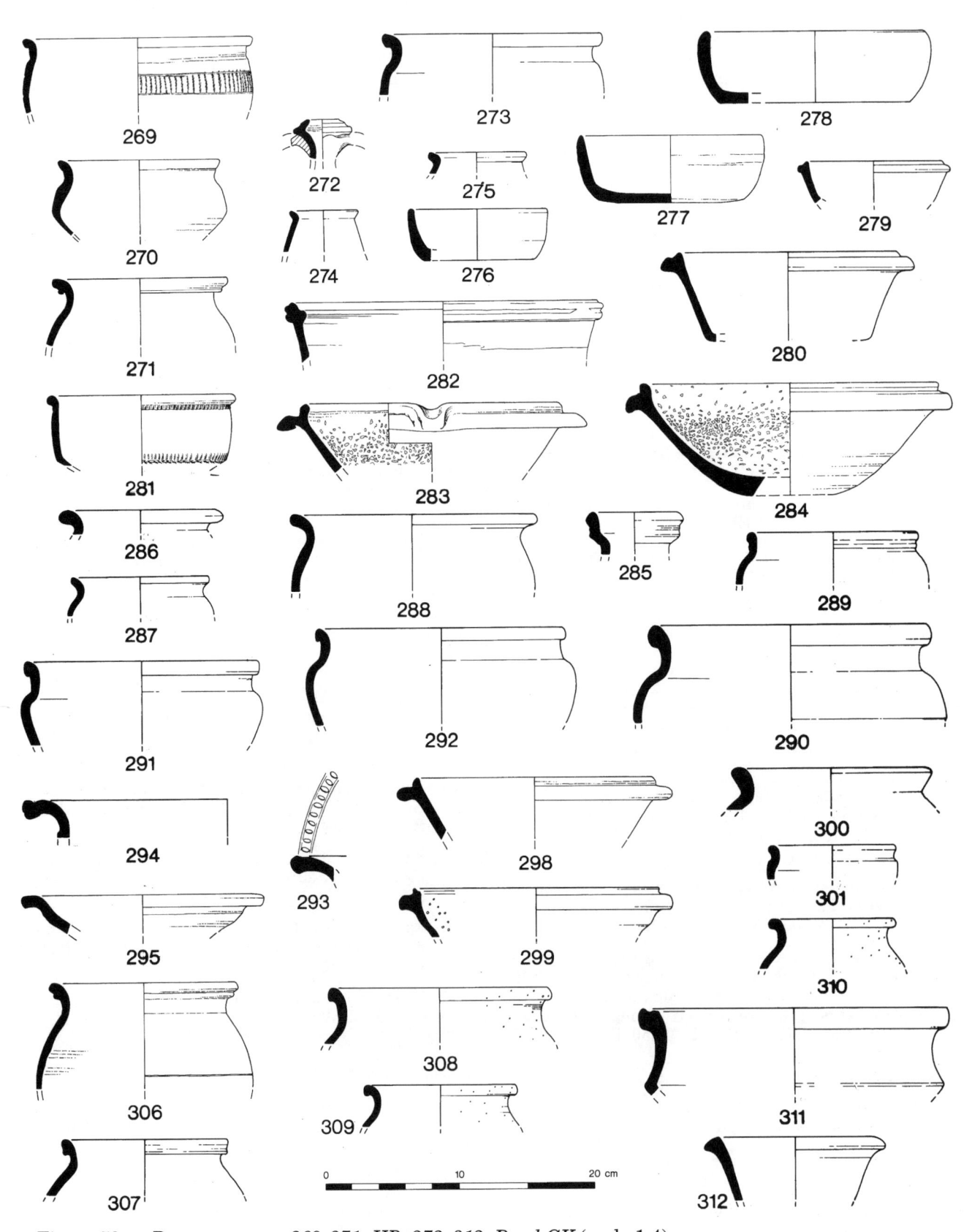

Figure 52   Roman pottery; 269–271, HB: 272–312, Pond GK (scale 1:4).

132

Shell-tempered wares

313 Fabric 58: hook-rim jar. Medium grey core with dark brown-grey surfaces; vesicular. (GK 2). R.EVE =0.13.

314 Fabric 58: s-profile jar with squared rim. Patchy dark brown-black ware. Decoration: rilling on the shoulder. (GK 1). R.EVE = 0.17.

315 Fabric 58: necked jar with 'figure of 7' rim. Grey core with buff-brown surfaces. Decoration: rilling begins under the rim. (GK 14). R.EVE = 0.17.

316 Fabric 58: similar form and fabric to **313**. (GK 1). R.EVE = 0.32.

317 Fabric 58: hook-rim jar. Fabric as **315**. (GK 2). R.EVE = 0.10.

318 Fabric 58: hook-rim jar. Patchy grey to light brown ware; worn surfaces. Decoration: rilling on the shoulder. (GK 1). R.EVE = 0.23.

319 Fabric 58: large storage jar with thick, bead-rim. Patchy buff to dark brown fabric; vesicular. (GK 15).

320 Fabric 58: form and fabric as for **319**. (SHL GK 1, 14). R.EVE = 0.12.

321 Fabric 58: straight-sided dish. Pinkish-beige fabric. Baldock No.843; late fourth to fifth century. (GK2). R.EVE = 0.07.

322 Fabric 58: similar form to **321**. Black exterior surfaces with pinkish beige interior. (GK1). R.EVE = 0.43.

323 Fabric 58: small, flanged bowl; straight squared flange. Patchy pale grey to beige fabric; slightly vesicular. Decoration: faint rilling under the flange. (GK 6). R.EVE = 0.10.

324 Fabric 58: flanged bowl; squat squared flange. Dark grey to black core and exterior; interior reddish-brown. Decoration: rilling below flange. (GK 1). R.EVE = 0.10.

325 Fabric 58: flanged bowl; down-turned flange. Patchy reddish-brown to buff fabric; vesicular. (GK 1). R.EVE = 0.07.

326 Fabric 58: shallow, flanged bowl; short squared flange. Grey core with patchy beige-brown surfaces; vesicular. Decoration: rilling under the flange. (GK 10). R.EVE = 0.16.

GK+ LEVELS OVER POND
(Fig. 53)

Hadham wares

327 Fabric 9: round-bodied jar; almost upright rim. R.EVE = 0.37.

328 Fabric 10: bowl with folded-over, moulded rim. R.EVE = 0.34

Misc. oxidised wares

329 Fabric 19: hemispherical bowl with sieve-like holes. Finely granular reddish-orange fabric. Abraded surfaces. R.EVE = 0.27.

Shell-tempered ware

330 Fabric 58: deep, almost straight-sided dish. Pinkish-buff fabric. R.EVE = 0.22.

Nene Valley wares

331 Fabric 22: mortarium with horizontal reeded rim. Worn trituration grits. R.EVE = 0.28.

332 Fabric 22: larger version of **331**; undercut rim. R.EVE = 0.32.

OTHER LATE ROMAN POTTERY
(Fig. 53)

Nene Valley wares

333 Fabric 5A: necked jar. White paste with dark brown-black colour-coat. N.V. No.75; fourth century. (RY 1). R.EVE = 0.21.

334 Fabric 5A: straight-sided dish. Fabric as for **333**. (RY 1). R.EVE = 0.05.

335 Fabric 5A: flanged bowl; hooked flange. Fabric as for **333**. N.V.No.79. (RY 1). R.EVE = 0.19.

Oxfordshire wares

336 Fabric 8: necked bowl. Hard; grey core and red surfaces; abraded, almost no colour-coat remaining. Decoration: impressed rosette. Young type C.75; 325–400+. (AAK 1). R.EVE = 0.11.

Hadham wares

337 Fabric 9: disc-mouthed flagon. Bright orange fabric; very abraded. (ZT 1). R.EVE = 0.20.

338 Fabric 9: small straight-sided dish. Profile. Fabric as for **337**. (EAB 1). R.EVE = 0.35.

339 Fabric 9: mortarium with upstanding rim and short hooked flange. Dark orange fabric; worn grits. Abraded. (CG 1). R.EVE = 0.07.

Misc. oxidised wares

340 Fabric ?25: flagon with moulded rim. (CQ1). R.EVE = 0.07).

Misc. grey wares

341 Fabric 37: wide-diameter straight-sided dish. Profile. Light grey core with medium grey surfaces; smoothed. (EAC 2). R.EVE = 0.12. B.EVE = 0.15.

342 Fabric 49: s-profile jar with squared rim. Dark grey core with patchy reddish brown to dark orange surfaces; sandy and abrasive. (EAF 1). R.EVE = 0.65.

343 Fabric 37: s-profile jar with hooked moulded rim. Medium grey fabric; smoothed surfaces. (ZF 1). R.EVE = 0.30.

344 Fabric 49: flanged bowl; short down-turned flange. Light grey core with dark grey-brown surfaces; very sandy and abrasive. (EAF 1). R.EVE = 0.25.

UNSTRATIFIED POTTERY
(Fig. 53)

Oxfordshire ware

345 Fabric 8: round-bodied cordoned bowl. (DG+). R.EVE = 0.08.

346 Fabric 8: miniature necked bowl; groove on top of rim. Soft bright orange-red fabric, extremely abraded. Young type C.75; 325–400+. (DG+). R.EVE = 0.15.

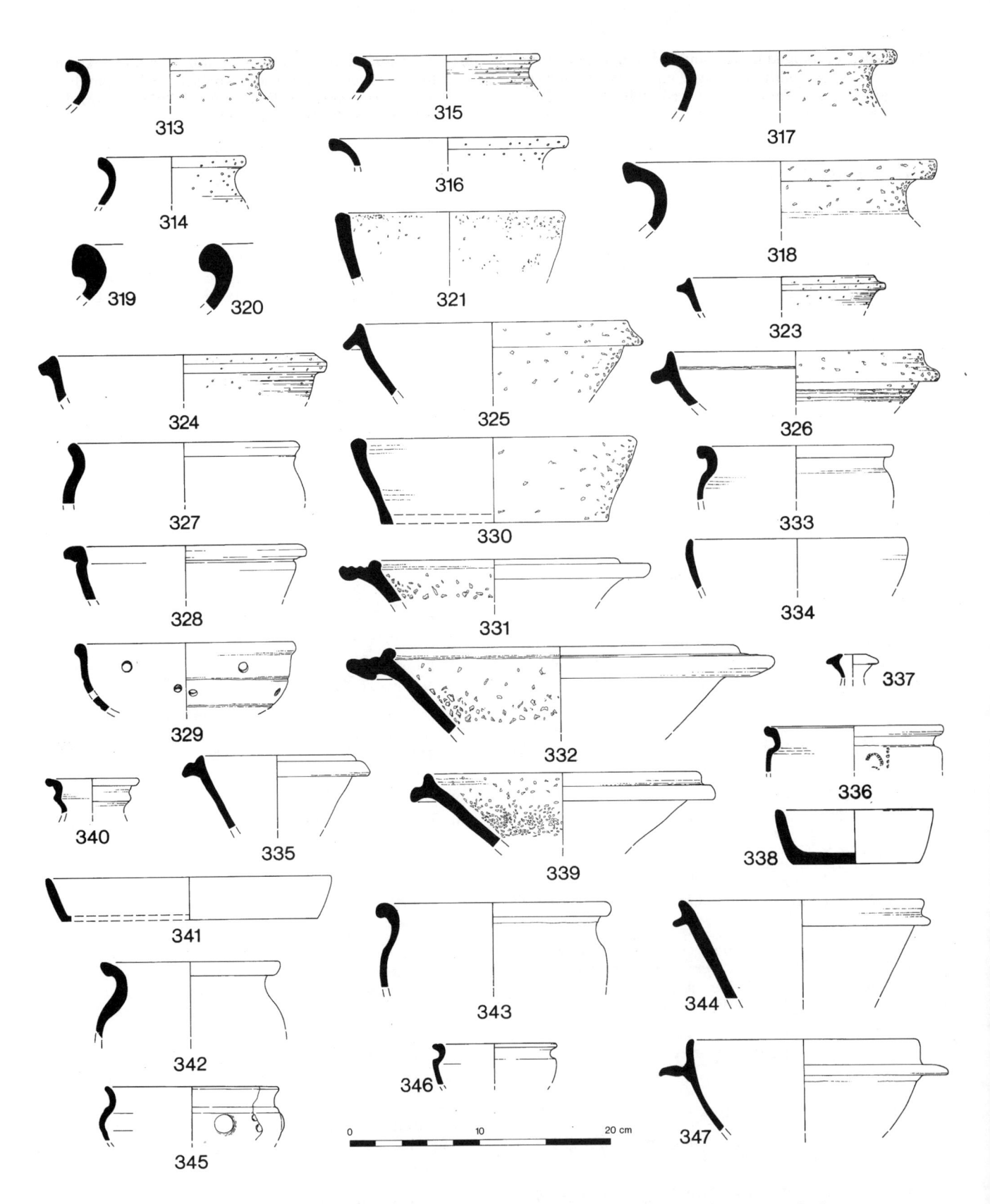

Figure 53   Roman pottery; 313–332, Pond GK: 333–347, other late Roman & unstratified pottery (scale 1:4).

347 Fabric 8: flanged bowl; moulded flange. Hard; grey core with reddish-orange surfaces; colour-coat fairly worn. Young type C.51; 240–400+. (DF+). R.EVE = 0.07.

THE CEMETERY
(Fig. 54)

348 Fabric 57: bead-rim jar; almost upright rim, thickened internally. Baldock No. 570; Hadrianic. (GAI 1). R.EVE = 0.44.

349 Fabric 11: shallow dish or platter with narrow out-turned rim. (GAN 2). R.EVE = 0.35.

350 Fabric ?33: necked jar with thickened rim; rilled zone around shoulder. Almost complete. Very abraded surfaces. Dark grey with reddish patches. Baldock No.558; Hadrianic–Antonine/Antonine. (GAM 1). R.EVE = 0.65. B.EVE. = 0.85.

351 Fabric 49: smaller version of **350**. Complete except for damaged rim. Abraded surfaces. Sooty patches on exterior surface. Found within **350**. (GAM 1). R.EVE = 0.95. B.EVE = 1.00.

352 Fabric 17: small shallow flanged bowl. Fine pale orange-red fabric. All surfaces completely worn away; very friable. (GBI 3). R.EVE = 0.85.

Vessels from disturbed graves

353 Fabric 37: round-bodied beaker with short everted rim. Narrow groove around girth. Medium grey. Similar to Baldock No. 354; first century. (GBE 1). R.EVE = 0.21.

354 Fabric 33: small bowl with bead-rim. Dark brown to ochre surfaces. Slightly abraded. (GBE 1). R.EVE = 0.05.

355 Fabric 37: shallow, curved dish. Parallel grooves under rim. Medium grey fabric. (GBE 1). R.EVE = 0.13.

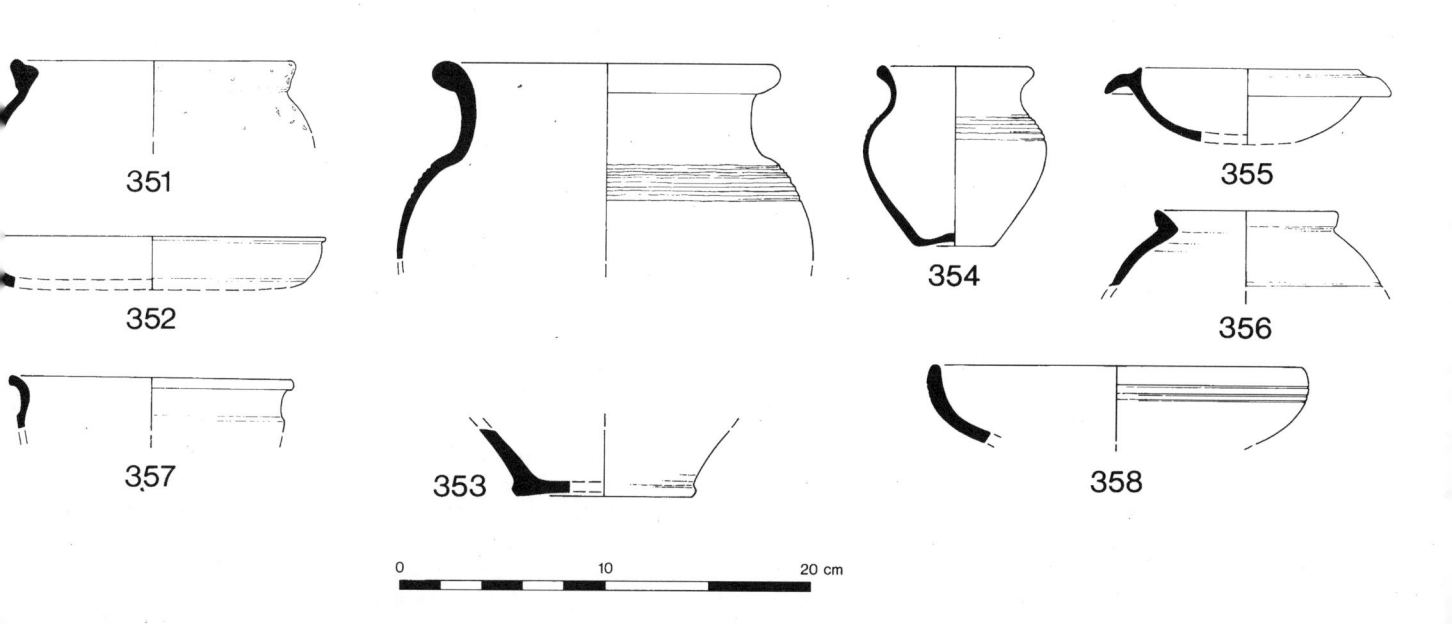

Figure 54 Roman pottery; 348–355, Cemetery (scale 1:4).

Plant Remains and other Macrofossils

Peter Murphy

Summary

Limited sampling at the Chells excavation produced remains of spelt (Triticum spelta) *with traces of barley* (Hordeum sp.), *bread-type wheat* (T. aestivum s.l.) *and an associated weed flora. A corn drier, fuelled with wood and spelt chaff, is thought to have been used for drying prime grain prior to storage or milling, and perhaps also for parching spelt malt. Samples from the aerated fills of a well produced carbonised cereals, arable weeds and a grassland flora, but the feature was too deep (14.5 m+) for its presumed basal organic fills to be excavated. Plant remains from other contexts were assessed, but not studied in detail, being apparently typical Roman rural assemblages.*

Introduction

Although plant remains from rural Roman sites have been quite extensively studied in East Anglia and elsewhere, there is comparatively little information on arable farming on heavy boulder clay soils, even though field survey indicates that in some areas such soils were densely settled and under arable production (Williamson 1984) during the Roman period. Limited sampling was therefore undertaken at this site to obtain relevant assemblages of plant remains.

Sampling and retrieval

The deposits from this site mainly comprised very stiff decalcified clay, and disaggregation of these deposits proved difficult. Consequently, very large-scale bulk sampling and flotation was impractical. Samples were, however, collected from the corn drier, well and some other features, for examination in the laboratory.

From the corn drier and associated layers, twenty one-kilogramme samples were examined. These were taken from layers within the flue [GF], stokehole [JA] and an overlying layer [JE] (Fig. 55). The composition of the assemblages of plant material present were recorded in detail in an attempt to reconstruct the function(s) of the structure. Plant remains and other macrofossils present are listed in Table 13.

The deposits at the site provided rather poor conditions for the preservation of biota, and one objective of the excavation of Well CAB was to expose structured organic deposits from which, it was anticipated, a wider range of macro- and microfossils would be obtained. In addition, 1–2 kg samples were taken from the upper aerated fills at 150 mm vertical intervals for possible land mollusc analysis, and assessment of types of refuse deposition. Unfortunately, the great depth of the feature (14.5+m) meant that excavation had to be stopped for safety reasons before basal organic fills were reached, and consequently only the samples from the upper fills were available for analysis. Samples were selected for assessment from this series at regular vertical intervals.

The samples were found to have largely decalcified clay matrices, so mollusc shells were not preserved, except in the basal chalky sample at 14.25–14.4 m, and where the shell structure had been modified by burning. No useful shell assemblages were obtained. However, the samples did contain carbonised plant remains, which are listed in Table 14. Following this assessment, it was not thought that further work on the remaining samples could be justified.

Other contexts sampled are listed in the site archive. One-kilogramme samples were initially examined with the aim of distinguishing contexts which included high densities of plant material which might relate to particular types of crop-processing activity. In the event, the samples were found to contain only small quantities of carbonised crop plant remains and weed seeds, which are thought to represent no more than a diffuse 'background scatter' of material, derived from a variety of sources. Full quantitative analysis was not thought to be worthwhile.

The samples were air-dried, then immersed in hot water. Some clay aggregates were not broken down by this method, and retrieval of plant material was therefore incomplete. Plant remains were extracted by manual flotation/washover, using a 0.5 mm collecting mesh.

THE CORN DRIER
Samples from this feature (Table 13) produced abundant carbonised remains of spelt wheat *(Triticum spelta)*, comprising mainly spikelet fragments with some grains, occasional culm fragments and a few remains of weeds, mainly the common weed grasses *Bromus mollis/secalinus* and *Avena fatua* type. Damaged and fragmentary remains of wheat were also present, but the only crop definitely identifiable was spelt. The counts given in Table 13 should be regarded as minimum numbers of specimens, for there were many small unquantifiable fragments. Silica residues of awns and inflorescence bracts were present in most samples, and some produced white vesicular siliceous material, thought to represent silica

derived from cereals, which had been fused at high temperatures.

Assemblages from structures of this type have been reviewed by van der Veen (1989), who concludes that 'corn driers' were in fact multi-purpose structures used for both drying grain for consumption or storage and for parching malt. Characterising functions depends on detailed recording of sample composition, location (Fig. 55) and the percentage of sprouted (germinated) grains.

The plant remains from the stokepit [JA] are assumed to represent fuel. Charcoal, including oak (*Quercus* sp.) and hazel or alder (*Corylus/Alnus* sp.) was present, but cereal remains were also abundant: JA 2 is estimated to have contained approximately 200 grains and 10,500 glume bases per kilogramme of soil. The use of cereal-processing waste mixed with wood as a fuel for grain-parching is well attested historically, and palaeobotanical evidence indicates that Roman corn driers were similarly fuelled (van der Veen, op. cit.).

The distribution of plant material in samples from the basal flue fill [GF 18] is shown in Fig. 55. It is quite clear that the density of cereal remains was greatest at the southern end of the flue, close to the stokepit, and fell away northwards. A probable interpretation of this distribution is that charred plant material from the stokepit was carried along the flue by the draught. Consequently, samples from this layer are of little help in characterising plant remains which had fallen from the drying floor. The samples from GF 17 (5, 6, 7, 8) are also of limited use, for they include fragments of fused siliceous material, thought to indicate very high temperatures and hence, probably, preferential combustion of spikelet fragments.

This leaves the two samples from GF 16 (9 and 10). Sample 10 came from directly adjacent to the stokepit, and is likely to have included material derived from fuel. Sample 9, however, came from the end of the eastern arm of the flue, at the furthest point from the stokehole, and is much less likely to include fuel residues. No siliceous material was noted, though this does not necessarily exclude differential preservation of glumes and grains. However, the sample did contain a relatively high proportion of grains (c.180 per kg), with few glume bases (c.12 per kg). The grain to glume ratio, at 14.6:1, is conspicuously high. A few of the grains present had germinated prior to carbonisation, though poor preservation makes the determination of the exact proportion of sprouted grains difficult. This is, in fact, a general problem with the samples from this structure. Of the 152 grains identifiable as wheat from GF and JA, 42 (27.6%) showed signs of germination, but in addition most samples included grain fragments and detached sprouts, so this percentage is probably misleadingly low.

Taking all these results together, it may be concluded that:

1 The structure was used for large-scale processing of spelt wheat: no other crops were represented;
2 The absence or rarity of culm fragments and weed seeds indicates that ears/spikelets had been separated from straw and weed seeds before processing in the corn drier;
3 The fuel used was spelt chaff, mixed with wood or charcoal;
4 Most samples from the flue included some fuel residues carried from the stokepit by the draught;
5 Sample 9 [GF 16] included a high proportion of grains, most of which showed no obvious signs of sprouting. *If* differential preservation of grains and glumes can be discounted, this indicates drying of prime grain (with a few glumes as contaminants) prior to storage or milling (van der Veen's functions 4 and 5);
6 The proportion of sprouted grains is difficult to determine, due to probable fragmentation of germinated grains and their 'sprouts'. The parching of spelt malt is therefore impossible to establish with certainty, but remains a possibility.

The layer overlying the structure included small quantities of cereal remains, probably derived from the earlier deposits, but also quite a large amount of charcoal. This included charcoal of oak *(Quercus* sp.*)* and ash *(Fraxinus* sp.*)* from mature wood with some fragments of roundwood, c.20–25 mm diameter, of hazel *(Corylus* sp.*)*, perhaps derived from the superstructure.

THE WELL

Carbonised plant remains from well fills at depths between 0.27 and 14.40 m are listed in Table 14. Samples from the upper fills produced mammal bone fragments, occasional scraps of mussel shell *(Mytilus edulis)* and low densities of carbonised cereal and other plant remains. These included spikelet fragments of spelt *(Triticum spelta)*, indeterminate wheat grains, a rachis internode of barley *(Hordeum* sp.*)*, hazel nut shell fragments *(Corylus avellana)*, and a few weed seeds. Although only small (1 kg) samples were examined for assessment purposes, it appeared that processing larger samples would be unlikely to add anything to the interpretation of these deposits, which appear to have contained food waste and crop-processing residues, probably derived from a variety of sources.

Below this, bone and marine mollusc shell fragments were not observed in the samples, although samples from 2.3–3.7 m had somewhat higher densities of carbonised plant remains. At this level, cereal grains and spikelet fragments (of *T. spelta, T. aestivum*-type and *Hordeum* sp.) were associated with seeds of arable weeds and grassland plants. Grassland taxa represented were *Ranunculus* sp(p) (buttercups), *Stellaria graminea* (lesser stitchwort), *Linum* cf. *catharticum* (purging flax), small-seeded Leguminosae, *Rumex acetosella* (sheep's sorrel), *Plantago lanceolata*

TABLE 13: Plant remains and other macrofossils from corn drier Flue GF, Stokehole JA and overlying deposit JE.

Species		Context: Sample no:	GF 17 5	GF 17 6	GF 17 7	GF 17 8	GF 17 9	GF 16 10	GF 16 11	GF 18 12	GF 18 13	GF 18 14	GF 18 15	GF 18 16	GF 18 17	JA 2 2	JA 4 3	JA 5 4	JA 8 5	JA 8 6	JA 10 7	JE 1 3
Cereal indet.		ca. fr	+	+	+	+	+	+	+	+	+	+	+	+	+	+	+	+	+	+	+	+
		ca	2	4	1	4(2)	27	1	2	6	7	4	2	1	4	6	8	6	7	2	12	2
		spr	–	–	–	–	2	–	–	–	–	–	6	3	8	5	1	3	1	1	13	–
		cn	–	1	–	–	–	–	1fr	1+fr	–	1	–	–	–	1fr	–	–	–	–	–	–
		cb	1	–	–	–	–	–	–	–	–	–	–	–	–	–	–	–	–	–	–	–
		ib(si)	–	–	–	–	–	++	+	+	+	+	+	–	–	+	+	+	+	+	+	+
Triticum sp(p)		ca	7	2(1)	4(1)	8(2)	17(1)	7(3)	6(1)	3(2)	2(1)	8(3)	9(5)	5(1)	6(2)	7(1)	19(4)	6(3)	11(3)	3	22(8)	17(3)
		spb	–	–	–	–	–	1	–	1	–	4	3	7	10	33	2	1	4	2	5	–
		gb	–	1	1	–	–	1	1	3	2	12	39	31	27	87	9	12	5	10	32	1
		ri	–	1	–	–	–	1	2	3	–	8	21	14	15	40	3	3	2	6	3	–
		afr	–	–	–	–	+	++	+	+	+	+	+	+	+	+	+	–	+	+	+	–
		afr(si)	–	–	–	–	+	+	+	+	+	+	+	–	–	+	–	–	–	–	–	–
Triticum spelta L.		spk	–	–	–	–	–	1	–	1	–	–	–	2	3	–	–	–	–	–	–	–
		spf	–	–	–	–	–	–	–	–	–	–	–	–	–	4	–	–	–	–	–	–
		spb	–	–	–	–	–	–	1	–	–	–	–	–	–	4	–	1	–	–	1	–
		gb	–	–	3	7	3	14	12	7	2	66	142	126	115	484	40	42	74	63	170	17
		ri	–	–	–	1	–	–	–	2	2	9	12	9	–	40	2	3	8	6	12	–
Cruciferae indet.			–	–	–	–	–	–	–	–	–	–	–	1	–	–	–	–	–	–	–	–
Chenopodiaceae indet.			–	–	–	–	–	–	–	1	–	–	–	–	–	–	–	–	–	–	–	–
cf. Trifolium–type			–	–	–	–	–	–	–	2	–	–	–	–	–	–	–	–	–	–	–	–
Vicia / Lathyrus sp(p)			–	–	–	–	–	–	–	–	–	–	2	–	–	–	–	–	–	–	1	–
Polygonum sp.			–	–	–	–	–	–	–	–	–	–	2	–	–	–	–	–	1fr	–	1	–
Rumex sp.			1	–	–	–	–	1	–	–	–	2	–	–	1	–	–	–	–	–	2	–
Anthemis cotula L.			–	–	–	–	–	–	–	–	–	–	–	–	–	3	–	–	–	–	–	–
Tripleurospermum maritimum (L) Koch			–	–	–	–	–	–	–	–	–	–	–	–	–	1	–	–	1	–	–	–
Lapsana communis L.			–	–	–	–	–	–	–	–	–	–	–	1	–	–	–	–	–	–	–	–
Compositae indet.			–	–	–	–	–	–	–	–	–	3	2	1	3	–	2	–	–	–	1	–
Bromus mollis / secalinus			–	–	–	–	–	–	–	–	–	–	1	1fr	–	–	2	1	–	–	–	–
Avena fatua-type		fb	–	–	–	1	–	–	–	1	–	1	–	–	–	2	2	–	1	–	–	–
Avena sp(p)		ca	–	–	–	–	–	–	–	–	–	–	1	1	–	2	–	1	1	1	6	1
Avena sp(p)		fb fr	+	++	+	+	–	+	+	+	+	+	+	+	+	+	+	+	++	++	+	–
Avena sp(p)		afr	–	–	+	–	+	+	+	–	–	+	–	+	+	+	+	+	+	+	+	–
Avena / Bromus		ca	–	–	–	1	–	1	–	–	–	1	–	–	2	2	3	1	1	1	2	1
Gramineae		ca	–	–	–	1	–	1	–	–	1	–	5	4	2	1	–	1	–	1	7	–
Indeterminate seeds, etc.			–	1	–	–	1	1	2	–	–	–	2	2	–	4	1	–	–	1	5	–
Charcoal			+	+	++	+	+	+	+	+	+	+	+	+	+	+	+	++	++	++	++	+++
Siliceous fused material			+	+	+	+	–	+	–	+	+	+	–	–	–	–	–	+	+	–	–	–
Small mammal/amphibian bone			–	–	–	–	–	–	–	–	+	–	–	–	–	–	–	–	–	–	–	–
Vallonia sp (burnt shell)			–	–	1	–	–	–	–	–	–	–	–	–	–	–	–	1	–	–	–	–
% flot sorted			100	100	100	100	25	25	100	100	100	100	12.5	3.125	6.25	6.25	100	100	12.5	6.25	6.25	100

138

All samples 1 kg. All taxa represented by carbonised macrofossils except where indicated.
Figures in brackets refer to numbers of grains which definitely had germinated before carbonisation.

Abbreviations:

afr	awn fragments
ca	caryopses
cb	culm bases
cn	culm nodes
fb	floret bases
fr	fragments
gb	glume bases
ib	cereal inflorescence bract fragments, including glume tips
ri	rachis internodes
si	silica residues
spb	spikelet bases
spf	spikelet forks
spk	spikelets containing grain
spr	'sprouts'

TABLE 14: Carbonised plant remains and other macrofossils from Well CAB.

Species		Sample depth (cm)	1.501 27-30	2.503 45-60	3.506 90-105	4.509 135-50	5.512 180-95	5.515 225-40	6.518 270-85	6.521 315-30	8.523 200-15	9.524 230-45	10.525 235-50	11.533 360-70	11.538 405-20	11.543 450-65	12.535 360-75	15.572 885-900	15.584 1065-80	19.608 1425-40
Cereal indet.	ca fr		+	+	+	+	+	–	+	+	–	+	+++	+	+	–	+	–	–	–
	ca		–	2	2	1	–	–	–	–	–	–	21	3	6	–	–	–	–	1
	spr		1	–	–	–	–	–	–	–	–	–	–	–	–	–	–	–	–	–
Cereal/grass	cn/fr		–	–	–	–	–	–	–	–	–	–	–	–	–	–	–	–	–	–
Triticum sp(p)	ca		–	7*	8	2	1	–	–	+	–	3*	++	+	2+	–	+	–	–	1
Triticum aestivum s.l.	ca		–	–	–	–	–	–	–	–	–	–	64*	13	4	–	1	–	–	–
Triticum sp(p)	gb		1	–	–	–	1	–	2	1	–	1	6	2	2	–	1	–	–	–
	spb		1	–	–	–	–	–	–	–	–	–	11	–	–	–	–	–	–	–
	ri		–	–	–	–	–	–	–	–	–	–	2	–	–	–	–	–	–	–
	rn		–	1	–	–	–	–	–	–	–	–	4	–	–	–	–	–	–	–
	afr		–	–	–	–	–	–	–	–	–	–	–	–	–	–	+	1	–	–
Triticum spelta L.	gb		7	29	6	1	–	1	–	–	1	5	7	3	2	1	2	–	–	–
	spb		–	1	1	–	–	–	–	–	–	1	–	–	–	–	–	–	–	–
	ri		–	1	–	–	–	–	–	–	–	1	4	–	–	–	–	–	–	–
	spf		–	–	–	–	–	–	–	–	–	–	5	–	–	–	–	–	–	–
	spk		–	–	–	–	–	–	–	–	–	–	1	–	–	–	–	–	–	–
Hordeum sp(p)	ca		–	–	–	–	–	–	–	–	–	–	4	–	–	–	–	–	–	–
	ri		–	–	1	–	–	–	–	–	–	–	–	–	–	–	–	–	–	fr
Ranunculus acris/repens/bulbosus			–	–	–	–	–	–	–	1	–	–	2	–	–	–	–	–	–	–
Agrostemma githago L.			–	–	–	–	–	–	–	–	–	–	fr	–	–	–	–	–	–	–
Stellaria graminea L.			–	–	–	–	–	–	–	–	–	–	–	–	–	–	–	–	–	–
Atriplex patula/hastata			–	–	–	–	–	–	–	2	–	3	51+fr	3	fr	–	1	–	–	–
Chenopodiaceae indet.			–	–	–	–	–	–	–	–	–	–	7	–	–	–	–	–	–	–
Linum cf. catharticum L.			–	–	–	–	–	–	–	1	–	1	1(cap)	–	–	–	–	–	–	–
Medicago-type			–	–	–	–	–	–	–	–	–	–	–	–	–	–	–	–	–	–
Medicago/Lotus/Trifolium sp(p)			–	–	–	–	–	–	–	–	–	–	19	–	2	–	–	–	–	–
Vicia/Lathyrus sp.			–	–	–	–	–	–	–	2	–	–	–	–	–	–	–	–	–	–
Leguminosae indet.			–	–	1	–	–	–	–	–	–	–	–	–	–	–	–	–	–	–
Aphanes sp.			–	–	–	–	–	–	–	–	–	–	1	1	–	–	–	–	–	–
Crataegus monogyna Jacq			–	–	–	–	–	–	–	–	–	–	–	–	–	–	–	–	–	–
Polygonum aviculare agg.			–	–	–	–	–	–	–	–	–	–	5	–	–	–	–	–	–	–
Polygonum convulvulus L.			–	–	–	–	–	–	–	–	–	–	1	1	–	–	–	–	–	–
Polygonum sp.			–	–	–	–	–	–	–	–	–	–	5	–	–	–	–	–	–	–
Rumex sp(p)			–	–	–	–	–	–	–	–	–	3	14	–	1	–	–	–	–	–
Rumex acetosella agg.			–	–	–	–	–	–	–	2	–	2	23	–	–	1	–	–	–	–
Polygonaceae indet.			–	–	–	–	–	–	–	1	–	–	3	2	2	–	–	–	–	–
Corylus avellana L.			–	+	–	–	–	–	–	–	–	1	–	–	–	–	–	–	–	–
Lithospermum arvense L.			–	–	–	–	–	–	–	1	–	–	–	–	–	–	–	–	–	–
Euphrasia/Odontites sp.			–	–	–	–	–	–	–	–	–	–	13	–	–	–	–	–	–	–
Plantago lanceolata L.			–	–	–	–	–	–	–	–	–	–	4	–	–	–	–	–	–	–
Sherardia arvensis L.			–	–	–	–	–	–	–	–	–	–	–	1	–	–	–	–	–	–
Valerianella sp.			–	–	–	–	–	–	–	–	–	1	1	–	–	–	–	–	–	–
Tripleurospermum maritimum (L) Koch			–	–	–	–	–	–	–	–	–	2	46	1	–	–	–	–	–	–
Chrysanthemum leucanthemum L.			–	–	–	–	–	–	–	–	–	–	4	1	–	–	1	–	–	–
Carex sp.			–	–	–	–	–	–	–	–	–	–	–	1	–	–	–	–	–	–
Anisantha sterilis (L) Nevski			–	–	–	–	–	–	–	–	–	4	4	–	–	–	–	–	–	–
Bromus mollis/secalinus			1fr	4	–	1	–	–	–	–	–	1	1	–	–	–	–	–	–	–

	afr																
Avena sp.		–	–	–	–	–	–	–	–	–	+	–	–	–	–	–	–
Gramineae indet.		1	–	–	–	1	5	–	5	44	3	1	–	–	–	–	–
Indeterminate seeds, etc.		1	2	–	–	–	1	–	1	34	7	1	–	1	–	–	–
Bone fragments		++	–	–	+	–	+	–	–	–	–	–	1	–	–	–	1
Small mammal/amphibian bone		–	–	+	–	+	+	–	–	–	+	–	–	–	–	–	–
Mytilus shell		–	+	–	–	–	–	–	–	2	–	–	–	–	–	–	–
Vallonia costata		–	–	–	–	–	–	–	–	–	–	–	–	–	–	–	–
Vallonia excentrica		–	–	–	–	–	–	–	–	1	–	–	–	–	–	–	1
Cochlicopa sp.		–	–	–	–	–	–	–	–	1	–	–	–	–	–	–	1
Charred insect		–	–	–	–	–	–	–	–	–	–	–	–	–	–	–	–

* indicates sprouted grain present.

All samples 1 kg.
The following additional samples produced only small charcoal fragments:

10.525	(235–250)	15.566	(795–810)
11.538	(405–520)	15.578	(975–810)
3.536	(360–375)	15.578	(975–990)
13.545	(480–495)	16.590	(1155–1170)
15.548	(525–540)	17.596	(1245–1260)
15.554	(615–630)	19.602	(1335–1350)
15.560	(705–720)

Abbreviations:

afr	awn fragments
ca	caryopses
cb	culm bases
cn	culm nodes
fb	floret bases
fr	fragments
gb	glume bases
ib	cereal inflorescence bract fragments, including glume tips
ri	rachis internodes
si	silica residues
spb	spikelet bases
spf	spikelet forks
spk	spikelets containing grain
spr	'sprouts'

(ribwort plantain), *Chrysanthemum leucanthemum* (ox-eye daisy) and various Gramineae (grasses). These included one calcicole species *(L. catharticum)* and two plants more characteristic of sandy soils *(S. graminea, R. acetosella)*. This may reflect the variability of soil types towards the margin of the Boulder Clay plateau. The fruits and seeds of grassland plants were associated with culm fragments of grasses and/or cereals. It appears that the fills at this depth included a mixture of residues from cereal processing and spoilt hay, burnt as refuse.

Samples from below about 5.0 m consisted of quite clean decalcified clay with flints and chalk, containing only occasional small charcoal fragments, very rare cereal remains and weed seeds, and a few land mollusc shells.

OTHER CONTEXTS

One-kilogramme samples from other contexts (listed in the site archive) were assessed but not examined in detail. They contained almost uniformly low densities of carbonised plant material, typically containing spikelet fragments of *Triticum spelta*, wheat grains, and weed seeds, mainly *Bromus* and *Avena,* associated with variable quantities of charcoal and bone fragments. Assemblages of plant material of this type are commonplace at rural Roman sites: they cannot be regarded as primary refuse deposits, but rather represent material dispersed across the site from areas of crop processing, such as the corn drier. No concentrations of material worth detailed analysis were detected.

Pit RC was interpreted by its excavator as a cess pit, and samples from this context were therefore inspected in the hope of finding mineralised plant material. Layers RC 2–4 produced carbonised cereals and weed seeds, but no mineralised macrofossils, which implies that the field interpretation was incorrect. RC 4 did, however, produce a few seeds, not apparently mineralised, of *Lemna* sp. (duckweed). Survival of these seeds in a deposit which would not have been permanently waterlogged is surprising, though it is possible that the clay matrix of the fill resulted in development of locally anaerobic conditions. Assuming that there is no possibility of recent contamination, these seeds point to the presence of standing stagnant water in the feature, which may have been a sump or shallow well intercepting surface drainage.

Conclusions

The samples from the corn drier, well and other contexts clearly establish that spelt was being processed on a large scale at this site: the majority of samples examined contained, at least, low densities of spelt glume bases and other spikelet fragments. Remains of barley occurred only sporadically in small quantities. The results from this site thus establish that on this area of the Hertfordshire clay plateau spelt production was the main element of the arable economy, as elsewhere in East Anglia. Specific interpretation of the corn-drier assemblages proved difficult, but clearly a late stage in spelt processing is represented: apparently drying of prime grain for storage and milling, and perhaps also parching of spelt malt.

The weed flora associated with the cereal remains included a range of taxa very characteristic of Roman sites, though given local soil conditions the rarity of *Anthemis cotula* (noted in only one sample, from Stokepit JA) is surprising. This plant is a particularly characteristic weed of boulder clay soils (Kay 1971), yet in the samples examined from Chells the other common mayweed *Tripleurospermum maritimum* is more frequent and abundant. Given the limited scale of mapping it is perhaps unwise to make too much of this, though it is possible that the heaviest clay soils of the Hornbeam and Hanslope associations (Hodge *et al* 1984) in this area were not under cultivation.

Some evidence for the disposal of waste or spoilt hay was provided by carbonised macrofossils from the well fills.

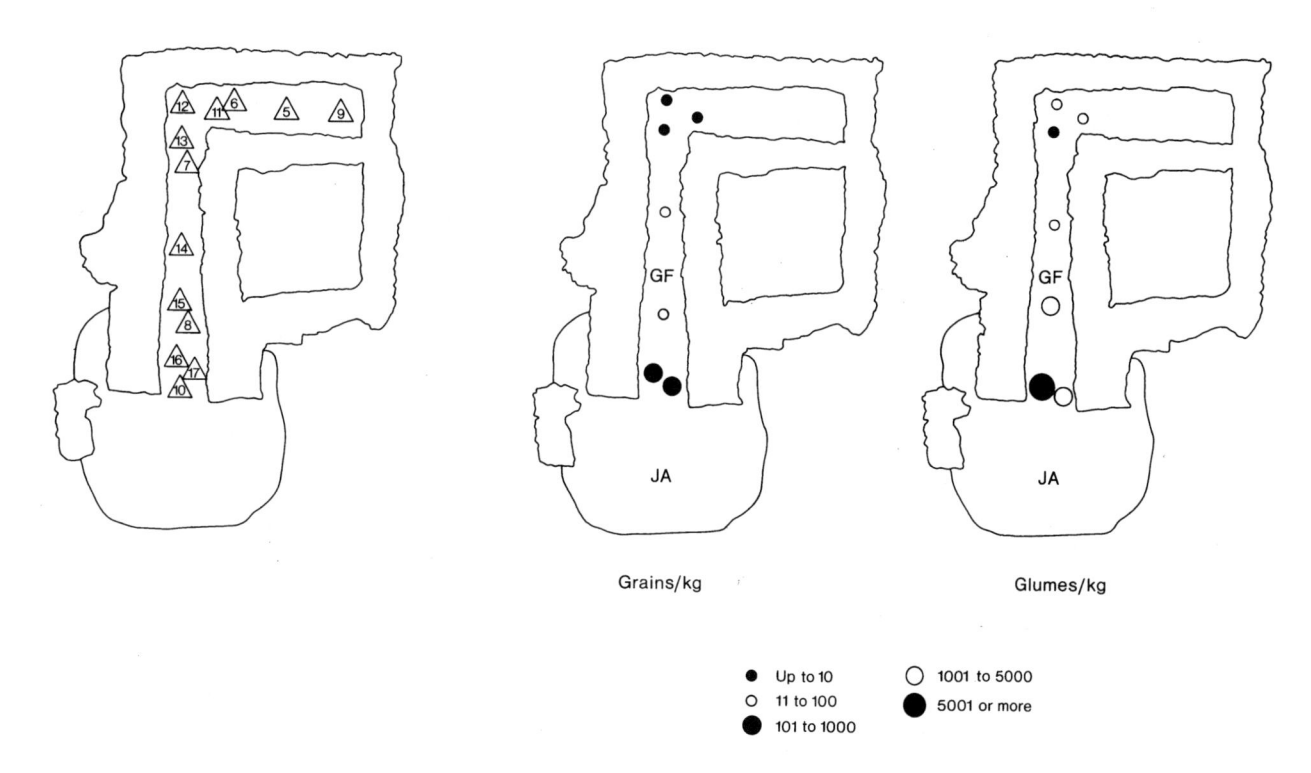

Figure 55   *The Corn Drier: location of samples from the basal flue fill.*

Cremated Bone

Jacqueline I. McKinley

[July 1991]

Introduction

Cremated bone from twenty-one burial contexts was received for examination. The site had suffered from extensive plough damage, which was clearly reflected in the condition of the bone from most of the cremation burials. Full details of the analysis of the cremated bone are contained in a report in the excavation archive; a summary of the findings appears below, and in the report on the cemetery excavation.

Methods

Bone from each context was passed through sieves of 10, 5 and 2 mm mesh size. The weight of bone collected from each sieve (presented as a percentage of the total weight in Table 16), and maximum skull and long bone fragment sizes, illustrate the degree of bone fragmentation. The identifiable bone was separated for further examination, being divided into the categories of skull, axial skeleton, upper and lower limb. Much of the bone in a cremation burial will be unidentifiable other than as fragments of long bone or spongy bone; only those fragments which could be identified fully have been subject to further examination. The percentage of identifiable bone from each context is given in Table 16, the percentage of identifiable bone from each of the four skeletal areas is also shown. This may illustrate any deliberate bias in the skeletal elements collected for burial, though it should be remembered that these percentages would be far from equal in a complete skeleton. Full details of all identified bone have been presented in the archive report, including i) any variation in colour from the normal buff/white for individual bones; ii) detailed descriptions of pathological lesions with diagnoses where appropriate; iii) any measurements other than those presented in Table 16. Some preliminary comment by the writer on the cremated animal bones occasionally recovered may be found in the archive report and Table 15.

A brief note on type of deposit and inclusions has been made with each context. Age was assessed from the stage of ossification and epiphyseal bone fusion (Gray 1977; McMinn and Hutchings 1985; Webb and Suchey 1985); and the general degree of cranial suture fusion and degenerative changes to the bone. Age categories rather than age in years are used, in view of the difficulties surrounding the accurate assessment of age for adults over 25/30yr (that is following final epiphyseal fusion), a problem compounded where the entire skeleton has not been recovered, as it rarely is in cremations. The degree of degenerative changes in the bone particularly may vary considerably dependent on the individual and/or the group. Where possible, a combination of methods was used to achieve the most accurate assessment.

The age categories used are:
infant	–	0–4 yr
juvenile	–	5–12 yr
subadult	–	13–18 yr
young adult	–	18–25 yr
mature adult	–	25–40 yr
older adult	–	40 yr+

Groups often had to be combined/linked because of poor bone recovery, resulting in reduced evidence of age.

The sex of the adults was assessed from the sexually dimorphic traits of the skeleton (Bass 1987), including maximum cranial vault thickness – '1a' and '1b' according to Gejvall (1981). Caution must be applied in the use of the latter measurements for reasons outlined elsewhere by the writer (McKinley 1994a). As with age assessment, a combination of methods and scoring of traits has been used where possible in order to overcome any methodological bias or variations in sexual morphology within the group. Three levels of reliability have been used; ?? for possible, ? for probable, and unquestioned. These levels are felt necessary because of the paucity of information in some cases, and unclear or contradictory dimorphism in others. The sexing of immature individuals has not been attempted, as sexual dimorphism does not tend to develop until after puberty.

Results

All the cremation burials examined contained human bone, but only eighteen contained identifiable fragments. The basic results are presented in Table 15.

Key to abbreviations of pathological conditions:
o.p.   osteophytes
o.a.   osteoarthritis

The small number of individuals recovered and high level of disturbance to the burials, resulting in the probable loss of much of the bone, renders any demographic discussion impossible. Only four (28%) adults had sufficient evidence to allow for any sexing.

The greatest weight of bone recovered was 773.0 g, *ie* less than 40% of the maximum weight of bone expected from an adult cremation (McKinley 1993). Though it is usual to find only a percentage of the bone was deposited, the recorded weights of bone in this case are doubtless considerably less than the deposited weights since all

TABLE 15: The Cemetery; human and other bone.

Context	Total weight (g)	Number individuals	Age	Sex	Pathology	Animal bone
GAB	183.8	1	older mature/older adult	?	o.p – atlas	–
GAC	612.1	1	mature adult	?	–	–
GAD	443.7	1	older mature/older adult	?	o.p. – sacrum	–
GAE	183.3	1	adult	?	–	–
GAF	292.7	1	adult	?	–	–
GAG	25.7	1	subadult/adult	?	–	–
GAH	52.4	1	older mature/older adult	?	–	–
GAI	128.8	1	older adult	?	o.a. – atlas	–
GAJ	37.1	1/?2	1) infant: 2) adult	?	–	–
GAL	773.8	1	adult	?female	–	?bird bone
GAO	9.8	1?	juvenile – adult	?	–	–
GAQ	325.2	1	adult	??female	–	–
GBA	674.2	1	older mature/older adult	??male	–	–
GBF	54.4	1	older infant – young subadult	?	–	–
GBH2	763.7	1	older mature/older adult	?female	o.p. – thoracic, radius head o.a. – atlas/axis exostoses – femur	?
GBH4	528.6	1	older adult	?	–	–
GBH6	18.3	1?	infant	?	–	–
GBI	265.8	1	adult	?	–	–

TABLE 16: Fragmentation of cremated bone.

Context	Total weight (g)	% total in 10 mm sieve	% total in 5 mm sieve	% total in 2 mm sieve	Max. frag. skull (mm)	Max. frag. l'bone (mm)	% total ident. bone	% ident. bone: skull	% ident. bone: axial	% ident. bone: u. limb	% ident. bone: l. limb
GAB 1	183.8	13.1	37.9	49.1	25.0	19.0	5.4	80.0	8.0	3.0	9.0
GAC 1	612.1	25.7	46.5	27.8	18.0	28.0	11.5	44.5	10.7	5.7	39.0
GAC 2	7.8	8.6	62.9	28.6	18.0	0.0	12.9	100.0	0.0	0.0	0.0
GAD 1	443.7	14.6	40.2	45.1	21.0	31.0	8.2	43.4	18.2	20.2	18.2
GAE 1	183.3	33.4	42.8	23.8	28.0	38.0	14.6	1.2	8.9	25.4	57.5
GAF 1	292.7	41.5	37.3	21.2	21.0	38.0	25.0	19.8	20.2	20.2	39.7
GAG 1	25.7	2.3	55.6	42.0	0.0	12.0	3.1	0.0	0.0	0.0	100.0
GAH 2	52.4	46.9	38.5	14.5	25.0	34.0	25.9	57.3	1.5	11.0	30.1
GAI 1	128.8	7.4	56.1	36.5	28.0	22.0	11.2	80.7	3.7	0.0	15.5
GAJ 1	37.1	1.9	30.7	67.4	13.0	0.0	14.0	100.0	0.0	0.0	0.0
GAL 1	773.8	25.0	43.7	31.2	21.0	40.0	7.4	33.9	8.2	25.3	32.6
GAK 1	184.2	15.7	47.8	36.5	0.0	0.0	0.0	0.0	0.0	0.0	0.0
GAN 1	17.9	12.2	67.0	20.7	0.0	0.0	0.0	0.0	0.0	0.0	0.0
GAO 1	9.8	50.0	33.7	16.3	9.0	0.0	4.1	100.0	0.0	0.0	0.0
GAQ 1	325.2	9.3	47.5	43.2	26.0	21.0	3.3	86.8	0.0	0.0	13.2
GBA 1	674.2	27.1	43.1	29.8	28.0	45.0	14.1	68.9	6.0	1.3	23.6
GBF 1	54.4	2..9	44.5	52.6	11.0	0.0	3.1	100.0	0.0	0.0	0.0
GBH 2	763.7	32.8	41.6	25.6	34.0	31.0	15.5	31.1	30.6	8.3	29.9
GBH 4	528.6	26.0	44.8	29.1	18.0	24.0	15.2	85.9	3.1	2.3	8.7
GBH 6	18.3	19.4	48.5	32.8	16.0	0.0	15.5	100.0	0.0	0.0	0.0
GBI 1	265.8	12.4	57.1	30.4	20.0	35.0	4.9	78.6	0.0	7.6	13.7

cremation burials were disturbed to some degree, and it is impossible to ascertain how much has been lost. The fairly small fragment sizes recorded are also probably the product of plough damage rather than being representative of the size of deposited fragments. Recent work by the writer on undisturbed urned cremation burials (McKinley 1994b) demonstrated the amount of bone fragmentation which occurs during even very careful excavation. It was also shown that plough damage to cremation burials reduced fragment size. The bone appeared well oxidized, presenting a fairly uniform white/buff colour. The quantities of burnt flint and charcoal in the fills, both representing pyre debris (the soil type was clay-with-flints), implies the fairly close proximity of the pyre sites to the burials. No scorching of the pit sides was noted, which may imply that burial occurred after the ashes had cooled. Only one cremation burial appeared to contain the remains of more than one individual, but the evidence was uncertain. The burial contained very little bone, and the high level of plough damage may have led to contamination. Probable animal bone was recognised in two cremation burials, one of which may be bird bone. Cremated animal bone is not an unusual feature in burials of this period (McKinley forthcoming a, b and c).

Osteophytes (bony growths around joints) and exostoses (bony growths at tendon/ligament insertions), were noted in the bones of four individuals, and are probably age-related lesions. Two individuals had osteoarthritis in the atlas/axis joint; again, the diseased was probably age-related.

Animal Bone

Nick Winder and Marta Moreno-Garcia

Introduction

The animal bone assemblage from Chells was initially examined by Nick Winder, and a copy of his comprehensively detailed study is retained in the site archive. The following report, which summarises Winder's work, was prepared by Marta Moreno-Garcia.

The assemblage consists of 10,245 bone fragments, weighing 133 kg. Of these, 11 kg (4871 fragments) are unidentifiable. As a consequence, the identifiable fraction comprises 5,377 fragments, of which only 37% (2,015 fragments, including loose teeth) is identifiable to taxa. Table17 shows the proportions of identified and unidentified material for each period.

Methods of Analysis

Animal bone fragments were identified and counted by skeletal element for each taxon using the NISP method of quantification (Grayson 1984). Although attempts were made to identify the bone to taxa level, this was not always possible with some skeletal elements, such as long-bone shaft, rib, vertebrae and skull fragments. These were recorded under additional categories, for example 'oxo', which comprises animals of large artiodactyl and perissodactyl size, *eg* horse, red deer and cattle, 'lar', which includes large artiodactyles (red deer, fallow deer and cattle) and 'sma', which consists of beasts of smaller size, such as sheep, goats, roe deer, dogs and pigs (Table 18).

In addition, another method of quantification was used. This involves the counting of 'indicators' (Luff 1993) which comprise the following skeletal parts where more than fifty per cent is present: horn core, mandible tooth row, scapula glenoid cavity, distal epiphyses of humerus, radius and metacarpal, pelvic acetabulum, distal epiphyses of femur, tibia, metatarsal and the proximal epiphysis of first phalanx. Indicators are bones that preserve well, and thus highlight those elements from which Minimum Number of Individuals (MNI) could most reliably be calculated, providing differences in butchery techniques between taxa are allowed for, and also the fact that different taxa are composed of different numbers of bones. As indicators were counted for each taxa per period they also provide an overview on the general state of preservation across the site.

Bone weight was also recorded as a means of assessing fragmentation, since higher fragmentation would result in smaller and lighter fragments per taxa per anatomical element. However, the high degree of recent breakage made this unreliable as a taphonomic indicator for this site.

The age of the cattle and sheep/goat remains was determined by Silver's (1969) figures for the fusion of long bones. The method used to assess the age of the mandibles is described below (*Ageing of cattle...*).

The measurements used in this report are based on von den Dreisch 1976.

Finally, the surface condition of the bone was examined and note was taken of eroded, gnawed, burnt, butchered, worked or recently broken material.

TABLE 17: General description of bone assemblage, by period.

Date	Bone	TOTAL NISP	%	Total no. teeth	TOTAL WEIGHT (g)	%
mid to late first century	Identified	149	51	4	983	81
	Unidentified	146	49	4	236	19
	TOTAL	295		8	1219	
late first to early/mid second century	Identified	133	52	24	2297	93
	Unidentified	123	48	–	186	7
	TOTAL	256		24	2483	
mid second to mid third century	Identified	302	68	19	6471	95
	Unidentified	143	32	–	356	5
	TOTAL	445		19	6827	
mid to late third century	Identified	25	36	35	216	79
	Unidentified	45	64	5	59	21
	TOTAL	70		40	275	
fourth century	Identified	4111	48	572	111945	92
	Unidentified	4395	52	10	10327	8
	TOTAL	8506		582	122272	
All periods	IDENTIFIED	4720	49	654	121912	92
	UNIDENTIFIED	4852	51	19	11164	8

TABLE 18: Quantification of the animal bone assemblage.

Date	Taxa	NISP	Teeth	Weight (g)	Inds	R. Br.	Eroded	Gnawed
mid to late first century	Horse	–	1	21	–	–	–	–
	Cattle	7	3	179	1	4	2	–
	OXO	37	–	510	–	11	19	–
	LAR	2	–	19	–	–	2	–
	SMA	61	–	57	–	34	–	1
	Pig	1	–	20	1	–	–	–
	Dog	41 (PB)	–	177	9	12	–	–
	Unidentified	146	4	236	–	–	–	–
late first to early/mid second century	Cattle	19	13	1480	7	14	–	1
	OXO	31	–	330	–	6	1	–
	Sheep/goat	9	7	144	4	2	–	2
	SMA	49	1	89	–	1	–	1
	Pig	5	3	72	1	–	–	–
	Dog	20 (PB)	–	182	6	3	–	–
	Unidentified	123	–	186	–	–	–	–
mid second to mid third century	Horse	5	–	1466	2	2	–	–
	Cattle	28	2	2611	10	15	1	2
	OXO	91	–	1546	–	8	–	1
	Sheep/goat	21	9	305	13	3	–	1
	Goat	1	–	–	1	–	–	–
	SMA	99	–	367	–	1	–	–
	Pig	6	8	108	1	5	–	–
	Dog	4	–	40	3	2	–	1
	Human	39	–	17	–	–	–	–
	Chicken	3	–	7	–	–	–	–
	Bird	8	–	2	–	–	–	–
	Unidentified	143	–	356	–	–	–	–
mid to late third century	Cattle	4	1	79	1	2	1	–
	OXO	16	18	68	–	–	–	–
	Sheep/goat	–	9	38	–	4	–	–
	SMA	4	3	8	–	1	–	–
	Pig	1	4	23	–	1	–	–
	Unidentified	45	5	59	–	–	–	–
fourth century	Horse	62	61	6315	20	29	–	–
	Cattle	820	173	61160	265	473	5	14
	Red deer	1+(21ant)	–	516	4	16	–	–
	OXO	1987	9	36421	–	620	–	–
	Sheep/goat	176	272	2803	87	95	1	7
	Sheep	1	–	6	–	–	–	–
	Goat	10	–	297	2	4	–	–
	Roe deer	3+(2ant)	–	54	–	1	–	–
	SMA	896	29	3181	–	28	–	–
	Pig	88	27	1021	5	18	–	5
	Dog	9	–	101	4	3	–	2
	Carnivore	1	–	1	–	–	–	–
	SCR	1	–	17	–	1	–	–
	LAG	1	–	1	–	–	–	–
	TIM	2	–	4	–	–	–	–
	Human	1	1	4	–	–	1	–
	Chicken	12	–	16	3	–	–	–
	Bird	17	–	14	–	1	–	–
	Unidentified	4395	10	7075	–	–	–	–

KEY:

ant	antler fragment
PB	partial burial
OXO	large artiodactyl and perissodactyl size: horse, red deer and cattle.
LAR	large artiodactyls: red deer, fallow deer and cattle.
SMA	sheep, goats, roe deer, dogs and pigs.
SCR	small carnivore.
LAG	lagomorph.
TIM	tiny mammal.

Distribution of Bone

The animal bone from Chells was assigned to five periods, spanning from the mid to late first century AD until the end of the fourth century. Table 19 describes the distribution of the animal bone by period and context type.

As can be seen in the table, most of the identifiable material for the whole site came from Period V (4111 nisp and 572 loose teeth, 87% of the total number of fragments), and in particular from the pond and the well, which also produced a large number of unidentifiable bone (3244 nisp).

Preservation and Recovery

STANDARDS OF RECOVERY

Although sieved samples were taken during the excavation of the site, they were not presented to Nick Winder for assessment or detailed study. Thus, only the hand-picked material is considered in this report.

The standard of trench recovery can be measured by quantifying the presence of the smaller bones such as phalanges, carpals, tarsals and teeth, as well as the presence of bird and fish bones. Since the samples for Periods I to IV were very small, only the samples from the well and the pond will be considered in this section.

Tables 20 and 21 show the number of skeletal elements per taxa present in both the well and the pond. A lack of carpals and tarsals, as well as phalanges for sheep/goat, is evident in both deposits. The number of first phalanges for cattle is bigger than for ovicaprids, but carpals and tarsals are also missing for this species.

The number of bird bones recovered from Period V is limited to twenty-nine fragments, of which seventeen were unidentifiable. Neither fish nor small mammals were recovered.

In contrast, numbers of loose teeth and unidentifiable fragments are very high. One could argue that this fact is more likely related to the fragmentation that the maxillae and mandibles underwent whilst lying on the ground or during the

TABLE 19: Distribution of bone by period/context type.

Date	Context	NISP	Loose teeth	Weight (g)
mid to late first century	Ditches ABL–ABM	77	4	606
		137 uni	4	210
	Clay deposits	5	–	96
		6 uni	–	21
	Well CAB	67	–	281
		3 uni	–	5
late first to early/mid second century	Hollow	–	1	5
		13 uni	–	22
	Palisade	–	1	20
	Quarry EAA	1	–	3
		1 uni		
	Raft ABR	16	1	94
		56 uni	–	41
	Ditches	42	18	1357
		44 uni	–	113
	Unnamed	6	–	30
	Well CAB	68	3	788
		9 uni	–	10
mid second to mid third century	Demolition material	43	2	135
		6 uni	–	10
	Quarry EAA	234	17	3782
		137 uni	–	346
	Well CAB	25	–	2554
mid to late third century	?Building	25	35	216
		45 uni	5	59
fourth century	Unnamed	87	23	1353
		105 uni	–	311
	Building complex	562	56	8742
		566 uni	–	1189
	Corn drier	257	35	6498
		383 uni	–	760
	Pond GK	1845	361	52578
		2240 uni	8	5500
	Pits	156	20	3469
		97 uni	–	214
	Well CAB	1204	77	39305
		1004	2	2353

Key:
uni – unidentified

excavation process, than to good standards of recovery.

PRESERVATION OF THE ASSEMBLAGE

In general, the surfaces of the bone are not eroded, but much of the material has been damaged by modern ploughing. The factor most affecting the bones is that of recent breakage, as can be seen in Table 22.

Frequently, the fragments could be put together so that the original bone was constructed. The bone was quantified as one, and not by the number of fragments of which it was comprised, in order that the NISP was not inflated.

Gnawing marks are very scarce. This, together with the few eroded bones, shows that the bones were not left lying around, but were buried in a short period of time.

In Tables 17 and 22, it can be seen quite clearly that the bone assemblage was considerably fragmented. Oxo, sma and unidentifiable categories comprise most of the bone. It is evident that for all periods these represent an important proportion of the total sample. In addition, another factor to take into account in assessing fragmentation is the number of loose teeth. They were abundant for all taxa in all periods. It is worth noting that in the pond (Table 21) the number of sheep/goat teeth is more than double the number of bone fragments for this species. Teeth are also the most abundant skeletal element for horse in this same deposit.

The state of preservation has reduced the number of bones that can be measured quite dramatically. Ageable mandibles have also been affected. In spite of the fact that the assemblage has been quantified in Table 18, it is unlikely that the proportions of the species originally deposited are well reflected in the results obtained, given the taphonomical processes affecting them. The number of indicators for Periods I to IV shows the scant information available for interpreting diet or animal husbandry standards at Chells at this time. Although indicators increase in Period V, their numbers are still too low to draw any real conclusions.

Results by Period

PERIOD I (mid to late first century AD)

Bone was recovered from three features dated to this period: the trackway ditches [ABL, ABM], the clay dumps and the well [CAB] (Table 19). The assemblage of identifiable bone is very small (149 nisp and 4 teeth). From Table 19 and Table 18 it can be seen that the only remains found in the well were those of a dog. No metrical data was obtained from this skeleton due to its fragmentary state. Nearly half of the bones were damaged, almost certainly during the excavation. Indeed, the total percentage of recent breakages in this period (41%) is the highest of all. The number of small fragments is the next biggest category to be recorded after the unidentifiable bone. It is worth noting that rib fragments probably belonging to dog were recorded under this category.

PERIOD II (late first to early/mid second century)

The sample of bone dated to this period is slightly smaller than for the previous period. In addition, it is spread over more contexts. The unidentifiable bone fragments are larger in number in all contexts except for the well. There, the remains of two partial dog burials were found. One of the dogs had suffered from osteoarthritis. In general, bones from this period were less fragmented (19%), although recent breakage affected most of the cattle bones recovered from the ditches and the well (74%). The fragments that were identified as cattle were mainly mandibles. Their fragmentation is reflected in the number of loose teeth for this species (Table 18).

PERIOD III (mid second to mid third century)

Most of the material came from Feature EAA. Although the sample is small, the identifiable fragments doubled the unidentifiable in number. The excavator noted the presence of large amounts of pottery (Figs 48, 49) and oyster shells, small bones and ash in the fills of this feature. These, together with the eleven pins recovered (**Bone 3–13**), lead him to surmise that they represent domestic rubbish. Whether these fills represent separate phases of deposition, or tip lines produced as refuse was dumped in a single concerted action, is not clear.

The percentage of recently broken bone (12%) is the lowest for all periods. However, species such as horse, cattle and pig show high proportions of damaged bone (Table 22), which prevents any measurements being taken.

It is worth mentioning that a semi-complete horse skull was recovered from the well, in addition to thirty-nine fragments of neonatal human bone from contexts in the north part of the site. The latter may have been associated with the cemetery, detailed elsewhere in this volume.

PERIOD IV (mid to late third century)

Period IV dates were assigned to contexts in Structures ABO/ABP and ABQ. All the bone was recovered from the circular gullies that surrounded Structure ABQ. Most of it has been ploughed out, and a very small amount of bone survives. In fact, the number of loose teeth fragments was greater than the amount of bones.

The bone recovered from this period does not warrant any further comments.

PERIOD V (fourth century)

The bulk of the material comes from the pond and the well (Table 19). Tables 20 and 21 describe in detail the skeletal elements per taxa present in each of these deposits.

Twelve chicken bones were identified from this period. Other taxa present, apart from the usual domesticates, are both red and roe deer. They are represented mainly by antler fragments, some of them naturally shed and many subject to plough damage (73% recently broken). One plough-damaged antler fragment from undated layers showed traces of sawing.

The two human bones comprise a slightly carious and worn molar tooth from the well fill, and an eroded cranial fragment that may have been originated from the cemetery.

The Well
(Table 20)

(a) *Horse:* only eleven fragments of horse were recovered, including a jaw, femur, tibia and possibly the humerus and pelvis of another young individual.
(b) *Cattle:* the most abundant skeletal element is the mandible (83 fragments). According to indicators first phalanges are the highest in number, followed by sixteen ageable mandibles and thirteen metacarpals. The ageing and metrical data of cattle bones is considered in detail below.

A minimum number of eleven individuals was calculated from the mandibles.

It is worth noting the low number of skull (4) and maxilla (5) fragments. This is also signified by splitting loose teeth into lower and upper ones. From thirty-five loose teeth, only six are upper ones, as opposed to twenty-nine from the mandible.

The lack of vertebral elements, carpals and tarsals stands out. The former were recorded most likely under the 'oxo' category, but the small carpals and tarsals are absent.

It is quite clear that limb bones comprise most of the sample for this species. According to the NISP and indicators, forelimb bones, *ie* scapula, humerus, radius, ulna and metacarpal are slightly more frequent than hind-limb bones, pelvis, femur, tibia and metatarsal.

(c) *Oxo:* under this category a considerable number of ribs (181), long-bone shafts (122) and vertebrae (80) are recorded. They are probably

TABLE 20: Skeletal element per taxa in Well CAB (fourth century).

BONE	TAXA Horse	Cattle	Red deer	Oxo	Shp/Gt	Roe deer	SMA	Pig	Dog
Skull	–	4	–	1	3	–	1	–	–
Horncore	–	1 (1)	–	–	–	–	–	–	–
Antler	–	–	15	–	–	–	–	–	–
Maxilla	–	5	–	–	3	–	2	5	–
Mandible	2 (1)	83 (16)	–	22	29 (13)	2	2	6 (1)	1
Hyoid	–	3	–	–	1	–	1	–	–
Scapula	1 (1)	14 (6)	–	26	1	–	2	–	–
Humerus	–	13 (9)	–	13	–	1	2	1	–
Radius	–	10 (3)	0	5	3	–	5	1	–
Ulna	–	6	–	3	–	–	1	–	2
Carpal	–	1	–	–	–	–	–	–	–
Metacarpal	3	29 (13)	–	–	4 (1)	–	1	–	–
Pelvis	–	21 (3)	–	15	2 (1)	–	–	–	–
Femur	1 (1)	7 (4)	–	2	1	–	4	–	1
Patella	–	–	–	–	–	–	–	–	–
Tibia	3 (1)	7 (5)	–	6	1 (1)	–	10	–	–
Fibula	–	–	–	–	–	–	1	–	–
Astragalus	1	4	–	–	–	–	–	–	–
Calcaneus	–	6	–	–	–	–	–	–	–
Tarsal	–	–	–	–	–	–	–	–	–
Metatarsal	–	23 (8)	–	–	5	–	–	–	–
Metapodial	–	12	–	4	–	–	2	6	–
Rib frag.	–	–	–	181	–	–	50	–	–
Costal frag.	–	–	–	–	–	–	23	–	–
Atlas	–	1	–	–	–	–	–	–	–
Axis	–	1	–	–	–	–	–	–	–
Cervical vx	–	2	–	–	–	–	–	–	–
Thoracic vx	–	–	–	–	–	–	–	–	–
Lumbar vx	–	–	–	5	–	–	–	–	–
Caudal vx	–	–	–	–	–	–	–	–	–
Sacrum	–	6	–	2	–	–	–	–	–
Vertebra	–	–	–	80	–	–	5	–	–
Sternum	–	–	–	–	–	–	–	–	–
Longbone fragment	–	–	–	122	–	–	105	–	–
1st phalanx	–	32 (24)	–	4	–	–	–	–	–
2nd phalanx	–	5	1	1	–	–	–	–	–
3rd phalanx	–	1	–	2	–	–	–	–	–
u/d phalanx	–	–	–	66	–	–	–	–	–
TOTAL	**11 (4)**	**297 (92)**	**15ant+1**	**560**	**53 (16)**	**3**	**217**	**19 (1)**	**4**
Loose teeth	7	35	–	–	26	–	–	8	–

Indicators in brackets
ant – antlers

associated with cattle and not horse, since remains of the latter were not that abundant. From the fragments that could be identified to a certain skeletal element, the trend previously observed in cattle is repeated. Forelimb bones outnumber those of the hindlimb.

In general, the whole sample is very fragmented, as there are sixty-six unidentifiable fragments recorded as oxo.

(d) *Sheep/goat:* this species makes only a small contribution to the well assemblage, apart from the number of jaw fragments (29). Thirteen mandibles were indicators, and reflected a minimum number of eight individuals. Ageing and metrical data for sheep/goat are dealt with in detail below.

The number of loose teeth indicates the fragmentation of the bone deposit, and these are quite high in relation to NISP. In contrast to cattle, there are similar numbers of upper and lower teeth (12 and 14 respectively).

(e) *Sma:* over 80% of the bone recorded as sma consists of long bone and rib fragments. In contrast to oxo there are few vertebrae. Their absence, together with the lack of carpals, tarsals, calcanei, astragali and phalanges reflects poor standards of recovery for ovicaprids.

(f) *Pig:* not much can be said about this species. Only nineteen fragments were recovered, of which six are metapodials. Only one jaw is an indicator.

The Pond
(Table 21)

(a) *Horse:* most of the horse from the site was recovered from this deposit. It is worth pointing out hat there are more loose teeth than actual bone fragments. Mandibles seem to be most affected by recent fragmentation, since no indicators could be recorded. The presence

TABLE 21: Skeletal element per taxa in Pond GK (fourth century).

BONE	Horse	Cattle	Red deer	Oxo	Sheep/goat	Sheep	Goat	SMA	Pig	Dog
Skull	–	2	–	–	–	–	–	–	–	–
Horncore	–	35 (2)	–	3	–	1	10	–	–	–
Antler	–	–	3	–	–	–	–	–	–	–
Maxilla	–	5	–	2	7	–	–	–	6	1
Mandible	14	78 (1)	–	51	31 (1)	–	–	12	19 (2)	–
Hyoid	–	1	–	2	–	–	–	1	–	–
Scapula	3 (2)	36 (11)	–	37	–	–	–	3	2	–
Humerus	–	23 (11)	–	35	2 (2)	–	–	5	2	1
Radius	3 (2)	16 (7)	–	15	8 (2)	–	–	11	3	–
Ulna	1	6	–	9	2	–	–	–	–	–
Carpal	–	–	–	–	–	–	–	1	–	–
Metacarpal	2 (1)	17 (8)	–	–	3	–	–	2	–	–
Pelvis	1	19	–	38	1	–	–	12	–	2
Femur	–	18 (8)	–	39	–	–	–	1	1	–
Patella	–	1	–	–	–	–	–	–	–	–
Tibia	6 (3)	19 (5)	–	14	6 (1)	–	–	16	2	1
Fibula	–	–	–	–	–	–	–	1	–	–
Astragalus	–	5	–	–	1	–	–	–	–	–
Calcaneus	–	9	–	–	1	–	–	–	1	–
Tarsal	–	3	–	1	–	–	–	–	–	–
Metatarsal	3	20 (8)	–	5	12 (1)	–	–	–	–	–
Metapodial	1	13	–	5	–	–	–	6	6	–
Rib frag.	–	–	–	106	–	–	–	41	–	–
Costal frag.	–	–	–	–	–	–	–	–	–	–
Atlas	–	4	–	1	–	–	–	–	–	–
Axis	–	4	–	–	–	–	–	–	–	–
Cervical vx	1	–	–	–	–	–	–	–	–	–
Thoracic vx	–	–	–	–	–	–	–	–	–	–
Lumbar vx	–	–	–	–	–	–	–	–	–	–
Caudal vx	–	–	–	–	–	–	–	–	–	–
Sacrum	–	2	–	–	–	–	–	–	–	–
Vertebra fragment	–	–	–	95	–	–	–	6	–	–
Sternum	–	–	–	–	–	–	–	–	–	–
Longbone frag.	–	–	–	349	–	–	–	327	–	–
1st phalanx	2 (2)	16 (10)	–	–	1 (1)	–	–	–	–	–
2nd phalanx	–	5	–	–	–	–	–	–	1	–
3rd phalanx	–	3	–	–	–	–	–	–	–	–
Phalanx uni/d.	–	–	–	52	–	–	–	–	–	–
TOTAL	**37 (1)**	**360 (80)**	**3ant**	**859**	**75 (17)**	**1**	**10**	**445**	**43 (2)**	**5**
Loose teeth	44	103	–	2	168	–	–	29	15	–

Indicators in brackets.
ant - antlers

TABLE 22: Factors affecting bone breakage.

Date	Taxa	NISP	Recently broken NISP	%
mid to late first century	Horse	-		
	Cattle	7	4	57
	OXO	37	11	30
	LAR	2		
	SMA	61	34	56
	Pig	1		
	Dog	41 (PB)	12	29
	TOTAL	**149**	**61**	**41**
late first to early/mid second century	Cattle	19	14	74
	OXO	31	6	19
	Sheep/goat	9	2	22
	SMA	49	1	2
	Pig	5		
	Dog	20 (PB)	3	15
	TOTAL	**133**	**26**	**19**
mid second to mid third century	Horse	5	2	40
	Cattle	28	15	53
	OXO	91	8	9
	Sheep/goat	21	3	14
	Goat	1		
	SMA	99	1	1
	Pig	6	5	83
	Dog	4	2	50
	Human	39		
	Chicken	3		
	Bird	8		
	TOTAL	**305**	**36**	**12**
mid to late third century	Cattle	4	2	50
	OXO	16		
	Sheep/goat	–		
	SMA	4	1	25
	Pig	1	1	100
	TOTAL	**25**	**4**	**16**
fourth century	Horse	62	29	47
	Cattle	820	473	58
	Red deer	21 ant + 1	16	73
	OXO	1987	620	31
	Sheep/goat	176	95	54
	Sheep	1		
	Goat	10	4	40
	Roe deer	2 ant + 3	1	20
	SMA	896	28	3
	Pig	88	18	20
	Dog	9	3	33
	Carnivore	1		
	SCR	1	1	100
	LAG	1		
	TIM	2		
	Human	1		
	Chicken	12		
	Bird	17	1	6
	TOTAL	**4111**	**1289**	**31**

KEY:
ant — antler fragment
LAG — lagomorph
PB — partial burial
SCR — small carnivore
TIM — tiny mammal

of fragments of a very young horse metatarsal were recorded.

(b) *Cattle:* the remains of two semi-complete skulls were found. Only two horn cores were complete enough to be indicators. The MNI obtained from the mandibles is seven, slightly smaller than the figure obtained for the well. However, the pattern of skeletal elements present is very similar to that observed in the well. Jaws have suffered much fragmentation, and skulls are still very rare. Vertebral elements have been recorded under 'oxo', and front leg bones (inds: 37) outnumber hind leg bones (inds: 21).

Only three tarsal bones were recovered, and first phalanges are less than in the well.

(c) *Oxo:* the trend described for he well was also observed for the pond. The only change is that with the pond there are more long bone fragments and less ribs than in the well.

(d) *Sheep/goat:* the number of loose teeth (168) indicates the general fragmentation of the bone. There are many mandible and metatarsal fragments; however, only one metatarsal and ten jaws were indicators, which give an MNI of five.

One sheep horn core was identified, together with ten fragments of goat horn core.

(e) *Sma:* once more, long-bone fragments comprise most of the sample. Hardly any vertebrae (6) and carpals (1), and no calcaneum, astragalus, tarsal or phalanges were recovered.

(f) *Pig:* this is slightly more abundant than in the well fills, but there are still insufficient remains to draw any conclusions on the role this species played.

Ageing of Cattle and Sheep/Goat

No age profile can be obtained from the small sample of bone present in the first four periods. The only material available comes from Period V. Due to the lack of whole bones and high fragmentation among sheep/goat, only *cattle* epiphyseal fusion data is described in Table 23.

The epiphyseal fusion data suggests that 77% of the fourth-century cattle survived more than $1\frac{1}{2}$ years. Those older than 3 years slightly decreased to 68%, and 61% survived for more than 4 years.

The sample is small, but it is tempting to suggest that the presence of mature animals may be an indication of beef production on the site. In a dairy-producing economy, one would expect a high proportion of young calves killed early in the first year of life, and most of the adults would be female, only a very small number of males being retained for breeding purposes. In contrast, in a beef-producing economy a smaller proportion of the herd would be killed during the first two years. Most animals would be slaughtered in late adolescence or early adulthood, when they had reached bodily maturity. Only a small number of adults would be kept for breeding purposes. Since we are dealing with a rural site, one cannot forget the role of cattle as traction animals.

The ageing profiles derived from the analysis of dental eruption and wear conform to the previous results. Mandibles were grouped into four stages. The first group comprises the immature jaws where deciduous molar 3 was present; the second group covers the initial eruption and coming into wear of the third permanent molar; in the third group are those mandibles with the third molar in wear (Grant 1982, stages g, h, j, k); and the last

TABLE 23: Cattle epiphyseal fusion data.

	Unfused	Fused	% fused
Early fusion (1½ years)			
Distal humerus	4	17	81
Proximal radius	3	7	70
Total	7	24	77
Mid fusion (3 years)			
Distal tibia	6	14	70
Distal metacarpal	11	22	71
Distal metatarsal	6	13	68
Total	23	49	68
Late fusion (4 years)			
Proximal femur	5	1	17
Proximal humerus	2	6	75
Distal radius	4	6	60
Proximal ulna	–	3	100
Distal femur	8	8	50
Proximal tibia	4	12	75
Total	23	36	61

TABLE 24: Cattle measurements.

Bone	Distal width	Distal thickness
METACARPAL	60.0	32.0
	58.0	32.0
	65.0	30.0
	51.5	30.0
	70.5	35.5
	64.0	35.0
	55.0	28.5
	57.0	30.0
	57.0	31.5
	53.0	30.0
	52.0	30.5
	51.0	27.5
	67.0	36.0
METATARSAL	50.0	30.0
	50.5	31.0
	50.0	30.0
	52.0	29.0
	54.0	32.5
	47.5	28.0
	56.0	30.0
	59.0	33.5
	49.5	28.0
	62.0	34.5
	50.5	29.0
	47.0	27.5

one groups jaws with very worn third molars (Grant's stages i or m). The following table gives a summary of the results obtained.

Date	Stage	Mandibles	loose dP4	loose LM3
fourth century	immature (dP4)	2	2	–
	LM3 not in wear	4	–	3
	LM3 in wear	25	–	11
	LM3 very worn	1	–	–

The same grouping was done for sheep/goat mandibles and loose teeth. The following table summarises the results for sheep/goat.

Date	Stage	Mandibles	loose dP4	loose LM3
fourth century	immature (dP4)	5	1	–
	LM3 not in wear	11	–	11
	LM3 in wear	8	–	20
	LM3 very worn	–	–	–

It is difficult to outline the role ovicaprids played at Chells. From the mandibles, it appears that they were killed when still young, at 2–3 years of age. At this time they would have been approaching bodily maturity. If they were kept primarily for meat, this is the time they would have been slaughtered, since continuing to feed them beyond this age would not have increased meat output.

Metrical Data

As has been stated previously, the fragmentary nature of the bones considerably reduced the number of measurements that could be made. *Cattle* measurements are included in Table 24. All the bone was from Period V. All measurements are in millimetres.

Although the sample is small when these measurements are plotted against each other for both metacarpal and metatarsal, two distinct groupings can be seen in the scatterplots (Figs 56 and 57), one cluster at the lower left of the graph and a smaller group to the top right. This is indicative of more females than males. The presence of castrates is difficult to assess in such a reduced sample.

Mean, standard deviation, range and coefficient of variation have been calculated from the distal width measurement:

The mean obtained from the distal width of the metacarpal (n=8, x=58.9) is similar to that from the Roman villa at Shakenoak, Oxon. (Luff 1982), but is bigger than the mean (n=30, x=48.6) from Exeter (Maltby 1979). The metatarsal distal width mean is similar to that (n=13, x=53.3) from Thistleton Roman villa (Luff 1982).

Withers height could not be recorded due to the lack of whole bones.

Four measurable ovicaprid metapodia were recovered, for which the same measurements were taken as for cattle metapodia. One metacarpal belongs to Period III, the rest to Period V.

Conclusion

Domestic animals dominate the Roman animal bone assemblage from Chells. Of these, cattle were the most numerous in all periods (Fig. 58), and would have provided most of the meat. Sheep and pig would have played a smaller part in the subsistence economy of the site. The presence of a small number of young horse bones in the pond and well during the fourth century suggests that horses may have been raised at the site.

However, it is important to note that the study was hampered by two factors. Firstly, the very fragmentary nature of the bones did not allow the retrieval of metrical data needed for intra- and inter-period/context comparisons. Secondly, as no sieved samples were studied, the presence and contribution of bird and fish species to the diet at Chells could not be assessed. In addition, the small sample of bone recovered from Periods I to IV prevents any discussion on changes through time in the economy of the site. Although the Period V assemblage is larger, the same taphonomic processes, *ie* recent breakages, affect the bones. If conditions of preservation, sample size and recovery standards were better, one might have been able to comment further on the general outlines of the subsistence system present at this Roman rural site.

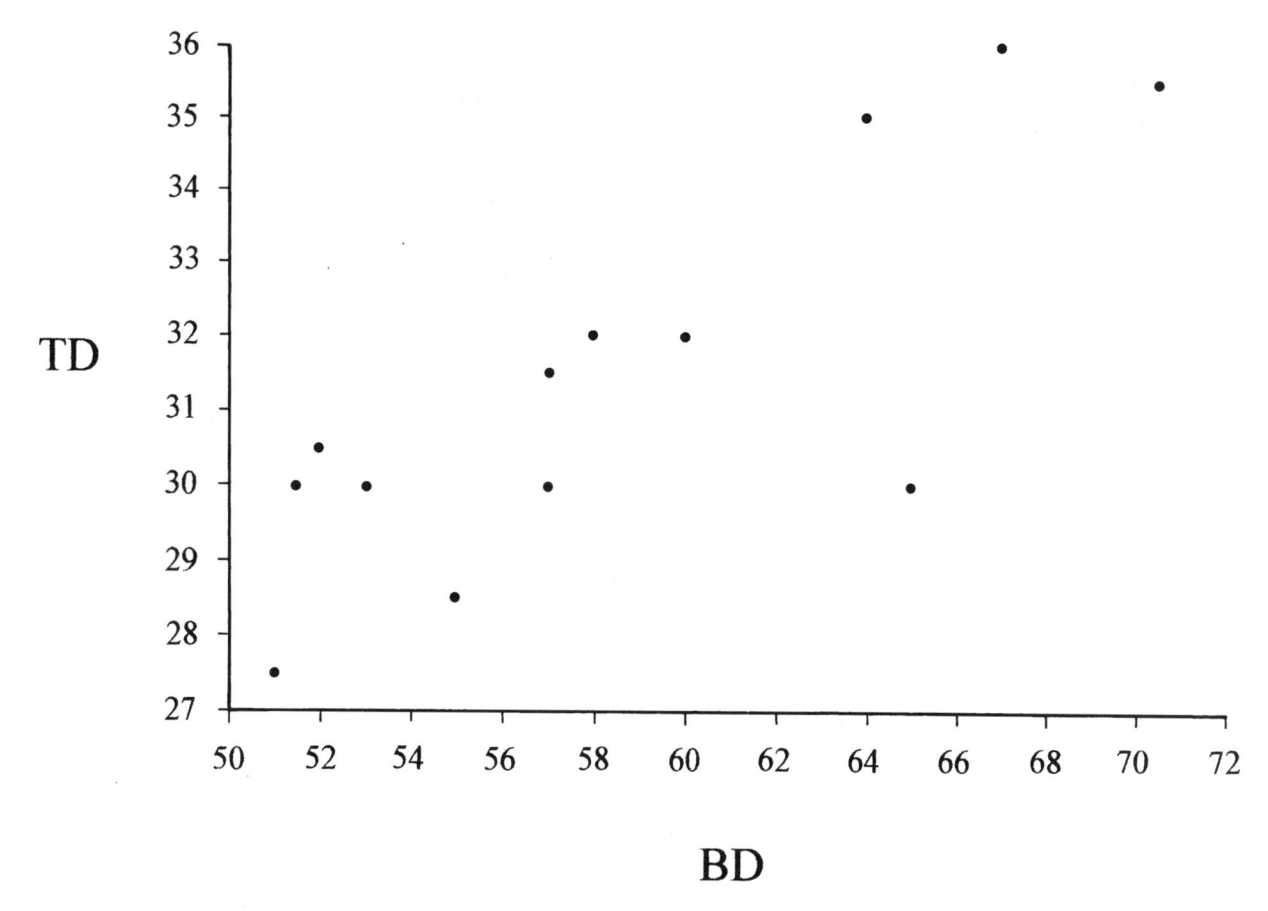

Figure 56   Scattergram of cattle metacarpal distal thickness (TD) against distal width (BD).

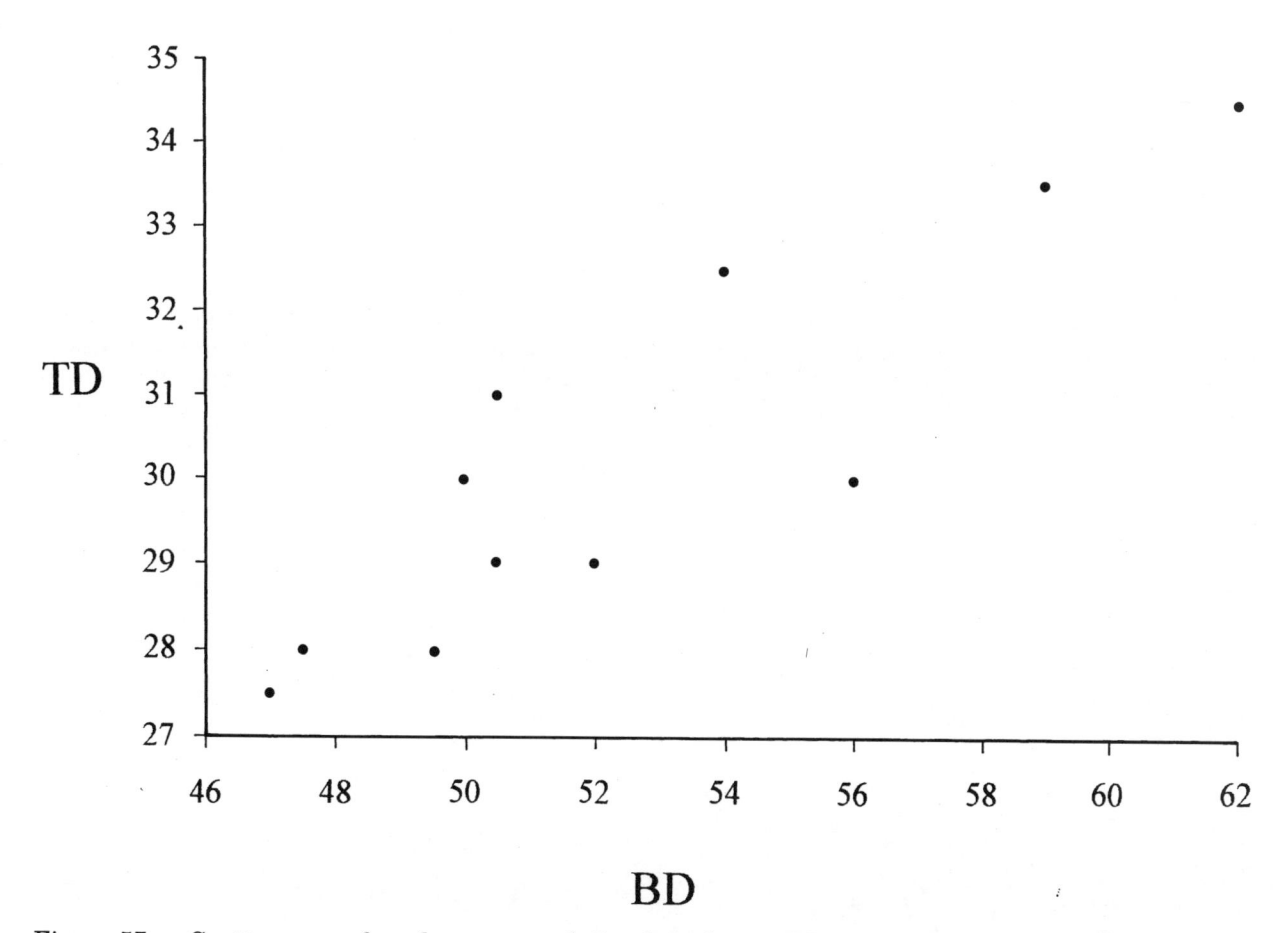

Figure 57   Scattergram of cattle metatarsal distal thickness (TD) against distal width (BD).

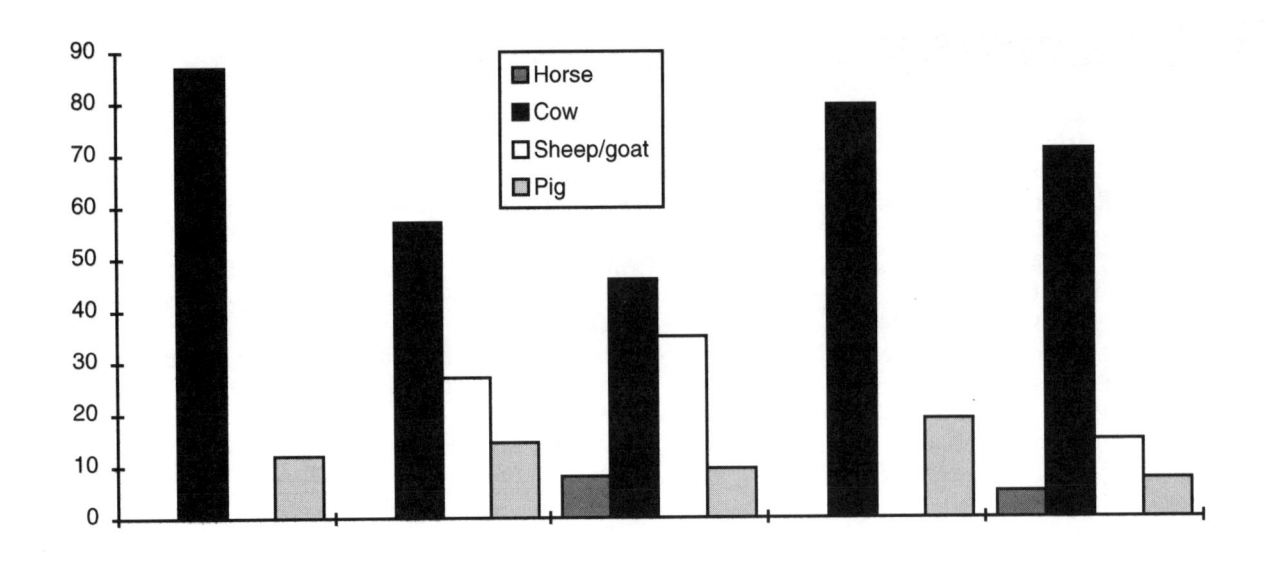

Figure 58   Percentage number of bone fragments (NISP) for the main domesticates per period.

Bibliography

Abbreviations used:
BAR   British Archaeological Reports.
CBARR   Council for British Archaeology Research Report.
RRCSAL   Report of the Research Committee of the Society of Antiquaries of London.

Allason-Jones L. 1989 *Ear-rings in Roman Britain*. BAR **201** (Oxford).

Allason-Jones L. and Miket R. 1984 The catalogue of small finds from South Shields, Newcastle upon Tyne (Newcastle upon Tyne).

Amandry M., Rigault R. and Trombetta P.J. 1985 'Le trésor monétaire de l'Ecluse de Creil', *Bull. de la Soc. archaeol., hist. et géog. de Creil et de sa Région* **127–8**, 65–111.

Anderson A.C. 1980 *A guide to Roman fine wares*. Vorda Res. Ser. **1**.

Anon. 1978 *Southwark excavations 1972–74*. London Middlesex Archaeol. Soc/Surrey Archaeol. Soc. Joint Pub. **1** (2 vols) (London).

Applebaum S. 1972 'Roman Britain' *in* Finberg, H.P.R. (ed) 1972 *The agrarian history of England and Wales* vol. **1.2**, AD43–1042, 5–277 (Cambridge).

Arthur P. 1978 'The lead glazed wares of Roman Britain' *in* Arthur and Marsh 1978, 293–355.

Arthur P. and Marsh G. 1978 *Early fine wares in Roman Britain*. BAR **57** (Oxford).

Atkinson D. 1942 *Report on the excavations at Wroxeter (the Roman city of Viroconium) in the county of Salop, 1923–1927* (Oxford).

Avent R. and Howlett T. 1980 'Excavations at Roman Long Melford, 1970–1972', *Proc. Suffolk Inst. Archaeol. Hist.* **34**, 229–249.

Bass W.M. 1987 *Human osteology*. Missouri Archaeol. Soc.

Besly, E.M. and Bland, R.F, 1983 *The Cunetio Treasure*. British Museum Publications (London).

Bland R.F. 1988 '8. Stevenage, Hertfordshire' *in* Bland and Burnett 1988, 43–73.

Bland R.F. forthcoming 'Denominational relationships in the early third century AD' *in* King, C.E. and Wigg, D. (eds) forthcoming *Proc. 13th Oxford Symposium on Coinage and Coinage History*.

Bland R.F. and Amandry M. 1992 'Monnaies romaines rares du médailler du Musée Saint-Remi' (with M Amandry), *Journées Numismatiques Reims, 6–8 Juin 1992 (Bulletin de la Société Française de Numismatique* **47**, 6 Juin 1992), 333–339.

Bland R.F. and Burnett A.M. (eds) 1988 *The Normanby hoard and other Roman coin hoards from Roman Britain*. British Museum Publications (London).

Boon G.C. 1974 *Silchester, the Roman town of Calleva* (Newton Abbot & London).

Brenot C. 1963 'Le trésor de Vannes (Morbihan)', *Revue Numismatique*, 159–163.

Brown A.E. and Sheldon H.L. 1969 'Post-excavation work on pottery from Highgate', *London Archaeol.* **1. 3**, 60–65.

Brown A.E. and Sheldon H.L. 1970 'Highgate Wood 1970–71', *London Archaeol,* **1.13**, 300–303.

Bushe-Fox J.P. 1932 *Report on the excavations of the Roman fort at Richborough, Kent*. RRCSAL **10** (Oxford).

Bushe-Fox J.P. 1949 *Fourth report on the excavations of the Roman fort at Richborough, Kent*. RRCSAL **23** (Oxford).

Castle S.A. 1972 'Excavations at Brockley Hill, Middlesex. Sulloniaciae (NGR TQ 174941) 1970', *Trans. London Middlesex Archaeol Soc.* **23.II**, 148–157.

Castle S.A. 1973 'Trial excavations in Field 410, Brockley Hill, Part 1', *London Archaeol.* **2**, 78–83.

Charlesworth D. 1972 'The glass' *in* Frere 1972, 203–7.

Charlesworth D. 1975 'Glass', *in* Hobley, B, 1975 '"The Lunt" Roman fort and training school for Roman cavalry, Baginton, Warwickshire'. *Trans. Birmingham Warwickshire Archaeol. Soc.* **87**, 1–56.

Charlesworth D. 1984 'The glass' *in* Frere 1984, 145–173.

Clarke G. 1979 *The Roman cemetery at Lankhills*. Winchester Studies **3**: pre-Roman and Roman Winchester, Part II (Oxford).

Cocks A.H. 1921 'A Romano-British homestead in the Hambleden valley, Bucks', *Archaeologia* **71**, 141–198.

Cool H.E.M. 1991 'Roman metal hairpins from southern Britain', *Archaeol. J.* **147**, 148–182.

Cracknell S. and Mahany C. (eds) 1994 *Roman Alcester, southern extramural area, vol. 1, 1964–1966 excavations, part 2. Finds and discussion*. CBARR **97** (London).

Crummy N. 1983 *The Roman small finds from excavations in Colchester1971–9*: Colchester Archaeol. Rep. **2** (Colchester).

Cumont G. 1898–1907 'Découvertes d'antiquités romaines et gallo-romaines a Castre-la-Chaussée', *Annales Cercle archaeol. d'Enghien* **6**, 256–298.

Cunliffe B.W. 1968 *Fifth report on the excavations of the Roman fort at Richborough, Kent*. Research Report of the Society of Antiquaries **16** (London).

Curle J. 1911 *A Roman frontier post and its people, the fort of Newstead in the parish of Melrose* (Glasgow).

Curnow P. 1974 'Coin lists: some problems of the smaller site' *in* Casey, J. and Reece, R. (eds) 1974 *Coins and the archaeologist*. BAR **4**, 52–63 (Oxford).

Curnow P. 1990 'The coins', *in* Neal *et al* 1990, 105–112.

Down A. 1979 *The Roman villas at Chilgrove and Upmorden*. Chichester excavations **4** (Chichester).

Down A. and Rule M. 1971 *Chichester excavations I*. (Chichester).

Drury P.J. 1976 'Braintree: excavations and research 1971–6', *Essex Archaeol. Hist.* **8**, 1–143.

Drury P.J. 1978 *Excavations at Little Waltham, 1970–71*. CBARR **26** (London).

Evans J. 1890 'On a small hoard of Roman coins found at Amiens', *Numismatic Chron*, 267–272.

Fabre G. and Mainjonet M, 1953 'Trésor de Noyers-sur-Serein (Yonne)', *Revue Numismatique*, 131–134.

Fabre G. and Mainjonet M, 1954 and 1958 'Le trésor de Rouvroy-les-Merles (Oise)', *Revue Numismatique*, 183–187: 187–189.

Farrar R.A.H. 1973 'The techniques and sources of Romano-British black-burnished ware' in Detsicas A. (ed) 1973 *Current research in Romano-British coarse pottery*. CBARR **10**, 67–103 (London).

Fox C.F. 1923 *The archaeology of the Cambridge region* (Cambridge).

Fowler E. 1960 'The origins and development of the penannular brooch in Europe', *Proc. Prehist. Soc.* **26**, 149–77.

Fowler H. 1891 'The Six Hills, Stevenage' *Trans St Albans Architect. Archaeol. Soc,* 40–48.

Fremersdorf F. 1958 'Römische buntglass in Köln', *Die Denkmaler des Römischen Köln III* (Cologne).

Fremersdorf F. 1959 *Römische glaser mit fadenauflage in Köln* (Cologne).

Frere S.S. 1972 *Verulamium excavations I*. RRCSAL **28** (London).

Frere S.S. 1973 *Verulamium excavations II*. RRCSAL **41** (London).

Frere S.S. 1984 *Verulamium Excavations III*. Univ. Oxford Comm. Archaeol. Monog. **1** (Oxford).

Freudenberg J. 1867 'Fund von römischen Silbermünzen', *Jahrbücher d. Vereins v. Altertumsfreunde im Rheinland* **42**, 211–212.

Fulford M.G. 1979 'Pottery production and trade at the end of Roman Britain: the case against continuity' in Casey J. (ed.) 1979 *The end of Roman Britain*. BAR **71**, 120–32 (Oxford).

Gage J. 1834 'A letter from John Gage to Hudson Gurney', *Archaeologia* **25**, 1–23.

Gallup S. 1973 'Der Frankische Friedhof in Olk', *Trier Zeitschrift* **36**, 223–275.

Gejvall N.G 1981 'Determination of burnt bones from prehistoric graves'. *Ossa Letters* **2,** 1–13.

Gillam J.P. 1977 'Coarse fumed ware in north Britain and beyond', *Glasgow Archaeol. J.* **4**, 57–80.

Gilljam H. 1987 'Antoniniane des Saloninus Augustus', *Mitteilungen der Osterreichischen numismatischen Gesellschaft* **27.6**, 77–83.

Going C.J. 1987 *The Mansio and other sites in the south-eastern sector of Caesaromagus: the Roman pottery*. Chelmsford Archaeol. Trust Rep. **3.2**: CBARR **62** (Chelmsford and London).

Going C.J. 1988 'The countryside around Great Dunmow' *in* Wickenden 1988, 86–88.

Going C.J. and Ford B.A. 1988 'The Roman pottery' *in* Wickenden 1988.

Grant A. 1982 'The use of tooth wear as a guide to the age of domestic ungulates' *in* Wilson B., Grigson C. and Payne S. (eds), 1982 *Ageing and sexing animal bones from archaeological sites*. BAR **109**, 91–108 (Oxford).

Gray H 1977 *Anatomy* (New York).

Grayson D.K. 1984 *Quantitative zooarchaeology* (Orlando).

Green C. 1978 'Flavian "ring and dot" beakers from Londinium: Verulamium form 130 and allied types' *in* Arthur and Marsh 1978, 109–118.

Green M.J. 1978 *Small cult-objects from the military areas of Roman Britain*. BAR **52** (Oxford).

Greene K.T. 1972 *Guide to pre-Flavian fine wares c.AD40–70*. second impression: private publication (Cardiff).

Greep S.J. 1982 'Two early Roman handles from the Walbrook, London', *Archaeol. J.* **139**, 91–100.

Greep S.J. 1986 'The objects of worked bone' *in* Zienkiewicz, D, 1986 *The legionary fortress baths at Caerleon; vol. II, the finds*, 197–212.

Greep S.J. 1987 'Lead sling-shot from Windridge Farm, St Albans, and the use of the sling by the Roman army in Britain', *Britannia* **18**, 183–200.

Greep S.J. 1995 'Objects of bone, antler,and ivory' in Blockley, K, M and P., Frere, S.S. and Stow, S, 1995 *Excavations in the Marlowe car park and surrounding areas. Part II: the finds*. Archaeology of Canterbury **5** (Canterbury).

Gricourt, D. and Hollard, D. 1987 'L`articulation des frappes de bronze et de billon dans la production de l`atelier II de Postume', *Cahiers Numismatiques* **93**, 302–314.

Grose D.D. 1973 *Roman glass of the first century AD. A dated deposit of glassware from Cosa, Italy*. Annales du Sixième Congrés de l'Association Internationale pour l'Histoire du Verre, 31–52.

Guido, M, 1978 *The glass beads of the prehistoric and Roman periods in Britain and Ireland*. RRCSAL **35** (London).

Haevernick, T.E, 1981 *Beitrage zur Glasforschung. Die wichtigsten Aufsatze von 1938 bis 1981*.

Hammerson M. 1988 'The Roman pottery' in *Excavations in Southwark 1973–76, Lambeth 1973–79*. London Middlesex Archaeol. Soc/Surrey Archaeol. Soc. Joint Pub. **3**, 197–209.

Harden D.B. 1967 'The glass jug' *in* Biddle M. 1967 'Two Flavian burials from Winchester', *Antiq. J.* **47**, 238–40.

Harden D.B. 1974 'Window glass from the Romano-British bath-house at Garden Hill, Hartfield, Sussex', *Antiq. J.* **47**, 280–281.

Harden D.B. 1979 'Glass vessels' *in* Clarke 1979, 209–220.

Harden D.B. 1983 'The glass hoard' *in* Johnson, S, 1983 *Burgh Castle, excavations by Charles Green 1958–1961*. East Anglian Archaeol. Rep. **20**, 78–89.

Harden D.B. and Green C. 1978 *A late Roman grave-group from the Minories, Aldgate*. Collectanea Londiniensia;London Middlesex Archaeol. Soc. Spec. Pap. **2**, 163–175.

Harden D.B. and Price J. 1971 'The glass' *in* Cunliffe B.W. *1971 Excavations at Fishbourne 1961–1969, Vol ii, The Finds*. RRCSAL **27**, 317–374 (London).

Hartley B.R 1972 'The samian ware' *in* Frere 1972, 216–262.

Hartley B.R. Pengelly, H. and Dickinson, B. 1994 'Samian ware' *in* Mahany, C, 1994 *Roman Alcester: southern extramural area: 1964–1966 excavations*. CBARR **96**, 93–119 (York).

Hartley K 1972 'Stamped mortaria' *in* Castle 1972, 156–157.

Havis R. and Brooks H. forthcoming *Excavations in advance of the extension of London's third airport, Stanstead, Essex*.

Hawkes C.F.C. and Hull M.R. 1947 *Camulodunum, first report on the excavations at Colchester, 1930–39*. RRCSAL **14** (Oxford).

Hawkes S.C. and Dunning G.C. 1961 'Soldiers and settlers in Britain; fourth to fifth century', *Medieval Archaeol.* **5**, 1–70.

Hodge C.A.H. *et al* 1984 *Soils and their use in Eastern England*. Soil and Survey Bulletin **13** (Harpenden).

Hollard D. 1986 'Le trésor de Rocquencourt et la transformation du monnoyage d'imitation sous le règne de Postume', *Trésors Monétaires* **8**, 9–46.

Holmes J. 1954 'Stevenage: Romano-Belgic burials', *Trans. East Herts. Archaeol. Soc.* **13.2**, 209–11.

Holwerda J.H. 1923 *Arentsburg* (Leiden).

Howe M.D., Perrin J.R. and Mackreth D.F. 1981 *Roman pottery from the Nene Valley: a guide*. Peterborough City Mus. Occ. Pap. **2** (Peterborough).

Hull M.R. 1963 *The Roman potters' kilns of Colchester*. RRCSAL **21** (Oxford).

Hunn J. 1993 'The Romano-British farmstead at Boxfield Farm, and other settlements in the Stevenage Area', *Hertfordshire's Past* **34**, 25–31.

Isings C. 1957 *Roman glass from dated finds* (Gröningen).

Jackson R. 1985 'Cosmetic sets from late Iron Age and Roman Britain', *Britannia* **16**, 165–191.

Jackson R. 1986 'A set of Roman medical instruments from Italy', *Britannia* **17**, 119–67.

Jackson R. 1990 'Roman doctors and their instruments: recent research into ancient practice', *J. Roman Archaeol.* **3**, 5–27.

Jessup R.F. 1936 'Romano-British barrows', *Antiquity* **10**, 1936.

Johnson D.E. 1972 'A Roman Building at Chalk, near Gravesend', *Britannia* **3**, 112–149.

Juhász G. 1935 *Die sigillaten von Brigetio*, Dissertationes Pannonicae Ser. **2.3** (Budapest).

Kay Q.O.N. 1971 'Anthemis cotula', *J. Ecol.* **59**, 623–6.

Kars H. 1980 'Early mediaeval Dorestad, an archaeo-petrological study', *Berichten van de Rijksdienst voor het Oudheidkundig Bodemonderzoek* **30**, 393–422.

Kern J.H.C. 1963 'Römische modioli des 1 Jahrhunderts N.Chr.', *Mnemosyne* **16**, 400–405.

Kienast D. 1962 *Die Fund münzen der römischen Zeit in Deutschland, Abt III. Saarland*. (Berlin).

King D. 1986 'Petrology, dating and distribution of querns and millstones. The results of research in Bedfordshire, Buckinghamshire, Hertfordshire and Middlesex', *Inst. Archaeol. Bull.* **23**, 65–126.

Knorr R. 1919 *Töpfer und Fabriken verzierter Terra-Sigillata des ersten Jahrhunderts* (Stuttgart).

Knorr R. and Fr Sprater 1927 *Die westpfälzischen Sigillata Töpfereien von Blickweiler und Eschweiler Hof* (Speyer).

Lallemand J. 1986 'Le trésor de Bras', *Archaeologia Belgica* **II**, 205–211.

Lawson A.J. 1976 'Shale and jet objects from Silchester', *Archaeologia* **105**, 241–75.

Le Gentilhomme P. 1962 'Variations du titre de l'antoninianus au IIIe siècle', *Revue Numismatique* 141–166.

Lloyd-Morgan G. *1981 Descriptions of the collections of the Rijksmuseum G M Kam at Nijmegen IX: The Mirrors* (Nijmegen).

Ludowici W. 1905 *Stempel-Bilder römischer Töpfer aus meinem Ausgrabungen in Rheinzabern*.

Luff R.M. 1982 A zooarchaeological study of the Roman north-western provinces. BAR **S137** (Oxford).

Luff R.M. 1993 *Animal bones from excavations in Colchester, 1971–1985*. Colchester Archaeol. Trust Rep. **12** (Colchester).

Lyne M.A.B. and Jeffries R.S. 1979 *The Alice Holt/Farnham Roman pottery industry*. CBARR **30** (London).

Mackreth D.F. 1988 'The brooches' *in* Trow S.D. 1988 'Excavations at the Ditches hillfort, North Cerney, Gloucestershire, 1982–3', *Trans. Bristol Gloucestershire Archaeol. Soc.* **106**, 19–85.

Manning W. 1972 'The iron objects' *in* Frere 1972, 163–195.

Manning W. 1985 *Catalogue of the Romano-British iron tools, fittings and weapons in the British Museum* (London).

Maiuri G. 1932 *La casa del Menandro e il suo tesora di Argenteria* (Rome).

Maltby M. 1979 *The animal remains from the excavations in the City of Exeter*. Exeter Archaeological Reports **2** (Exeter).

Marsh G. 1978 'Early second-century fine wares in the London area' *in* Arthur and Marsh 1978, 119–224.

Mattingly H. 1939 'The great Dorchester hoard of 1936', *Numismatic Chron.*, 21–61.

McKinley J.I. 1993 'Bone fragment size and weights of bone from modern British cremations, and its implications for the interpretation of archaeological cremations', *Int. J. Osteoarchaeology* **3,** 283–287.

McKinley J.I. 1994a *The Anglo-Saxon cremation cemetery at Spong Hill, North Elmham. Part VIII; the cremations.* East Anglian Archaeol. **69**.

McKinley J.I. 1994b 'Bone fragment size in British cremations and its implications for pyre technology and ritual', *J. Archaeol. Sci.* **21.3**, 339–342.

McKinley J.I. forthcoming (a) 'The skeletal material' *in* Chander, C, forthcoming *Excavations at the Romano-British walled cemetery, Worthview Hospital, Purton* (report for Thamesdown Archaeology, January 1991).

McKinley J.I. forthcoming (b) *Romano-British cremation burials from Baldock; Area 15* (report for Baldock Project, 1991).

McKinley J.I. forthcoming (c) *St Stephen's Cemetery, St Albans; the human bone* (report for St Albans Museum, May 1992).

McMinn R.M.H. and Hutchings R.T. 1985 *A colour atlas of human anatomy.* Waye Medical Publications).

Millett M. 1979 'An approach to the functional interpretation of pottery' in Millet (ed) 1979 *Pottery and the archaeologist.* Inst. Archaeol. Occ. Pub. **4**, 35–48.

Neal D., Wardle A. and Hunn J. 1990 *Excavations of the Iron Age, Roman and mediaeval settlement at Gorhambury, St Albans.* English Heritage Arch. Rep. 14, 105–112 (London).

Niblett R. 1993 'A forgotten ruler venerated at *Verulamium*', *Hertfordshire's Past* **35**, 5–7.

Olivier A.C.H. 1988 'The brooches' *in* Potter and Trow 1988, 35–53.

O'Neill H.E. 1947 'The Roman villa at Park Street near St Albans, Herts', *Archaeol J.* **102**, 21–110.

Orton C. 1975 'Quantitative pottery studies. Some progress, problems and prospects', *Science and Archaeol.* **16**, 30–35.

Oswald F. 1936–7 *Index of figure-types on terra sigillata ("Samian ware")* (Liverpool).

Oswald F. and Pryce T.D. 1920 *An introduction to the study of terra sigillata* (London).

Parkhouse J. 1976 'The Dorestad quernstones', *Berichten van de Rijksdienst voor het Oudheidkundig Bodemonderzoek* **26**, 181–188.

Partridge C. 1977 'Excavations and fieldwork at Braughing, 1968–73', *Herts. Archaeol.* **5**, 22–108.

Partridge C. 1979 'D. The pottery", *in* Partridge 1979 'Excavations at Puckeridge and Braughing, 1975–79', *Herts. Archaeol.* **7**, 103–128.

Partridge C. 1981 *Skeleton Green.* Britannia Monog. Ser. **2** (London).

Peacock D.P.S. 1980 'The Roman millstone trade: a petrological sketch', *World Archaeol.* **12**, 43–53.

Peacock, D.P.S. and Williams D.F. 1986 *Amphorae and the Roman economy: an introductory guide.*

Petru S. 1972 *Emonske Nekropole.* Dissertationes et Monographiae Societe Archeologique Jugoslavie. Tome **XIV**.

Pocock J.A. 1987 *A geophysical survey at Chells Manor, Stevenage.* Univ. Bradford Schools of Physics and Archaeol. Sciences.

Potter T.W. and Trow S.D. 1988 'Puckeridge-Braughing, Hertfordshire. The Ermine Street excavations 1971–72', *Herts. Archaeol.* **10**.

Price J. 1977 'The Roman glass' *in* Gentry A., Ivens J. and McClean H. 1977 'Excavations at Lincoln Road, London Borough of Enfield, November 1974–March 1976', *Trans. London Middlesex Archaeol. Soc.* **28**, 101–189.

Price J. 1980 'The Roman glass' *in* Lambrick G. 1980 'Excavations in Park Street, Towcester, 1963–8', *Northamptonshire Archaeol.* **15**, 35–118.

Price J. 1981 'The glass' *in* Jarrett M.J. and Wrathmell S. 1981 *An Iron Age and Roman farmstead in South Glamorgan*, 149–162 (Cardiff).

Price J. 1985 'The Roman glass' *in* Pitts L.F. and St Joseph J.K. 1985 *Inchtuthil: the Roman legionary fortress.* Britannia Monog. Ser. **6**, 303–12 (London).

Price J. 1987 'The glass vessels from Felmongers, Harlow', *Annales du dixième Congrès de l'Association Internationale pour l'Histoire du Verre* (1985),185–206.

Price J. 1990 'Roman vessel and window glass' *in* McCarthy M.R. 1990 *A Roman, Anglian and medieval site at Blackfriars Street.* Cumberland Westmoreland Antiquarian Archaeol. Soc. Res. Ser. 4, 163–79.

Price J. and Cool H.E.M. 1983 'Glass from the excavations of 1974–76' *in* Brown A.E. and Woodfield C. 1983 'Excavations at Towcester, Northamptonshire: The Alchester Road Suburb', *Northamptonshire Archaeol.* **18**, 115–124.

Price J. and Cool H.E.M. 1985 'Glass' *in* Hurst H.R. 1985 *Kingsholm.* Gloucester Archaeol. Reps 1, 41–54 (Gloucester).

Price J. and Cool H.E.M. 1989 'The Romano-British glass project', *The Glass Cone* **21**, 3–5.

Price J. and Cottam S. 1994 'Glass' *in* Cracknell and Mahany 1994, 224–229.

Reece R. 1972 'A short survey of the Roman coins found in fourteen sites in Britain', *Britannia,* **3**, 269–76.

Reece R. 1982 'The coins from Cow Roast, Herts – a commentary', *Hertfordshire Archaeol.* **8**, 60–66.

Rees S. 1979 *Agricultural implements in prehistoric and Roman Britain* (2 vols). BAR **69** (Oxford).

Roes A. 1960 'Horn cheek pieces', *Antiq. J.* **40**, 68–72.

Ricken H. 1948 *Die Bilderschüsseln der romischen Töpfer von Rheinzabern.* Tafelband (Speyer).

Ricken H. and Fischer C. 1963 *Die Bilderschüsseln der Römischen Töpfer von Rheinzabern.* Textband zu Katalog **6** (Bonn).

Rigby V. 1986 'The pottery' in Stead and Rigby 1986, 223–380 (London).

Rogers G.B. 1974 *Poteries sigillées de la Gaule centrale,* Gallia Supplement **28** (Paris).

Rook A.G. 1970a 'A Belgic and Roman site at Brickwall Hill', *Herts. Archaeol.* **2**, 23–30.

Rook A.G. 1970b 'Investigation of a Belgic site at Grub's Barn, Welwyn Garden City', *Herts. Archaeol.* **2**, 31–36.

Rook A.G. 1973 Excavations at the Grange Roman-British cemetery, Welwyn, 1967', *Herts. Archaeol.* **3**, 1–30.

Rook A.G. 1987 'The pottery' *in* Rook 1987 'The Roman villa site at Dicket Mead, *Herts. Archaeol.* **9**, 79–175.

Ross A. 1968 'Shafts, pits, wells – sanctuaries of the Belgic Britons' *in* Coles J.M. and Simpson D.D.A. (eds) 1968 *Studies in Ancient Europe: essays presented to Stuart Piggott*, 155–285 (Leicester).

Ross A. and Feachem R. 1976 'Ritual rubbish? The Newstead pits' *in* Megaw J.V.S. (ed.) 1976 *To illustrate the monuments*, 229–237 (London).

Shiel N. 1979 'The coinage of Saloninus as Augustus', *ANS Museum Notes* **24**, 117–122.

Silver I.A. 1969 'The ageing of domestic animals' *in* Brothwell D. and Higgs E.S. (eds) *1969 Science in Archaeology*, 283–302 (London).

Skilbeck C.O. 1923 'Notes on the discovery of a Roman burial at Radnage', *Buckinghamshire Antiq. J.* **3**, 334–337.

Sommer U. 1990 'Dirt theory, or archaeological sites seen as rubbish heaps', *J. Theor. Archaeol.* **1**, 47–60.

Stanfield J.A. and Simpson G. 1958 *Central Gaulish potters* (London).

Stanfield J.A. and Simpson G. 1990 *Les potiers de la Gaule Centrale*. Revue Archaeol. Sites, Hors Serie **37** (Paris).

Stead I.M. 1976 'The earliest burials of the Aylesford Culture' *in* Sieveking G. de G. *et al* (eds) 1976 *Problems in social and economic archaeology*, 401–16.

Stead I.M. and Rigby V. 1986 *Baldock: the excavation of a Roman and pre-Roman settlement, 1968–72*, Britannia Monog. Ser. **7** (London).

Stead I.M. and Rigby V. 1989 Verulamium: the King Harry Lane site, *English Heritage Arch. Rep* **12**.

Stevenson M.D. 1978 'Romano-British pottery rediscovered', *Herts. Archaeol.* **6**, 116–119.

Szaivert W. 1983 'Der Beginn der Antoninianpragung in Viminacium', *Litterae Numismaticae Vindobonenses* **2**, 61–67.

Terrisse J-R. 1968 'Les céramiques sigillées gallo-romaines des Martres-de-Veyre (Puy de Dôme)', *Gallia Suppl.* **19** (Paris).

Thirion M. 1966 'Le trésor de Basècles', *Helenium* **4.3**, 193–217.

Tomason A.J. and Avery B.W. 1970 *The soils of Hertfordshire* (Harpenden).

Thompson I. 1982 *Grog-tempered 'Belgic' pottery of south-eastern England (2 vols)*. BAR **108** (Oxford).

Thorpe W.A. 1933–4 'A glass jug of Roman date From Turriff', *Proc. Soc. Antiq. Scotland* **68**, 439–43.

Tyers P. 1983 *Verulamium Region-type white ware fabrics from London*. Early Roman pottery from the City of London **4**. DUA/Museum of London.

Vanderhoeven M. 1961 *Verres Romains (Ier–IIIme siècle) des Musées Curtius et du Verre à Liège* (Liege).

Vanderhoeven M. 1975 *De terra sigillata de Tongeren* (Tongeren).

van der Veen M. 1989 'Charred grain assemblages from Roman period corn driers in Britain', *Archaeol. J.* **146**, 302–19.

van Naeman F. 1892–93 'Découverte de monnaies gallo-romaines a Belsele', *Annales Cercle archaeol. Pays de Waes* **14**, 41–73.

VCH 1914 *Victoria County History of Hertfordshire*, vol. **4** (London)

von den Driesch A. 1976 *A guide to the measurement of animal bones from archaeological sites.* Peabody Museum Bull. **1** (Cambridge, Mass.).

Wait G.A. 1985 *Ritual and religion in Iron Age Britain.* Brit. Archaeol. Rep. **149** (Oxford).

Ward J. 1911 *The Roman era in Britain* (London).

Webb P.A. and Suchey J.M. 1985 'Epiphyseal union of the anterior iliac crest and medial clavicle in a modern multiracial sample of American males and females.' *Amer. J. Phys. Anth.* **68**, 457–466

Welker E. 1974 *Die römischen Gläser von Nida-Heddernheim.* Schriften des Frankfurter Museums für Vor- und Fruhgeschichte (Frankfurt).

Westell W.P. 1937 'Roman occupation site at Wymondley', *Trans. East Herts. Archaeol. Soc.* **10.1**, 11–15.

Wheeler R.E.M. 1930 *London in Roman times.* (London).

Wheeler R.E.M. and T.V. 1936 *Verulamium: a Belgic and two Roman cities.* RRCSAL **11** (Oxford).

Wickenden N.P. 1988 *Excavations at Great Dunmow, Essex: A Romano-British small town in the Trinovantian Civitas.* East Anglian Archaeol. Rep. **41**.

Wild F. 1975 'Samian ware' *in* Robertson A.S. 1975 *Birrens (Blatobulgium)*, 141–177 (Edinburgh).

Williams D. 1977 'The Romano-British black-burnished industry; an essay on characterisation by heavy mineral analysis' *in* Peacock D.P.S. 1977 *Pottery and early commerce: characteristics and trade in Roman and later ceramics.*

Williamson T.M. 1984 'The Roman countryside: settlement and agriculture in N.W. Essex', *Britannia* **15**, 225–230.

Williamson T.M. 1986 'The development of settlement in north-west Essex. The results of a recent field survey', *Essex Archaeol. Hist.* **17**, 120–132.

Wilson M.G. 1972 'The other pottery' *in* Frere 1972, 263–370.

Wilson M.G. 1973 'The pottery used for dating' *in* Frere 1973, 294–342.

Wilson M.G. 1984 'The other pottery' *in* Frere 1984, 201–276.

Young C.J. 1977 *Oxfordshire Roman pottery.* BAR **43** (Oxford).

Zeepvat R. J. 1987 'Shale' *in* Mynard D.C. (ed.) 1987 *Roman Milton Keynes, excavation and fieldwork 1971–82.* Buckinghamshire Archaeol. Soc. Monog. Ser. **1**, 145 (Aylesbury).

INDEX

Illustrations are denoted by page numbers in *italics* or by *illus* where figures are scattered throughout the text.

agriculture, 4, 37, 142, 153, 154
animal bone
    age profile, 153-4
    analysis, methods of, 146-7
    in cremation, 33, 145
    discussion, 154
    distribution, 148
    metrical data, 154
    preservation and recovery, 148-9, 152
    results: by period, 149-50; pond, 151, 153; well, 15, 35, 150-1
animal husbandry *see* agriculture
animal processing, 21
antler fragments, 70, 72, *73*, 149-50
antler working, 70, 150
ash deposits, 23, 25, 34
Aston, settlement evidence, 37
awl?, 62, *63*

beads
    glass, 76, 77, *79*
    shale, 80, *81*
belt fittings, 56, *57*
bone *see* animal bone; human bone
bone working, 70
boundaries *see* ditches; fence-lines; land allotment
box fittings, 31, 33, 60, *61*
Box Wood, mound, 37
bracelets
    copper alloy, 54-5, *57*
    shale, 80, *81*
Broadwater, settlement evidence, 37
brooch pin, 63, *64*
brooches
    by type: Aucissa, *52*, 53; bow (iron), 63, *64*; Colchester, 51, *52*; Colchester Derivative, *52*, 53; Hod Hill, *52*, 53; La Tène III, 27, 51, *52;* Langton Down, 51, *52;* Nauheim Derivative, 51, *52;* Penannular, *52*, 53; Thistle, 51, *52*
    discussion, 53
buckle, 56, *57*
buckle plate, 54, 56, *57*
buildings *see* structures
burial sites, local, *5*, 36-7
burials *see* cremations

casket fittings, 31, 33, 54, 60, *61*
cemetery
    catalogue of cremations, 29-33
    excavation and discussion, 29, *30*, 33-4
    pottery, 29-33, 107, *135*
    see also human bone
cereal processing, 9, 23, 25, 136-7, 142
cereal remains, 136-42
cess pits?, 25, 142
chain fragments
    copper alloy, *59*, 60
    iron, *65*, 66
charcoal, 25, 34, 137; *see also* plant remains
'cheek piece', 72, *73*
chisels, 62, *63*
Church End Common, settlement evidence, 37
clamps, 66, *67*
cleat, 66, *67*
cleaver, 62, *64*
cloth seal, 68, *69*
cobbles, 15

coin hoard
    excavation, 29, 35
    report, 45-6, *47-8*, 49-50
    strays from, 40
coins
    Iron Age, 27, 40, 41
    Roman: catalogue, 41-4; discussion, 21, 40-4
comb fragment, *71*, 72
Corey's Mill, burials, 36
corn drier
    excavation and discussion, 23, *24-6*, 27, 36
    plant remains, 136-7, 138-9, 142-3
cosmetic grinder, 54, 58, *59*
cremation sites, local, *5*, 36
cremations
    bone report, 144-5
    catalogue, 29-33
    excavation and discussion, *29*, 33-4
cult object *see* votive object

Datchworth, settlement evidence, 37
dating evidence
    pottery, 100-1
    summarised: Early Roman period, 14-15, 27; Roman period, 16, 23, 29; Later Roman period, 19, 20-1, 25, 29; post-Roman period, 21
dew pond
    excavation and discussion, 27, *28*, 29, 35
    pottery summarised, 102-4, 105
ditches
    Early Roman period, *13*, *14*, 15, 35
    Roman period, 15-16, 22, 23, *24*, 36
    Later Roman period, *23*, 25, 27
    see also enclosures; gullies
droveway *see* trackway

earrings, 54, 55, *57*
enclosures
    Early Roman, 8, *11*, 13, 35
    Roman (sub-enclosure), 8, *12*, 22-3, 36
    Later Roman (around corn drier), *23*, *24*, 27, 36
evaluation, 2
excavation methods, 9

fence-lines, 18, 20, 25, *28*, 29, 36
ferrules
    iron, *65*, 66
    lead, 69
field system, 35, 36
finger-rings
    bone, *71*, 72
    copper alloy, 55, *57*
fire, evidence for, 9, 25, 36
fleshhook, 64, *65*
flints, 13, 27, 34
funerary ritual, 33-4
furniture fittings, 54, 60, *61*

geophysical survey, 2
glass
    beads, 76, 77, *79*
    hairpin, 76
    vessels, 32, 33, 74-7, *78*
    window, 74, 76, 77
Great Collens Wood, settlement evidence, 37
Great Wymondley, occupation evidence, 36, 37

gullies
> Iron Age, 13, 35
> Early Roman, 13, 14-15, 35
> Roman, 22-3
> Later Roman, 18-19, 20, 21, 23, 36
> *see also* ditches

hairpins
> bone, 27, 70, *71*, 72, *73*
> copper alloy, 54, 55-6, *57*
> glass, 76, *79*

hammer, 62, *63*
handle, 72, *73*
hearth, 25
hedge?, 36
hinge fragments, 66, *67*
hipposandals, 62, *63*
hoard *see* coin hoard
hobnails, 63
holdfasts, 66
hollows
> prehistoric, 13, 35
> Early Roman, 13, 14
> Later Roman, 20, 25, 27
> *see also* dew pond; pits; ponds

honestone, 82
human bone, 33, 144-5, 149, 150

inscription, cloth seal, 68, *69*

joiner's dog, 66, *67*

key, 65
knives, 62-3, *64*; *see also* handle

land allotment, 37
latrine *see* cess pits
lead fragment, indeterminate, *69*
leatherworking tool, 62, *63*
ligulae, 54, 58, *59*
linch pin, 62, *63*
locks, 32, 33, *65*
loops, double-spiked, 66, *67*

metalling *see* raft
millstones *see* quernstones/millstones
mirror, 54, 56, *59*
molluscan evidence, 20, 136; *see also* shellfish
mounts, 54, 60, *61*

nail cleaners, 58, *59*
nails, 32, 60, *61*
needles
> bone, *71*, 72
> copper alloy, 54, *59*, 60
> iron, 64, *65*

Ninesprings villa, 36, 37

ox goads, 62, *63*, *65*, 66

padlocks *see* locks
patches, lead *see* plugs
pathology, 145
phasing, 10
pin?, 64, *65*; *see also* brooch pin; hairpins; linch pin
pitchfork tip, *65*, 66
pits
> Early Roman, 13-14, 15, 27, 35
> Later Roman, 19, 20, 21, 25, 27, 29, 35, 36
> post-Roman, 21, 36
> *see also* dew pond; hollows; ponds; sand quarrying pits

plant remains
> discussion, 142
> sampling and retrieval, 136
> > corn drier, 136-7, 138-9, 142, 143; well, 137, 140-2

plate fragments
> copper alloy, 60
> lead, 69

plough damage, 29
plough share?, 62, *63*
plugs, lead, 68, *69*
ponds
> Early Roman, 35
> Roman: animal bone, 151, 153; excavation and discussion, 15-16, 18, 19-20, 21, 35-6; pottery summarised, 104-6
> post-Roman, 21, 36
> *see also* dew pond

postholes
> prehistoric-Early Roman, 22
> Early Roman, 13-14
> Roman, 15
> Later Roman: Area 1, 18, 19, 20, 36; Area 2, 25, *27;* Area 3, *28*, 29, 36
> *see also* stakeholes

potters' stamps, 85-6, *87*
pottery, prehistoric, 13
pottery, Roman
> catalogue (*illus*), 111-35
> fabric incidence, 98, 107-10
> fabrics: amphorae, 96; buff wares, 92-3; colour-coated wares, 89-91; glazed wares, 89; grey wares, 93-5; grog-tempered wares, 95-6; mica-dusted wares, 91; red wares, 91; sandy wares, 93; shell-tempered wares, 96; slipped red wares, miscellaneous, 91; white wares, 91-2; white-slipped red wares, 91
> key groups, 96-7
> > cemetery, 107; dew pond, 102-4, 105; penannular ditch, 106; pond, 104-6; well, 97, 99, 101-2, 103
> methodology, 88-9
> samian, 84-5, *86-7*, 97

pruning hooks, 62, *63*
punch?, 62, *63*
Purwell Mill *see* Ninesprings villa

quarries *see* dew pond; sand quarrying pits
quernstones/millstones, 25, 36, 82-3

raft, flint and chalk, 15, 18, *19*, 35, 36
reaping hooks, 62, *63*, *64*
recording system, 9
rings *see* finger-rings
ritual deposition, well, 15, 35, 99, 101-2; *see also* votive object
rivets
> iron, 66, *67*
> lead, 69

Robins Hall, settlement evidence, 37

sacrifice, 35
sampling, plant remains, 136, *143*
sand quarrying pits, 27, *28*, 35
scoops/spatulas, cosmetic, 54, 58, *59*
settlement sites, local, 5, 36-7
share *see* plough share
sheet metal
> copper alloy, 60
> lead, 69

shellfish, 27, 29, 137, 149
'Six Hills' *tumuli*, 36
sling-shot, 68, *69*
smithing tools, 62, *63*
soils, 4
spindle fragment, 72, *73*
spindle whorls, 80, *81*
split socket, 62, *63*

164

spoon, 54, *59*, 60; *see also* scoops/spatulas
spud, 62, *63*
spur, 62, *63*
stakeholes, 25; *see also* postholes
stand, miniature, 54, *59*, 60
staple, flat-headed, 66, *67*
steelyard (*statera*), 54, 58, *59*, 60
Stevenage, Roman activity, 36-7
strap-end, 56, *57*
strips, copper alloy, 60
structures?
    Early Roman, 14
    Roman, 15
    local evidence for, 36
    see also corn drier
studs
    lion-headed, 32, 33, 54, 60, *61*
    plain, 60, *61*
stylus, 63, *64*
sub-enclosure *see* enclosures

tack, 60, *61*
toilet implements, 54, 58, *59*

topography, 4, *5*
trackway, 13, *14*, 15, 35
tumuli, 36
tweezers, 58, *59*

vessel fragments (copper alloy), 54, *59*, 60; *see also* glass
villa sites, local, *5*, 36, 37
votive object, 54, *59*, 60; *see also* ritual deposition

Walkern, settlement evidence, 37
weights, 68, *69*
well
    excavation and discussion, 14-15, 16, *17*, 18, *19*, 35
    finds: animal bone, 150-1; plant remains, 136, 137, 140-2; pottery summarised, 97, 99, 101-2, 103
Weston, settlement evidence, 36
whistle?, 72, *73*
windbreak, 25
Wymondley, settlement evidence, 37
Wymondley Bury, settlement evidence, 36, 37

yard *see* raft